The Many Faces
of Socialism

The Many Faces of Socialism

Comparative Sociology and Politics

Paul Hollander

Transaction Books
New Brunswick (U.S.A.) and London (U.K.)

Library of Congress Catalog Number: 82-19458
ISBN: 0-87855-480-7 (cloth)
Printed in the United States of America

Library of Congress Cataloging in Publication Data
Hollander, Paul.
  The many faces of socialism.
  Includes bibliographical references and index.
  1. Sociology—United States—Addresses, essays, lectures. 2. So-
cialism—Addresses, essays, lectures. 3. Comparative government—
Addresses, essays, lectures. 4. Totalitarianism. I. Title.
HM22.U5H625 1983   301   82-19458
ISBN 0-87855-480-7

Contents

Acknowledgments   vii

Introduction: The Appeals of Socialism and
the Discontents of American Life   1

PART I: THE FACES OF SOCIALISM

1. Privacy: A Bastion Stormed   17
2. Models of Behavior in Stalinist Literature: A Case   33
   Study of Totalitarian Values and Controls
3. Leisure: The Unity of Pleasure and Purpose   55
4. Bureaucracy, Totalitarianism, and the Comparative   67
   Study of Communism
5. Border Controls: An Integral Part of the Soviet   79
   Social-Political System
6. Politicized Bureaucracy: The Soviet Case   105
7. Criticism and Self-Criticism   115
8. Comparing Socialist Systems: Ends and Results   127
9. Family and Feminism in Soviet Society   145
10. The Subordination of Literature to Politics: Socialist   163
    Realism in a Historical and Comparative Perspective
11. Public and Private in Hungary: A Travel Report   175
12. How Banal Is Evil? Solzhenitsyn's Contribution to the   187
    Sociology of Coercion
13. Afghanistan and the Myth of "The Return" of   193
    the Cold War
14. Poland: Coercion and the Stability of Marxist   197
    One-Party States
15. Marxist Societies: The Relationship between Theory   201
    and Practice

PART II: CONTRASTS

16. Sociology, Selective Determinism, and the Rise of   241
    Expectations
17. The Ideological Pilgrim—Looking for Utopia,   253
    Then and Now

18. American Society and Soviet Power   283
19. Revisionism   295
20. Reflections on Anti-Americanism in Our Times   299
21. Comparative Sociology in the United States and   313
       Why There Is So Little of It
22. Society and Intellectuals: The Persistence of   323
       Estrangement and Wishful Thinking
Name Index   345
Subject Index   350

Acknowledgments

I express my appreciation for a research grant by the John M. Olin Foundation which assisted in the preparation of this volume.

The author gratefully acknowledges the following publishers and publications for granting permission to reprint copyrighted material:

"Privacy: A Bastion Stormed." *Problems of Communism* 12(6) Nov.–Dec. 1963: 1–6.

"Models of Behavior in Stalinist Literature: A Case Study of Totalitarian Values and Controls." *American Sociological Review* 31(3) June 1966: 352–64.

"Leisure: The Unity of Pleasure and Purpose" (originally: "The Uses of Leisure"). *Survey.* July 1966.

"Bureaucracy, Totalitarianism, and the Comparative Study of Communism" (originally: "Observations on Bureaucracy, Totalitarianism, and the Comparative Study of Communism"). *Slavic Review* 26(2) June 1967: 302–307. [American quarterly of Soviet and East European studies.]

"Border Controls: An Integral Part of the Soviet Social-Political System." *Ost-Europa.* October 1969.

"Criticism and Self-Criticism." From *Marxism, Communism, and Western Society: A Comparative Encyclopedia.* New York: McGraw-Hill. 1972. © McGraw-Hill. Used with the permission of McGraw-Hill Book Company.

"Comparing Socialist Systems: Ends and Results." In *Comparative Socialist Systems.* C. Mesa-Lago and C. Beck (eds.). University of Pittsburgh Center for International Studies. 1975.

"The Subordination of Literature to Politics: Socialist Realism in a Historical and Comparative Perspective. "Reprinted from *Studies in Comparative Communism* 9(3) Autumn 1976: 215–25. By permission.

"How Banal Is Evil? Solzhenitsyn's Contribution to the Sociology of Coercion." *Contemporary Sociology.* July 1980: 498–501.

"Marxist Societies: The Relationship between Theory and Practice." *Annual Review of Sociology* 8. 1982: 319–51.

"Sociology, Selective Determinism, and the Rise of Expectations." *The American Sociologist* 8. November 1973: 147–53.

"The Ideological Pilgrim: Looking for Utopia, Then and Now." *Encounter.* November 1973: 3–15.

"American Society and Soviet Power" (originally: "The Future of East-West Relations"). *Survey.* Summer–Fall 1976.

"Revisionism." *Commentary.* May 1978.

"Reflections on Anti-Americanism in Our Times." *Worldview.* June 1978: 46–51.

"Comparative Sociology in the United States and Why There Is So Little of It." *Current Perspectives in Social Theory* 2. JAI Press. 1981: 21–29.

Introduction:
The Appeals of Socialism and the
Discontents of American Life

It is never difficult for an author to convince himself that his shorter writings scattered in various journals or collections deserve to be brought together in one volume to be rescued from oblivion and have their impact magnified by their combination.* At the same time, such an undertaking is not without its dangers. The author may expose a paucity of original thinking, he may reveal the "recycling" of ideas which might otherwise have gone unnoticed. Most of us, however, will opt for taking such risks in the hope that, on the contrary, displaying our enduring preoccupations will provide yet another example of the parts adding up to a whole that is not only different from but also superior to the parts. Thus putting together a collection of essays is one way of affirming the ancient belief in the whole illuminating and outshining the parts and infusing them with new meaning that could not be discerned while they were separated.

Besides the hope that the combination of scattered pieces may reveal something that was not perceptible before, authors also tend to aver that their collections are held together by certain "unifying themes" and concerns lending coherence to their writings. This certainly applies to the selection of my shorter writings included in *The Many Faces of Socialism.*

The essays of this collection share several attributes. For one thing, most belong to the subdiscipline of political sociology and deal with a particular type of society (of which more will be said later on). Many of them are comparative explicitly or by easily discernible implication. They deal with two kinds of societies: for the most part with those that are socialist (or state socialist) but also with Western or pluralistic ones. The major Western example is the United States, the major socialist one the Soviet Union.

While there is bound to be a historical component to essays written over a period of twenty years, most of them address issues which are of enduring interest in both socialist and pluralistic societies.[1] Thus, for

1

example, the relationship between the private and public, the techniques of social and political controls, the problems of value orientation in secular societies, the timeless tension between professed value and observed behavior and between social ideals and government policies, the roles of intellectuals (in Western societies) and the various ways in which individuals, groups, and political systems grope for a sense of purpose in the contemporary world—all are matters which remain in the forefront of current concerns.

My interest in the type of social systems loosely called "socialist" and in cross-cultural comparisons[2] is not the only tie that binds these essays (and much of the rest of my work) together. A concern of mine, possibly an underlying orientation which finds expression in many of these essays, has been the desire (bordering on morbid fascination) to examine and understand some of the least appealing phenomena in political and social life. Thus political violence and coercive institutions and practices claimed my attention repeatedly, as indicated by my writings on totalitarianism, concentration camps, border controls, politicized bureaucracies, the regimentation of arts and literature, group controls, and other assaults on privacy and personal freedom. My basic, intuitive perspectives on organized (and unorganized) social existence have not been permeated by too many rays of optimism; I have never been inclined to overestimate harmony, rationality, and collective kindness in human affairs. Correspondingly, I never believed that violence, repression, and irrationality were incidental, marginal, or transient aberrations which higher levels of social organization, political wisdom, material abundance, or good intentions would cure at some future time. My background and past experiences (which included living through World War II, and narrowly escaping extermination as a Jew, as well as experiencing various unpleasant turns of life in Stalinist Hungary) obviously sensitized me to the ubiquitousness of conflict and its nastier varieties. Having such an enlarged awareness of conflict in human affairs did not, however, make me a "conflict sociologist" as the term is used these days, meaning "Marxist," particularly since I also believe strongly in the causal importance and autonomy of ideas in social and political life. Thus in view of such a close association between the "conflict school" and the Marxist inspiration, "conflict sociologist" is a label I cannot comfortably wear. (More will be said later on about such labels and affinities.)

In bringing together these essays, I was also motivated by the awareness that these writings represent and highlight areas or subfields of American sociology which have suffered some neglect within the profession: the study of socialist societies (in particular the Soviet Union and societies of Eastern Europe), comparative studies in general, the sociology of coercion and political violence, and the sociology of literature. Working with such topics, and my approach toward them, puts me outside the various "reigning paradigms" of American sociology, and this too may lend some added interest to this volume. Substantively, I am also removed from the mainstream of the discipline because, unlike most of my fellow sociologists, American society is not my consuming and singular preoccupation, the source of all data and of all ideas about the nature of the social world.[3] In my methodology too I belong to another nebulous minority, those who may be called "qualitative" sociologists who are interested in matters difficult to quantify for either practical or theoretical reasons. Certainly, I am not one who believes that "nothing is worth knowing unless it can be counted."[4] Many things worth discussing, thinking, or writing about cannot be counted, while many quantifiable things are not very enlightening.

While nonquantitative sociologists often find home in one or the other of the two major theoretical-conceptual streams of American sociology, that is, the structural-functionalist or the Marxist, I cannot claim to be attached to either of these schools. To be sure, it may be said (and it has been) that in some ways "we all are functionalists," that is, we are looking for certain patterns, connections, and regularities in social life or the life of societies. It may also be said that in a similar general sense we all are Marxists too, as, for example, when we acknowledge the weight of social structure and class on individual behavior, or the impact of how people make their living on many of their attributes. But functionalism in practice tends to be more: an approach that implies or posits a view of society far too harmonious, complacent, and cozy for me. It is hard for me to believe that social institutions most of the time represent "solutions" to problems, that societies tend toward orderliness, that social systems abound with ingenious problem-solving devices, that value-consensus is the major cement holding societies together. Nevertheless, while regarding conflict as far more central to the interaction of human groups and societies, I am not a Marxist either, finding the Marxist vision of conflict narrow and contrary to the variety and multiplicity of its sources and manifestations. I would like to think that my interest in both conflict and the part played by ideas (and values) in human affairs places me in the sociological tradition of authors like Weber (very much aware of conflict without reducing its sources to material-economic factors). Weber also succeeded in probing problems of social existence, both timeless and historically significant, which are difficult to quantify.

As noted previously, these days if an American sociologist is neither a quantitative-empiricist nor a structural-functionalist he is likely to become, almost by a process of elimination, a Marxist of some variety. Thus some further comments are in order to account for my avoiding the Marxist inspiration and disclaiming the Marxist label.

I grew up in a society which was officially Marxist, legitimated itself by Marxism, and claimed to shape its institutions by the guidelines this theory provides. This circumstance may help to explain why it was fairly easy for me to withstand the intellectual (and nonintellectual) temptations of Marxism one is exposed to in Western academic life and the social sciences especially if one is not inclined to either structural-functionalism or quantitative studies.

The claims and the practices of the "Marxist" society I got to know as I was growing up discredited Marxism (and Marxism-Leninism) in two principal ways. First, we were force-fed in school and college (and sometimes even at work) a watered-down Marxism (which nevertheless had something to do with the more genuine article). Forced intellectual diets produce strong reactions of distaste and nausea as do most diets administered under compulsion. Moreover, the rigid and relentless application of Marxist perspectives and criteria to most fields of learning—and especially the humanities and social sciences—was genuinely stultifying, painfully constricting, and thoroughly unenlightening.

Second, and more important, Marxism was discredited for me (and the vast majority of the population, intellectuals included, in my native Hungary) by the vivid contrasts between the promises, ideals, propositions, and values derived from it (both from the esoteric and watered-down versions) and its discernible applications in daily life. It was a contrast, a gap, indeed an abyss that could not fail to make a deep impression. Workers now owned the means of production, the factories where they worked, did they not? If so, why were they searched for stolen goods on the way out at the gates? Would they steal from themselves? By whom were they searched or arrested if they tried to strike, if they criticized their wages or working conditions? By other workers temporarily doing duty for "the armed militia" Lenin spoke of in *State and Revolution?* Or was there perhaps more than one working class, some still working with their hands in the factories, and others guarding them, searching them, planning for them, arresting them, and regulating them? And if the workers were the new masters of the land and their lives, why did they go to work on streetcars or on bicycles while the managers of the factories, the ministers in the distant ministries, and Party functionaries at the Party headquarters were driven to work in chauffeured limousines? Why did workers even have to ask permission from the foreman to turn on a light on dark days in their own workshops in their own factories?[5] Why were there so many more new rules, regulations, restrictions, and prohibitions, so many policemen and special policemen (those guarding "state security," not the "people's security")? Why were the government and the Party so mistrustful of the masses who were in theory the beneficiaries of every policy, every move the regime made? Why was it necessary to jam foreign radio broadcasts, prevent access to foreign newspapers, purge the libraries and book shops, and literally fence in the whole nation? Were people that easily corruptible if exposed to the "wrong" ideas (assuming that they were wrong)? Why was there so much mistrust—which, in turn, gave rise to the gigantic bureaucracy—so little self-determination, autonomy, and freedom? If all these turns of events and policies had anything to do with Marxism, *then* the philosophy or theory was obviously no good. But if, as is often said in the West, that was not what Marx (or even Lenin?) had in mind, why was it so easy to misuse, to misapply their ideas (and not only in Hungary)? Was not there something also wrong with a theory which lent itself so easily to such monstrous distortion and misuse wherever it was tried out? It should not be surprising that Herbert Padilla's recent reflections born out of similar experiences (in Castro's Cuba) concerning the relationship between theory and practice strike a responsive chord in me:

> The 19th century socialist utopias now seem to me precursors of the forced labor camps and the ideal City of Man in which the New Man was to be created. Their works seem to me now like luxuriant verbal constructions, no less distant from reality than those of the socialist thinkers Georg Lukács, Herbert Marcuse and Theodor Adorno: empty Scholasticism.[6]

At this point one may ask: are these essays really about "the faces of socialism" or perhaps something else? Are the societies, the countries dealt with in this book (the USSR, China, Cuba, Hungary, Poland, etc.,) socialist? In what sense? It is safe to say, even without reviewing the vast literature on the nature of socialism, that there will be many readers and critics who will, in time-honored fashion, dispute calling these countries socialist.[7] They will argue that these countries, and the Soviet Union in particular, are not only not socialist, but have besmirched the good name of socialism.[8] In deviating from the ideals and blueprints of socialism, so the argument runs, such countries have become highly coercive: the powers of the state have flowered, not withered. These systems have also failed to create even a semblance of material abundance, and they have also fallen short of introducing equality, social justice, widespread and meaningful political participation. The unfolding of human potential envisioned on a mass scale has receded into the very distant future.[9] At the same time, those among the putatively socialist countries which managed to develop a more "human face"—that is, become more tolerant of dissent and cultural diversity—and succeeded, to a limited degree, in improving the material standard of living (like Hungary) appeared to have made these advances by abandoning some of the ideals of socialism. They allowed a far greater share to private enterprise (and the profit motive) than socialist principles would condone.

It may also be recalled that another distinctive characteristic of socialist societies, and another claim to their superiority, was supposed to be the more painless transition, indeed shortcut, to modernity. As I put it elsewhere;

> Central to the appeals of socialism is the promise and expectation that it can and will bring about better material living conditions in combination with the maintenance (or renewal) of community and thus provide the blessings of technology, industry and urban life without the ruptures, conflicts and disturbances associated with them under capitalism.[10]

That has hardly been the case. It would be difficult to define socialism as the painless and rapid path to modernity. Modernization under socialism (or under Marxist one-party systems) proved as arduous and disruptive as the corresponding process under capitalism. Indeed, it may be argued that its "forced march into modernity" exacted even more hardship, bloodshed, dislocation, loss of meaning, and social cohesion than the capitalist variant. There was much resistance to overcome: people in the Soviet Union as in China and Indochina (and most recently the Indians of Nicaragua)[11] clung to their old ways of life, place of residence, religion, and kinship ties. They were prodded, pushed, "mobilized," and regimented in the name of a better future and in order to make state power more secure. Vast population relocations took place: peasants were uprooted from the countryside, ethnic groups were moved from one part of the country to another, city dwellers were sent to rural areas (on the largest scale in China but in Eastern Europe as well).

By what criteria then did I choose to call these countries socialist? First, there was common usage. Rightly or wrongly, they are called socialist in the news media, by most scholars, and the educated public. This has been accomplished in part by the persistence of the regimes concerned, by the sheer force of self-identification.

Second, I believe that the claim that they are socialist is not entirely hollow. These countries did take one major step in the direction of socialism prescribed by the creators of these theories: they did liquidate the private ownership of the means of production, a measure which, at least in institutional terms, goes to the heart of the socialist program of transformation. That few of the results followed which had been anticipated is another matter.

Thus we have a terminological problem if we refuse to call these countries socialist. What are the alternatives? Certainly, "socialist" has its difficulties, but other efforts at finding a widely accepted definition or appellation have failed. We could call them "Marxist one-party states or dictatorships" (as I have done in another essay of this volume, pp. 201–237), but, as I noted before, some people would have no less trouble deciding what is a "true" Marxist society than deciding upon which country to confer the "socialist" label.

While many of the countries dealt with in these essays could still be characterized as totalitarian—as much of the evidence presented in this volume suggests—I preferred to use the "socialist" appellation although not without hesitation. For one thing, specialists of the countries concerned are nowadays reluctant to designate them as such (whatever the justification for this shift),[12] and therefore the concept is less part of the scholarly discourse than used to be the case. Furthermore, as noted before, some of them (i.e., Hungary and Poland) certainly ceased to fit the criteria used to define "totalitarianism." Finally, insofar as these countries have been attractive to Western intellectuals, it was on account of their perceived socialist character. Hence in looking at the appeals of these countries (as I proposed to do in some of the essays)—and at the corresponding discontents of American (and Western) life—it is necessary to put into sharp focus their socialist character, or whatever affinity they have with the ideals of socialism.

At the same time, I continue to believe that totalitarianism is a far from useless concept in our times. And while Western scholarly experts may question its applicability, people who live in the countries so designated invariably find the concept valid (when exposed to it) since they feel that the kinds of controls which circumscribe their lives have a distinctiveness of their own which justifies the use of a new word. Let me add that I am not arguing now, nor have I done so in the past (as these essays make clear), that totalitarian political systems should be thought of as those which achieve total control over the lives of their citizens. Instead I believe, as did other writers on this subject, that we need a concept with which to denote a characteristic contemporary mode of government that has succeeded in exacting exceptionally high levels of conformity from its population by various organizational and coercive techniques, pressures, and mechanisms. Totalitarianism is also distinctive, in addition to its refinement of techniques of social-political control, because it represents what may be called the culmination of the contemporary idealization of politics, or, more familiarly put, the ascendance of ideological politics.

While the proper applicability of the term "socialist" to various countries may be subject to debate, it is not a matter of dispute that the ideals and values associated with the concept of socialism continue to exert a powerful attraction in many parts of the world, foremost in those which in no sense and by no claim can be considered socialist. The appeal of such ideas is especially strong among academic intellectuals in Western Europe and the United States as well as in some Third World countries and Japan. As I wrote two years ago:

> The appeals and values associated with socialism . . . have provided the most powerful incentive for the suspension of critical thinking among large contingents of Western intellectuals. . . . Such intellectuals appear to assume an affirming, supportive stance as soon as a political system (or movement) makes an insistent enough claim to its socialist character. . . . The word "socialism" has retained, despite all historical disappointments associated with regimes calling themselves socialist, a certain magic which rarely fails to disarm or charm these intellectuals and which inspires renewed hope that its most recent incarnation will be *the* authentic one, or at least more authentic than previous ones had been. (There is little evidence that intellectuals, or for that matter non-intellectuals, living in countries considered socialist are similarly charmed or disarmed by the idea of socialism.)[13]

While the recent defection of Susan Sontag from the ranks of those still beholden to these attitudes could be used to challenge the argument here presented, the hostile reactions to her statement[14] testify to the strength and durability of the attachments here described. While Sontag did not attack the idea of socialism as such, she did label virtually all countries claiming to be socialist as having an "essentially despotic nature," and that was too much for her audience, ready perhaps to reject some of the countries concerned but not *all of them,* since doing so would cast serious doubt on the realizability of the ideal. The angry reactions to Sontag's public soul-searching reflected once more the lack of alternatives for the alienated who must embrace some set of ideas with which to relieve the gloom of estrangement. These social critics still have nowhere to turn but to the ideals of socialism, as far as collective solutions to the real and perceived defects of their society are concerned.

It is virtually impossible in our times to separate the appeal of socialism from the social-critical impulse among Western intellectuals. Feeling deprived of a sense of purpose, community, and wholeness, many intellectuals are ready to discover these states elsewhere. Correspondingly, the more recent attractions of certain Third World countries had more to do with these hopeful projections (of wholeness, purpose, and community) than with some other, more traditional appeals of socialism.

Thus since the 1960s the discontents of American life have predisposed to the veneration of these new, putatively improved versions of socialism that can be found in largely underdeveloped countries. If such an industrial underdevelopment was a liability from the standpoint of Marxist theory and its applicability, it had particular appeals for the intellectual sensibility here alluded to. The recent admirers of the distant incarnations of socialism were less interested in expunging the irrationalities of the capitalist modes of production than in harmony, uncorrupted simplicity, and authenticity the "Third World" seemed to offer. It may well be said of these intellectuals what was observed about German technocrats who became supporters of nazism: "For these people part of the appeal of National Socialism [here one may substitute 'Third World socialism'] was not a total rejection of modernity but a promise to embrace it selectively in accordance with specific national traditions."[15] In other words, they were attracted, as were many Nazi sympathizers, to a mixture of tradition and modernity where tradition stood for community and sense of purpose, while modernity for the marvels of technology used to advance political-ideological objectives.[16]

Thus one is led to reemphasize the enormous importance of the romantic element in both the persistent appeals of socialism and the current forms of estrangement among intellectuals. This peculiar combination of antirationalism and prosocialism was also evident among the groups and movements partaking of the spirit of what used to be called the New Left and the counter culture, no less antinomian and eclectic in its values than were the romantic technocrats and bureaucrats of Germany in the early 1930s.[17] Thus what used to be called "reactionary modernism" in the German context and what may be called countercultural romanticism have more in common than meets the eye, including the selective acceptance of technology.[18]

Thus socialism in our times has come to stand for a remarkably wide variety of dreams, hopes, and longings many of which have little to do with the earlier, more rigorously felt and formulated concerns of socialism with equality and social justice, or material progress. Somewhat paradoxically and indirectly, the appeals of socialism have also been replenished by what a philosopher-economist, Albert Hirschman, called the "recoil from consumerism" or "backlash of affluence,"[19] that is to say, the disappointment that attends consumption and the satisfaction of material desires increasingly taken for granted. The developments in the 1960s in the United States (and their lingering aftereffects) are a good example of this process in which disappointment over security, affluence, and consumption creates an intensification of estrangement, social criticism, and involvement in "activism," that is, public social protest of some kind which, in turn, creates

> a heady feeling of excitement . . . generated when the consciousness of selflessly acting for the public good is combined with the sensation of being free to overstep the traditional boundaries of moral conduct, a sensation that is closely related to that of power. . . . The greatest asset of public action is its ability to satisfy vaguely felt needs for higher purpose and meaning, . . . especially of course in an age in which religious fervor is at a low ebb in many countries.[20]

In the 1960s and early 1970s, such activism centered on Vietnam, racial injustice, and feminism. In the early 1980s, it has been focused on the nuclear "freeze" and disarmament. In all these instances and causes, the bulk of the participants in the protests came forth from the ranks of the comfortable middle classes displaying the readiness "to get involved." Indeed, the very term "involvement" achieved during the 1960s a new meaning and association with "good," "praiseworthy," and "socially desirable" even when lacking in any specification as to what one should be involved in. The same happened with the words "activism" and "activist," also widely used as praiseworthy states or dispositions indicative of some deeply felt but often unspecified commitment to some undeclared higher purpose.

All of this leads back to the two major converging themes and concerns of these essays (and much of my work published elsewhere). They are the nature of "socialism" and, increasingly, the discontents of American life which predispose intellectuals and aspiring intellectuals to entertain misconceptions of political systems which claim the socialist ideological-philosophical heritage. As far as the nature of these societies is concerned, I was preoccupied with the loss of personal and group freedoms in historical situations when political movements of high aspiration and idealism attained and consolidated their power. In our times, such movements have been predominantly anchored in the ideology, spirit, and values of Marxism-Leninism. While philosophically speaking the political systems inspired by these ideas may be running out of steam, they still possess sufficient dynamics, organizational skills, and military power (here I am thinking primarily of the Soviet Union) to threaten the freer parts of the world. What has in fact been happening in the West has been a striking transformation of what may be called the threshold of threat perception. While twenty years ago the existence of some half-dozen pro-Soviet countries in Africa might have been viewed with alarm and the emergence of more such countries in Central America as intolerable, since Vietnam many influential intellectuals, foreign policy makers, politicians, and media people have joined forces to redefine what is threatening to the United States and made considerable headway in allaying apprehensions about the growth of Soviet power in many parts of the world. The propensity to play down Soviet advances is directly proportional to the unwillingness to engage American power or resources to counter such trends.

This brings us once more to the second preoccupation that will be found in these essays and especially the more recent ones. It is the condition of American (and other Western) intellectuals and their disenchantment with the world they live in and know best, their reflexive disparagement not only of the pleasures of consumption (perhaps more deserved), but also of the benefits of intellectual and personal freedom. Recognizing that such estrangement is closely tied to high levels of idealism, expectation, and good intentions especially among Americans does not make the phenomenon any less consequential and corrosive. As Edward Luttwak observed:

> Alienation, once the recondite anxiety of the few, has certainly become as common as the common cold. . . . Those of the Western intellectual elites who are motivated by the impulse of self-hatred perhaps see the hostile forces now converging upon the West as some sort of solution to the predicament of their own alienation. Hence the peculiarly aggressive *Kulturpessimismus,* the willful demoralization and the eager attention given to every trace of weakness in Western society.[21]

Certainly, since my study *Political Pilgrims* was published (in 1981), its central concern, the estrangement of Western and especially American intellectuals, has shown no signs of receding. Paradoxically, the election of Ronald Reagan to the presidency of the United States, which initially signaled a shift away from the attitudes and views of the 1960s, has turned out to be a superficial and transient shift in public mood. His election and the attendant change in administration policies and values have reinvigorated alienation and the outpouring of social criticism, further inflaming intellectuals and probably enlarging the adversary culture. Their social criticism gained new substance and acquired new themes. President Reagan has come to stand for and symbolize everything these groups detest: a simple-minded patriotism, ties with and sympathy for big business, unashamed love of conspicuous consumption, a lack of guilt about American power, the ethos of Hollywood and public relations, and a generally unapologetic attitude about American institutions and middle-class American values. There were, of course, also the specific policies of the Reagan administration which provoked hostility, such as the transfer of resources from the civilian to the military sectors of the economy and the attempted global reassertion of American power. In short, the early 1980s in the United States have witnessed an upsurge of the discontents of American life because of the decline of the economy and the hardships it has created, and also on account of the way of life and values symbolized by Ronald Reagan in the White House.

Thus the appeals of socialism and the discontents of American life remain intertwined. While, as most of these essays suggest, knowledge of the particulars of socialism so far realized could rapidly erase its appeals, such information even when it becomes widely available tends to be neutralized by the intimately known and strongly felt discontents of American (and Western) life. Even if it is recognized that "disappointment is a central element of the human experience"[22] (and it often is not recognized), people, including intellectuals, can only be disappointed with what they know. This simple truth continues to explain the recurring interplay between political disenchantment and infatuation Western intellectuals so predictably display.

Notes

*The justification of making the elusive accessible is also frequently invoked and certainly applies here. Many of the essays reprinted in this book were published in relatively inaccessible or highly specialized journals. One of the essays had previously been published only in a foreign language, and several had never been published at all, lending further support to the enterprise.

1. While all the essays have been reprinted here in their original form (with minor editing and cuts designed to improve their style rather than substance), I added postscripts to many of them and especially to the older ones. Such postscripts serve the purpose of placing these writings in the context of the present, reflect my current thinking on various topics, and occasionally update them with more recent information and ideas.

2. Of my comparative frame of reference, it may be said that it has something to do with not being a native American but one who grew up in Eastern Europe (Hungary), attended college in England, and arrived at these shores to go to graduate school.

3. More is said about these preoccupations in my essay concerning the neglect of comparative sociology in the United States on pp. 313–322.

4. Stanislav Andreski, *Social Sciences as Sorcery* (New York: St. Martin Press, 1973), p. 111.

5. See also Miklos Haraszti, *Worker in a Worker's State* (New York: Universe, 1978).

6. Herbert Padilla, "After 20 Cuban Years," *New York Times,* Op-Ed page, 17 Sept. 1981.

7. Jean François Revel in particular argues forcefully against confusing Communist with socialist regimes. He wrote: "If the contrast between Marx's thought and the actions of the regimes that call themselves Marxist [and socialist—P.H.] causes more scholarly debate than political change, it is because it is easier to bend philosophy to fit reality than to do the opposite." While denying the socialist appellation to the regimes which have quite successfully claimed it for varying lengths of time, he identifies them as Communist regimes "defined as those in which all the power is in the hands of a single political party that calls itself Communist" (*The Totalitarian Temptation* [New York: Penguin, 1978], p. 60).

8. Similar definitional problems and disputes arise when one tries to define what a "Marxist society" is. See Ch. 15 of this volume.

9. Alex Inkeles made similar observations comparing the promise and reality of the Soviet system. See his "Fifty Years of the Soviet Revolution," in *Social Change in Soviet Russia* (Cambridge: Harvard Univ. Press, 1968).

10. Paul Hollander, *Political Pilgrims* (New York: Oxford U. Press, 1981), p. 418. See also Peter Berger, "The Socialist Myth," *Public Interest* (Summer 1976).

11. See, for example, Leonard Sussman, "Nicaragua's Brutal Abuse of Miskito Indians" (Correspondence), *New York Times,* 18 March 1982; Alan Riding, "Nicaraguan Indians Clash with Regime," *New York Times,* 18 June 1981. Another article reporting on the resettlement of the Indians and the burning of their villages by the government troops also noted that "foreign reporters have not been allowed to visit the region" (Alan Riding, "Nicaraguans Say Incursions Prompted Indians' Eviction," *New York Times,* 22 March 1982).

12. For further discussion of this shift, see pp. 73–76.

13. Paul Hollander, *Political Pilgrims,* pp. 416–17.

14. "Communism and the Left," *Nation,* 27 Feb. 1982, pp. 229–38.

15. Jeffrey Herf, "Reactionary Modernism—Some Ideological Origins of the Primacy of Politics in the Third Reich," *Theory and Society* 10 (1981): 813.

16. Such ambivalence toward both modernity and tradition may be linked to the longstanding ambivalence of Western intellectuals toward material progress "both celebrated and vilified." See Albert O. Hirschman, *Shifting Involvements—Private Interest and Public Action* (Princeton: Princeton University Press, 1982), pp. 49–50.

17. The following comment about the Nazi ideological discourse of the 1930s could be readily transposed to the counter-cultural context of the 1960s in the United States: "Reason was always preceded by the adjectives 'lifeless' or 'soulless' and was juxtaposed to vaguely defined but highly valued essences such as 'life,' 'will' or 'soul'" (Herf, "Reactionary Modernism," p. 814).

18. Bennett Berger, *The Survival of the Counter Culture: Ideological Work and Everyday Life among Rural Communards* (Berkeley: University of California Press, 1981), pp. 115–16.

19. Hirschman, *Shifting Involvements,* pp. 53, 46.

20. Ibid., pp. 101, 126.

21. Edward N. Luttwak, *Strategy and Politics—Collected Essays* (New Brunswick, N.J.: Transaction, 1980), p. 205.

22. Hirschman, *Shifting Involvements,* p. 11.

Part I
THE FACES OF SOCIALISM

1.
Privacy: A Bastion Stormed

Nothing illuminates the essence of totalitariansm more clearly than the characteristic compulsion of totalitarian regimes to extend their control into every nook and cranny of the life of the citizen—his daily activities, his thoughts and attitudes, his moral conduct, his relationships with others, private as well as public. The Chinese Communist regime is far from an exception in this regard: in fact, of all totalitarian systems to date, it appears to be the most ambitious and determined in its drive to impose officially prescribed patterns of morality on marital, familial, and sexual relationships. Its apparent aim is to "politicize" all personal relationships and to obliterate any distinction between private and public concerns.

The attitudes and the aspirations of the Mao regime in the areas of morality and interpersonal relationships may be gleaned from a survey of official statements and comments publicized in the Chinese mass media. These pronouncements also shed considerable light on the difficulties that have been encountered in the effort to implement the Party line in these spheres; at the same time, they are suggestive of the inadequacy of the psychological premises on which the regime's policies appear to rest.

The main pillar of the Chinese Communist ideological position is the Party's view of human nature. This view has remained unchanged since the early 1950s and—barring a fundamental transformation of the political system—is not likely to undergo significant modification.

Understandably enough (for reasons to be touched upon later), the party ideologists have sought first of all to combat the notion of a universal human nature, positing in its place a Marxist class interpretation. Thus, to quote an article published in the Chinese Communist youth organ:

> Every class has its own human nature. . . . Bourgeois individualists always dream of absolute "freedom of personality" and set this against organization and discipline. . . . [However,] one's personality can be developed freely, rationally and healthily only in a revolutionary organization, under public supervision and with collective help. . . . All absurd theories of human nature must be completely exposed.[1]

17

Similarly, a writer in the Party theoretical journal *Hsueh Hsi* (Study) takes issue with a "revisionist" philosopher named Pa Jen for erroneously suggesting that human feelings are universally shared:

> He [Pa Jen] writes: "What are human feelings? I think that human feelings are common to all men. Men share a common want for food, a common liking for fragrant flowers. . . . These wants, likings . . . stem from human nature."

> True, these wants, likings . . . stem from human nature, but do the hostile classes in class society have wants and likings . . . of the same character? Some want to obtain food through exploitation and do not allow others to eat to the full. Some want to drink water and expect others to drink it also; but some want to drink the blood of others. Is there anything in common between them?[2]

Another article sets out specifically to refute the idea that such feelings as devotion to one's parents, the "longing for love," "concern for friends and friendship," "homesickness," and even "the joy of living and hatred of dying" are universally shared human emotions. Thus, for example, the same unfortunate Pa Jen is again taken to task, this time for thinking it "only human that one is unable to carry out a firm struggle against his reactionary family." The article says:

> Actually, this is in every way a sign of vacillation in a revolutionary stand. A loyal, heroic and staunch fighter of the proletariat is capable of drawing a line of distinction between himself and his counterrevolutionary parents.[3]

Turning to love, the article goes on to quote the words of a "folk song" about proletarian love in an effort to differentiate it from that of the "exploiting classes":

> "The girl carries away the soil as the boy dredges the pond. Sweat drips from their bodies along with muddy water. The girl does not complain of fatigue though she has carried a thousand loads; nor does the boy feel the chill of the mud. It is inconvenient for them to talk to each other because there are too many people, but they understand each other at heart. Both the boy and the girl are heroic fellows. They work until the stars disappear and the sun rises."

> Can this kind of love engendered in common labor be found in the exploiting classes?

As for the view that fear of death is universal, the article associates such claims with "the dirty soul of the revisionists who measure men by the meanest psychology of individualism." Here too Pa Jen is condemned with special severity for maintaining that "when his life is at stake, even a proletarian hero would 'get nervous' and 'waver'; otherwise he would be inhuman." Apparently, the Chinese Communist ideologues are not content to demand that the citizen be willing to sacrifice his life for the Party; they also expect him to do so cheerfully and without flinching.

It is not difficult to see why the concept of widely shared human qualities is repugnant to the regime, for any admission that all human beings have much in common would tend to inhibit the intense hatred which the Chinese Communists seek to inculcate toward certain classes, groups, and individuals. As many observers have noted, a major goal of totalitarian propaganda is to make people forget that their alleged "class enemies" belong to the same species as themselves, and the denial of the universality of human nature is essential to the achievement of this goal. For only if people are led to believe that different classes have different "human natures" will they accept the idea that interclass antagonisms are irreconcilable, and only then can they be relied upon to carry out the struggle against those defined as "enemies" with the necessary consistency and relentlessness. As will be shown later in this study, the rigid differentiation of social groups on the basis of class and political criteria is a cornerstone of Communist morality as preached by the regime.

Judging from the numerous discussions about it and the intensity with which it is condemned in the Party press, individualism is regarded as one of the basic traits of bourgeois mentality and a major threat to the regime's efforts to inculcate "correct" behavior patterns. On closer inspection, this individualism reveals itself as an assortment of apolitical aspirations, ambitions, and attitudes, especially aspirations toward greater material and spiritual comforts. Examples would be a preference for urban rather than rural living (manifested in the shirking of "hardship positions" in the countryside); the desire to obtain higher education, or a better job more in line with one's special training, without regard for the current needs of the economy; or even the simple wish to choose one's friends or spouse from among persons of like background and education.

The desire for greater material well-being—often stimulated, para-doxically enough, by the very claims and promises of the regime—appears to be ranked as one of the most insidious forms of individualism. As an illustration of this sort of improper attitude, an article in the CCP organ *Chung-kuo Ch'ing-nien* (China Youth) quotes at length from a letter supposedly written by a young woman Party member, calling it representative of the thinking of some young comrades:

I often cherish this beautiful hope: with the progress of each five-year plan . . . material wealth will accumulate, wages will increase and hours of labor will decrease, and living conditions will improve further. By that time our small family will be even happier than now. We shall live in a modern flat well furnished with bookshelves, a radio receiver and a television set. Every day, after our work, either my husband or I will bring home some fruits and tasty chocolate, and while relaxing on a comfortable sofa we will watch television, listen to the radio, or read some books. . . . On Sundays we will bring our child home from the nursery . . . and buy her some things to eat and to wear. Both my husband and I would have nothing more to desire. Neither do we entertain any illusions about doing great meritorious service to win greater rewards from the people, nor do we long for the wanton life of the bourgeoisie. All we hope for is such a peaceful life. . . . Yet this ideal of ours is criticized by our comrades. . . . I feel that . . . if one serves the people all his life, leaves a place after it has been built and then builds another without even enjoying a family life, such a hard life is quite meaningless. . . . Revolution and construction should serve the future and the people, but they should also serve the present and ourselves.[4]

Castigating the attitude expressed by the letter writer, the article sarcastically remarks: "Yet, compared with the big family of socialism, how insignificant the small family hankered after by Hsiao Wen is!"

The repeated admonitions voiced in Party journals against such manifestations of "individualism"—manifestations rooted, apparently, in the rising expectations of the people—make it plain that the regime views the preoccupation of "certain comrades" with the attainment of material comforts and "ease" as detrimental to revolutionary morale. Thus, for example:

There is a section of the people who, with the steady improvement in livelihood, are indulging themselves in material enjoyment and forgetting the revolutionary tradition of diligence and courage. . . . The temptation of material life corrupts morale.[5]

The same article, giving an interesting twist to the Stalinist thesis of the sharpening of class struggle following the victory of socialism, brands aspirations for a better material life as evidence of a recrudescence of bourgeois ideological tendencies:

In the present complicated class struggle, the greater the improvement in our living standard, the more vigilant we must be against the infiltration of bourgeois thought . . . [and] the more we must be determined to inherit and promote an austere revolutionary style of the proletariat. . . . In our times, aspiration to ease is an expression of the exploiting ideology of the bourgeois class, and diligence and thrift are expressions of the great revolutionary will of the proletarian class.[6]

Another attitude which Chinese Party propaganda denounces as a survival of the "exploiting ideology" of "bourgeois individualism" is aversion to physical labor, or the idea that physical labor is inferior to mental work. Indeed, the manner in which the regime has sought to propagate a cult of physical labor would seem to suggest that growing numbers of Chinese have come to harbor premature ambitions of escaping the hardships of physical toil and earning their livelihood in some "easier" and more dignified way.

The official exaltation of manual labor cannot be explained simply as a rationalization of economic need reflecting China's retarded technological development—or a cautious estimate of future technological progress. Party propaganda on the subject consistently abstains from holding forth the prospect, even in the distant future, of that state of "ease" which might permit relief from heavy toil; in fact, it makes a point of insisting on the permanent value of manual labor. For example, a discussion in *Chung-kuo Ch'ing-nien* asserts:

> Some bourgeois intellectuals think that with the development of mechanization and automation manual labor will be eliminated. This kind of viewpoint is wrong in the extreme. Marxism-Leninism holds the view that manual labor will never be eliminated.[7]

Thus the stress on manual labor goes beyond the accommodation to current economic realities and appears to take on the character of a cult of "hardship for hardship's sake," which is expressive of totalitarian concepts of discipline and service. Behind the regime's fulminations against the corrupting influence of material pleasures and its insistence on hard labor as a necessary element in building Communist character, one may also detect fear of loss of revolutionary zeal, or of the "bourgeoisification" attributed—rightly or wrongly—to Khrushchev's Russia.

It is significant in this context that Chinese propaganda sermons on the salubrious effects of manual labor are directed, more often than not, at the intellectuals. The regime's requirement that intellectuals participate in such labor is clearly motivated by ideological and political rather than economic considerations. No secret is made of the fact that the primary purpose of assigning intellectuals to occasional periods of work on farms, in factories, or on construction projects is to effect their ideological "remolding."[8]

An interesting aspect of most Chinese commentaries dealing with "survivals" of bourgeois ideology is their implication—for the most part unexplained—that the acquisition of correct Communist views and attitudes is no permanent safeguard against deviationist backsliding. There are constant warnings that no matter how well-indoctrinated a person may have become or how sincere his intentions, evil ideas and attitudes are always ready to engulf him, and that self-control and ideological "rectification," therefore, cannot for a moment be relaxed. For example: "if learning is not reinforced and constant vigilance is not maintained, one might very easily be influenced by non-proletarian ideology."[9] Indeed, the guardians of Party orthodoxy seem to regard it as more natural for people to err, especially in the area of morality, than to think and behave "correctly." Even the phraseology of many of the articles on these subjects is suggestive of a belief in the basic fallibility of man: "people slide back," they "succumb to wrong ideas," are easily "tempted," "corrupted," and so on.[10]

The Chinese Communist approach to human behavior and morality is thus characterized by the imposition of class and political-ideological criteria. This is perhaps most vividly illustrated by the way in which Party ideologues and propagandists treat the subject of intimate relations between the sexes—or what they commonly refer to as "the love problem."

Here, the Party appears to be waging a battle on two fronts. On the one hand, it denounces promiscuity and the treatment of women as "playthings" as survivals of the corrupt moral standards of capitalist society; love is to be regarded as a serious affair and must be handled "correctly." On the other hand, the Party simultaneously argues that people in love should not allow their emotional involvement to assume overwhelming proportions because the idea that love transcends everything is also a bourgeois notion!

More specifically, the official ideologues insist that love should never interfere with work or with one's dedication to the Party and its leaders, to the collective, and to the political tasks at hand; nor should it be allowed to get in the way of the prescribed detestation of class enemies.[11] Going a step further, they argue that love cannot be enduring and worthwhile unless it is based on a shared commitment to goals transcending the individuals concerned—unless it is integrated with the goals of the collective, that is, of the Party. Love, or any strong attachment to another person, it is held, cannot be isolated from the individual's political attitudes; and anyone who is not concerned with the collective, who lacks the appropriate political motivation, cannot truly love.

Published discussions of "the love problem" in the Party journals provide ample illustration of these official attitudes. In one such discussion, for instance, the following example is cited to show the sort of social-political criteria which, in the Party's view, ought to take precedence over mere personal feelings as a basis for love and marriage:

> Hsieh Ta-sa knew for sure that Kuo Kuo-liang was an agricultural expert of the Ili Chi collective farm, while Kuo Kuo-liang also knew from press reports that Hsieh was a model worker at the Red Guerrillas' collective farm.[12]

Again, an article in a women's magazine clearly points to political background as a major qualification of a desirable bridegroom:

> He was a very enthusiastic, smart, and capable man. *More important still* was the fact that he had participated in the revolution since 1939 and was a member of the Communist Party. All these things held attraction for a young girl.[13] (Emphasis added)

One even finds the suggestion that when love is based on correct socialist criteria, physical separation ceases to be a hardship. In an article entitled "How I Handle My Love Problem," a young woman Party member writes:

> Not long ago I received a letter from Lao Tang telling me that he had already registered himself to participate in the work of dredging Tungting Lake. This news gives me so much joy. I believe that he will cultivate himself through collective labor to become an active builder of socialism. Our future is bright and full of happiness.[14]

The official effort to "politicize" love appears, indeed, to have encouraged some young Party members to go farther than even the Party thought desirable in trying to form love relationships on the basis of political considerations. In the mid-1950s particularly, Party journals frequently published letters sent in by young women activists telling of their efforts to cultivate love affairs with their "team-leaders" or with "politically advanced" cadres. Evidently, some male comrades—presumably less advanced—began cultivating similar affairs, and the Party finally felt compelled to reaffirm the "principle of voluntariness in love life."[15]

More than anything else, the official line on love is a reflection of the Party's fundamental opposition to any sort of emotional attachment between individuals which might compete with, and perhaps overshadow, their dedication to the Party and the regime. Yet the curious fact is that the regime itself, by sweeping aside the traditional familial marriage controls, was largely responsible for encouraging the kind of romantic love which it now opposes. Romantic attachments are, by nature, highly individualistic and tend to absorb a substantial share of the interest, energies, and time of the participants at the expense of their wider social commitments. Hence it is understandable that such relationships should be discouraged by a regime that seeks to make total claims upon its citizens.

It is interesting to observe, however, that the Party, while it frowns upon intense romantic relationships between individuals, encourages a highly emotional and unrestrained attachment toward the Party and its leaders. The model citizen, as portrayed in the official mass media, keeps his love for wife or sweetheart, family or friends, within circumscribed bounds. Yet in contrast to this reserve in his personal relationships, the same model citizen displays, and quite obviously is expected to display, the most intense emotional attachment to the leading figures of the Party. Consider, for example, this reaction to a visit by Party Chairman Mao Tse-tung:

> "If it was not Secretary K'o, who could it have been?" But when I saw the felicitous smile on Yang Hsin-fu's face, my heart started to pound wildly. "It could not have been Chairman Mao?" . . . Chairman Mao? At first, I was dumbfounded, and then I embraced Yang Hsin-fu tightly. . . . I felt as if my blood was starting to boil . . . and my heart was leaping out of my chest.[16]

Or, the following account of a visit to a factory by Liu Shao-ch'i,[17] as related by one of those present:

> I was suddenly called . . . [and] informed . . . that Comrade Shao-ch'i would look at the wall-newspapers . . . and would come to our plant to acquaint himself with the "blooming and contending" situation here. This was unexpectedly good news. Despite the pressure of work every day, this comrade of the central leadership could manage to squeeze out time to read wall-newspapers and survey the "blooming and contending" situation. How could we not be moved? . . . I could hardly restrain the thumping of my heart as I pondered the matter. . . . No sooner had he emerged from the meeting room than there arose a thunder of handclapping. Comrade Shao-ch'i waved his hand. . . . Young workers, forgetting a day's toil and their empty stomachs, were seized with an agony of exaltation. Some of these young fellows still lingered on the street at the front gate of the plant staring in the direction of his car after it had already driven far off. . . . My mind is still full of whirling thoughts all these days since Comrade Shao-ch'i left. I can never forget the most impressive lesson he has imparted to us.[18]

In light of these examples, it may not be too farfetched to suggest that the cult of personality, as developed in Communist China and other totalitarian societies, represents in part an instrumentality for the transference of emotionalism from the sphere of interpersonal relations to that of the citizen's relations to the leaders of party and state.

As has been shown, then, the model Chinese Communist citizen is expected to avoid the pitfalls both of a casual attitude toward sex and of overintense romantic involvement. It would be wrong, however, to infer from this that what the regime wishes to see is the single-minded dedication of the citizen to the pleasures and preoccupations of family life. To devote too much attention to one's family is also regarded as an error, and the Party propaganda machine drives this home in no uncertain terms. For instance:

> A man called Li Chien-hua, praising this kind of vulgar, selfish "happiness," cried out: "Is there any other place in the world which is warmer than the family?" He contended that "it is the family that gives you love and brings you up, . . . that gives you everything." . . .He believed that the family can bring people "infinite joy." This is really a big lie.[19]

Another Party journal offers the reader a sharply contrasting "positive" example in the person of a Mrs. Chu:

> She [Mrs. Chu] often says to her sons and daughters-in-law: "You must listen to the party and do what it tells you to do. . . . The group is the important thing. Our family is not so important." Having a mother who loves the group so much, the sons and daughters are little concerned over their own family affairs. Whenever they meet at home after returning from work, they talk about production and challenge one another to do better. They think of nothing else. The old woman is pleased to see all this. There was a time when, during her leisure, she collected forty cartloads of high-quality manure and delivered all of it to the production team.[20]

Not surprisingly, the tendency to devote too much time and attention to family life has sometimes been pictured as only part of much more serious "deviationism," as in the case of a man whose own wife finally denounced him to the Party as a "masked counterrevolutionary." Writes the wife in one of the Party journals:

> In his leisure hours he would either read stories or play with the child, caring nothing for the ideological struggle. . . . I was seized with remorse for showing affection to a counterrevolutionary. . . . I began to review my past carefully and to lay bare all information in my possession.[21]

As indicated earlier, the Party holds political compatibility to be the cornerstone of a correct marital relationship. It also seeks to encourage later marriages, partly in order to allow a longer period of full-time dedication to political work and education, and partly on the ground that this will contribute to a healthful avoidance of sexual overindulgence:

> If people get married when they are older . . . their minds will have assumed greater control over their bodies, enabling them to handle problems more intelligently and to curb their sex urge so that they will not have their health impaired through excess. . . . By getting married late, young people [also] can in the meantime spend more energy in caring about state affairs and group life, in studying political theory, and in taking part in political struggles. . . . Thus, late marriage provides a favorable objective condition for political progress.[22]

Understandably enough, the Party displays an even greater aversion to premarital sexual "excesses" and preoccupations.[23]

The combination of pragmatism and puritanism that characterizes the Party's approach to sex is further evident in the regime's response to popular complaints against the use of certain contraceptives. Occasional letters from readers, published in Party journals, indicate that the contraceptive devices available to the public were objected to by many as "troublesome" and diminishing the gratification of the husband. The complainants were sharply rebuked in the Party organs for their short-sighted, pleasure-seeking attitudes and were told to think of the interests of the country and the economy.[24]

As a matter of fact, most of the published discussions regarding the proper conduct of married life are refreshingly candid and make it quite clear that the Party expects marital bliss to be subordinated to the requirements of the economy and the "collective" interest. For instance:

> Love for the group and proper participation in collective production involve another important matter, which is . . . making proper arrangements for family life. . . . When proper arrangements are made . . . people will feel happy, free from worries, and energetic in production. If the arrangements for family life are improper, production will be adversely affected.[25]

If the essence of totalitarianism is the maximization of political controls and the obliteration of any demarcation line separating the private affairs of the citizen from the public concerns of the state, the preceding survey of the Peking regime's attitudes concerning the "proper" conduct of the citizen's sexual and family relationships would seem to justify the conclusion that Communist China today presents the most authentic example of a thoroughly totalitarian society.

While professing to be disciples of Stalin, the Chinese Communist leaders appear to have gone farther than even the Soviet regime of Stalin's day in attempting to prescribe norms for the conduct of the most intimate aspects of the citizen's life, in imposing collectivist attitudes, and setting standards of personal morality governed by political criteria. In fact, there would seem to be hardly any area of the Chinese citizen's life in which the regime feels that it can allow him to make his own choices without benefit of official "guidance."

The essential characteristic of the Chinese Communist prescriptions on morality and personal relationships is their highly practical or *functionalized* character. Love, affection, friendship, and the pleasures of emotional and sexual bonds are not viewed as valuable *in themselves*: at best they are looked upon as means to other ends, at worst as potentially troublesome or useless individualistic preoccupations. The human need for love and affection is given a certain degree of recognition (except, of course, with respect to "class enemies"), but at the same time the Party is careful to stipulate that the satisfaction of this need must not interfere with the citizen's political loyalty or his dedication to the goals and tasks set by the regime. Friendship is acceptable as long as it helps to cement collective unity, to promote efficient teamwork, and to bolster the fighting spirit of the group. The importance of sexual gratification is acknowledged, but the citizen is called upon to refrain from "excesses" that might reduce the energies he can devote to productive tasks and political work. The family is tolerated, subject, however, to a drastic curtailment of its traditional role: the regime ridicules and condemns excessive preoccupation with family affairs, stresses that family ties must be subordinated to the citizen's primary commitments to the Party and to the collectivity. The regime has also taken various measures to limit both the family's traditional autonomy and its child-rearing function.

The evident determination of the Chinese Communists to subject even intimate personal relationships to official scrutiny and control may have behind it something more fundamental than the mere desire to prevent these relationships from interfering with the citizen's dedication to Party-prescribed tasks. It may be the recognition that there is a certain incompatibility between authoritarianism and rigidity in political relationships and the tolerance of freedom, diversity, and mobility in relationships between individuals. Thus while the conservation of sexual and emotional energies for political and economic purposes is undoubtedly an important objective of totalitarian regimes, these regimes must also be prompted by the realization that laxity of controls in one sphere of the citizen's life is incompatible with the maintenance of rigid discipline and restrictions in all others.

Besides delineating the Chinese Communist approach to personal relationships and morality, the evidence presented here affords some insight into the problems that have been encountered in implementing it. The frequent exhortations, complaints, and rebukes addressed to the public, or certain segments of it, by the Party organs suggest that the Chinese masses are not quite so docile and so easily reconciled to the severe limitations on their personal freedoms as some Western observers have supposed. If the evidence reviewed is any guide, there would appear to be a great many Chinese who are conscious of the harsh demands made upon them by the regime, who would prefer more leisure time, a fuller family life, better opportunities for education (and its utilization), the right to love or associate with whom they will, without political restriction—in short, who consider their personal lives important enough to resent official encroachments and interference.

It is especially noteworthy that already at this early stage people are "hankering after" the forbidden and unavailable material and physical comforts, that popular expectations, in other words, have been rising at a rate which the regime views as disquieting and is trying to check.

The complaints of the masses, as filtered through the official responses to them, are also suggestive of the flaws in the psychological premises of the regime. There may be no such thing as a universal human nature, yet it appears to be true that most people, at most times and in most places, sooner or later become conscious of the deprivations they suffer— particularly when they are being told that their lot has never been better.

Postscript 1982

It was entirely accidental that the first article I had ever published in English (almost exactly twenty years ago) had to do with Chinese affairs in view of the fact that I was not (and still am not) a specialist on China. Rather than a reflection of my interest in Chinese politics as such, "Privacy: A Bastion Stormed" grew out of my interest in the concept of and the practices associated with totalitarianism, or, more generally, the relationship between political controls and private lives. The Chinese Communist setting offered an excellent opportunity to look at these issues. (It was the same general desire for a deeper understanding of totalitarianism which led me to the study of various aspects of Soviet society both under and after Stalin—rather than an interest in Russian culture, history, or Soviet political institutions as such.)

There are certain matters of special interest in the preceding article for the present-day reader, besides the evidence it provides of the high degree to which the Chinese regime in the 1950s and early 1960s lived up to the theoretical models of a totalitarian society. Thus I think it is of some significance that the harsh and intolerant official attitudes and policies described previously had already prevailed in an era preceding the Cultural Revolution, which many outsiders assumed to be a somewhat discordant chapter in Chinese politics, an outburst of excess, repression, and collectivist frenzy virtually unrelated to policies preceding it. By the same token, we are beginning to learn more of the continuities (and specifics) of the official policies which both preceded *and* followed the Cultural Revolution and of the thoroughness of social-political controls over personal lives from the writings of authors like Simon Leys, Fox Butterfield, and Bernard Frolic.[26]

In reflecting over phenomena which stretch from the 1950s to the present, one may also single out the touchingly humble material and personal aspirations of Chinese people conveyed in some of the materials I have just quoted. There is reason to believe that today such aspirations are stronger, not weaker, than they were almost a quarter century ago.

Hopefully, such attitudes will be viewed more indulgently and with more tolerance by the new leaders who have undertaken to lighten the weight of Maoist totalitarianism over Chinese society.

Notes

1. Wang Tzu-yeh, "Hu Feng's 'On Human Nature'—Just a Lie," *Chung-kuo Ch'ing-nien* (China Youth), no. 18, 1955; English translation in *Selections from China Mainland Magazines* (hereafter cited as SCMM), U.S. Consulate General, Hong Kong, no. 15, pp. 7–8.
2. Kuan Feng, "On Human Nature and Class Nature," *Hsueh Hsi,* no. 17, 3 Sept. 1957; SCMM, no. 112, p. 11.
3. Red Flag Literary and Art Critique Group of Peking University, "Are There Sentiments Common to Mankind in a Class Society?" *Chung-kuo Ch'ing-nien,* no. 11, 1960; SCMM, no. 221, p. 14.
4. Wu Chih-p'u, "On the Ideal Life of Revolutionary Youth," ibid.; SCMM, no. 219, pp. 16–17.
5. Kan Feng, "In Discussing 'Too Many Pleasures Stifle Ambition,' " ibid., 16 Nov. 1960; SCMM, no. 249, pp. 22–23.
6. Cf. also Wu Chiang, "A Discourse on Public Interests and Individual Interests," ibid., 10 Dec. 1961; SCMM, no. 297; and Ma T'ien-ting, "Seek Pleasure and Happiness Through Struggles . . . ," ibid., 1 Feb. 1961; SCMM, no. 253.
7. Ch'ih Liao-chou, "The Militant Program for Cultural and Educational Work," ibid., 16 June 1960; SCMM, no. 219.

8. E.g., see Yen-Tzu-yuan, "Resolutely Turn Intellectuals into Laborers," ibid., 16 Dec. 1960; SCMM, no. 251. On the subject of difficulties connected with the reeducation of intellectuals, see Chou Chien-jen, "Widening the Scope of Knowledge *versus* Ideological Remodeling," ibid., 5 Feb. 1962; SCMM, no. 305. (The latter article combats the apparently not atypical view that higher intellectual attainments obstruct the acquisition of correct political-ideological attitudes.)

9. Yen Sheng, "The Need of Making a Correct Estimate of Oneself," ibid., 16 April 1962; SCMM, no. 315, p. 2.

10. E.g., see Kan Feng, "What If We Fail to Guard the First Pass?" ibid., 16 March 1962; SCMM, no. 309.

11. "Some people . . . ask: 'Why is it that people of antagonistic classes can also fall in love with each other? Doesn't this show that love has no class character?' In our opinion this is an entirely erroneous argument. There have been people from antagonistic classes who have fallen in love with each other. But such a thing could only happen when the world outlook of one party was influenced by another class to such an extent that a change set in, thus engendering some common ideological foundation."

    From an article authored by the Red Flag Literary and Art Critique Group, Chinese Department, Peking University, in *Chung-kuo Ch'ing-nien* (China Youth), no. 11, 1 June 1960.

12. Chung Tien-fei, "Be Smart and Firm, and Fight Against Such Bad Men as Ma Cheng-laing," ibid., 16 Aug. 1955; SCMM, no. 13, p. 8.

13. Liu Lo-ch'un, "Why Our Marital Relations Became Strained," *Hsin Chung-Kuo Fu-nü* (Women of New China), no. 11, 1955; SCMM, no. 22, p. 5.

14. Article by Chou K'e-hsien, *Chung-kuo Ch'ing-nien*, no. 11, 1955; SCMM, no. 22, p. 4.

15. "Respect the Principle of Voluntariness in Love Life," a summary of letters from readers, ibid., no. 10, 1956; SCMM, no. 14.

16. Wang Lin-ho, "I See Chairman Mao Tse-tung Every Day," *Shanghai Wen-hsueh* (Shanghai Literature), no. 8, 1960; SCMM, no. 228, p. 34. (Actually, on the occasion described, the author narrowly missed seeing Mao. The title of his article is more figurative than actual.)

17. Subsequently denounced and purged during the Cultural Revolution.

18. Yen Shang-hua, "A Most Impressive Lesson—Report on a Talk by Liu Shao-ch'i," *Chung-kuo Ch'ing-nien*, no. 21, 1957; SCMM, no. 41.

19. Wei Wei, "Backwater and Billows," ibid., no. 14, 1960; SCMM, no. 227, p. 41.

20. "Love the Group" (editorial), *Chung-kuo Fu-nü* (Women of China), 1 March 1962; SCMM, no. 320, p. 27.

21. *Chung-kuo Ch'ing-nien*, no. 24, 1955.

22. Yang Hsiu, "For Late Marriage," ibid., 1 June 1962; SCMM, no. 322, pp. 23–24.

23. E.g., see Ke Ch'ang-yueh, "Do Not Start Making Love Too Early," *Chung-hsueh Sheng* (Middle-School Student), no. 4, 1956; SCMM, no. 41. This article goes so far as to suggest that masturbation and nocturnal emissions are diseases.

24. E.g., see the article entitled "How to Approach the Problem of Birth Control," *Hsin Chung-kuo Fu-nü*, no. 4–5, 1955; SCMM, no. 2; and "Is Contraception

Still Necessary?" (editorial in reply to a reader's query) *Chung-kuo Fu-nü*, no. 14, 1959; SCMM, no. 184.

25. See editorial cited in note 20.
26. Simon Leys, *Chinese Shadows* (New York: Viking, 1977); Fox Butterfield, *China Alive in a Bitter Sea* (New York: N.Y. Times Books, 1982); Bernard Frolic, *Mao's People* (Cambridge: Harvard Univ. Press, 1980).

2.
Models of Behavior in Stalinist Literature: A Case Study of Totalitarian Values and Controls

This article seeks to link political sociology and the study of political socialization in particular to the sociology of literature by examining the official values and techniques of control in two totalitarian societies as revealed in the officially sanctioned literature and literary criticism. Our focus is on the omnipresent literary stereotypes: the recurring personifications of good and evil.

The approach is historical since it draws its data from Soviet (and "Sovietized" Hungarian) sources dating from the mid-1930s up to 1953, or the death of Stalin, which represented both a symbolic and a real closure of the era of full-blown Soviet totalitarianism. Although Stalinist totalitarianism has in the meantime become largely a matter of historical interest, the fact remains that the basics of Soviet industrialization were carried out under Stalin. As long as rapid industrialization remains a major preoccupation in more than half the world, it is hardly a matter of indifference what official values accompanied the process in the USSR and how the Soviet regime tried to inculcate them. Concern with the literary products of the period represents a concern with the by-products and repercussions of industrialization in the realm of values and social controls. Literature was one of the major arenas where the struggle to overhaul the popular value system was joined. The methodology of this struggle in the realm of the arts came to be known as socialist realism. Our interest centers on the ways in which Soviet literature sought to provide models of behavior incorporating the new values and desirable attitudes. What is the nature of these models and how are they balanced between the respective demands of industrialization *and* totalitarianism? In what way do they stand for a new departure in social control and political socialization?

Two points are stressed: first, the function of socialist realist literary works transcends political agitation and propaganda, and extends to a broader and more ambitious objective—the provision of models of behavior for the population. This objective can be viewed as a form of social conrol peculiar to totalitarianism and its paradoxical effort to supplement (but not to replace) coercion with "persuasion."

Second, the premises of socialist realism and particularly the literary stereotypes (the so-called positive and negative heroes, or the personifications of good and evil) offer unusual insight into the nature of the official system of values. The core of any value system is revealed when conceptions of good and evil are laid bare. More significantly, these polarized personality types betray an unmistakable affinity with the spirit, ideology, and institutions of a totalitarian society.

The positive and the negative hero inform us about techniques of social control because they are officially designated models of behavior[1]— one standing for the attitudes and modes of behavior to be emulated and cultivated and the other for those to be avoided or repressed. The models thus reflect a characteristic of totalitarian control systems: the desire to eradicate even the potential for deviance by undertaking to transform not only society but also its basic unit, the individual. For the totalitarian rulers, mere prohibition or suppression of undesirable behavior is not sufficient.

The positive hero (the literary equivalent of the "New Soviet Man") was thus created as a synthetic culture hero to aid the regime's efforts to get the new values internalized by the population. No other political system in this century set such goals for its literature or pursued them with the same determination (except, of course, the Chinese Communist regime). In no other modern society have the political power holders entrusted to the writers (and instructed them so well in the details of the task) the expression of their perceptions of good and evil, presenting in the process a summary of their whole system of values. No other modern society presents the sociologist with the double opportunity to examine the values of the rulers and the favored techniques of social control through the pages of fiction.

It is easy to see why models of behavior came to occupy an important place in the system of social control practiced under Stalin. There are many areas of life difficult to bring under adequate institutional control (particularly of a coercive kind), covered by explicit rules, political instructions, or ideological propositions. Personal relationships, for example, by virtue of their diffuseness and inherent privacy, are difficult to bring under satisfactory political-institutional control. This is one reason why literature was called upon to attempt a penetration of the corners of privacy and to provide guidance through the models of behavior.

Before turning to a detailed analysis of the models, we must outline the meanings of socialist realism, since it is in this context that the positive and negative heroes emerged as omnipresent literary stereotypes. Socialist realism may be viewed as a theoretical framework for the complete subordination of the arts to the political objectives upheld by the Soviet regime.[2] We may also look upon its principles as a set of rationalizations developed to justify the deprivation of art of any autonomy.[3] Specifically, it is the theory of the artistic representation of social reality *in terms of what it ought to be like* according to the prescriptions supplied by the Soviet ideological and power elite at any given time. From the sociological point of view, socialist realism is a vehicle for the monopolistic dissemination of the ideal patterns devised by the ruling groups.[4] Its main features are tendentiousness, optimism, simplification, the politicization of conflicts, and "typicality." The latter requires some explanation. The typical in socialist realism does not refer to a statistical average, but to the unfolding, the emergent, the developing— to phenomena that conform to certain ideological prescriptions and propositions. Typicality in socialist realism is, therefore, a device for presenting reality as it is supposed to be. As such, it is a means of evading or idealizing reality.

The most fundamental and far-reaching (and as yet unattained) goal of socialist realism is to alter people's perceptions of reality. This is the essence of indoctrination: to generate a capacity for selective or distorted perceptions. In a society which restricts the free flow of communication and in which the individual's ability to obtain reliable information of many aspects of social reality is severely curtailed, it is not entirely unreasonable to hope that a consistent and systematic misrepresentation of reality may lead one to question the soundness and generalizability of his personal experiences.

Source of Data

The choice of data was based on the following considerations. First, it seemed desirable to draw information from more than one Soviet-type society since the social-political phenomenon to be illustrated was Stalinist totalitarianism in general, not just its manifestation in the Soviet Union. We were also interested in finding out to what degree the Stalinist value system (as expressed in socialist realist literary works) could be transplanted into societies of a totally different cultural-historical background. Hungary was chosen for two reasons. One was the author's familiarity with the language, thereby making Hungarian literary works accessible. Supporting this practical consideration was the fact that

Hungary has been the furthest removed from Russian cultural influences among the East European nations which became, at least for a time, "Sovietized." Thus to the extent that Stalinist totalitarianism was manifest in Hungary we expected to encounter it in its "purest" form least affected by historical traditions and continuities. Since the study revealed no significant differences between Soviet and Hungarian literary heroes (negative or positive), we make no analytical distinction between Soviet and Hungarian sources. (There were, of course, differences in the historical backgrounds and settings presented in the Hungarian books, and in the social bases from which the heroes were drawn. Yet the overwhelming characterological similarities dominated the comparison.) Such similarity can be explained by the fact that the precepts and techniques of socialist realism are easy to imitate, and in the period surveyed there was a large enough group of writers in Hungary sufficiently familiar with Soviet socialist realist works and their theoretical inspiration, and devoted to the creation of such works.

The time span covered was not exactly the same for the two samples. Most of the books used, both Soviet and Hungarian, were published or written between 1948 and 1953. In both societies, these were years of intense Stalinist repression and cultural conformity. In Hungary, this was the only period of clear-cut Stalinist domination. In the Soviet Union, of course, Stalinism had roots further back in history; this prompted the inclusion of a few Soviet novels which appeared in the 1930s and were regarded as outstanding examples of socialist realism.

An effort was made to select works most authentically representing the Party line, most favored by the literary policy makers. Three criteria, not always combined, were used: (1) literary prizes (Stalin prize for the USSR and also for some of the Hungarian writers; Kossuth prize for Hungarian writers); (2) position beyond membership in the respective writers' union (another unmistakable sign of political reliability); and (3) favorable criticism in the press and literary journals. At least one of the three criteria applied to all writers selected. In the case of writers who have written over a long period (like Sholokhov), books written before the Stalinist period were excluded from consideration.

A second consideration entering into the selection was the desire to diversify the sample with regard to settings and social types. Thus, for example, in order to broaden the basis from which to generalize about the negative hero, we included Soviet works with American or other non-Soviet settings, with wartime as well as peacetime situations, stories taking place in farms, factories, universities, barracks, and so on.[5]

The Positive Hero

"Party-mindedness" is perhaps the most important trait of the positive hero. It means unswerving loyalty to the Party and whatever position it takes at any given time, an unconditional and complete identification with the Party. Since the Party is above all a political entity, Party-mindedness also means the permeation of consciousness with political criteria, a sharpened sensitivity to the political content or connotation of every issue, situation, and relationship. From this identification with the Party (and also from the identification with the collective, to be discussed later in this volume) follows a highly instrumental approach to the self. Party-mindedness, based on the assimilation of the goals of the Party, means also readiness to expose the self to the Party. The positive hero has no secrets from the Party and little sense of privacy (except for the sexual sphere). Significantly, Party-mindedness is a trait applicable not only to Party members. While the model citizens presented in the novels surveyed are mostly Party or Komsomol members, the positive hero's Party-mindedness derives not from membership, but from his acceptance of everything the Party stands for and demands from the population. This attitude does not presuppose membership. (It would in fact be quite dysfunctional for the regime to limit such expectations to Party members.) Expressions of Party-mindedness can range from collecting scrap metal to the willingness to move to remote areas of the country; from acceptance of new production norms (with an attendant cut in the standard of living) to spying on one's neighbor; from heroism on the battlefield to self-effacing conformity in the administrative apparatus.

Patriotism is a variation on the theme of loyalty to the regime. The patriotism of the positive hero is hardly distinguishable from patriotism as known and cherished in other lands and at other times (unless one gives credence to the ritualistic affirmations of proletarian internationalism which often accompany definitions of Soviet patriotism), except that it has an intensity which patriotism in other countries acquires only at times of crisis and conflict. This intensity (not limited to patriotic sentiment) indicates the positive hero's readiness to cross from the plane of belief to that of action and symbolizes the crucial link between theory and practice, the declared hallmark of the Soviet system and the new Communist man.

The positive hero is also a staunch and consistent *collectivist* (or *antiindividualist*), ready to surrender—or, rather, continuously engaged in surrendering—his personal interests. To be sure, if one accepts the official premises concerning the nature of Soviet society, then the notion of "surrendering" personal interests becomes redundant since there can be no conflict between personal and collective (or social or public) interest (as defined by the Party); everything the regime does is bound to benefit the citizen sooner or later.

The collectivist orientation of the positive hero is usually exemplified by his apologetic attitude toward his private problems (ranging from toothache to divorce), and his shame over any personal sorrow or suffering that is unrelated to larger causes. This antiindividualism is also expressed in his readiness to expose himself to the Collective (as, for example, in the context of criticism–self-criticism), his dislike of privacy, and his preference for group activities and constant company.

Vigilance is another trait of the positive hero directly related to the politicization of his personality. Vigilance refers to the permanent readiness to discover and uncover the activities and representatives of the enemy, a constant awareness that he is dangerous, ubiquitous, and cleverly camouflaged. Vigilance represents a delicate balance between indiscriminate suspiciousness and a state of mind which attributes all mistakes of individuals and the malfunctioning of institutions to malevolence rather than accident. It is a trait typical of the paranoid atmosphere of Stalinism.

The propensity to hate is closely related to vigilance since it is the hateful qualities of the enemy which call forth and justify vigilance. Hatred of the enemy may also be viewed as a corollary of love of the Party and the Fatherland. This hate has two dimensions. On the one hand, the positive hero is supposed to possess a large reservoir of hate, kept at a constant level and ready to be discharged against the abstract figure of the enemy. On the other hand, hate can take the form of violent flare-ups against specific targets designated from time to time in accordance with changes in the Party line. Naturally, the hate of the positive hero must always be directed against the appropriate, centrally assigned objects. A noteworthy aspect of the capacity for hate is the apparent ease with which the positive hero can switch it on and off. He can hate at a moment's notice without any need for a gradual buildup of negative emotions. It is enough to be told by the appropriate authorities that somebody he would never have suspected is an agent (conscious or unwitting) of the enemy, and he is at once filled with an intensely personal hatred. Such demands to display hate on short notice are particularly striking when it is directed against outstanding public figures, leaders who shortly before had been the equally compulsory objects of deep affection and respect. There is never a residue of doubt or slowness to respond when new objects of hate are introduced. The unqualified willingness to hate all those labeled as the enemy is tantamount to the support of whatever policies the regime wants to pursue. The propensity to hate is also a prerequisite of efficient, highly motivated fighting spirit.

Activism and the love of work. The love of work follows from the absorption of Marxism (and one of its central propositions that work invests man with his distinctive human qualities) and from the overall compulsion of the Soviet regime to increase production and productivity in every possible realm. Translated into personality traits, the love of work becomes a more diffuse activism, an attitude that shuns reflection and contemplation, giving the impression that activity is valued for its own sake. The cult of activism also follows from the purposefulness of the positive hero, who is keen on transforming his environment and himself. It may also be linked to what Leites calls the fear of goal fulfillment,[6] or the suppressed existential anxiety of the consistent philo-sophical materialist who, rejecting a transcendental meaning of life, must always set himself new goals—since the accomplishment of any is never an end in itself.

Without *discipline* none of the commitments, attitudes, and goals of the positive hero could be translated into reality. Readiness to submit to discipline is related to the ability to obey easily—another highly functional feature of the positive hero. It finds expression in carrying out cheerfully and without hesitation all instructions received from the authorities; in adhering rigidly to the Party line of the day; in curbing whatever personal impulses, wishes, or idiosyncrasies might prevent him from carrying out his Party-assigned tasks; in subordinating matter to the mind, flesh to the spirit, the personal to the collective interest. (As such, discipline is also an adjunct to antiindividualism.)

The link between *modesty* and collectivism is easily established, for if a person conceives of himself (as the positive hero does) as serving causes and organizations immeasurably higher and more important than himself, or as an instrument of historical and political designs, he is bound to be modest. Modesty is also demanded of the positive hero as an antidote to overconfidence or—as Stalin put it—to "dizziness with success." The latter can be dangerous insofar as it can lead to the relaxation of effort or to an underestimation of the magnitude of the tasks always ahead.

The positive hero is *optimistic*, as any man must be if he is assured of living in the historically most advanced society, working and fighting under the leadership of the collective wisdom of a historically unique organization—the Party—and guided by infallible leaders. The ideology, the official system of values he internalized, assure him of being on the right, the victorious side of history, supported by invincible social forces.

From the regime's point of view, optimism is a desirable quality of the citizen since it helps him to forget or gloss over the imperfections and frustrations of the present and accept, without skepticism, promises of a better life to come. Thus optimism is also tied to future orientation.

The *puritanism* of the positive hero has numerous manifestations. Certain aspects have already been touched upon: devotion to work, dedication to a superpersonal cause, discipline, the submission of the self to a collective. Puritanism, in addition, entails disdain for frivolous and hedonistic activities and attitudes, and the capacity for self-sacrifice. The core of the concept lies in the various manifestations of self-denial. What emerges is a person not unlike the Western conceptions of the puritan: intensely concerned with spiritual (ideological) values, minimizing the importance of self in humility to a superpersonal cause, constantly on guard against violations of his moral code, impatient with those violating it. Yet he is also impatient with himself, and here lies the main psychological source of self-denial. Self-denial is expressed in his indifference to personal danger and in the mortification of the flesh, sometimes bordering on clear-cut asceticism. For example, he can live practically without sleep and with little food. The positive hero also extends his working hours beyond what would appear the limits of human endurance, and he rarely succumbs to illness or fatigue.

Puritanism is also expressed in the sexual relations of the positive hero. Sex plays little part in his life; sexual goals and desires are never allowed to compete with nonsexual ones. While some positive heroes in our sample shun sex almost completely, for others it seems to be a matter of no significance. It would seem, by implication, that he considers sex a potentially dangerous, disruptive force. (For example, it is probably not an accident that female negative characters are often presented as sexually alluring, as seductresses who use sex for ulterior purposes.) It is clear, however, that sexual self-denial need not go so far as to interfere with procreation. No information is provided in the novels surveyed on the degree of sexual compatibility between the positive characters; it can only be inferred that when politically-ideologically compatible mates are joined in marriage, all other problems of compatibility are solved at one stroke and sex falls into its—deservedly—secondary place.

The sexual continence of the positive hero is a highly functional component of the model. First, intense sexual preoccupations tend to go hand in hand with intense private emotional preoccupations. A personal relationship fortified by strong sexual involvements can, and often does, make collective public causes and undertakings seem insignificant. Intense and frequent enjoyment of sex can also lead to, or form a part of, a generally hedonistic approach to life, equally undesirable in a Soviet-type society. It can also result in a depletion of physical energy, in channeling energy away from work. And last, promiscuously intense sexual activity can weaken family ties and repudiate the goal of procreation. Freedom in emotional and sexual relations is also difficult to reconcile with regimentation and discipline in other areas of life.[7]

Selective Emotionalism. In popular imagination, the stereotype of the positive hero merges with the image of the iron-willed Bolshevik, the impassive leader-functionary, or the dedicated, depersonalized robot. Such images and a superficial reading of socialist realist works of fiction may suggest that the positive hero is a rather unemotional being. After all, he is supposed to be highly rational in pursuit of the goals he is fed by the Party and his leaders, and unaffected by emotional appeals when means are to be chosen to attain the goals.

Yet the positive hero is far from unemotional. Rather, his emotions and emotionalism are channeled in the requisite direction.[8] He can be emotional when the occasion warrants it.

The key to the emotionalism of the positive hero lies in the implicit injunction to avoid it in his private life but release it in the public-political sphere. For instance, his attitude toward political symbols and their personifications, his leaders, is distinctly emotional. Not surprisingly, the hatred of the enemy is also highly emotionalized—he nurtures hate toward the enemy which is "passionate," "burning," "consuming," and "overpowering."

The explanation is not difficult to find. Private emotions siphon away psychic energy from tasks which demand total dedication. The essence of selective emotionalism is discrimination in allocating emotional energies and motivation. The regime does not want to extinguish emotionalism; it wants to control and manipulate it.

The propensity to feel shame is another undeclared characteristic of the positive hero which one does not find in the official requirements and suggestions made for writers. It obviously has some affinity with selective emotionalism: an unemotional, unfeeling person can hardly be shamed. This propensity finds frequent expression in the positive hero's tendency toward contrite, humble self-criticism. Indeed, shame is the prerequisite of the truly fruitful self-criticism which otherwise degenerates easily into a false ritual. The feeling of shame provides the strong motivation for self-criticism and the desire to correct one's shortcomings.

The positive hero's readiness to feel ashamed tacitly provides the population with a model of a person who always looks at himself when searching for the source of errors and shortcomings, rather than at the institutions of society and the leaders who control them. In this way, the propensity to feel shame is implicitly tied to the infallibility of higher authority, the supreme leadership, or the various collectives. Those in whom the feeling of shame can be quickly induced are easy to control.

As already indicated, the positive hero is always inclined to self-criticism (both in private and in public) and practically rejoices in being harshly criticized. Despite his "positiveness," he seems to carry in himself a deep, pervasive awareness of his fallibility, especially in relation to his superiors, the Party, and the magnitude of the tasks ahead. The most familiar situations in which he is overcome by shame are those of committing slight political errors or mistakes in his work. He is particularly prone to feel shame and embarrassment in the presence of his great leaders.

Credulousness and instant enthusiasm. Once more, we would search in vain for any explicit encouragement to present the positive hero as credulous. Yet a reading of the novels of the period conveys this characteristic. The positive hero is forever ready to believe every statement or suggestion emanating from the appropriate authorities. History may change with each new edition of the Soviet Encyclopedia (or the History of the Communist Party of the USSR), today's invincible doctrine turn into falsehood tomorrow, beloved infallible leaders of yesterday become today's traitors and deviants, nevertheless, he stands his ground with no inclination to develop the capacity for skepticism.

The credulousness of the positive hero is implicitly justified by the credibility of the Party. He can trust the Party, the Party knows best and fulfills all its promises. This attitude has its logic. The positive hero's frames of reference are all located outside himself, he surrenders his autonomy demonstratively and with seeming relish. The merits of credulousness in the citizen are evident for a totalitarian regime. It is the true believer who has the best chance to transcend the discontinuity between theory and practice.

Lack of spontaneity. Once more, this is not an explicit official prescription, but a partially unintended cumulative result of the other requirements. For the political activist, spontaneous action is risky, if not outright dangerous.[9]

The lack of spontaneity of the positive hero manifests itself in various ways. Its degree is determined to some extent by his social-political position and relationship to the Party. The closer he is to the Party (and its spirit), the more he partakes of the omniscience, restraint, and foresight of its leaders. Lack of spontaneity (almost like wisdom) seems to grow with high office. It shows up in the unwillingness or inability to act on impulse, feel or show surprise, or be carried away by talk. He is usually taciturn although capable of volubility and eloquence when a particular situation justifies it (e.g., the need to exhort fellow workers or soldiers).

Thus the positive hero's attitude toward speaking—as toward most things—is highly utilitarian.

One specific source of the lack of spontaneity is his constant reliance on theory (Marxism-Leninism), his persistent effort to translate theory into the practices of his daily life—hardly an effort that allows much display of spontaneity. The propensity to plan and predict (or the frantic desire to do so) is yet another manifestation of the lack of spontaneity. The latter is not limited to the sphere of his political or professional activities. It also enters into his relations with people, where lack of spontaneity merges with vigilance, the most effective damper on any spontaneity in personal relations.

Adaptability and the drive for self-improvement. The positive hero in action (as portrayed in the pages of fiction rather than in the articles of theoretical and literary journals and magazines) amazes the reader by his ability to change himself and his ways of life radically in response to external demands—of the Party or other institutions represented by it—and in response to circumstances. He is also continuously bent on improving himself. Self-satisfaction and smugness are the great characterological evils the Party warns against. This desire for self-improvement takes three expressions. If he is a worker, he continuously tries to increase his output and perfect his methods. If an administrator or Party worker, he similarly strives for greater efficiency and better relations with his subordinates. Self-education is the second expression. We find most positive heroes engaged in some form of study, private or organized. Such endeavors may bear immediate relation to his work or they may involve some edifying intellectual-cultural pursuit, such as learning to play a musical instrument, exploring the classics of Russian literature, or studying the flora of the region where he lives. Such aspects of his life suggest that in him we are witnessing the rebirth—on a new and ever-widening scale—of the Renaissance Man, the well-rounded man that will characterize Communist society in which, as Marx hoped,

> everyone has no exclusive circle of activity but can train himself in any branch he wants to . . . do[ing] one thing today and another tomorrow; to hunt mornings, fish afternoons, raise cattle evenings, criticize after dinner, in whatever way [he pleases] without ever having to become a tradesman, a herdsman, or a critic.[10]

Such facets of his life also intimate that whatever his excellence in a particular field *he is never merely a narrow specialist,* but a man of broad and inquisitive mind, a "lover of life and beauty," as it is sometimes put. However, none of these pursuits is undertaken for its own sake.

What appears a purely aesthetic enjoyment is functional, whether it involves the improvement of the mind or recreation to increase his efficiency at work. (Thus even these attitudes symbolize the atrophy of spontaneity.)

A third, and perhaps most significant expression of his desire for changing himself for the better is his constant immersion in the classics of Marxism-Leninism which answer all questions, fulfill all spiritual needs, and offer solutions to a wide range of practical problems.

Self-criticism also serves the purpose of improving oneself and at the same time transforms self-improvement into a quasi-communal task. In the last analysis, the positive hero always praises the Collective for whatever progress he makes in any sphere. From the point of view of a totalitarian regime, the adaptability of the citizen—the elasticity of response to the changing demands the regime is always prepared to make on him—is an important, perhaps the most important, virtue. As long as the monopoly of controlling and guiding change lies with the infallible leadership and as long as policies are changeable, the best citizens are the most adaptable ones.

The Negative Hero

The model of the enemy, the negative hero (or negative character) occupies in the scheme of political socialization through literature a place no less important than the positive hero. This is because the personification of virtue must have its counterpart, the personification of evil, if the regime wants to instruct the population not only in the modes of behavior to be emulated but also in those to be avoided or repressed. Besides, the population has to be taught to identify the enemy in everyday life. In addition, the stereotyped figure of the enemy—in literature and elsewhere—serves the traditional function of providing a target for popular resentment and frustration, whatever its source. The literary elaboration of the figure of the enemy provides visible reminders of his existence and serves to justify institutionalized intolerance of any dissent or opposition.

Detailed and lengthy discussions and instructions on the portrayal of the enemy are not as numerous as those devoted to the positive hero. Perhaps it is easier to depict vice convincingly than virtue: hence, there is less need to advise the writers on how to do it.

The major official requirement of the literary presentation of the negative hero is to convey repugnance and dangerousness. The literary rendering of the enemy should evoke profound hostility, preferably hate and disgust, or at least ridicule. Repugnance should be achieved by what we call clustering of negative traits. With the full-blown negative hero, there can be no saving grace, no inner struggle between good and bad, but only unmitigated repulsiveness. The reader is not invited to feel any pity or empathy toward him. Socially, the enemy represents the past: either by actually deriving from the defeated ruling classes, or by being one of their lackeys, or by being contaminated by "survivals"; he may also be a representative or tool of foreign powers and interests.

Most of the enemy's features that make him repugnant would also evoke negative feelings in societies other than the Soviet. In other words, he is repugnant not so much on political-ideological grounds as on human, ethical ones. We present now a summary of the traits of negative characters as observed in fiction and as derived from the official recommendations to writers.[11]

Unscrupulousness and amorality. The negative hero adheres to no moral standards or ethical norms. Typically, this is reflected either in the murderous methods he uses to promote his political aims, or, if the historical setting does not justify his presentation as a politically active individual, his amorality is reflected in his completely selfish, parasitic outlook on life. These two manifestations may be combined. Even when the negative hero pursues political goals, great pains are often taken to portray him as basically unprincipled. He must be denied any idealism, he cannot be granted ideological-philosophical motivation that transcends narrow self-interest. Presumably, this ensures that the negative hero evokes no sympathy and avoids the appearance of a tragic hero; after all, a man in pursuit of his principles who uses repugnant means is usually more appealing than one using these same means to attain merely personal or material gain.

The repugnance of the negative hero is sometimes highlighted by his *physical unattractiveness.* He need not be really ugly, but somehow strange or slightly abnormal in his looks. A touch of deformity sensitizes the reader to the grievous air of evil that hangs over him. An advanced variation on this theme is the monster image, spectacularly manifested in the "zoological" description of political enemies, the famous victims of various purge trials.[12] Such extremes were reserved for the most hated groups and individuals whom the regime wanted to remove from the sphere in which human values, norms, and understanding apply. Pity and compassion have no place in the arena of class struggle.

Cowardice and duplicity are related, yet each serves different purposes. Cowardice is part of the repugnance syndrome, an obvious characterological defect. Combined with duplicity, it highlights the dangerousness of the enemy who tends to be camouflaged. The negative hero is also hypocritical and insincere. These traits are reflected in his pretended support of the regime, and in the insincerity of his repentance when unmasked. Since repentance invites a measure of compassion and forgiveness, his cannot be genuine. The duplicity (or "double dealing") of the enemy may also be seen as a generalized manifestation of dishonesty.

The capacity for hate. Nothing makes people more hateful than their ability to hate others. Thus the negative hero's propensity to hate becomes a major source of his repugnance, enhanced by the fact that he lacks the capacity to love. Sometimes he even hates himself. At the same time, his hatred of the new society and its leaders is a major explanation of his activities. The source of this boundless hatred is often not fully explained. Sometimes jealousy, competition, and drive for power are invoked, or the fact that the regime struck at his social roots and that he or his family lost a position which they had earlier enjoyed. Occasionally, his corruption by foreign influences explains his hatred. On the whole, however, the negative hero's hatred is treated as a trait secretly harbored practically from birth.

Hedonism, sexual depravity. The private moral standards of the negative hero are as repugnant as his public ones. His sexual-emotional life is close to pathological, frequently highlighted by his being unmarried, divorced, or separated. He is often represented as friendless, a social pariah. Negative heroes and heroines are often promiscuous, ready to indulge in sex at any time on a purely hedonistic basis or to use it to further other aims, without any feeling of tenderness, affection, or love. Corrupting and corrupt sensuousness in the negative hero is the logical antithesis of the puritanism or family-oriented sex of the positive hero. The sexual depravity of negative characters also serves to illustrate the general moral decay associated with capitalist societies. The hedonistic, unemotional approach to sex is at the same time associated with a more general hedonism—the yearning for an easy life whose fulfillment lies in material and sensual comforts. In this frame of reference, sex becomes a form of escapism and makes no meaningful contribution to human relationships.

Activism. The classical negative hero is characterized by systematic, resourceful, and ceaseless activism against the regime. He is constantly scheming, planning acts of sabotage, or speading false and malicious rumors to cause panic or discredit the system. He commands considerable organizational skills, and is ready and able to corrupt and recruit the weak or faltering. This emphasis on systematic, unceasing activity serves to demonstrate his dangerousness and determination, suggesting that his misdeeds are not the results of momentary rage or a lapse of loyalty, but the fruits of highly calculated irrepressible hostility toward the regime.

His *willingness to be a tool* is a further indication of his lack of integrity and suggestive of his dangerousness.

Historical changes—even within the Stalin period—have exerted some influence on the presentation of the negative hero. He has changed more than the positive hero—and not only with regard to the settings he occupies or the typical occupations he holds—but also with regard to some basic attitudes. A brief summary should indicate the direction of change.

The consolidation of the Soviet system—both in the brief interval between the end of the purges and the beginning of World War II, and in the postwar period—made it implausible to treat the negative hero as actively engaged in fighting the regime. With the introduction of the Stalin Constitution in 1936, it was officially declared that antagonistic social classes had been liquidated, and their "cornered" remnants were eradicated in the purges. From the late 1930s onward, it became increasingly difficult to claim that members of the old ruling classes survived and actively struggled against the regime. To the extent that these antagonistic social groups disappeared, by either natural extinction or coercive policies, the social base of the negative hero had to change. If negative heroes now had to come from the working class, peasantry, or intelligentsia, raised under the Soviet regime, they could not be as actively destructive as members of the old ruling classes or as actively hostile as infiltrators from abroad. Thus emphasis shifted from the active negative hero (the enemy) to what might more appropriately be called the negative character. In the latter case, "negativeness" consisted of basic characterological defects rather than defects of social origin and/or political activity and ideological hostility. The emerging features of the negative character in the late Stalin period were:

1. Political indifference, which replaced articulate and conscious ideological hostility;
2. Careerism within the framework of Soviet institutions at the expense of collectivism;
3. Inauthenticity, which replaced treacherousness;
4. Cosmopolitanism in cultural orientation, replacing active service of foreign political powers;
5. Individualism, presented more as a characterological than political trait (including hedonism, sexual depravity) joined with irresponsibility; and
6. Parasitism, loafing, shirking of work.

In concluding the discussion of the negative hero, it must be noted that—reflecting the degree to which his personality was politicized—he exhibited some surprising similarities to the positive hero. All such similarities had a political basis.The dedicated activism of the positive hero had its counterpart in the ceaseless scheming and subversion of the negative character. The discipline of the former had its distorted reflection in the latter's capacity for being a willing tool. If the positive hero sometimes had to disregard the means to be chosen in the struggle, his negative counterpart deliberately chose unappealing means because he was amoral or sadistic. If the positive hero hated his enemies intensely and with good reason, the negative hero did the same, *without* justification, or at least with no justification transcending his narrow self-interest. Immersion in political-organizational activities made both prototypes unspontaneous and calculating. What was self-control for the positive hero became insincerity and duplicity for the negative hero. To the extent that they were committed to political actions and beliefs, both were purposeful. Finally, both stereotypes resembled an "authoritarian personality"[13] in that both had a tendency to view everything in power terms (as does the Party and its ideology); both were highly sensitive to the implications and dimensions of submission and dominance in most situations and relationships; both looked upon their social environment in categorical and simplified perspectives shaped by their respective fears; and both were rigid and intolerant.

When political motivation engulfs the whole personality, such similarities need not be puzzling. For this reason, many of the features of the positive hero were unconsciously projected onto his foe, who often became his distorted mirror image. Frequently, they differed only in motivation rather than overt behavior. Socialist realism thus reflects an unarticulated belief in the fundamental similarity of the ways in which political interests are expressed and promoted.

Conclusion

Hopefully, this chapter has shown that literature produced in totalitarian societies offers much interest to the sociologist. Socialist realism in view of its limited artistic value lends itself far more readily to sociological than to literary analysis. This is so regardless of its success or failure in reeducating the population. For a variety of practical reasons, it would have been fruitless to pursue the latter issue; hence we were limited to a discussion of the functions of the models as inferred from their characteristics and from the official-theoretical guidance rendered for their formulation. There is no reason to doubt that insofar as citizens assimilated the virtues of the positive hero and were repelled by the vices of the negative hero, the regime gained dedicated supporters. Positive heroes also served the regime by verbalizing and articulating specific short-term programs and policies—a function we have not discussed. Suffice it to say that much of Soviet history, including shifts in official objectives, could be reconstructed from the activities and manifestations of positive heroes. The negative heroes, in turn, assisted the regime by inspiring hate toward its real or alleged enemies and by helping to identify them both in sociological terms (insofar as they tended to be members of specific social groups) and in characterological ones (through the exhibition of undesirable traits).

The totalitarian inspiration of both models of behavior was expressed in the improbable interdependence and integration of their personality traits. One could find no saving features in the personality of the negative hero and no jarring ones in that of the positive. We labeled this tendency "clustering." The polarized mode of character portrayal was indicative of the totalitarian intolerance of ambiguities.

The qualities of the positive hero could be best explained in terms of the requirements of a totalitarian society which desires to maximize control over its citizens. Patriotism and Party-mindedness, antiindividualism, capacity to hate any officially designated target, acceptance of subordination, unquestioning loyalty to leaders, lack of any *genuine* initiative, obedience, adaptability, susceptibility to shame—all these are qualities which facilitate control over the individual. Industrialization as such does not require this personality structure, but industrialization in a totalitarian framework does.

This study has also raised other problems bearing on the nature of Communist morality and its internalization. The totalitarian effort to internalize values turns out, on closer inspection, to be paradoxical and potentially self-defeating. Morality in a totalitarian society—as we have seen—has no stable reference points. It is defined by decree. At the same time, the truly value-oriented person who has internalized values has no use for external agencies defining and redefining the norms of his behavior. Value-oriented behavior means internal—not external—guidance. This is an anomaly in a totalitarian society where the rulers reserve the right of guidance for themselves. The dynamic nature of totalitarianism also militates against the internalization of values. Its climate is unfavorable for the persistence of value commitments. In the long run, a totalitarian society is not compatible with the internalization of values other than obedience, trust in the superior authorities (that is, State, Party, or Supreme Leader), and productivity. Practically every other value is subject to redefinition or replacement. Thus in light of the fluctuating policies pursued by Soviet-type totalitarian societies, it is less than expedient to breed generations of citizens who follow internalized values, since their utility as guides to behavior fades when policies change. In other words, the problem a Soviet-type regime faces in internalizing values in the population is that once it succeeds, the individual acquires a degree of autonomy and independence from external control and manipulation.

Therefore, we have to modify our original proposition. The Soviet attempt to exercise social control through the internalization of values is more limited in scope than appeared at first sight. The values which Soviet totalitarianism has attempted to internalize in its citizens are not so much ultimate values as guidelines to behavior or "instrumental values"—that is, obedience, loyalty, trust, discipline, and productivity.[14]

The New Man in Soviet society is supposed to have internalized only the notion that the most desirable behavior pattern consists of responsiveness to the commands and cues of the regime. Perhaps, in the long run, serious value commitments[15] and totalitarianism as known in the Soviet Union and Eastern Europe under Stalin are incompatible. This, of course, need not endanger the stability or persistence of such regimes. Thus far, the stability of Soviet-type totalitarian regimes has rested primarily on the control of behavior and not on that of ultimate values.

Postscript 1982

"Models of Behavior in Stalinist Literature" remains one of the very few attempts to explore the specifics of the Soviet effort to create a "New Man" and the particulars of the values and attitudes he was supposed to display. There have been even fewer attempts on the part of social scientists (or anyone else) to examine the part played by literature in this process. This has been all the more regrettable since, as noted in the article, using such materials also lends itself to an inquiry into the issue of which attitudes were required for industrialization and which ones were required to meet the need for political conformity in a totalitarian society. In other words, an examination of the ideal modes of behavior derived from socialist realist literature (and the official discussions and instructions on how to cultivate it) could have made a useful contribution to the debate which sought to establish to what extent the characteristics of the Soviet system under Stalin were to be explained by the imperatives of modernization and to what extent by the demands of a totalitarian political milieu.[16]

While the neglect of socialist realist literature as sociological data is regrettable, it is not surprising. American social scientists (and sociologists in particular) have never shown much interest in the sociology of literature, let alone the literature produced in the Soviet Union and the countries under its control. Moreover, American sociologists have also remained generally uninterested in Soviet society, the study of which attracted only a handful. There have been, of course, a few notable exceptions: scholars from other disciplines such as Vera Dunham, Alexander Gerschenkron, and Xenia Gasiorowska, who combined the study of certain aspects of Soviet society with the use of literary materials.[17]

Perhaps part of the problem has been that the perusal of literary works conceived in the spirit of socialist realism offers few temptations to those interested in literature and little in the way of respectable data, as most social scientists define such matters.

While my study[18] has helped to codify the official values of the Soviet political elite under Stalin (which probably have changed little over the last quarter century), the issues raised at the end of my essay regarding the success of the official program of political education (of which literature was an important part) remain unresolved. We know that the Soviet regime has retained the capacity to control and regulate the behavior of its population—but to what mixture of coercion, apathy, or internalization (of the official values) we can ascribe this we can only guess.

Since the article was written, socialist realism as practiced under Stalin has lost its stranglehold over Soviet literature (and even more so over that produced in Hungary and some other East European countries), and the realm of what is permissible in the arts has somewhat expanded as less politicized works have been allowed to appear. It would be a matter of considerable interest to learn to what extent the ideological authorities in the USSR continue to view socialist realism as a device for the political education of the population and what the more recent socialist-realist literary stereotypes have in common with the older ones. Research into such matters may throw unexpected light on the ambivalent attitudes of the Soviet regime toward the relaxation of political controls and the tolerance of greater diversity and pluralism in the realm of ideas.

Notes

1. It is likely that the function of such models could be traced back to Lenin's conception of the "force of example." Cf. Alfred G. Meyer, *Leninism* (Cambridge: Harvard University Press, 1957), p. 55. See also Alexander Gurvich, "Sila polozhitel'naya primera" (The power of the positive example), *Novy mir* (Sept. 1951), and Georgii Malenkov, *Otchetnyi doklad XIX s'ezdu partii o rabote tsentral'nogo komiteta VKP (b)* (Report to the Nineteenth

Party Congress on the work of the Central Committee of the Communist Party) (Moscow: Gospolitizdat, 1952), p. 73.

2. On socialist realism see: Abraham Tertz, *On Socialist Realism* (New York: Pantheon, 1960; Praeger, 1959); Rufus W. Mathewson, *The Positive Hero in Russian Literature* (New York: Columbia University Press, 1958); Ernest J. Simmons, ed., *Continuity and Change in Russian and Soviet Thought* (Cambridge: Harvard University Press, 1965), pp. 398–469; Gleb Struve, *Soviet-Russian Literature: 1917–1950* (Norman, Okla.: University of Oklahoma Press, 1951); Marc Slonim, *Soviet Russian Literature: Writers and Problems* (New York: Oxford University Press, 1964).

3. Even today, this issue is far from settled as the recent sentences in the trial of the two Soviet writers Sinyavski and Daniel illustrate. Their dialogue with the judge highlighted the persisting official refusal to grant autonomy to the arts and the apparent inability of the officials to view literature outside a political context.

4. The concept of "ideal patterns" is used here in two senses: (a) a normative sense, referring to the correct, desirable, or prescribed ways of behavior, and (2) the situational sense, referring to the official conceptions of what the world, society, and its institutions are supposed to be like. This is a modification of the concept as used by Levy. Cf. Marion J. Levy, Jr., *The Structure of Society* (Princeton: Princeton University Press, 1952), pp. 123–25.

5. Works used by Hungarian authors were:

> Tamas Aczel, *Vihar es napsutes* (Storm and sunshine) (Budapest, 1950).
> Lajos Barta Ifj, *Tabornok ur konyvet ir* (The general writes a book) (Budapest, 1950).
> Klara Feher, *Az elso het tortenete* (The story of the first week) (Budapest, 1948).
> Sandor Gergely, *Vitezek es hosok* (Knights and heroes) (Budapest, 1948).
> Gyula Hay, *Az elet hidja* (The bridge of life) (Budapest, 1951).
> Mihaly Horvath, *Tatar Peter* (Peter Tatar) (Budapest, 1950).
> Bela Illes, *Tuz Moszkva alatt* (Fire under Moscow) (Budapest, 1949).
> Ferenc Karinthy, *Komuvesek* (Brickmasons) (Budapest, 1950).
> Lajos Mesterhazi, *Huseg* (Loyalty) (Budapest, 1952).
> Sandor Nagy, *Megbekeles* (Reconciliation) (Budapest, 1950).
> Laszlo Nemes, *Ket vilag* (Two worlds) (Budapest, 1950).
> Istvan Orkeny, *Hazastarsak* (The couple) (Budapest, 1953).
> Pal Szabo, *Tavaszi szel* (Spring wind) (Budapest, 1950).
> Erno Urban, *Tuzkeresztseg* (The watershed) (Budapest, 1952).
> Endre Veszi, *Uj hid a Dunan* (New bridge on the Danube) (Budapest, 1951).

Works used by Soviet authors were:

> Vassily Azhaev, *Daleko ot Moskvy* (Far from Moscow) (Moscow, 1948).
> Semyon Babaevsky, *Cavalier of the Gold Star* (London, 1956; published in the USSR, 1948).
> Ilya Ehrenburg, *The Ninth Wave* (London, 1955; published in the USSR, 1948).

Alexander Fadeev, *The Young Guard* (Moscow, 1958; rev. Russian language ed., 1951).

Boris Gorbatov, *Donbas* (Moscow, 1953).

Emanuel Kazakevich, *Spring on the Oder* (Moscow, 1953).

Boris Lavrenyov, *Golos Ameriki* (The voice of America) (Moscow, 1948).

Nikolay Ostrovsky, *The Making of a Hero* (New York, 1937).

Fydor Panfyorov, *And Then the Harvest* (London, 1939).

Pyotor Pavlenko, *Happiness* (Moscow, 1950).

Boris Polevoi, *A Story about a Real Man* (Moscow, 1952).

Constantin Simonov, *Russky vopros* (The Russian question) (Moscow, 1947).

Mikhail Sholokhov, *Seeds of Tomorrow* (New York, 1942; first Soviet ed., 1932).

Nikolay Spanov, *Podzhigateli* (Arsonists) (Moscow, 1952).

Yuri Trifonov, *Students* (Moscow, 1953).

6. Nathan Leites, *A Study of Bolshevism* (Glencoe Ill.: Free Press, 1953), pp. 132–41.

7. The same observation had also been made in the Chinese context in relation to the official admonitions regarding love and marriage.

8. See also Raymond A. Bauer, *The New Man in Soviet Psychology* (Cambridge: Harvard University Press, 1962), p. 168.

9. Cf., for example, Vladimir Ilyich Lenin, *What is to be Done?* (New York: International Publishers, 1929), pp. 52–53.

10. Karl Marx and Friedrich Engels, *The German Ideology* (New York: International Publishers, 1960), p. 22.

11. Here we also relied on a third source of information that falls between pure fiction and the ideological-literary discussions of the enemy, viz., the purge trials, in which the prosecution described in meticulous detail the character of the "real life" enemy. Subsequent historical evidence justifies our treating the allegations made in these trials as almost pure fiction. The sources used are: *Report of Court Proceedings in the Case of the Anti-Soviet Trotskyite Center* (Moscow: Peoples Commissariat of the USSR, 1937); *Report of Court Proceedings in the Case of the Anti-Soviet Bloc of Rights and Trotskyites* (Moscow: Peoples Commissariat of Justice of the USSR, 1938).

12. The historical (Stalinist) tradition of portraying the live personifications of the enemy reasserted itself in 1966 in connection with the trial of the writers Sinyavski and Daniel. We collected the following terms applied to them from one article: "unprincipled," "poisonous," "blasphemous," "malicious," "hypocritical," "Jesuitical," "double-dealing," "morally degraded," "morally deformed," "scum," "hooligans," "not merely moral monsters but active henchmen" who were also characterized by "shameless duplicity" and "the hatred of our [the Soviet] system." *Izvestia*, 13 Jan. 1966, trans. in *Current Digest of the Soviet Press*, 2 Feb. 1966, pp. 11–12.

13. The affinity of the authoritarian personality to totalitarian modes of thinking has been demonstrated by Edward Shils in "Authoritarianism, Right and Left," in Richard Christie and Marie Jahoda, eds., *Studies in the Scope and Method of the Authoritarian Personality* (Glencoe Ill.: Free Press, 1954).

14. The similarity between all such totalitarian values was noted by Isaiah Berlin, "Political Ideas in the Twentieth Century," *Foreign Affairs* 28 (April

1950):83. "The new Stalinist values were similar to those proclaimed by Mussolini: loyalty, energy, obedience, discipline."

15. We are not referring to the commitment of the rulers, for we are not disputing the likelihood of *their* commitment to ultimate values. On the contrary, we considered their commitment an important characteristic of totalitarianism.

16. The persistence of these issues and the debates associated with them have been strikingly demonstrated in a number of recent contributions to a scholarly journal, some of which sought to reemphasize the imperatives of modernization in Soviet history under Stalin and in doing so to rehabilitate Stalin to a startling degree. (See Theodor H. von Laue and Alfred G. Meyer, in *Soviet Union* 8 (1981):1–17 and 18–24.) For a further discussion of these issues, see pp. 73–77, 131–34 of this study.

17. Vera Dunham, *In Stalin's Time: Middleclass Values in Soviet Fiction* (England: Cambridge Univ. Press, 1976); Alexander Gerschenkron, "Reflections on Soviet Novels," in *Economic Backwardness in Historical Perspective* (New York: Cambridge Univ. Press, 1965); Xenia Gasiorowska, *Women in Soviet Fiction* (Madison: Univ. of Wisconsin Press, 1968).

18. "The New Man and His Enemies: A Study in the Stalinist Conceptions of Good and Evil Personified." Ph.D. Dissertation, Princeton University, 1963.

3.
Leisure:
The Unity of Pleasure and Purpose

The emergence of leisure as an issue of public discourse, ideological concern, and sociological analysis is one of the obvious products of post-Stalin social change. While Stalin's jovial proposition in 1936 (about life having become better and gayer) somewhat overstated the case at the time of the Great Purge, from the late 1950s, life for the Soviet citizen did become less of a burden; consequently, a quest for its available and unavailable pleasures began to gain momentum. The results, for Soviet ideologues, are yet another demonstration of the way in which "consciousness lags behind existence," or of the degree to which individual behavior emancipates itself from the influence of institutions which were designed to guide it into appropriate channels. Given more (if still not enough) leisure, a great many Soviet citizens either have chosen to follow a path that shows a disturbing similarity to the ways in which citizens corrupted by capitalist societies spend their time, or they have exhibited symptoms of sincere bewilderment and paralysis of initiative. One student of such matters recently noted in *Pravda*:

> It is not a secret that among some of our scientists and practical workers the conviction prevailed . . . that an increase in free time automatically leads to a rise in people's cultural and technical level[s] and in their labor productivity. However, special research conducted by the USSR Academy of Sciences and Philosophy Institute showed that it is impossible to avoid serious negative consequences when the working day is shortened without simultaneously expanding the places for cultural recreation and amusement, without improving the organisation of leisure, especially for young people, and without conducting the appropriate ideological preparation.[1]

By now, a veritable inventory of the undesirable responses to more leisure has been compiled by Soviet ideologues, journalists, Party and Komsomol officials, and social scientists. Particularly noteworthy are the time-honored reliance on alcohol, the spread of hooliganism, street-corner malingering, excessive television watching, and unseemly dances. In this essay, we shall deal primarily with those aspects of Soviet leisure which reflect peculiarly Soviet conditions.

How did leisure acquire such prominence in post-Stalin Russia? First of all, as Soviet spokesmen themselves point out, "non-working time" (of which leisure is a part)[2] acquires new importance in proportion to its quantitative increase. The reduction of the workday caused citizens to spend less time in such well-defined settings as the place of work. The official recognition of the ideological-political significance of leisure must also be viewed in the context of diminished coercion. Since overt coercion has ceased to be the most favored way of exacting conformity, persuasion has come to occupy a more prominent place in social controls. Leisure-time activities provide, at least in theory, good opportunities for persuasion, yet the official intention to make it functional from the regime's point of view clashes with the popular preference for making it private and apolitical.

The insistence that Communist society is not far away also has implications for leisure (even though this insistence has become somewhat more muted since the end of the Khrushchev era). Blueprints of communism must entail, besides projections of material abundance, what people will be able to do with their free time.

The current official interest in leisure is also a by-product of the concern with the younger generation. Free time plays a much greater part in the lives of the young than in those of adults, and the ways in which they spend this time have a lasting influence upon the formation of their character. Soviet spokesmen find the misuse of free time a source of antisocial attitudes. "We must always remember that the morale and work of young people depend on how they spend their free time."[3] And, no doubt, how they spend their free time also depends on their morale. "Under socialism every worker can make use of his free time as he sees fit. This does not, however, mean that society takes a passive attitude towards the ways in which he utilises his time."[4] Two major themes permeate the official discussion of leisure. One is the interdependence of leisure and work, that is, the contribution which well-spent leisure time can make to efficiency at work; the other is the relationship between leisure and the "all-round development of the personality." Thus the desired functionalization of leisure takes two forms: the morale-building, which has economic, productive relevance, and the ideological, which promotes the integration of the personal and political, or the personal and collective spheres of life. The official approach is frankly utilitarian:

> Free time does not amount to idleness. . . . This is the time devoted to study, the raising of qualifications, self-education and self-development

(attending lectures, cultural groups, museums, the reading of fiction, journals, newspapers, etc.), to sports and hobbies (hunting, fishing, photography, etc.), to active rest and rational leisure (visiting places of entertainmment, walks and excursions, travelling, open air festivals, creative discussion, and bringing up children, etc.), and also to participation in the life of society.[5]

An opinion poll on the preference of theatergoers included this question: "Has any production you have seen helped you to decide a vital, personal problem for yourself?" Among the appropriate and exemplary answers we read:

> After seeing "Irkutsk story" I firmly resolved to get my husband to return to school for further study even though we had a year old child and lived in our own apartment. . . . When I saw "Judge between us, people" I decided to go to night school. . . . The production of "Colleagues" . . . helped me to understand what it means to choose an occupation suited to one's desires and abilities.[6]

While not insisting that all forms of entertainment should have such far-reaching effects on the audience, Soviet spokesmen continually stress its utilitarian rationale. The official conception of the rational uses of leisure time is prim and didactic:

> If in the time spent studying the worker does not learn anything useful and does not raise his qualifications he has spent his time in an irrational way. Time spent on domestic games is rational if it is devoted to such interesting and elevating games as chess, riddles (rebus), viktorina [?], crosswords, charades, etc. Time spent on entertaining or visiting is rational if it is devoted not to gossip, scandalmongering, and guzzling liquor, but to interesting conversation about the achievements of science and technology, about international and domestic political events, about the needs of production, to the exchange of experience about the upbringing of children, to the exchange of opinions about books read, films and plays seen, etc.[7]

To summarize, free time as seen by Soviet ideologues and social scientists should be used for the following purposes:

1. Recreation which helps to restore energy for production and various useful social purposes.
2. Activities which contribute to the all-around development of the personality (i.e., to the creation of the truly new Soviet Man described in the 1961 Party program as one "who will combine harmoniously spiritual wealth, moral purity, and perfect physique").
3. Activities which raise educational and professional qualifications: formal and informal study, reading.

4. Participation in communal-public affairs of direct or indirect political and economic relevance (e.g., voluntary work for some communal project such as planting trees, improving housing, building cultural facilities, attending meetings, etc.).

The collectivization of leisure is encouraged. It follows from the disapproval of undesirable trends in its use, for example, the development of the capacity for reflection, individualistic proclivities, and the taste for privacy. In the official Soviet interpretation, leisure appears more like work than play.

The desires of the Soviet government and the recommendations of its ideologues are far from being the sole determinants of how Soviet citizens actually spend their time. Among the conditions affecting leisure, we find factors which are independent of the official policies or which represent the unintended consequence of them. For example, the expenditure of free time is negatively affected by poor living conditions, the scarcity of consumer goods and household labor-saving devices, as well as the time-consuming nature of routine tasks such as shopping. The priorities of the economy are further reflected in the acknowledged inadequacy of facilities for entertainment and recreation, particularly in the rural areas, small towns, and new industrial settlements. At the same time, there is a whole set of factors which exert pressure toward greater popular demand for more and better leisure. If the home, in terms of privacy, comfort, and recreation, leaves a great deal to be desired, public places of entertainment become all the more important and alluring.

The limited resource allocation for private telephones, cars, and household articles is also relevant here: all these services and facilities encourage private leisure. This is not to suggest that the economic factors behind these policies are not more weighty than the official fear of privacy; but when funds are available and choices have to be made, the public sector will be given primacy largely for ideological reasons. This is best shown by the contrasting development of telephones and television. The former is an instrument of private and informal communications, a device for the maintenance of social life and personal relationships. Television, by contrast, is a centrally controlled instrument of one-way communication, the contents of which are highly standardized. The figures speak for themselves: the number of telephones (this includes close to 3 million public phones and an unknown but high proportion of official ones) is 7 million, while that of TV sets is 15 million. It is unlikely that these discrepancies have much to do with the costs of installing phones versus manufacturing TV sets and setting up TV stations.

A major study conducted among industrial workers of six cities, Erevan, Novokuznetsk, Kostroma, Sverdlovsk, Krasnoyarsk, and Norilsk, provides many examples of the persisting deficiencies in the use of nonworking time. Among them is the fact that free time constitutes only 16.8 percent of nonworking time, while domestic work and household care consume 22.3 percent. Activities related to work, that is, transportation, changing from one shift to another, also account for an excessive amount of nonworking time: together with domestic work and personal care, they consume twice the amount of free time. Here lies one of the principal causes for concern and the mainspring of such studies: the large areas of inefficiency which surround the place of work and which would create problems, even if it were assumed that at the workplace itself exemplary order and organization prevailed. Among the sources of the irrational use of time—which leads to its being swallowed up by domestic work and other trivia—a Soviet specialist on leisure mentions the underdeveloped state of "housing, communal, sanitary-medical, commercial, cultural, transport and other kinds of services . . . those of children's and pre-school establishments, enterprises for communal feeding, places of entertainment, and so on."[8] This is seen as largely a problem of regional differences, and in particular of the surviving gap between rural and urban areas. Indeed, as all the studies show, the widest gulf in the pattern of recreation appears to be between the rural and urban population as a whole. Collective farm peasants are the most disadvantaged group, if not in terms of absolute amount of time available for leisure, then in the accessible opportunities for its use. The most alarming expression of this lack of opportunities is the escape of the young from the villages and the resulting manpower shortage, and the reluctance of professionals and experts to accept rural assignments. However, the problem has broader implications. The current rural (and to some extent even the urban) leisure situation is the product of modernization, which has proceeded to a sufficient degree to undermine or destroy traditional forms of peasant recreation, yet not far enough to provide adequate substitutes. This has resulted in a sense of cultural confusion and occasionally actual nostalgia for some of the old rural ways. Not infrequently, the maintenance and enrichment of well-organized, nonreligious, traditional holidays in the countryside is recommended. *Izvestia*, in an article entitled "Holidays need talents," concluded that

> the time has come at last to enlist our best artists . . . masters in all the arts, in the creation of Soviet ceremonies, holidays and celebrations. . . .

> Thrilling holidays and poetic ceremonies are legitimate spiritual require-
> ments of the people.[9]

The article also noted the appearance of a book entitled *New ceremonies
and holidays*, which was published "to aid rural club workers." The
other category which has yet to benefit significantly from whatever leisure
revolution has taken place is women, in almost all strata of the population.
While devoting an amount of time to work equal to that of men, women
continue to carry their traditionally unequal share of domestic labor,
which must, naturally, be done in nonworking time.

> Women in Novosibirsk wash, mend, darn, and iron in the evenings and
> on Sundays. . . . Many women also spend their free time in papering
> walls, whitewashing and painting. . . . How much time does a woman in
> Novosibirsk work each day after she has put in a normal working day on
> the job? Two hours are spent standing in lines, two more hours in preparing
> supper, breakfast, and dinner (in order to be on time for work in the
> morning, breakfast and dinner are cooked the evening before), an hour in
> cleaning the apartment and another hour in washing, ironing, and other
> work. Almost a whole "overtime" work day! Is this normal? . . . It is
> necessary to spend an hour and a half to two hours in the stores after
> work every day just to purchase groceries for the next day. . . . In order
> to dine at any dining-room in Novosibirsk, it is necessary to stand in line
> for two hours.[10]

Even *Pravda* turned its attention to the matter, noting that

> sociologists, who are now honoured in our country, have conducted a spot
> investigation and calculated that many of us spend 70% of our non-working
> time on everyday concerns—on shopping, doing laundry, cooking, getting
> clothes repaired, paying bills, waiting for buses and the like. That means
> that . . . only 30% is left for books, the theatre, sports and rearing of
> children. Isn't that too little?[11]

But the problem does not lie only in inadequate services and facilities.
The handicaps of women in the realm of leisure are also closely related
to the persistence of yet another feature of traditional peasant societies,
namely, the masculine disdain for household work. *Izvestia*, in a recent
article, criticized this state of affairs and called its urgent solution "a
political task."

Besides revealing the inequities in the distribution of free time, the
sociological studies illustrate the ways in which popular preferences
regarding the use of free time continue to outweigh the official ones. It
is particularly interesting to compare the amount of time spent on "social
work" (i.e., communal, public, quasi-political activities), 3–5 hours a

month, with that which is spent on entertainment, namely, 33.5 hours a month! A limited preference for the diversions offered by the mass media is reflected by the relatively short time devoted to radio and television—6 hours a month—against frequenting places of entertainment: 9.9 hours a month, and visiting friends and relatives: 8 hours a month. (A study conducted in Leningrad among young people similarly showed that "the majority of those polled preferred to spend their free time at home or visiting relatives.")[12] Another interesting finding of the same study was that only two hours a month were occupied by sports. In the category of self-education, a significant discrepancy appeared between the reliance on reading as a means to this goal, fourteen hours a month, and attendance at lectures, seminars, and study circles, totaling two hours. An article in *Kommunist* noted the contrast between substantial participation in civic-communal activities at the place of work and the small amount of the same at the place of residence.[13] (Such a discrepancy indicates the superior strength of organized pressures at the place of work against the relatively unorganized character of the residential units where people feel freer to withdraw from public-communal activities.) But the lack of adequate participation in collectivized leisure time at the place of work is also apparent:

> Particularly unsatisfactorily organised in some enterprises is mass cultural work—collective attendance at theatres, cinemas, museums, touring trips, country excursions and picnics, meetings with well-known people, and so on: public organisations are little interested in the life and daily existence of the workers, and do not exert enough influence on the use of non-working time. As a rule, therefore, workers at these enterprises use their non-working and especially their free time less rationally. The raising of the general level of work of party, komsomol, and trade union organisations is an essential reserve of the further rationalisation of the use of non-working time of the workers.[14]

If the use of free time by industrial workers is so different from the prescriptions, the discrepancy is bound to be more marked on collective farms. As a recent investigator reports with regret, "the kolkhozniki prefer in their free time to sit at home in their warm apartment, in a circle of friends or acquaintances over a cup of tea, or for that matter, over a glass of vodka." Sitting at home per se is not, of course, regarded as undesirable, but is deplored in light of the further finding that "because of the insufficient penetration among rural workers of such games as chess and checkers, crosswords and rebuses, table tennis and billiards, particular success is enjoyed by lotto, dominoes, and cards, which give nothing to the mind or heart."[15]

Both Soviet commentators and Western travelers agree upon the extraordinary importance of reading, one of the most favored uses of leisure. Several explanations may be advanced. One is undoubtedly the policy of the regime. Rates of literacy are high, reading matter is available in abundance, and reading is a highly respectable activity. We may also suspect that it provides an irreproachably legitimate escape from the unpleasant realities of life and that it can be highly apolitical. The popularity of technical, scientific, classical, and foreign literature supports this. The Russian classics are especially loved among the older generations of collective farm peasants, while the current vogue of science fiction, detective, and adventure stories reported by the press underlines the escapist quality of some Soviet reading habits.[16]

Housing difficulties may account for yet another typical and highly popular Soviet pastime, going to municipal parks and parks of culture. This, along with the high rates of cinema and theater attendance, is among the major public, though not necessarily collectivized, forms of recreation to which Soviet people are predisposed. Undoubtedly, this is one result of the lack of facilities for small-scale private leisure which has to be based on the uncrowded, comfortable apartment (or house) or the family car or boat.

Some of the problems associated with leisure are not peculiar to Soviet society but are also manifest, often in a more pronounced way, in other modern, secular societies. The privileged (or leisured) classes of the past always had "leisure problems" of their own, but these did not become major concerns for society at large because the number of people so afflicted was very small. Furthermore, they usually managed to devise elaborate, if not truly satisfactory, ways to chase boredom away.

To the extent that in every modern society the young, adolescents in particular, have more free time than the adults, it is to be expected that Soviet leisure problems are also primarily those of the young. The predominance of the leisure of youth in Soviet writings attests to this.[17] The proper upbringing of the future builders of communism is part of the general concern with the upbringing of the new generations.[18] The words of the first secretary of the Komsomol merit our attention in this context:

> It would be a big mistake to think that the very fact of living in the land of the Soviets, in the conditions of socialist reality, presupposes a communist world outlook in a young person. . . . It would also be a mistake to think that the growth of political awareness and conviction in the young person is always directly proportionate to the growth of his general educational and cultural level.[19]

The remedy is conceived of largely as one of facilities and proper guidance. However, even when the facilities are available they are not often used to capacity. Recreational programs are frequently poorly organized, those in charge are inadequately trained (in 1964, of eighty-nine thousand club leaders, thirty-five thousand did not have a high school education), and as to other forms of organized entertainment, a recurring theme of Soviet discussions on the various media is dullness. The producers of Soviet films, plays, TV, radio, and club programs are haunted by the revolt against tedium. In the Aesopian language of the officials: "Young people expect from writers, artists and composers from the theatre and the screen, works which show our heroic times and will create an image of the contemporary world worthy of emulation."[20] It is one of the new developments of the post-Stalin period that this question of dullness has been officially discovered and analyzed. The problem for the authorities is to find a balance between providing stimulating leisure-time activities and at the same time preserve (and possibly increase) their didactic functions.

The use of leisure becomes a problem not only among collective farm workers but also among young people of such metropolitan areas as Leningrad:

> Pastimes that are not connected with spiritual interests and that are accompanied by drinking lead to no good. Last year more than 2,000 intoxicated young men were arrested in one Leningrad borough alone. Out of ten violators of public order nine are drunk. . . . Study of the causes of divorce in Leningrad has shown that approximately half of the divorces result from the husband's drinking. . . . On Mondays and the days after holidays labour productivity usually falls off markedly. . . . These difficulties arise in large part because we have too few recreational facilities that are genuinely cultural and are capable of attracting young people. . . . The correct organization of leisure for city youth is unthinkable without Clubs and Palaces of Culture. . . . According to data from the poll, fewer than 25% of the young workers and only 2% of the intelligentsia visited the clubs last year and they came mainly for films and dances. The conclusion is not very comforting: The majority of boys and girls spend a large part of their free time in the courtyards and streets.[21]

Drunkenness is certainly not a new phenomenon in Russian society. Its spread to the younger age groups, however, is more of a novelty and reflects both their greater purchasing power and their desire for escape from boredom.

Another study conducted among one thousand secondary school students in Smolensk presents other aspects of the leisure problem: "The teenagers' weekdays and Sundays are taken up mainly by passive activities:

reading, watching television, listening to the radio, etc. Activities requiring intellectual output . . . were in the 10th and 20th place."[22] Only 3 percent of those polled expressed a desire to engage in public activities. The article discussing the study reached the melancholy conclusion that there is a strong relationship between free time and juvenile delinquency.

Not surprisingly, Soviet spokesmen also discern a relationship between domestic leisure problems and the penetration of Western models of leisure. The trend toward the Westernization of leisure poses many dilemmas for the guardians of the ideological purity of Soviet citizens. What is the nature of the appeal of Western models of leisure? How "subversive" are they and to whom do they appeal?

As far as the Soviet public and the young in particular are concerned, interest in Western forms of leisure is part of the ambivalent yet voracious interest in things Western. Western forms and accessories of leisure are associated not only with material abundance and comforts, but are also seen by many as more exciting and "modern." Such propensities in the population are obviously unwelcome to Soviet ideologues. Borrowing from the West in the realm of leisure is undesirable because it amounts to borrowing styles of life which are tainted by apolitical and escapist values and lacking in purpose. To be sure, escapism in the Western sense is not yet an issue. The escapist tendencies in the Soviet leisure are of a more primitive kind: they originate in the desire to forget the drabness of life rather than in the anxiety generated by questions which arise *after* material and environmental harshness is conquered. The spiritual maladies—ennui, spleen, and general world weariness—which, according to Aldous Huxley, have always afflicted the leisured classes are not yet afflicting the Soviet masses. There are, however, some indications that the Soviet social system does not confer invulnerability on them. Huxley's ironic comments on the optimists of his day, who believed that "the leisured masses of the future . . . will do all the things which the leisured classes of the present so conspicuously fail to do," invite application to similarly unrealistic Soviet expectations.

The further Westernization of Soviet leisure is most likely, except in the improbable event of radically retrogressive political changes. It is not surprising that the more affluent and consumption-oriented societies will continue to be the models in this realm. After all, in these societies people have the most leisure and the most varied means for its use. Thus in the final analysis, Soviet spokesmen are not far off the mark when they utter warnings about the "pernicious microbes" transmitted by the Western mass media and, by implication, by many Western forms of entertainment.[23] These are the "microbes" against which the Soviet leadership wants to immunize the population. However, immunization cannot take place without exposure; "the man of the future cannot be raised in a bell-jar." Yet exposure in this context means a more permissive attitude toward the infiltration of Western ideas and models of leisure. As is often the case, Soviet authorities face a problem analogous to the squaring of the circle.

Postscript 1982

The political significance of leisure under socialism, as exemplified by the Soviet case, lies in its potential misuse associated with a variety of social problems. Thus Soviet ideologues and social scientists have linked the misuse of leisure with juvenile delinquency, alcohol abuse, the inequality of women (who have less free time), inefficiency and lack of discipline at work, as well as certain deformations of character such as the capacity for boredom, individualism, and hedonism.

To be sure, there are prescribed forms of leisure, highly functionalized and politicized, which remain the official ideal, not unlike the positive heroes of socialist realist literature. It is most likely that despite the concern of the authorities, leisure-time activities have become more private over the past sixteen years—with improvements in housing and greater access to private automobiles. Insofar as drinking has persisted and even increased, the misuse of free time has continued to trouble the authorities. The special place occupied by alcohol abuse among Soviet social problems may be explained by the absence of other forms of escapism. In particular, the Soviet mass media—dull, didactic, and politicized—do not lend themselves to the gratification of escapist impulses.

Western forms and accessories of leisure (tapes, records, types of clothing, consumer goods of various kinds) remain attractive for Soviet people, the young in particular, and are viewed with somewhat less alarm by the authorities than a decade and a half ago. Such an increase in the official level of permissiveness suggests a more tolerant attitude toward manifestations of apolitical escapism among the population.

Notes

1. Trans. in *Current Digest of the Soviet Press* (hereafter abbreviated as CDSP), 6 April 1966, p. 5.
2. "*Non-working time* . . . that which is not directly absorbed by participation in socially productive activities. . . . It includes routine activities of daily life and free time. . . . Free time is the part of non-working time which includes study . . . voluntary public activities, leisure, hobbies, creative activities, etc. . . . Leisure is one of the parts of free time connected with

the restoration of the psychic and physical energies of man" (*Sotsiologiya v SSSR* [Moscow, 1965], 2:485, 495).

3. CDSP, 8 Dec. 1965, p. 15.
4. G. S. Petrosian, *Vnerabochee vremya trudiashchikhsya v SSSR* (Moscow, 1965).
5. Ibid., p. 16.
6. CDSP, 23 Dec. 1964, p. 10.
7. Petrosian, *Vnerabochee*, p. 126.
8. Ibid., pp. 64, 78, 127, 129. Many of his findings, and especially those connected with the inadequate availability and/or utilization of free time, were confirmed by recent articles in *Komsomolskaya Pravda* reporting the results of the newspaper's opinion poll institute. Cf. issues for Feb. 24, 25, 26, 1966. Among the interesting findings of the newspaper was that despite reduction of the workday, a high proportion of the respondents continue to work long hours at the expense of their free time.
9. CDSP, 9 Feb. 1966, p. 32.
10. CDSP, 2 June 1965, p. 30.
11. CDSP, 16 Feb. 1966, p. 29.
12. CDSP, 8 Dec. 1965, p. 14.
13. *Kommunist*, Aug. 1965, p. 55.
14. Petrosian, *Vnerabochee*, p. 180.
15. V. G. Baikova, A. C. Duchal, and A. A. Zemstov, *Svobodnoe vremya i vsestoronee razvitie lichnosti* (Moscow, 1965), p. 267.
16. Ibid., p. 257. Similar reading preferences were found among industrial workers in a survey by L. N. Kogan, in *Esteticheskie potrebnosti Sovetskogo rabochego* (Moscow, 1963), p. 190. The popularity of detective stories prompted *Komsomolskaya Pravda* to recommend their use for constructive purposes: "Adventure literature should become a powerful means of propagandizing the Soviet way of life" (CDSP, 22 July 1964).
17. Cf. F. G. Durham, *The Use of Free Time by Young People in Soviet Society*, M.I.T. Center for International Studies Monograph (Cambridge, Mass., 1966).
18. Cf. Merle Fainsod, "Soviet Youth and the Problem of Generations," *Proceedings of the American Philosophical Society* 108, no. 5 (October 1964).
19. CDSP, 26 Jan. 1966, p. 10.
20. CDSP, 22 Sept. 1965, p. 15.
21. CDSP, 8 Dec. 1965, p. 14.
22. CDSP, 25 Aug. 1965.
23. For example, the detective story is seen as "a weapon that has been used long and successfully by our ideological enemies" (CDSP, 22 July 1964, p. 16).

4.
Bureaucracy, Totalitarianism, and the Comparative Study of Communism

Though I am a sociologist, not a political scientist, I share with Professor Meyer an interest in Soviet society, convergence, totalitarianism, and the comparative study of communism and have followed the development of his views on these matters.[1] I therefore welcome an opportunity to comment on his recent paper (published in the Symposium of the March 1967 issue of the *Slavic Review*), having felt both critical of and sympathetic toward the views put forward in it. His thoughtful analysis of the study of Communist societies is all the more worthy of discussion since it reflects some broader contemporary issues in American social sciences and in our general thinking about communism.

First, I want to make clear that I am in sympathy with his call for comparative studies of Communist societies and his championing a more discriminating use of the concept of "totalitarianism." We are at a stage in the study of Communist societies, and the Soviet society in particular, when the old model has lost some of its validity, whereas a new model of similar explanatory power has not yet arisen. The emerging consensus, at any rate among students of Soviet society, lies in a preference for combining several models, several approaches, depending on the purposes and interests at hand.[2] The question of the day is not so much which models to use but what emphasis to give any one of them. In agreement with those who call for a more restricted use of the totalitarian model, I would stress its growing inapplicability to areas of life which lie outside the realm of politics proper. It is in itself an indication of change that today we can speak with more certainty of such areas. In particular, I have found that totalitarianism cannot adequately explain what sociologists call social problems, that is, juvenile delinquency, crime, family instability, problems of leisure, alcoholism, and rural migration. When dealing with these features of Soviet society (and some other Communist societies), we are compelled to fall back on concepts or processes which have no direct political relevance or derivation: secularization, urbanization, social mobility, the decline of informal social controls, and so forth—concepts which are unrelated to totalitarianism. At the same time, I would like to argue that we have not yet reached the stage in which the totalitarian model can be abandoned or even demoted to a very subordinate role in the analysis of Communist societies. I would also like to argue that its declining popularity is associated with circumstances other than the changes in Communist societies that are usually cited as the main justification for its abandonment.

I also would like to suggest that, since American social sciences are as dynamic as American society itself, we tend to be impatient with concepts, models, or theories which have been around for a long time; they make us restless and even anxious. Social scientists (sociologists probably even more than political scientists) want to be in the mainstream of the latest developments. We are fearful of being left behind with an old, obsolete "model"; we long for the latest. The analogy is deliberate— the fear of becoming obsolete is as pervasive in the social sciences as in the realm of consumption. The quest for new models and theories is not its only expression. We are also addicted to verbal innovation and to the spurious sense of novelty that comes with each new publication. None of this has any direct relevance to the issue at hand, least of all to Professor Meyer's work and opinions, for which I have much respect. I have made the aforementioned observation merely to indicate the broad background against which the current debate might be considered and to increase the appreciation of our receptivity to innovation.

To trace further the general context in which we confront the call for comparative studies of communism and new models with which to carry it out, I would like to comment on the influence of the cold war which Professor Meyer mentioned. It seems to have become almost axiomatic, for Professor Meyer and others, that the concept of totalitarianism is inextricably linked to the cold war and that this relationship has been detrimental to the development of scholarship on the Soviet Union and Communist countries in general. We hardly need to be reminded that the emergence of the concept of totalitarianism preceded the cold war, having evolved originally from the experiences of nazism and fascism. It is true, however, that subsequently it has been wholeheartedly applied to the Soviet system and that the early applications coincided with the beginning of the cold war. What remains to be demonstrated is that the use of this model did any lasting or temporary damage to the study of Communist societies. It so happens that thus far the best studies, of Soviet society at any rate (of which I am most acquainted), made use of the concept of totalitarianism and were employed by authors of such divergent views as Merle Fainsod, Alex Inkeles, Barrington Moore, Adam Ulam, and many others. I am sure Professor Meyer would agree with me that their use of the model did not impair their scholarship, objectivity, or the value of their work. And I would agree with his probable rejoinder that if in the past there was justification for the model, this may not hold for the present. In any case, I merely wanted to draw attention to the fact that the concept of totalitarianism in itself need not carry the stigma of the cold war and an attendant unscholarly ideological fervor.

In relation to the effects of the cold war on Soviet studies, I would like to take up another point Professor Meyer implies in his paper and has made more explicit elsewhere. I feel that his diminishing liking for the totalitarian model is closely linked to a belief that its use inclines us to self-righteousness and blindness to the defects of our own society. His remark in support of the bureaucratic model supports this proposition: "In preferring the latter [that is, the bureaucratic model], we point to striking similarities the bureaucratic model has with organizations familiar to all of us, and we imply that in criticizing the Communist way of life we should not be blind to analogous failings in our own." I am in complete agreement with Professor Meyer's feeling on this: the study of foreign societies, Communist or otherwise, should not become a vehicle for an indulgent evaluation of our own. Yet I do not think that the overgenerous use of the bureaucratic model necessarily saves us from this temptation. I submit that neither in the American nor in the Communist case is bureaucratization the major evil which should provoke the sharpest social criticism. This does not mean that we should ignore the ill effects of bureaucratization, American or Soviet. I simply suggest that each society has far more serious shortcomings than those which can be derived from the bureaucratic model and that adopting it for the analysis of Communist societies may not be of much utility in redressing the balance between self-indulgence and the stern criticism of others.

I would now like to offer more direct criticisms of the model and the approach Professor Meyer prefers—sometimes, it would seem in contradiction to his own insight into both the differences between Communist and non-Communist societies and the similarities between those that are Communist. It seems to me, in brief, that the totalitarian model is not quite as obsolete, and irrelevant to the political landscape, as he and others believe. The model became problematic primarily because of its emphasis on coercion, or, more precisely, permanent *mass terror*. The question remains: does this invalidate the model entirely or can it be "patched up"? While the decline of coercion has had far-reaching social consequences and while the purge turned out to be impermanent, massive and highly differentiated coercive institutions have not been eliminated, nor have new institutional arrangements been made to place obstacles in the path of arbitrary force.[3] I would nonetheless agree with Professor Meyer that, despite this, a return to Stalinist forms of government is for many reasons unlikely. In any case, however, the potentiality of coercion remains a major incentive to conform in Communist societies. These features cannot be reduced to the characteristics of complex bureaucracies. This brings me to my central contention, namely, that replacing the totalitarian model with the bureaucractic one is not an improvement. To be sure, Professor Meyer did say at one point that the two are complementary rather than mutually exclusive and may well be applied jointly. If this is the case, I have little to disagree with. I might even be inclined to suggest a verbal innovation such as a model of pluralistic versus totalitarian bureaucracy. Still, on the whole, Professor Meyer explicitly prefers the bureaucratic model.

Should we decide to abandon the middle-aged and decreasingly useful concept of totalitarianism in favor of one that focuses on the bureaucracy, we would do little to sharpen our understanding of Communist societies viewed either in isolation from each other or jointly. It would, however, achieve what I think Professor Meyer favors, a lowered estimation of the differences between Communist and non-Communist societies. Even if one aspired to construct a scheme to accommodate both Western and Communist societies, I wonder whether the bureaucratic model would be a more promising starting point than the concept of convergence. I have argued, together with Ezra Vogel,[4] that Communist bureaucracies— at any rate the Soviet and Chinese—are radically different from both the classical sociological models of bureaucracy and contemporary Western bureaucracies. While many counterarguments are possible and many similarities between all bureaucracies can be noted, we concluded that the differences outweigh the similarities. This is not the place to repeat my arguments (or to draw on those of Vogel), but merely to recall that we both found the decisively distinctive feature of Communist bureaucracies to be their thorough politicization, from which follow many other features setting them apart from Western bureaucracies. What I am suggesting here is that we cannot provide a unifying conceptual scheme for the analysis of Communist and non-Communist societies which is based on the alleged similarities of all complex, large-scale bureaucratic organizations once such similarities, or their importance, are open to serious question. We might end up with a situation worse than that which faces us currently with the totalitarian model: we would have to qualify the generalizability of the bureaucratic model out of existence.

I would now like to say something positive to recommend the retention of the totalitarian model, at least until we have something better or until further changes in the Communist world reduce its usefulness more significantly. I see the remaining virtues of the totalitarian model in that it draws together the following features of Communist systems: (1) strong ideological commitment of the leadership combined with apparent belief in a quasi-utopian social order (some participants in the symposium referred to this as a drive to create a new man); (2) intensity of controls, which, even if not outright terroristic, cannot be adequately described as merely bureaucratic; (3) concerted drive for industrialization (Nazi Germany obviously is a special case); (4) absence of legitimate and significant pluralism; and, most important (5) deliberately created interdependence of all social, economic, political, administrative, and cultural institutions and activities. I am aware that some of these features of totalitarianism might be found in non-Communist, developing societies and that we might end up with the unsatisfactory finding that totalitarianism is more than ever a matter of degree and not a pure type. However, the same objection can be made to other ideal-type concepts: democracy, capitalism, bureaucracy, feudalism, underdevelopment, modernization, and so on. The present time is characterized by such a high degree of interchange and mutual borrowing between different societies that pure types are increasingly difficult to find. In the final analysis, the question of which model we find the most useful boils down to often intangible factors of personal interests, disposition, and values. The preference for the totalitarian versus bureaucratic model clearly depends on whether we are more interested in discovering similarities or differences between Communist societies, whether we consider their internal similarities more important than their resemblances to non-Communist societies. Unavoidably, the issue of the distinctiveness of Communist versus non-Communist societies does have ideological implications, but the differences discerned need not be viewed in terms of superiority and inferiority, even when we compare our own society with Communist ones.

What I am suggesting is that we can and should recognize and study the differences between Communist societies without falling back on the bland, homogenizing approach toward all modern societies, Communist and non-Communist alike, implied by the bureaucratic model. Little is gained if we exchange one set of oversimplifications for another.

I would also like to comment on Professor Meyer's perception of the ethnocentrism which, in his opinion, has characterized Western and presumably primarily American, studies of communism. He says:

> Most work done in the past, I would submit, has not been comparative in this sense but has been ethnocentric. In dealing with the Communist world, our notions of what a political system is and does have been

suspended. For describing that world we have used concepts and models reserved for it alone or for it and a few other systems considered inimical.[5]

I will propose exactly the opposite. To apply without reservation the concepts and models developed in the context of Western political institutions and traditions to Communist and other non-Western societies might be a good deal more ethnocentric than the practice criticized by Professor Meyer. By following his advice, we would project terms and perspectives which derive from a particular and limited historical experience and scholarship and which may have little relevance to the phenomenon they try to describe. It seems to me more ethnocentric to build and apply concepts on the assumption that "basically" all societies are like our own (of course, it depends on what is "basic"). Consequently, one could argue that the concept of totalitarianism arose not out of the desire to arm ourselves with a new pejorative term with which to describe our enemies, but from the recognition that a somewhat new sociopolitical phenomenon had appeared which could not be described adequately by the traditional vocabulary Western social scientists had developed and applied to their own societies. In addition, I sense a contradiction between the plea for sharper distinctions between Communist societies, on the one hand, and, on the other, the proposal to analyze them with concepts which would make them less distinctive in comparison with non-Communist societies.

In the end, the major, and the most sensitive, issue that emerges is not so much the variability of Communist societies but the degree and the ways in which they differ from non-Communist ones. (I am in full agreement with Professor Meyer concerning the growing differentiation of European Communist movements and societies as their respective social-cultural bases reassert themselves.) I submit that we can retain and even increase our appreciation of the differences between Communist systems without overestimating their similarities to Western societies (which may occur through undue reliance on the bureaucratic model) and also without succumbing to the even stronger temptation of lumping them together with all "developing" countries. The lure of the latter is particularly strong because it promises to maximize the yield of theoretical generalizations in the framework of a subtle revival of evolutionary theory.[6]

To sum up, I believe that as of now the comparative study of Communist systems in itself does not necessitate a rejection of the totalitarian model, which, while timeworn, continues to direct our attention to many important features these systems have in common. Moreover, although the model can be improved upon (or supplemented by others), little will be gained by treating Communist systems as modern, complex bureaucracies. Finally, if we wish to promote greater sensitivity in distinguishing between Communist systems, the developmental model might not be the most useful, unless we are content with a more sophisticated version of economic determinism.

Postscript 1982

Time has been on the side of Professor Meyer: his aversion to the concept of totalitarianism has become more widely shared in the course of the last fifteen years since the previous article was written. Nowadays, few American political scientists or sociologists would be caught dead applying the term to Soviet society or other socialist countries. This by itself, however, does not settle the issue. As I argued in the article, the use of concepts is influenced by matters other than their intrinsic intellectual merit or usefulness. The debate about totalitarianism in the Soviet Union—and more broadly about the best ways to characterize or conceptualize the Soviet system (and others similar to it)—has over the years died down without being resolved. True enough, fewer scholars use the term "totalitarianism" with reference to the Soviet Union (or other Communist states), but it is far from clear whether or not such preferences came about as a result of the evolution of the Soviet political system or in response to the changes in the climate of opinion within American society and especially the academic community.

Six years after I wrote the previous article (in 1973, that is), I added the following comments on the reluctance to apply the concept of totalitarianism to the Soviet Union, paralleled by the grudging attribution of pluralism to American society:

> Totalitarianism . . . has come under heavy criticism both by those who have come to believe that it has *never* been a useful concept and by those who think that it has been rendered obsolete by social change in the Soviet Union. The applicability of pluralism to American society in turn has been questioned most forcefully by C. Wright Mills and his numerous followers. Note that the growing denial of pluralism in American society by one group of social scientists has been paralleled by an increasing imputation of pluralism to the Soviet society by another group. Indeed the search for signs of pluralism (however feeble or minor) in the Soviet Union has been just as determined and purposeful as the pursuit of data to prove its nonexistence in the United States! These two endeavors have been carried out by different groups of scholars, yet they spring from the same underlying "Zeitgeist," which prompts many American intellectuals to approach their own society in the most critical spirit and other societies fearful of being critical—increasingly haunted by the spirit of self-righteousness.[7]

I think the passage of time strengthened rather than dated these observations. Although public opinion has not become more favorable toward the Soviet Union, the writings of a few Soviet specialists aimed at a partial moral rehabilitation of the Soviet system met less astonishment or rejection than one might have expected. The most far-reaching among these revisionist approaches toward the Soviet system (going far beyond the repudiation of the totalitarian model) could be found in the work of Jerry Hough. He believes, for example, that the Soviet leadership (under Brezhnev) "almost seems to have made the Soviet Union closer to the spirit of the pluralist model of American political science than is the United States." Not surprisingly, Hough also regards political participation in the Soviet Union as meaningful as it is in the United States and discerns a flourishing of debate on major policy questions as well as a striving for the creation of constitutional restraints within the Soviet leadership.[8]

Equally symptomatic and perhaps even more startling have been the recent attempts at the moral-historical rehabilitation of Stalin performed by historian Theodore von Laue (and seconded, with some reservations, by political scientist Alfred G. Meyer). Von Laue's vision of Stalin is part of his longstanding perception of a forever victimized, underdog Russia which produced and determined the role to be played by Stalin as a tough-minded redeemer of this victimized nation. Consumed by his abiding fear of being unduly (or at all) judgmental of the Soviet Union, von Laue is apprehensive that by being critical of the USSR he might somehow absolve the United States of any misconduct in domestic or international affairs. He writes:

> American and Western historians have sat solemnly and self-righteously in judgement of Stalin. One wondered by what right, by what standards, by what power of their imagination? How can the bookish tribe of scholars judge the harsh realities which shaped Stalin and his judgement?
>
> . . . what people instinctively take to be their morality—particularly their political morality—is relative. This truth never emerges more clearly than in the judgement of Stalin.
>
> Our sights cleared at last, we are left to praise Stalin as a tragic giant set into the darkest part of the twentieth century. . . .
>
> Praise then to the strength and fortitude of mind and body that raised Stalin to such heights—and compassion too for his frailties.[9]

In such statements and many others Professor von Laue has undertaken the task of "putting Stalin in responsible focus" and of saving us from the "guilt of moral imperialism."

The reassessment of Stalin undertaken by Professor von Laue represents the bizarre culmination of an extreme and one-sided historical determinism which froze, once and for all, the Soviet Union in the role of the victim-underdog, the halo of which has come to be extended to Stalin himself. The latter in the grip of alleged historical necessities is now absolved of all responsibility for the incalculable pain he inflicted on his nation and other parts of the world too. Von Laue exemplifies an extreme and selective historical determinism which seeks to account for virtually every major facet of the Soviet system—including the political terror—by the effort to modernize the country against supposedly insuperable odds, and by the need to protect itself against external threats. Given the disposition to avoid being "judgmental" about the Soviet regime and concurrently to be savagely critical of the United States (or, generally, the West), such a one-sided scheme of historical determinism provides an admirable set of double standards which enable the observer to judge or refuse to judge.

As far as the conceptual issues relating to the study of the Soviet Union are concerned, I believe that what I wrote in 1967 is still true: "We are at a stage in the study of Communist societies, and the Soviet society in particular, when the old model has lost some of its validity, whereas a new model of similar explanatory power has not yet arisen." It seems to me that Soviet authoritarianism is very different from, say, the authoritarianism of the governments in Bolivia, Morocco, or the Philippines, and far more similar to the authoritarian states of Eastern Europe, Cuba, North Korea, or China. How should one refer to the distinctive characteristics of Soviet authoritarianism which it shares with other one-party dictatorships which legitimate themselves by the recurring incantation of Marxism-Leninism? One could call the Soviet regime, and others similar to it, "Marxist one-party dictatorships" (as I had done in one of the essays that follow), but it so happens that such regimes come close to what used to be called totalitarian systems even if *some* of them deviate more noticeably from the model than used to be the case. Such deviations are to be found in the reduction of governmental coercion (and the slackening of controls over certain cultural activities and population movements), but the instruments of coercion are still intact, powerful, and in place. The high levels of institutional integration and interdependence that totalitarian states create still characterize most of the states I called Marxist one-party dictatorships.[10] Some of them like Hungary (or Poland, briefly but significantly) strayed relatively far afield from the totalitarian model, but most of them did not. Thus, for example, much of the new information coming out of China gives vigorous support to the applicability of the totalitarian model to that society, and the same goes for Indochina as a whole and Cuba too.

The theoretical or conceptual problems associated with the use of the concept of totalitarianism have much to do with the durability of the Soviet system and its peculiar mixture of rigidity and flexibility, pragmatism and idealism, stagnation at home and dynamism abroad, or conservatism at home, and commitment to change in many places around the globe. Thus, while in certain ways the Soviet system has become traditional, that is to say, it has been taken for granted by the population and assumed a certain immutability, it has retained much of its totalitarian institutional arrangements and the right to virtually unlimited interference in the life of the citizen.[11]

In short, we still need some word with which to signify that the Soviet system and most other Marxist one-party dictatorships are different from non-Marxist dictatorships and still have more in common with one another than with other authoritarian regimes.[12] Today, there is still no widely agreed upon word or concept with which to highlight these differences (or the commonalities).

Notes

1. As set forth in Alfred G. Meyer, "USSR, Incorporated," in Donald W. Treadgold, ed., *The Development of the USSR: An Exchange of Views* (Seattle: Univ. of Washington Press, 1964); and Meyer, *The Soviet Political System: An Interpretation* (New York: Random House, 1965).
2. See Alex Inkeles, "Models in the Analysis of Soviet Society," *Survey*, July 1966.
3. Allen Kassof elucidated the distinctive qualities and consequences of totalitarian coercion in the post-Stalin period in his article "The Administered Society: Totalitarianism without Terror," *World Politics*, July 1964; see also Herbert Ritvo, "Totalitarianism without Coercion?" in A. Brumberg, ed., *Russia under Khrushchev* (New York: Praeger, 1962).
4. See Ezra Vogel, "Politicized Bureaucracy: Communist China," and Paul Hollander, "Soviet Bureaucracy: The Pursuit of Efficiency and Political Control" (Papers delivered at the 1966 Meeting of the American Political Science Association, New York). See also pp. 105–114 of this volume.
5. Meyer, "The Comparative Study of Communist Political Systems," *Slavic Review*, March 1967, p. 11.
6. Reinhard Bendix, *Nationbuilding and Citizenship* (New York: Wiley, 1964), esp. pp. 2999–301 and 6–15; Wilbert E. Moore, *The Impact of Industry* (Englewood Cliffs, N.J.: Prentice Hall, 1965), esp. pp. 10–19; see also Stanislav Andreski, "Old and New Elements in Totalitarianism," "Factors of Liberalization," and "Communism and Capitalism: Are They Converging?" in *The Uses of Comparative Sociology* (Berkeley: University of California Press, 1965).

7. Paul Hollander, *Soviet and American Society: A Comparison* (New York: Oxford Univ. Press, 1973), p. 110.

8. Quoted in David E. Powell, "In Pursuit of Interest Groups in the USSR," *Soviet Union* pt. 1 (1979), pp. 111–12. Hough was also in the front ranks of those experts who offered the most sanguine assessments of the good natured reasonableness that will attend to the leadership of Andropov (see for example *The New Republic*, 27 Dec. 1982, p. 10). Hough's rise to the position of the favorite academic Soviet specialist of the national news media (reflected in his frequent appearances in papers such as the *Washington Post* and *The New York Times*) has been symptomatic of the recent upsurge of wishful thinking about the nature of the Soviet Union. Jerry Hough emerged as the Soviet expert willing to lend his academic authority to all those in the news media and politics, who sought to redefine the Soviet system as far more benign and unthreatening than has generally been assumed. In turn such wishful thinking was greatly reinforced by the desire for disarmament, which attempts to give reasons why armaments are unnecessary, and in doing so ends up redefining the threat (which had earlier justified the armaments) as delusory.

9. Theodore H. von Laue, "Stalin among the Moral and Political Imperatives, or How to Judge Stalin?" *Soviet Union* pt. 1 (1981), pp. 2, 17.

10. George Feiffer spoke of the KGB "as coordinator in all matters of . . . importance" in his *Message from Moscow* (New York: Random House, 1969), p. 65.

11. Zbigniew Brzezinski noted, along these lines, that "the contemporary Soviet system . . . combines residual elements of revolutionary totalitarianism with features reminiscent of the more traditional autocracy" (in Paul Cocks et al., eds., *The Dynamics of Soviet Politics* [Cambridge: Harvard Univ. Press, 1976], p. 342).

12. Jeane Kirkpatrick made a good case for the enduring usefulness of the distinction between authoritarian and totalitarian systems in her article entitled "Dictatorship and Doublestandards," *Commentary*, November 1979.

5.
Border Controls:
An Integral Part of the
Soviet Social-Political System

I

Soviet society and the Soviet political system cannot be properly understood without some knowledge of the system of border controls the regime has developed. The border controls (and the associated restrictions on travel and emigration) are an integral part of the entire network of political controls. They represent an aspect of the "totalitarian syndrome" that has been largely neglected by students of totalitarianism and the Soviet political system. The major function of these controls, the prevention of unauthorized departures and entries, is a revealing and indispensable characteristic of the totalitarian organization of society. Border controls and prohibitions aptly symbolize a general obsession with controls and the official anxiety aroused by the spectacle of the citizen "voting with his feet." Considerable secrecy surrounds the nature of these controls, many vital aspects of which are undocumented and unpublicized. It would be in vain to search in published sources for data on the number of border violators per annum, statistics of their punishments, or backgrounds. Nor do we know how many Soviet citizens have applied for exit visas over the years, how many of them were granted and refused. This article is based on the available fragments of information both from Soviet and Western sources including those of a personal nature provided by former Soviet citizens.

Lines of demarcation and physical barriers (natural or man-made) separating human groups from one another are presumably as old as mankind itself. Several stages may be discerned in the development of such barriers and boundaries. In the more distant past and in the primitive societies of the present, the functions of boundaries have been primarily economic-defensive. The emergence of the nation-state vastly increased the significance of boundaries since they often alone defined the unity of the nation, not necessarily made up of ethnically and culturally homogeneous groups. Nation-states have stressed their territorial unity and integrity; guarding their frontiers represented a gesture directed at outsiders serving both symbolic and defensive military purposes. The third stage in the development of boundaries may be discerned with the emergence of modern dictatorships and particularly the totalitarian states of the twentieth century. It has been their historical innovation to add a new dimension to the functions of frontiers by turning them into auxiliary devices of domestic social-political control. This trend has been pioneered by the Soviet Union, though not without the help of pre-Soviet traditions of border control present in nineteenth-century Russia. The latter was the first among European countries to restrict legally the freedom of travel by requiring passports for travel abroad and also within the country. The police-military control of Russian frontiers from the second half of the nineteenth century went far beyond the corresponding deployments of such forces of other European countries, even though it fell short of the efficiency and territorial coverage introduced by the Soviet regime. Modern technology made it possible for the Soviet government to maximize the effectiveness of border controls, relying on mobile troops, sophisticated warning devices, sensitive mines, long-range fire power and advanced techniques of communications. But efficiency was not the only difference. What separates the czarist and Soviet border controls is part of the gap that divides the political controls of a traditional autocracy from those of a modern totalitarian society.[1]

Historical traditions and experiences are of importance in shaping Soviet policies in this area. There can be little doubt that the many foreign invasions of Russia were among the influences on the defensive aspects of Soviet border controls. The early Soviet experience of foreign expeditionary troops aiding the anti-Communist forces during the Civil War of the early 1920s continued to deepen the fear of foreign invasions. For some time after the Soviet Union came into existence, its territorial and political integrity could not be taken for granted by its leaders. Theirs was a young state, a new political formation, which, in search of cohesion, cultivated an intensified nationalism drawing both on traditional Great Russian nationalism and on the appeals of the new, somewhat artificial unit forged in and after the October Revolution. Nor did the German invasion in World War II help to reduce the concern with the inviolability of Soviet frontiers. Soviet leaders considered virtually all neighboring countries potentially hostile until the USSR created in the postwar period a group of client states in Eastern Europe and stationed troops in most of them. Nevertheless, the borders with these countries appear just as closely guarded as those with less friendly nations.

Preoccupation with defense has remained up to the present a cornerstone of Soviet border policies, although threats of foreign invasion have significantly declined since the Soviet Union emerged as the second greatest military power in the world following World War II. Nevertheless, the myth of "capitalist encirclement," carefully nurtured by Stalin (largely for domestic political purposes), has not diminished noticeably. In fact, the ever-present threat of imperialist aggression and hostility appearing in new guises has become enshrined and institutionalized in Soviet political thought. There remains a profound conviction that the frontier separating the Soviet Union (and other "socialist" countries) from other, nonsocialist countries represents more than conventional boundaries between nation-states: it divides two wholly different worlds from each other: "The state borders of the Soviet Union and of the socialist countries adjoining the capitalist states represent lines of demarcation between two camps opposed to one another by virtue of their political-economic system. They divide two worldwide social systems from each other."[2]

By the middle of the twentieth century, the Soviet example of border controls has had many imitators. Along with the one-party system and government controlled industrialization, it has been an important feature of the Soviet social order which many nations have borrowed. We can hardly find any country in the world today which, if committed to strict domestic political controls, allows even a moderately free movement of its citizens across its frontiers. Other things being equal (i.e., technology, size of the country, terrain, relationship with neighbors), there is an obvious connection between freedom of expression and association within the country and the strictness of border controls. This relationship is easy to grasp. On the one hand, authoritarian political systems are defensive and insecure, feeling unduly threatened by both their own population and hostile forces abroad. On the other hand, it is impossible to institute efficient domestic controls without controlling the movements of the population.

In this article we will examine in some detail the organization, functions, justifications, and consequences of Soviet border controls.

II

The organization of Soviet border controls fully reflects the magnitude and importance of its objectives. There are about 200,000 border guards who are provided with every military and technological device available to fulfill their task.[3] Enlisted men serve three years. An elite unit is given specialized and demanding training and the best food ("Norma no. 1.") available in the Soviet armed forces. The importance of the unit's political reliability is indicated, among other things, by the amount of time allocated for political instruction in the training of the guards. According to a former high-ranking officer in the Border Guards, out of sixty hours monthly instruction eighteen hours are allocated to political training, while the next two most important categories receive only ten hours each: "border (operational service) training" and "firing."[4]

To ensure the fullest possible effectiveness of border guards,

> They are recruited mainly from Soviet citizens of Russian nationality according to the principle of extraterritoriality: a border guard soldier must not serve in his district of origin regardless of where he would like to serve—he is not asked about the matter. He may be sent to any frontier in the Soviet Union, as a rule to as distant a frontier as possible; for example, if he comes from Vladivostok, he may be sent to the Western frontier, to the Kaliningrad oblast (East Prussia) or Lithuania; if he comes from Kaliningrad oblast, he might be sent to Kamchatka, the Kuriles or Central Asia.[5]

Interestingly, there is a tendency to avoid recruitment of the border guards from areas which were occupied by foreign troops during the war,[6] presumably on the assumption that their political reliability might in some manner have been impaired by the experience of occupation. Political reliability is also assured by careful screening by both local military authorities and the state security organs. "Preference is given to Komsomol members, Stakhanovites and outstanding workers in industry and farming, whose past, and whose parents' past is politically trustworthy."[7]

The officers serving in the border guards receive rigorous and highly demanding training under the auspices of the Ministry of Internal Affairs together with KGB officers. A more specialized institute for the higher training of border-guard officers is the Moscow Border School for Improvement of the Officer Corps (*Mosskovskaya Pogranichnaya Shkola Usoverstvovaniya Ofitserskovo Sostava*) founded in 1951.[8] Officers entering this school must be members of the Party. The schedule at the school is very taxing with twelve hours of training each day (including individual preparation). Study materials are not allowed to be taken out of the classroom, not even notebooks. The curriculum includes the following disciplines: "the organization of intelligence work in the USSR and abroad"; "intelligence work by the intelligence organs of foreign countries," particularly American and British; "investigation work by the intelligence organs of the Soviet State Security"; "the study of Soviet justice and judicial law"; and "specialized border problems." In addition, there is much time devoted to Marxism-Leninism, the organization of Party work among border troops, Soviet military science, tactics, fire training, and military topography.[9]

Characteristic of the symbolic (as well as tangible) status privileges of border officials are their travel arrangements. "Junior officers up to and including the rank of captain travel in wooden seat coaches but have reserved seats, while officers of the rank of major are given seats in coaches with separate compartments. Lieutenant colonels and colonels are entitled to cushioned seats."[10] Each year, officers also get one month leave with pay excluding travel time and free military tickets each way.

The actual system of controls along the border is complex and not limited to the supervision of the immediate area along the frontier. To begin with, there is a restricted zone along the entire frontier averaging 18½ miles in depth in which "special security measures apply."[11] This is what Artemiev calls "frontier-strip" (*pogranichnaya polosa*) which can be divided into restricted zones (*rezhimnye zony*).[12] Those who are not residents of the area in question can only enter it with special permission to be obtained in advance from the State Security. This is not a simple procedure, and application has to be accompanied not only by statements of the purpose of the visit but also by biographical information and photographs of the applicant. "Before the visa [the permit] is issued a careful check is made of the applicant which sometimes takes several weeks."[13] After entering the border area, the visitor must register and have his traveling papers stamped at the border command headquarters. In view of such restrictions, most would-be violators are likely to be caught well before they reach the vicinity of the border. Thus border violations are prevented by a combination of military and police measures. We already noted the system of special permissions to enter the entire border zone. Such areas are also saturated with KGB agents and informers, many recruited from the local population which is encouraged to report not only actual violators but any suspicious stranger. There are also various volunteer detachments, made up mostly of young people, recruited with the help of local Party and Komsomol organizations, including school children and pioneers, which lend open support to the authorities. When successful, such volunteers are rewarded with money, gifts, and certificates. The population of the border areas is ceaselessly encouraged to exhibit the utmost vigilance. The nature of civilian cooperation and the grounds for suspicion and arrest are well illustrated in a story in *Pravda*. The latter also provides some insight into the atmosphere of paranoia that prevails in the border zones, and has apparently infected at least some of the civilian population.

Tavakkyul Agayev, a railroad station attendant, saw a group of boys clustered around a stranger on the platform. As he approached, Agayev gathered from a few words here and there that they were talking about the road into the mountains. The stranger's inquiries appeared suspicious: One does not go into the mountains at nightfall, and besides, the border was in that direction.

Trying not to betray his suspicions, the railroad man greeted the stranger and, according to custom, invited him to rest up and have some tea.

The stranger was taciturn, increasingly so. But his host chatted easily about the local scenery, hunting and fishing. The guest must have sensed that something was wrong, because he began looking nervously out of the window and a few times stood up and tried to leave, but the "cordial host" sat him back down at the table each time.

Time passed. He had to act. As if remembering something urgent, the station attendant got up and headed for the door. Out of the corner of his eye, T. Ageyev saw the stranger's hand move toward his pocket. But the railroad man stopped him. Dishes were knocked off the table and crashed to the floor.

Border guards, summoned by T. Agayev, took the stranger away as a border violator.

On May 3 the command of the border unit presented a citation and a medal "for distinguished service in defense of the U.S.S.R. state frontier" to Tavakkyul Agayev, commander of one of the best rural people's volunteer detachments on the southern border of the country.[14]

As the story quoted shows, the "violator" was not actually caught on the border, nor did the article suggest that his papers were not in order. Merely he was alleged to talk "about the road into the mountains." The article hinted he might have been armed, "his hand moved toward his pocket," but for what reason we do not know. Had he been armed, it is unlikely that the report would have remained silent about this important fact. Nor does the article make it clear that he initiated the scuffle with his informer-host. Rather, it seems that it was the informer-host who attacked him to prevent his escape before the border guards got there. And finally, the article also failed to offer any further evidence such as might have been obtained subsequently to substantiate the claim that an authentic "border violator" was apprehended.

Restricted entry to the border zone and the vigilance of the local population are not the only obstacles the would-be violator has to surmount. Should he succeed in evading these, he would still face the formidable task of scaling the border defenses proper.

"Inside and all along the frontier one, two, or three strips 20 to 25 meters wide called 'control-track strips' (*kontrol'nosledovnye polosy*) are kept freshly plowed so that the footprints of anyone attempting to cross the border will be easily visible."[15] He may also encounter concealed barriers, or MZP (*malozametnye prepyatsviya*), which may consist of barbed wire, concealed wire netting, pitfalls, traps all of which may also be connected with an alarm system.

> The alarm may be transmitted either by sound or light; often it is of such a nature that it is not apparent to the frontier violator himself, but is received directly at the border posts. . . . Sometimes obstacles placed in narrow and difficult crossings, particularly in mountain areas, are so arranged that when they are touched they trigger off machine guns which fire automatically in a set direction and at a given range. In addition certain areas or zones are sown with small anti-personnel mines.[16]

There is also a "forbidden zone" (*polosa zapreschchennoi zony*) along the frontier itself the width of which varies with local conditions, geographic and demographic. Along the frontier there are also electric outlets from underground telephone cables, and the guards have telephone receivers they can plug into these outlets. Radio communications are kept to the minimum as far as patrols are concerned. Stationary frontier defenses include border posts, concealed posts, ambushes, patrols and larger patrols, observation posts, passport control posts, and maneuver groups.[17] A former resident of the Soviet-Rumanian border zone provides substantiating evidence of the nature of border fortifications and controls as they were set up after the Soviet annexation of Bessarabia.[18] The recollections of the author include descriptions of the often summary and violent punishment meted out to border violators.[19] It must be noted that such measures are taken only on the more sensitive borders while others in remote areas of little population or considerable natural barriers are more lightly guarded. Most of the security measures are taken on the European borders and more recently on some sectors of the Chinese.

III

The extent of the Soviet preoccupation with defection is reflected not only in the military and police measures surveyed so far. Going beyond them we find the efforts to induce or force defectors to return, sometimes to liquidate them. These efforts can be viewed as logical extensions of border controls. Their intensity varies, of course, with the importance of the defector. The kidnapping and assassination of defectors was particularly widespread under Stalin in the 1930s, as was reported, among others, by Barmine.[20]

The wide range of such activities has been recorded and reported by numerous ex-Soviet citizens and Western observers. Fisher describes, for example, what he calls the "great manhunt" after World War II in occupied Germany and Austria where large numbers of Soviet displaced persons were living, reluctant to return.[21] In the notorious case of the Petrovs in Australia, Soviet agents dragged Mrs. Petrov aboard the plane, while an astonished Australian crowd watched.[22] Kasenkina, teacher at the Soviet embassy in New York, after running away was forcibly taken back to the embassy and kept prisoner there until she jumped out of the window and thereby escaped.[23] Kaznachaev describes not only the dangers surrounding his own escape, but also the successful kidnapping of another Soviet official in Burma who tried to defect.[24] In March 1964, the chief mate of the Soviet ship *Vladivostok*, anchored in Cape Town, was "chased," "overpowered," "bound and gagged," and "carried back" to the ship by other members of the crew. Since the incident attracted attention, the captain explained later that "the chief mate had been under guard and medical attention for several months because his mind had been deranged."[25] Attempted kidnappings in the United States have also been reported by a Soviet pilot.[26] He also described the obviously fraudulent persuasion on the part of Soviet officials who promised to treat the affair—an escape by military aircraft—as a mistake if he returned voluntarily.

After World War II the Soviet ambassador advised to a group of Soviet sailors who got stranded in Sweden during the war and refused to return: "I warn you that if you show yourself so unpatriotic that you refuse to return of your own free will, you will be compelled to return under much less pleasant circumstances!"[27] More recently, a Soviet physicist who first expressed a desire to stay in Britain and later changed his mind was hustled aboard a plane by Soviet embassy officials after being pronounced sick.[28] While not every detail of the case is clear, it is beyond dispute that at one point Tkachenko was dragged into a Soviet embassy car and forced to board a plane (from which the British police removed him); he was given drugs by the embassy doctor, and his decision to return was preceded by strong pressure put on him by Soviet authorities and his wife. Once more, the theme of mental illness was much in evidence. A Soviet spokeman in London noted: "Certainly treatment in these cases is better in Russia than in a foreign country."[29] Said another: "These cases are very difficult. One must treat them gently."[30] It has been reported that "when the plane landed in Moscow Western reporters were not allowed near the aircraft and Dr. Tkachenko. Soviet security officials immediately put him in a waiting car which sped out of the airport. Passengers said the scientist spent most of the flight staring out of the window; he hardly spoke to his wife."[31]

Mental disturbance among defectors, who are either physically apprehended by Soviet authorities abroad or subject to serious pressure by them, is not necessarily a fabrication but often a reality. Sometimes such allegations exemplify the phenomenon of the self-fulfilling prophecy. Would-be defectors abroad experience extreme stress which is fully exploited and in part created by Soviet authorities themselves. Typically they are separated from their family whose safety is hardly enhanced by their decision not to return. Often Soviet authorities arrange for members of the family to make anguished personal appeals to the defector imploring him to return. Thus immense pressures are put on the defector which range from naked threats to appeals to family loyalty, patriotism, and public ostracism combined with predictions of a bleak future of isolation and universal contempt that await him abroad. In addition, decades of Soviet upbringing may also bear fruit as the defector finds himself torn between his desire to escape (whatever his immediate or long-term reasons for it) and the carefully inculcated beliefs which make him feel that he is a traitor.[32]

Even in the more liberal post-Stalin period, defectors have had reason to be concerned with the future and safety of their families left behind. This was illustrated by the case of Oleg Lenchevsky, a scientist who decided to stay in Britain in 1962 but whose family was not allowed to join him. Nor were they free of harassment by the Security Police. In his letter to Khrushchev, the scientist described a letter that reached him from his daughter:

> It had been dictated to my younger daughter Masha and only urged me to come back "before it is too late" in the hope that "we will be treated with humanity" though naturally "without much consideration." This reminded me of the conversation I had with members of our embassy at the Foreign Office last June. They too promised me humane treatment on condition that I return at once, and urged me repeatedly "to think seriously of what might happen to my family." I did not at that time appreciate all the implications of these warnings.[33]

For the potential defector separation from his family provides a powerful motivation to return. Another policy designed to establish some control over the Soviet citizen abroad has been group travel which facilitates supervision, particularly when the groups include representatives of the State Security who try to make sure that everyone will return. Viktor Nekrasov, the Soviet writer, commented sardonically on this phenomenon: "Poor, poor Ivan Ivanovich. . . . After all he had to keep track of all twenty of us. . . . Still and all our kind Ivan Ivanovich forgot one thing. . . . Excessive caution—let us call it that—does not bring people together, it drives them apart."[34]

According to Soviet sources, defense from external aggression is the major objective of border controls. Thus, for example, on a recent "Border Guards' Day" it was said that

> the protection of the USSR state borders is one of the most important measures carried out by the Communist Party and the Soviet government in the interests of strengthening the defensive capability of the Soviet Union and ensuring our people's peaceful creative labor. The border guards do not for a minute forget that the imperialists, headed by the USA, are exacerbating international tension and creating hotbeds of war, that the imperialist intelligence services have united their efforts in conducting espionage and subversive activity against the USSR and the countries of the socialist commonwealth. In these conditions, the fighting men of the border are increasing their vigilance to the fullest.[35]

As the previous quotation indicates, the major function of border controls is not so much to defend against actual *military* threats, but more against political or political-military ones, namely, subversion and espionage. It is difficult to assess how realistic these fears are at present. However, it must be noted that subversion and espionage are unwelcome in every modern state; yet measures taken against them do not result in such rigidly and tightly controlled borders as those of the USSR, except, of course, in countries which are modeled after the Soviet Union. It is especially noteworthy that the Soviet Union guards her borders with other "socialist" states as closely as those she has with non-Communist states. Such precautions make good sense only at the Soviet-Chinese frontier where external threats have more reality than, say, on the Soviet-Romanian, Soviet-East German, or Soviet-Polish borders.[36]

Defense against subversion has broader implications than preventing espionage or frustrating agents bent on sabotage. The control of frontiers assures, along with a number of other supplementary measures not only that hostile individuals will not circulate freely among the population, but also that unorthodox or unauthorized ideas will not enter either. Thus Soviet border controls also assist domestic political propaganda and socialization by screening off undesirable ideas and their carriers.

IV

While defense against the entry of hostile individuals and ideas is certainly one of the prime objectives, the border controls also serve to prevent unauthorized departures, and not only by spies or criminal fugitives from justice. That such is the case is suggested by the great difficulty of leaving the country not only illegally but also legally.

Hence the character of the Soviet system of border controls can be appreciated only when it is realized that it is not simply a means to prevent illegal entries and exits but that it supplements other controls over travel. It would indeed by a totally different situation if strict border control (designed to prevent illegal movements) would be accompanied by a liberal policy of granting to the population at large the legal means (passports, exit visas) and the right to travel abroad. This, however, is not the case. The vast majority of Soviet people do not have the opportunity to leave the country *either* legally *or* illegally. They do not, as a matter of course, carry passports for foreign travel (they do for domestic). Obtaining such a document is a privilege, not a right. Nevertheless, the number of Soviet citizens traveling abroad has increased over the last decades. Still, holidays abroad, especially in Western and non-Communist countries, remain a reward for the elite groups. A trip abroad is preceded by careful checks on the background and reliability of the potential tourist. "The procedure requires that the would-be tourist must fill out a series of questionnaires, write up biographical accounts and present numerous photographs. In addition, he must obtain references from the head of his place of employment, the chairman of the branch of the trade union to which he belongs, and the party secretary at his place of work. These documents are sent to the Committee for State Security (KGB), where a thorough investigation of the prospective tourist is conducted."[37] A further effort to promote proper behavior abroad is indicated by the existence of a booklet entitled "Rules of Behavior of Soviet Citizens Abroad."[38] And, as already noted, families are rarely allowed to go abroad together, particularly to Western countries.[39]

Thus border controls represent merely one facet of the overall policy of restricting travel and emigration abroad. Undoubtedly, if allowing Soviet citizens to leave the country legally were a matter of course, the need to supervise closely the frontiers would diminish since few would prefer illegal to legal exits. And conversely, if legal exits were restricted without a corresponding effort to prevent illegal ones, they would have little practical effect. On the whole, it might be generally proposed that the more restrictions there are on legal travel and emigration from (as well as immigration to) any country, the greater the corresponding need to make illegal border crossings impossible. Controls over legal and illegal travel must supplement each other if either is to be effective.

There is virtually no emigration from the Soviet Union abroad, neither to Western, nor to socialist, or neutral countries.[40] Theoretically, it is possible that Soviet people have no such desires. Yet in the absence of opportunities to translate such desires into reality, it is impossible to subscribe to such a proposition. Not only is it nearly impossible to obtain passports and exit visas, but the very idea of applying for a passport to leave the country is greatly discouraged. Such applications lead not only to lengthy and complex bureaucratic procedures, but they automatically create official ill will toward the applicant who desires to emigrate. Since his chances of being allowed to go are small, while the chances of incurring official displeasure are excellent, it is more than likely that most of those who entertain such ideas will not allow them free and public expression and will certainly not take the decisive and basically pointless step of applying for permission to leave.[41] The desire to leave the Soviet Union is an attitude that borders on treachery, as the officials see it. It amounts to a rejection of all the alleged benefits and accomplishments this historically most advanced society has allegedly provided for its citizens. It represents an intolerable ideological failure, an insult to the social order.

As far as illegal departures are concerned, the Soviet criminal codes are explicit. "Flight abroad or refusal to return from abroad to the USSR" is listed among "especially dangerous crimes against the state" comprising "treason" along with espionage, the transmission of state or military secrets to a foreign state, or conspiracy for the purpose of seizing power and rendering aid to a foreign state.[42] The law says, in effect, to the citizen: "If you do not like this country you are a traitor; if you do not want to live in this country you must be its enemy." There are few better illustrations of the totalitarian outlook on loyalty and treason than this unprecedented legal position. Severe punishment (ten to fifteen years of deprivation of freedom) is promised to those who do not wish to partake of life in the best possible of all societies in the history of mankind. An interesting contrast to the Soviet position was provided by a decision of the British government allowing Guy Burgess, a bona fide Soviet spy, "to transfer his private funds from London to Moscow by being classified as an emigrant."[43]

A favored Soviet method of discrediting (and possibly retrieving) defectors is to allege that they are common criminals in flight. Petrov recounts that Soviet spokesmen told the Swedish authorities that a sailor who jumped ship stole money.[44] In another case Radio Moscow claimed that Deriabin "disappeared from Vienna with a large sum of embezzled money." In addition, "those who worked with him in Austria report his great weakness for drink. . . . In a short period of time he had managed to marry four times, living with his two last wives simultaneously for two years. . . . He had speculated on the black market . . . in property stolen from his organization."[45] Such examples could be multiplied.

Although the desire to leave the country *legally* is not a punishable offense, official attitudes toward those seeking legal departures are hardly favorable. For example, a Soviet couple who apparently told foreign newsmen about the authorities' refusal to grant them exit visas were described as footloose people of poor moral character who slandered their country by complaining to foreigners. The article describing their unsavory attitudes and activities winds up with this warning: "We advise them to read the article in *Izvestia* (no. 217) on the fate that awaits certain renegades in the foreign 'paradise.' . . . You will wind up no better off than when you started, just like those no good jazzmen! [This refers to two Soviet jazz musicians who defected in Japan earlier in the same year.—P.H.] No one intends to hold you back."[46] In a follow-up article, they are described as "two nomadic families who cannot bear a settled way of life and who have defamed the lofty name of citizen of the Land of the Soviets with their ignoble behavior. . . . Soviet people are indignant at these people's scandalous behavior and write that they are unworthy of living side by side with honest Soviet toilers." Further along they are described as "scum," "rascals," and "exuding a stench of hatred for the Soviet people." And, to make sure that the Soviet reader will put such matters in a correct perspective, the article says: "They went abroad. They were indeed swept out like useless rubbish. But what happened in the last minutes before they boarded the plane, to their self-confidence, arrogance, bile and impudent tone? They became pitiful and unwanted tramps. They were rejected not only by us but also by those on whom they pinned their hopes."[47]

Evidently, official indignation in this case was particularly strong since the people in question were unafraid to talk to foreign newsmen about their desire to leave and about the difficulties encountered when trying to carry out their wish. We will never know whether they might have been allowed to leave without the publicity they created by their conversations with the Western journalists. In any event, it was deemed to be a good opportunity to remind Soviet newspaper readers of the character of those who want to leave their country and the sad fate that awaits them abroad. A contrasting case was reported in the previous year when "Soviet officials . . . returned a Greek national seeking repatriation outside the Greek Embassy to his home in Kazakhstan. . . . It is believed the man came to the Soviet Union after taking part in the post World War II insurrection on the Communist side."[48]

The Soviet propaganda apparatus devotes considerable effort to depicting the moral degradation of those who want to (or did) leave the country and to the unspeakable misery—moral, material, and emotional—that awaits them abroad. According to Soviet sources, it is simply impossible for an honest Soviet citizen to lead a decent and even moderately satisfactory life abroad. There are detailed reports of those who went abroad and either died there in penury and rejection or were begging the Soviet authorities to readmit them, no matter how harsh the punishment might be awaiting them, no matter how despised they would be by their fellow citizens after their return. Typically the official message to the citizen is that there is no such thing as an apolitical departure. According to the Soviet view, intelligence agents lurk everywhere in the West and woe to the Soviet visitor who relaxes his vigilance. Thus, for example, two so-called specialists on Marxism at an American university tried to pressure a Soviet exchange student to defect as part of a huge American project aimed at promoting defections.[49] Soviet fishermen washed ashore in Alaska were put under similar pressures. Despite the frantic efforts of their captors, they were rescued by Soviet embassy officials.[50]

Defectors in search of an easy life tend to find themselves in the clutches of Western intelligence agencies. This almost happened to a Soviet student on a tourist trip in West Germany who decided to stay. After his defection, he was given many fraudulent promises. After many disappointments, the young man went to the Soviet embassy saying, "I am guilty. Very guilty. I realize it all. I will make up for it. I will work in the forest. Only if I don't have to stay here too long." While one cannot vouch for the authenticity of the conversation described, it is possible that the official indoctrination equating defection with treason and other deformations of character is often successful, inculcating a sense of guilt in the Soviet citizen when he defects or even thinks about it. The article concluded that "riffraff like 'Mr. Zhunin' surely have a very strange understanding of their duty to the country that has given them everything. They are ready to turn what is most sacred to their own use. . . . The Soviet regime forgave him his treachery. Let him earn the forgiveness of people by his labor and his life."[51] The defecting jazz musicians mentioned earlier were characterized not only as traitors but also as "arrogant nobod[ies], cruel egoist[s]," "weak willed, characterless," "dirty, cruel men with empty crude souls," "riffraff, human rabble," "blithering idiots," "two-faced by nature, cunning and shifty," "two lowlifes," "two non-entities, who are nothing as musicians, who are unscrupulous in both political and moral aspects."[52] The article also includes references to a geologist who defected earlier and then repented, but who was not allowed to return, and to another who "wretchedly came crawling home." The article closes with almost biblical-style curses on the two defectors (or any others preceding or following them). "They will cry, bite their elbows . . . [and] will dream terrible dreams."

Soviet authorities often use court proceedings not only for judicial but also for educational and propaganda purposes. Thus the authorities were not satisfied by sentencing to death two young Armenians who attempted to defect by hijacking a plane; they were also induced to make sensational confessions in court to illustrate the depth of degradation to which defectors sink. As is not unusual in such cases, each item in the didactic confession seems to fit closely into the major propaganda themes current at the time. Thus one of the defendants said in response to the judge's question concerning their plans abroad:

> First I was going to hold a couple of anti-Soviet press conferences. A guide at the American Exhibition in Moscow [1959] told me Americans pay well for each press conference. Then I was going to publish an anti-Soviet book. I was also going to do some abstract painting. A couple of strokes with a brush and I would make money. If neither literature nor art had worked out, I would have tried to marry a rich girl.

The other defendant, in a similarly didactic manner, confessed his plan "to seek out a former Nazi general in West Germany and offer his services."[53]

In this way, the confessions of the would-be defectors were incorporated into the ongoing campaign against the United States (and its exhibits in the Soviet Union), West Germany, and abstract painting.

It is theoretically possible that all Soviet citizens who wish to leave or had left the Soviet Union are of exceptionally poor character. Much more likely, the Soviet authorities have undertaken to teach their people that those who want to leave their country are the scum of the earth and no person of integrity would wish to join them or identify with them. If they are dissatisfied in their homeland, it is because of their personal pathologies, their stupidity, greed, avarice, or susceptibility to misleading foreign propaganda. But, just for good measure, in case such admonitions are insufficient, the authorities also assure Soviet people that the defector's life abroad turns into disaster sooner or later, that he will either end up as a tool of Western espionage agencies or will repent too late and be doomed to end his life in a strange land, despised not only by his fellow countrymen at home, but also by those in his new country.

In recent years, the Soviet press has devoted special attention to those who may wish to or did leave for Israel and to their bitter experiences once there. Cases of such returnees to the Soviet Union have been reported in great detail. Life in Israel is painted in unusually harsh tones, even in comparison with the portrayals of other "capitalist" countries. (This attitude had been much in evidence even before the Arab-Israeli War of June 1967.) Thus immigrants who once lived in the Soviet Union described "the climate as so intolerably hot that 'even the palm trees which are native to Arabian deserts seem to founder under the heat and dryness.' The streets were said to be almost deserted except for long queues outside the Soviet Embassy of 'former citizens of the USSR, who for various reasons, left it and now dream of going back to their homeland.'"[54]

Many articles in Soviet papers detailed the somber warnings and bitter recollections of those who succumbed to anti-Soviet propaganda or the unscrupulous promises of Zionist agents. The papers also told of those who, out of misguided familial solidarity, wanted to rejoin relatives, or were actually misled by their relatives in Israel. The picture presented by the returnees in the Soviet press is one of unmitigated hardships: virtual starvation, life in shacks, unbearable climate, police state repression, Dickensian sweatshop conditions of work (for the few who can find any), relatives who "wave away" the newly arrived telling him, "Manage as best as you can. Everyone here thinks of himself"[55] and "thousands of graves" of the settlers in the desert.

In part, the anti-Israeli venom is related to the general Soviet policy on the Middle East, which, being pro-Arab, is bound to be hostile to Israel. More difficult to ascertain are the possible effects of traditional Russian anti-Semitism, dressed up as anti-Zionism. Yet, even after taking into consideration such circumstances, the fact remains that the fury of Soviet propaganda is in large measure provoked by Israel, being one and possibly the foremost among the countries where a large number of Soviet citizens (Soviet Jews) would consider going if the mere expression of interest in such a venture did not entail official disfavor and the resulting disadvantages. Exactly opposite was the case of a group of American-Armenians who after World War II decided to leave the United States and return to their ancestral homeland, Soviet Armenia. They soon regretted their decision. But fifteen years later, despite numerous efforts to obtain exit visas, only a small number of them (those with close relatives in the United States) were allowed to leave. Those still in the USSR were reported to suspect that "pride and fear of anti-Soviet propaganda is part of the reason why their applications for exit visas are met with obstruction, broken promises and cancelled appointments."[56]

V

Why are the Soviety authorities so determined to dissuade, not only by force and law, but also by word, the Soviet citizen from leaving his country or from expressing any desire to do so? Why, according to the official view, can only fools or the dregs of society entertain the desire to leave the Soviet Union? Why is it imperative to present the countries such people prefer in the most nightmarish colors? Why insist that the life of those who leave can only end in misery, unhappiness, or degradation? Why is it so important to persuade the Soviet people that leaving one's country (if it is a socialist one) is among the worst abominations a man can sink to and amounts to treason?

Three answers may be offered. One is practical. If leaving the Soviet Union were to be made easy, simple, and legitimate, it is possible that many valuable members of Soviet society might take advantage of the opportunity (in addition to the old, those who want to reunite with their families, or those with limited skills). Nobody knows how many people from various strata of the population would leave if they could. Possibly not many since Soviet people are patriotic in a nonpolitical sense and are attached to their homeland. On the other hand, it is likely that those leaving would include large numbers of highly trained scientists, technicians, or intellectuals seeking greater personal or intellectual freedom, or higher material rewards, or are simply curious to see the world. There would be a loss of skilled manpower and talent, and this in itself is to be prevented.

Nevertheless, this is unlikely to be the major reason for the policies examined since restrictions apply to everyone, even to the old and infirm, the socially, economically, and politically useless. (Rare exceptions have been made for those in such categories.) It is far more likely that a combination of ideological and psychological factors is behind this policy. Apparently for those thoroughly committed to the Soviet social order, who consider the Soviet Union the historically most advanced society, it is intolerable to be confronted with the citizen who wishes to leave it behind. Just as making a choice in the polling booth cannot be allowed, so "voting with one's feet" cannot be permitted either. Both modes of expressing dissent or disaffection are impermissible since they would conflict with the institutionalized claims of historical perfection and the allegations of the total devotion of Soviet people to the prevailing system. Where unquestioning political loyalty is held sacred, defection is "objectively" treason, no matter what the motives of the individual in question. Apparently, it is insufficient to denounce such people as pathological deviates, unscrupulous monsters, or spineless weaklings. Far better is *to prevent* the expression of their preferences for another mode of life, for another social environment. Allowing them to go would amount to letting people escape paradise or utopia. People *must* like what is good for them, and if they don't they still must live with it. The official attitude may be viewed as a form of extreme, bizarre paternalism. Possibly, the spectacle of defection disturbs the rulers because it confirms whatever unconscious doubts they might harbor about their legitimacy.

Presumably, the regime is also concerned with the possibility that those leaving, whatever the reason for their dissatisfaction, would contribute to unfavorable publicity not only by the very fact of their departure, but also by subsequent critical statements, disclosures, or complaints of one kind or another. This is not an unreasonable apprehension since indeed many of those who left made such statements in interviews, books, or articles.

In any event, departure from the Soviet Union (which becomes "defection" only because the regime makes it illegal and criminal by definition) is considered demoralizing from the point of view of both the population at home and the world outside. Defections clash with the image of Soviet society its leaders are anxious to convey to both their people and the world at large. According to this image, Soviet people are solidly behind their system and its leaders, contented and firmly committed to every official policy or program.

There is also a third likely explanation of these policies and attitudes. The freedom to leave a country represents an important and fundamental freedom of choice. The availability of this freedom may determine to a great extent one's attitude toward the society one lives in. The knowledge that as a last resort a person can extricate himself, by physical removal, from the social environment he finds unappealing has a profound bearing on his whole behavior and on the degree to which he is willing to adapt himself to the conditions around him. When there are no alternatives, the status quo is more likely to be accepted. Conformity flourishes when the rules and standards in question cannot be altered or evaded, when the individual knows that he cannot remove himself from their sphere of influence. In short, living in a literally "closed" society compels adjustment, helps to induce conformity, and thereby contributes to internal political stability, especially over time.

The case of East Germany offers a most graphic illustration of this proposition. Before the Berlin Wall went up, East Germans could, without much difficulty, get out of the country. Consequently, the exodus was considerable (no doubt far greater proportionally than any exodus from the Soviet Union would be), while political conditions were repressive, the economy inefficient, and the citizenry dissatisfied.[57] After the Wall went up and thus sealed the last major route of escape, productivity improved, people expressed less dissatisfaction, and even the police state aspects of the system became somewhat milder. The people of East Germany have tried to make peace with the regime since they had no alternative left. They tried to make the best of an unalterable situation which meant that they worked harder, criticized less, and even attempted to rekindle or create a sense of identification with the system with which they had to live. To be sure, the parallel is imperfect since East Germans had a far stronger motive to leave (than Soviet people), living in a divided country one-half of which was visibly better off than the other and also living under an externally imposed, imported system of government. Yet it is all the more striking that the Wall had a significant effect on compelling adjustment. From the official East German and Soviet point of view, the Berlin Wall has been a great success and openly celebrated.[58]

It may be noted that because of its obtrusive presence running through the middle of Berlin, the Wall has attracted a disproportionate amount of publicity in the Western world almost as if it were the first or only such undertaking. For most citizens of the West, the "Iron Curtain" has remained an abstraction, occasionally mentioned in the press but hardly a massive, visual presence. While the Wall has become a moral-ideological and "public relations" liability for East Germany,[59] the other "walls" surrounding the other East European countries and the Soviet Union have attracted comparatively little attention. Nor have other forms of border controls damaged the images of the countries concerned because of their relative invisibility. The control over the mass media has helped immensely the Soviet authorities to conceal their system of border controls and to minimize publicity about it. In five decades of Soviet rule, the "walls" surrounding the USSR have not received a fraction of the publicity given to the Berlin Wall. Yet the other walls are just as real and effective as that in Berlin, and they serve exactly the same functions. The different treatment of the Berlin Wall vs. other parts of the Iron Curtain illustrates the importance of concrete, visual experience and tangible information on public opinion formation and the political advantages of control over access to such information and experience. It also illustrates the political benefits of secrecy. People do not become morally indignant over abstractions.

The border controls and the associated restrictions on travel and emigration do create some problems. The idea of a country preventing the free movement of its own people, the occasional comparisons with a "big prison" are hardly flattering. Moreover, the preoccupation with preventing unauthorized departures (and denying legitimate exits as well) creates an exaggerated, inflated impression of what might be in reality a statistically modest trickle of Soviet citizens who might want to settle abroad.

The Soviet regime has handled the problem of the bad image abroad by a shrill and determined denial of the "Iron Curtain." Soviet officials would ardently deny that any adult Soviet citizen is prevented from leaving if he wants to go. Most typically, however, authorities do not admit that there might be citizens who want to leave. On the whole, the mixture of denial, secrecy, and invisibility has allowed the Soviet Union to maintain its system of border and travel controls without much embarrassment or damage to its reputation abroad.

The second disadvantage of the system is that it is presumably costly, requiring considerable resources and manpower (hundreds of thousands of troops and auxiliary informers) to maintain it. Such costs are gladly borne, however, given the perceived importance of the objectives.

Third, it might be argued that not letting people out who would like to leave is an unwise policy which bottles up discontent and deprives the system of a safety valve. This, however, is more a theoretical than real problem since discontent is far from explosive even on the part of those who would wish to depart. Nor does it have any organized expression. Active or effective political opposition is simply no problem in the Soviet Union after fifty years of totalitarianism.

Fourth, and perhaps more serious, is the ideological and psychological problem seclusion from the world outside creates among the population. The feeling of being cut off from what is beyond the frontiers leads to unrealistic views of life abroad. Frequently, it contributes to an over-estimation of things foreign (Western, that is,) and increases the attractiveness of the outside world. The highly restricted access to other lands is also reflected in the often staggering misinformation or lack of information among the population, deliberately increased by the official mass media.

Yet given the objectives of the regime, the advantages of the present system of border and travel controls clearly outweigh its disadvantages. Border controls and the associated travel restrictions have been among the most enduring characteristics of the Soviet political system. Even if their practical importance is limited, even if free movement out of the country would not lead to serious losses of manpower or to an increase of subversive activities by foreign agents, these controls and restrictions retain important symbolic and psychological functions. They are part of a coherent and interdependent pattern of institutional arrangements which eliminate some major, if only theoretically important, alternatives from the life of the citizen. It is difficult to conceive of a significant increase in domestic political freedom unaccompanied by a change in the official attitudes and policies toward travel and emigration. And it is just as difficult to conceive of a more relaxed attitude toward travel and emigration in isolation from a more relaxed attitude toward political expression and dissent at home. The fundamental alteration of Soviet border and travel policies would be among the unmistakable signs of the withering away of the totalitarian characteristics of Soviet society which survived the death of Stalin.

Postscript 1982

The changes which have taken place in the Soviet travel and emigration policies (if not the border controls as such) can be interpreted in quite contradictory ways. They may be viewed as being "among the unmistakable signs of the withering away of the totalitarian characteristics of Soviet society," or, exactly the opposite, insignificant modifications in the system of controls which in no way represent a "fundamental alteration" of the policies concerned.

Since this article was written, there have been two sets of changes in the policies that have just been examined. Beginning in the 1970s, the Soviet government decided to allow carefully selected portions of the Jewish population to emigrate to Israel. Thus in the past decade, approximately 200,000 Jews were given exit visas, sometimes without undue delay, sometimes after years of waiting. Many requests had been refused. Apparently, this policy was devised in part because it implies that Jews, being "alien" to begin with, are more acceptable candidates for emigration than the more authentic Soviet citizens. The second change in Soviet emigration policies has been the selective expulsion or exile of better-known political dissidents, people like Amalrik, Bukovsky (exchanged for a Chilean Communist leader), Chalidze, Grigorienko, Sinyavski, Solzhenitsyn, and others. Such better-known former Soviet citizens usually have been denounced in the Soviet press and deprived of their citizenship. At the same time, other groups intent on leaving have had greater difficulty gaining exit, in particular the Volga Germans, 100,000 of whom reportedly are seeking to leave (85,000 of them were allowed to go over the past decade). Their departures have been discouraged, as illustrated by the campaign described by a young German, which included "eight rejected applications [to leave], intimidation by local authorities, brief stints in jail and finally the surrender of Soviet citizenship at a cost per person of 500 rubles." As in similar instances in the past, the Soviet press also published articles on the hardships of repatriated Germans in West Germany including undernourishment and social isolation.[60]

At the same time, it seems that many Germans in East Germany (or the "German Democratic Republic") also remain desirous of leaving, as exemplified by the occasional stories of East Germans leaping into the sea from passenger boats and swimming to Western shores or ships and of families kayaking 100 miles across the Baltic under extremely adverse conditions.[61] Apparently, the East German authorities are so anxious to prevent illegal departures that at times they go after those in the West who assist would-be refugees in such undertakings. Thus it was reported that "a West German who is said to have helped hundreds of East Germans escape to the West was badly injured when a letter bomb went off." It was also reported that "at least two of [his] associates also involved in organizing the escapes have died in recent months." One associate was found hanged, another shot.[62] Such attacks represent, as it were, the extension of border and travel controls, other examples of which were noted earlier in the article. Another well-known example of this tradition of forced repatriation occurred in the mid-1970s off Cape Cod in the United States when Soviet crewmen were allowed to seize aboard an American Coast Guard cutter a Soviet-Estonian sailor who literally jumped ship and drag him back to their own boat. Defecting Soviet soldiers or KGB agents are usually tried in absentia and sentenced to death.[63] The Bulgarian secret police too have actively pursued some Bulgarian defectors in the West, and a few years ago they assassinated at least one (Georgi Markov) who was working for the BBC in London. It should be noted here that some socialist countries such as Hungary, Poland, and Czechoslovakia have introduced more liberal emigration policies in the course of the past decade and a half. Other socialist countries such as Cuba and Vietnam (and occasionally China) have practiced selective expulsions, alternating the granting or refusal of permission to some groups or individuals in response to what appear to be changing economic conditions. Despite such occasionally permissive policies, Cuba too produced its share of illegal escapees willing to risk departure under extremely hazardous conditions.[64] At the same time, other countries such as Albania, Bulgaria, or North Korea remain totally "closed" and guard their borders as strictly as ever. In fact, North Korea recently fortified its already well guarded border with South Korea to make it impossible even for a handful of its citizens to get through the demilitarized zone.[65]

Whether or not the border and travel control currently practiced by socialist societies is evidence of their totalitarian character, the fact remains that their governments continue to regard it as their basic right to place sharp limits on population movements both within their countries and across their international boundaries. Most of these governments also make legal exits extremely difficult and illegal ones extremely hazardous and severely punishable. These policies go well beyond, in their effectiveness and comprehensiveness, corresponding measures taken by other nonsocialist governments, both pluralistic and authoritarian.

Notes

1. For a discussion of this distinction, see Z. Brzezinski, "The Patterns of Autocracy," in *The Transformation of Russian Society*, ed. C. Black (Cambridge: Harvard University Press, 1960).
2. G. Afanas'ev, *Na Strazhe Rubezhei Rodiny—Iz Istorii Pogranichnich Voisk* (On guard of the borders of the fatherland—from the history of the borderguards) (Kazakhskoe Gosudarstvennoe Izdatel'stvo, Alma Ata, 1963), p. 24.
3. "Structure of Soviet Intelligence," *New York Times*, 10 Nov. 1967, p. 14; and *Radio Free Europe Bulletin* (September 1967), p. 4.
4. V. P. Artemiev and G. S. Burlutsky, "Personnel, Conditions of Service and Training in the Border Troops," in *The Soviet Secret Police*, ed. Simon Wolin and Robert M. Slusser (London: Methuen and Co., 1957), p. 286.
5. Artemiev and Burlutsky, in Wolin and Slusser, *Soviet Secret Police*, p. 280.
6. Ibid., p. 281.
7. Ibid.
8. Ibid., p. 309.
9. Ibid., pp. 317–18.
10. Ibid., p. 305
11. *Handbook on the Soviet Army*, Dept. of the U.S. Army, Pamphlet No. 30-50-1 (Washington, D.C., 1958), pp. 224–26.
12. Wolin and Slusser, *Soviet Secret Police*, pp. 260–61.
13. V. P. Artemiev, "The Protection of the Frontiers of the USSR," in Wolin and Slusser, *Soviet Secret Police*, p. 261.
14. "Incident: Violator Apprehended," *Pravda*, 4 May 1967, trans. in *Current Digest of the Soviet Press* (hereafter abbreviated as *CDSP*, 24 May 1967, p. 20; for similar incidents, see also "Everyone Guards the Borders," *Kazakhstanskaya Pravda*, 12 Jan. 1964, trans. in CDSP, 19 Feb. 1964, pp. 30–31; and Afanas'ev, *Na Strazhe*, pp. 160–73.
15. Artemiev, in Wolin and Slusser, *Soviet Secret Police*, p. 265.
16. Ibid., p. 265.
17. Ibid., pp. 267–68.
18. See Dumitru Nimigeanu, *Hell Moved Its Border* (London: Blanford Press, 1960), pp. 31, 32, 139–40.
19. Ibid., pp. 26–28, 145–46.
20. Cf. Alexander Barmine, *One Who Survived* (New York: Putnam, 1945), esp. pp. 12–16.
21. See Louis Fisher, *13 Who Fled* (New York: Harper and Brothers, 1949), pp. 14–15.
22. Michael Bialoguski, *The Case of Colonel Petrov* (New York: McGraw-Hill, 1955), pp. 222–29.
23. Oksana Kasenkina, *Leap to Freedom* (Philadelphia: Lippincott, 1949), pp. 261–90.

24. A. Kaznachaev, *Inside a Soviet Embassy* (Philadelphia: Lippincott, 1962), pp. 243–44; see also "Soviet Embassy 'Battle,' Burmese Reporters Manhandled," *Manchester Guardian*, 5 May 1959.
25. *New York Times*, 23 March 1964.
26. Cf. *Why I Escaped—A Story of Peter Pirogov* (New York: Duell, Sloan and Pierce, 1950), pp. 334–35.
27. Reported in Vladimir and Evdokia Petrov, *Empire of Fear* (New York: Praeger, 1956), p. 196.
28. *New York Times*, 17, 18, 19 Sept. 1967.
29. *Guardian*, 18 Sept. 1967, p. 1.
30. *Guardian*, 19 Sept. 1967, p. 1.
31. *Guardian*, 20 Sept. 1967, p. 1.
32. E.g., Kasenkina, *Freedom*, pp. 269–70.
33. *New York Times*, 30 Jan. 1962.
34. Quoted in Colette Shulman, "New Vistas for Soviet Readers," *Problems of Communism* (Nov.–Dec. 1965), p. 97.
35. Col. Gen. P. Zyryanov, "Today is Border Guards' Day: Our Frontiers Are Inviolable," *Pravda*, 28 May 1967, trans. in CDSP, 14 June 1967, p. 39.
36. See, for example, "Red Russia-Red China: The Bristling Border," *Atlas* (September 1967), pp. 15–19.
37. Mary Jane Moody, "Tourists in Russia and Russians Abroad." *Problems of Communism* (Nov.–Dec. 1964), p. 6.
38. Kaznachaev, *Soviet Embassy*, p. 15.
39. For a discussion of Soviet tourism abroad and the reliability of intourist figures, see Jill A. Lion, *Long Distance Passenger Travel in the Soviet Union*, M.I.T. Monograph (Cambridge, Mass., 1967), pp. 53–57; see also Moody, "Tourists."
40. See Postscript.
41. There are exceptions. Recently, two young Russians said in front of British television cameras: "We are all locked in here, . . ." "Two Young Russians on TV in Britain Call Soviet 'Prison,' " *New York Times*, 17 Nov. 1967.
42. "Article 64, Treason," in *Soviet Criminal Law and Procedure—The RSFSR Codes*, ed. Harold J. Berman (Cambridge: Harvard University Press, 1966), p. 178.
43. *New York Times*, 11 May 1962, p. 5.
44. Petrov, *Empire*, p. 199.
45. Peter Deriabin and Frank Gibney, *The Secret World* (Garden City, N.Y.: Doubleday, 1959), p. 268.
46. "The troublemaking Berezins and their benefactors," *Izvestia*, 4 Oct. 1964, trans. in CDSP, 28 Oct. 1964, p. 24.
47. "Weeds," *Izvestia*, 24 Oct. 1964, trans. in CDSP, 18 Nov. 1964, pp. 26–27; for a Western discussion on the same incident, see "Russians May Let Two Families Leave," *New York Times*, 9 Oct. 1964.
48. "World Briefs," *Christian Science Monitor*, 8 June 1963.
49. "Srabotano FBR," *Izvestia*, 30 Oct. 1964, p. 5.
50. "Around the World in Quest of Mushrooms," *Izvestia*, 12 Dec. 1965, trans. in CDSP, 5 Jan. 1966, p. 25.
51. "The Mellow Chime," *Izvestia*, 17 Jan. 1965, trans. in CDSP, 10 Feb. 1965, pp. 22–23.

52. "This is who will play in their jazz band," *Izvestia*, 11 Sept. 1964, trans. in CDSP, 7 Oct. 1964, pp. 35–36.

53. "Soviet Dooms Two Armenians for Trying to Hijack a Plane," *New York Times*, 11 June 1962.

54. *Vechernaia Moskva* (18 Aug. 1958), quoted in "Israel in the Soviet Mirror," *Jews in Eastern Europe*, a Periodic Newsletter (London, December 1965), p. 4.

55. "Israel in the Soviet Mirror," pp. 26, 30.

56. American-Armenians Who Left U.S. for Soviet Yearn to Return," *New York Times*, 18 March 1964; see also "Armenians Glad to Be Back in U.S.," *New York Times*, 22 March 1964.

57. For official figures on the exodus from East Germany, see "Escapees from the Soviet Zone," Federal Ministry for Expellees, Refugees and War Victims (Bonn, 1964).

58. Cf., for example "Reds to Acclaim the Berlin Wall" (on fifth anniversary), *New York Times*, 3 Aug. 1966.

59. This may explain the current efforts of the East German regime to "beautify" the Wall and eliminate some of its most jarring visual features, particularly those that could be seen most easily from the Western side. For a detailed description and diagram of the present remodeling—and strengthening—of the Wall, see "Berlin-Design for a Nightmare," *Time*, 8 Dec. 1967, p. 35.

60. " 'Release Us' Many Ethnic Germans Entreat Soviets," *New York Times*, 8 Nov. 1981. See also "Protest Is Staged by Soviet Germans," *New York Times*, 17 Nov. 1981. The protesting groups consisted of seven adults and one child who, after trying to unfurl banners in Red Square, were instantly seized and taken away in police cars.

61. "East German Flees to West," *New York Times*, 25 April 1982; "2 East German Couples Flee With Child Across Baltic Sea," *New York Times*, 21 Oct. 1981.

62. "German Refugee Aide Hurt by Letter Bomb," *New York Times*, 11 Feb. 1982.

63. Vladislav Krasnov, "Defectors: A Profile," *New York Times*, 25 Oct. 1981, Op-Ed. Page.

64. For a collection of such case histories, see Lorrin Philipson, *Freedom Flights* (New York: Random House, 1980).

65. "North Korea Blocks Defections Across DMZ," *New York Times*, 20 May 1982. In turn Chinese authorities showed growing concern with the rising number of defections among students allowed to attend American universities in recent years. Ten percent of them applied for political asylum. See "Peking Is Troubled by Rise in Defections to West," *New York Times*, 5 Dec. 1982.

6.
Politicized Bureaucracy:
The Soviet Case

The workers, having conquered political power, will smash the old bureaucratic apparatus, they will shatter it to its very foundations, they will destroy it to the very roots; and they will replace it by a new one, consisting of the very same workers and office employees against *whose transformation into bureaucrats the measures will at once be taken which were specified in detail by Marx and Engels: 1) not only election, but recall at any time; 2) pay not exceeding that of a workman; 3) immediate introduction of control and supervision by* all, *so that* all *shall become "bureaucrats" for a time and that therefore* nobody *may be able to become a "bureaucrat."*

Lenin, *State and Revolution*

Lenin's views about the transformation of bureaucracy in Soviet society (as expressed in *State and Revolution*) are among the best indicators of the distance that separates Soviet realities from the ideals and anticipations of the founders of Soviet society. Grasping the nature of Soviet bureaucracy is also indispensable for a better understanding of Soviet society as a whole, many features of which are the products of the process of bureaucratization in various spheres of life. From the theoretical point of view, the study of Soviet bureaucracy is important and challenging because it is a type of bureaucracy largely undreamed of in the philosophy of Western sociologists and which defies many of our major preconceptions about the nature of the beast.

The development of Soviet bureaucracy illustrates the interaction between political-ideological and economic forces in the creation of a new type of bureaucracy, the politicized one. A closer understanding of Soviet bureaucracy also provides unexpected help in reinterpreting the allegedly obsolete concept of totalitarianism to which it lends new meaning.

Several propositions will be offered in this paper. First, that Soviet bureaucracy represents a new type for which no generally accepted conceptual framework has yet been developed, partly because Soviet bureaucracy differs both from the existing Western bureaucracies and also from the theoretical portrait of bureaucracy created by Weber. Second, that Soviet bureaucracy can best be understood with reference to the political characteristics of the society which spawned it and that its features reflect the components of the ideology of Soviet leaders and founding fathers as well as developments they did not anticipate—in short, unintended consequences of their own policies. Third, Soviet bureaucracy is significantly different not only from Western bureaucracy, but also from the original, early Soviet conceptions of a new type "nonbureaucratic" administration.

Perhaps the major characteristic of Soviet bureaucracy from which most others follow is that it has developed primarily as a device of political control and only secondly as an instrument for the management of modernization. The contrast may seem slight and arbitrary, since, it could be argued, rapid modernization is impossible without political controls. These controls, however, had to be especially stringent in the Soviet case in view of the nature of Soviet modernization which was a forced, deliberate, and abrupt reorganization of an entire recalcitrant society, rather than a gradual response to technological or demographic change, to the diffusion of ideas, or to the slow accumulation of innovations. Soviet modernization was rapid and revolutionary based on intense attachment to chiliastic values. This type of modernization required, above all, the control and compulsion of people, rather than the "administration of things." Soviet bureaucracy has expressed from its beginning the ultimate aspiration of totalitarian rulers and thinkers: the maximization of controls and of predictability in social life. We know, of course, that the Soviet regime fell far short of these goals. Nevertheless, the presence of such goals left its imprint on the development of Soviet bureaucracy. The obsession with controls accounts for many features of Soviet bureaucracy: its enormous size, complexity, inefficiency, and permeation by particularistic criteria. It also helps to explain its instability, expressed in recurrent reorganization, the purges, demotions, transfers, the uncommon risks associated with high office, and the politically determined penalties for poor performance.

Among the important sources of the development of Soviet bureaucracy we find Lenin's (and his successors') abhorrence of the spontaneity of the masses and the corresponding efforts to keep it under control.

Since the Party has become the leading force in Soviet society, and the major repository of power, it has also become a model for other organizations as well as their controller. The principle and practice of Party control is a most direct explanation of many features of Soviet bureaucracy: in particular, the frequent slighting of competence in preference to political reliability, and the need to multiply bureaucratic roles. Bureaucratization of the whole society was both a response to the fear of spontaneity and a telling manifestation of the typically totalitarian preoccupation with every detail of social life. In other words, bureaucratization was a reflection of the mistrust of the masses, of their reluctance to lend active support to the regime, and of their reluctant participation in the social changes sweeping their country. Bureaucratization was also a logical correlate of the totalitarian atomization of society, of a process that destroyed old structures, institutions, associations, groupings, and informal devices of social cohesion and control. Bureaucratization represented the restructuring, the rebuilding of the fabric of society, deliberately as well as unwittingly destroyed in the crucible of war, revolution, and civil war. An atomized society lends itself to bureaucratization. We might also note that pre-Soviet Russia was already rich in bureaucratic traditions; the Russian state bureaucracy was highly developed.

A further examination of Lenin's ideas in relation to Soviet bureaucracy will be fruitful. At first sight, Lenin's major contribution appears purely negative: he simply failed to foresee the needs of the society he was trying to create: "In order to abolish the state, the functions of the civil service must be converted into the simple operations of control and accounting that are within the capacity and ability of the vast majority of the population and subsequently of every individual" (*State and Revolution*). So much for state bureaucracy. As for the economy, he noted that,

> Accounting and control—that is the main thing required for "arranging" the smooth functioning . . . of the first phase of communist society. . . . All that is required is that they [the workers] should work equally, do their proper share of work and get equally paid. The accounting and control necessary for this have been *simplified* by capitalism to the extreme and reduced to the extraordinarily simple operations—which any literate person can perform—of supervising and recording, knowledge of the four rules of arithmetic, and issuing appropriate receipts (*State and Revolution*).

It did not come to pass. Neither the administration of the state nor that of the economy conformed to Lenin's estimates. And yet, although Soviet realities represent a most striking repudiation of his prognosis, he did nevertheless exert an enduring influence. His imprint on the development of Soviet bureaucracy is twofold. The emphasis on controls and the suppression of spontaneity survived. So did his vision—in a modified form—concerning the simplicity of the bureaucratic operations. Not that they turned out to be simple. Yet his belief that special training and qualifications were not required for administration implicitly helped to justify the filling of important positions on the basis of political reliability and ideological convictions. To be sure, there have been limits, even in the earlier phases of Soviet society, to the application of this principle. Political reliability was not sufficient for running hydroelectric stations or steel plants. Nonetheless, the overall decisions about their construction, as well as those concerning resource allocation in general, continued to be made by nonexperts. The supervision of economic activities was also in the hands of the political elite. Not infrequently, the importance of political criteria directly impinged on the performance of economic tasks, when, for example, reliable industrial workers were given control of agricultural cooperatives or state farms, when regional Party secretaries controlled the fulfillment of five-year plans, and when army officers were promoted for their loyalty to Stalin. With the maturation of the Soviet system, universalistic criteria (or functional competence) became progressively more important. The ideal solution, as yet imperfectly implemented, has been to provide the high-level administrators with both political-ideological and technical training. Yet, to mention one example, it is not apparent in what ways Malenkov's engineering degree did influence him in his political roles and what amount of ideological neutrality it has imparted to his activities.

A major criticism of all bureaucracies, the unresponsiveness to the human needs they are supposed to serve, is particularly applicable to the Soviet case.[1] It follows from the whole institutional order of Soviet society that weighs heavily on the individual. The elitist nature of Soviet society militates against making heard the voice of the lone individual or that of the inchoate masses. The basic principle of elitism, that a small number of people know what is the best for the rest and, correspondingly, possess all power to implement this principle, affords excellent conditions for the growth of bureaucracy and its disregard for personal needs and wishes. Elitism is also inherent in the social structure of a backward society in which a high premium is put on the relatively small number of trained and competent individuals occupying leadership roles and in which contempt toward the untutored, hidebound masses is thinly disguised.[2]

Politicization continues to exert negative influence on performance, though its effects are becoming less pervasive. The result of politicization is most apparent in setting the goals for the bureaucracies. These goals, or policies, themselves may have questionable rationality. For instance, it may be argued that under Soviet conditions present forms of collectivized agriculture are not rational given the goal of rapidly increasing food production. Or given the goal of rapidly raising the standard of living, it is irrational to engage in space programs (which, on the other hand, are rational from the point of view of achieving international prestige and improvements in military technology). Neither was it rational to allow generalists, top leaders like Stalin and Khrushchev, to make the ultimate decisions regarding the economy, the arts, education, and so forth, areas in which decisions based on specific training yield better results.

Another typical Soviet source of bureaucratic inefficiency is the high level of insecurity associated with responsibility. This insecurity is due to the politicization of performance. While the regime has always been willing to treat good performance as one of the indexes of political loyalty, the opposite is also true: poor performance, error, and failure tend to be quickly associated with sabotage, with politically motivated hostility. The distinction between error and sabotage has always been tenuous. In a country that is supposedly engaged in building the best of all possible societies, it is understandable if poor performance is viewed with unusual sternness. Political sanctions against nonpolitical errors create a sense of insecurity that undermines administrative efficiency. Overcompliance, or "formalism" as Soviet sources call it, is one manifestation of this insecurity. Its function is to reduce risk by meticulous adherence to established procedures regardless of the circumstances. Insecurity also provides a powerful motivation for the avoidance of initiative, a failing of Soviet bureaucrats often castigated in the mass media. The paralysis of initiative (except in the realm of coercion) reached its peak during and after the Great Purges. Yet habits of administrative conduct developed over decades do not disappear quickly. As Armstrong noted in his study of the Ukrainian party apparatus, the "men of '38" are still there.[3]

It is paradoxical that Soviet bureaucracy is at once a barrier to significant change, a major pillar of the frozen stability of Soviet society, and at the same time an entity which—through erratic performance, inefficiency, and unresponsiveness—helps to maintain a level of unpredictability in Soviet life. Perhaps among the explanations of this duality, we find that in the final analysis the legitimation of all Soviet bureaucracies derives from the Party, which is beyond challenge and which determines the changing tasks of various bureaucracies. The second explanation may lie in the magnitude of the responsibilities of Soviet bureaucracy which greatly exceed those shouldered by the bureaucracies of pluralistic societies.[4]

Not surprisingly, perceptions of the Soviet system as a whole leave their imprint on the views taken of Soviet bureaucracy. A major vehicle of such perceptions in recent years, despite the number of qualifications with which it has been used, has been the theory of convergence. Among those who uphold it (to varying degrees), there has been a particularly strong temptation to discern growing numbers of similarities between the bureaucratic institutions of all industrial societies, but especially those of the United States and the Soviet Union. Professor Meyer's suggestive term "USSR, Incorporated"[5] reflects a view of Soviet society in which the bureaucratic features predominate and are reminiscent of those found in the giant corporations of capitalist societies, hence the word "incorporated."

Unavoidably, the extent to which we attribute uniqueness to Soviet bureaucracy (in comparison to forms found in pluralistic societies) depends on whether we prefer to explain most features of Soviet society with the help of the totalitarian model or that of a modern industrial society. Although we often assure ourselves that these two models are highly compatible, rarely in practice do we find an evenhanded combination of them: one or the other tends to be emphasized. Obviously, the uniqueness of Soviet bureaucracy diminishes in proportion with our belief in the similarity of all modern industrial societies and their shared functional imperatives which propel them to create similar structures and institutions.

Among the factors associated with the discernment of a growing number of similarities between Western (and particularly American) and Soviet bureaucracies we find once more the distaste for the concept of totalitarianism. The concept has been criticized for being vague, for allowing much disagreement in its interpretation, and for having confused an ideal, an aspiration, with social realities—a criticism, which incidentally, could well be made of many other concepts used by social scientists including bureaucracy itself. Some social scientists have become weary of the term "totalitarianism" because they feel that it is not sufficiently neutral. The concept of industrial society is, by contrast, more ambiguous, and it provides a great psychological convenience (for some) by accommodating the dislike of all modern, mass societies with seeming impartiality. Furthermore, the concept of industrial society is alluring for the theoretically minded scholar since it enables him to maximize theoretical generalizations about the contemporary social order.

To be sure, Western social scientific tradition supports the proposition that the similarities between Soviet and other bureaucracies are growing in number and importance. Weber regarded bureaucracy as a manifestation par excellence of modernity, a neutral tool at the disposal of different types of societies and their ruling elites, and an institution with its own internal dynamics and imperatives. In particular, he viewed bureaucracy as an instrument and expression of rationality, increasing complexity, and technological development. He drew our attention to the antithesis of traditionalism and bureaucratization. Weber had no conceptual framework for the strange amalgam of rationality and irrationality, neutrality and ideological commitment, expertise and political reliability that has entered into the formation of Soviet bureaucracy (as well as into that of other "socialist" bureaucracies).

The concept of totalitarianism offers considerable help in developing a new, amended perspective on Soviet bureaucracy. It is handy because, as we noted earlier, it has relevance for both the process of modernization *and* the extension of political controls. We will probably never satisfactorily resolve whether Soviet modernization has been a by-product of totalitarian values and motives or merely the implementation of modernization in a backward society that has produced totalitarianism. Undoubtedly, both are true. What we do suggest is that totalitarian principles of social organization help to explain most features of Soviet bureaucracy, which are otherwise difficult to understand. Today, Soviet totalitarianism expresses itself through bureaucratic rather than coercive controls, though, of course, the distinction is often quite imprecise.[6] The totalitarian inspiration behind these controls is still discernible.

The principle characteristics of Soviet bureaucracy—which help to differentiate it from the traditional, Western model—may be summed up in the following way:

1. In Soviet bureaucracies there is no legitimate place for ideological neutrality; political commitment is expected (also expressed in such *functionally diffuse* "bureaucratic" roles as that of the local Party secretary and other functionaries).
2. Sanctions for error are political: error in performance is judged partly on the basis of political-ideological criteria.
3. The Soviet bureaucratic system is contiguous and overarching: the whole society is bureaucratized, and all bureaucracies are interrelated and crowned by the commanding bureaucracy of the Party apparatus.
4. Some important bureaucratic controls are maintained both formally and informally; informal ones rely on the dispersion of Party members in every bureaucratic organization, especially in their higher echelons.

5. Reliance on rules is weakened, at times subverted, by
   (a) the response to emergencies, or situations *perceived as such*. The number of situations qualifying as emergencies in the USSR far exceeds that in the West;
   (b) the frequent interference by top leaders (such may become known subsequently as cases of "arbitrariness" or "harebrained schemes");
   (c) changing interpretation of doctrines (supplying the basis of policy and the blueprints for administrative structures).

These characteristics of Soviet bureaucracy are unlikely to disappear unless one day *Pravda* should startle us by announcing that both the state and the Party have withered away. (The most skeptical among us might remain dubious even after such an announcement.) In the meantime, the tension between political reliability and expertise remains unresolved.[7] In fact, the more industrialized Soviet society becomes, the greater this tension will become. Paradoxically, Party work and functions themselves have become more specialized. This means that those aspiring to high positions in political bureaucracies (or to political roles in predominantly nonpolitical bureaucracies) must have more rigorous training in more stratified and demanding Party schools. An ambitious Soviet citizen must make up his mind early about what he is aiming at: high position in the political hierarchy or the privileged life-style accorded to professionals. It is difficult to train at once (or in succession) for nuclear physics and the administration of an autonomous republic. The nonpolitical expert cannot move easily into political positions. Conversely, the political cadre is increasingly ineffective in positions of control that require specialized expertise. Yet the dilution of the "caste" of political bureaucrats by the infusion of technically trained experts is unlikely. It is more likely, as it happened on many occasions, that when the political hierarchy absorbs such experts, the relevance of their expertise diminishes and their assumed rationality will become dormant, or relatively ineffectual, in influencing major policy decisions.

It may appear in the eyes of the rational beholder that the Party has lost some of its functions in today's Soviet society. At the same time, the sense of purpose and integration achieved in Soviet society has its uncontested source in the Party. The Party bureaucracy is in de facto control, and its members are in the classical seats of vested interest. The Party has probably attained a degree of legitimacy as an agency of control; no other group or institution has. The Party bureaucracy will not liquidate itself for its declining number of functions or because it is a burden on society and a repository of privilege.

In analyzing the peculiarities of Soviet bureaucracy, I focused on the totalitarian desire to make power secure by a network of controls and double controls. I neglected some important distinctions that might have refined the propositions advanced, such as the differences between lower and higher echelons of bureaucracy, rural and urban areas, as well as the difference between the Party and state apparatus and their interrelationship. I also omitted a consideration of the role of bureaucracy in providing new avenues of social mobility and the possible part the avoidance of manual labor might have played in its expansion. Unavoidably, a general discussion of Soviet bureaucracy does considerable injustice to variations within the different realms of Soviet bureaucracy. Doubtless, the bureaucratic apparatus of the Central Committee of the Party is more politicized than that of the Fisheries Industry, as is film making bureaucracy more political than that associated with the production of footwear. The more sensitive an area of life to ideological criteria, the more politicized its administration becomes. But, as in every totalitarian society, far more areas of life are defined as politically sensitive than in other societies.

Postscript 1982

Since the previous article was written, there has been no great upsurge of Western social scientific interest in Soviet (or other forms of socialist) bureaucracy. Whatever attention Western sociologists have paid to socialist bureaucracies has been shaped by the orientation to assimilate them to the Western models and theories of bureaucracy (as in the case of the work of Professor Meyer) rather than highlight their distinctive features.

My article was intended to redress, to some degree, this imbalance by focusing on what is distinctive about Soviet bureaucracy, many attributes of which can, without undue difficulty, be generalized to the bureaucracies prevailing in other Marxist one-party states. Not surprisingly, some of the more recent and most original ideas about socialist bureaucracy are to be found in the works of East European authors such as Milovan Djilas, Svetozar Stojanovic, George Konrad, Ivan Szelenyi, and Miklos Haraszti.[8]

Among the omissions of my paper was its neglect of the connections between the development of Soviet bureaucracy and scarcity (forcefully elucidated by Trotsky in *Revolution Betrayed*) and also the functions of such bureaucracies in solidifying material and status privilege.[9] Of late, the work of Simon Leys, among others, has thrown new light on material privilege and bureaucratic position in China.

One more self-critical remark might be made about the foregoing. I seem to have had some trouble making up my mind about the relationship between bureaucracy and stability in the Soviet Union and may have exaggerated the instability entailed in the periodic overhaul of the various Soviet bureaucracies.

Notes

1. The comments of a character in a Tarsis novel capture these aspects of Soviet bureaucracy: "Our job, like that of twenty million other Soviet office workers, was to procrastinate as long as possible, give vague promises, disbelieve everything and everyone, insist on an infinite number of documents, detect, control, check and double-check. Krasnobryukov explained to me: 'You are the lowest form of life: you make the preliminary check on applicants'" (Valerii Tarsis, *The Bluebottle,* New York: Knopf, 1963).
2. A condition relevant to the formative periods of Soviet bureaucracy.
3. For a more recent discussion of the tenure in office of important Soviet bureaucrats, see Tibor Szamuely, "Five Years After Khrushchev," *Survey* 72 (Summer 1969): 51–69.
4. According to Fainsod, "The objective is nothing less than the use of political and administrative means to reshape man and society. . . . With totalitarianism we approach the apotheosis of politico-administrative social engineering as a means of achieving fundamental change" (Merle Fainsod, "Bureaucracy and Modernization: The Russian and Soviet Case," in Joseph La Palombara, ed., *Bureaucracy and Political Development* [Princeton: Princeton University Press, 1963], p. 233). More specifically, Brzezinski has stated that "the functional requirements of the company are far narrower than the demands of the revolutionary party with an ideology of total social and individual change going far beyond the demands of merely 'the industrial way of life'" (Zbigniew Brzezinski, "The Nature of the Soviet System," in Donald W. Treadgold, ed., *The Development of the USSR: An Exchange of Views* [Seattle: University of Washington Press, 1964], pp. 35–36.
5. Cf. Alfred G. Meyer, "USSR, Incorporated," in Treadgold, ed., *Development of the USSR,* pp. 21–28.
6. Soviet sources make a somewhat analogous distinction between "persuasion" and "administrative methods"—the latter is a euphemism for police terror, the former includes a mixture of threats and propaganda. In any event, both bureaucratic and "persuasive" methods are, in the final analysis, backed up by coercion—a circumstance that further dilutes the distinction.
7. In China, under Mao, this dichotomy was called "red versus expert."
8. Milovan Djilas, *The New Class* (New York: Praeger, 1957); Svetozar Stojanovic, *Between Ideals and Reality: A Critique of Socialism and Its Future* (New York: Oxford Univ. Press, 1973); and also by him, *In Search of Democracy In Socialism* (Buffalo, N.Y.: Prometheus Books, 1981); George Konrad and Ivan Szelenyi, *The Intellectuals on the Road to Class Power* (New York: Harcourt Brace Jovanovich, 1979); Miklos Haraszti, *Worker in a Worker's State* (New York: Universe Books 1978).
9. Mervyn Matthews, *Privilege in the Soviet Union: A Study of Elite Life-Styles Under Communism* (London: Allen and Unwin, 1978).

7.
Criticism and Self-Criticism

Introduction

Definition

Depending on who is engaged in it, the Soviet practice of criticism and self-criticism (CSC) can be both a signal for the initiation of new official policies *and* a substitute for genuine political participation and criticism on the part of the powerless. CSC is at once an instrument with which to improve the execution of broad national policies and also that of self-improvement at the most personal level. While political in its origin and intent, it can be used in the most diverse, non-political areas of life. Nor is it limited to Party members, though it is their special duty and right.[1] CSC is to be engaged in by all, Party and non-Party people, the young and the old, men and women, citizens of all and any educational level and occupation. Correspondingly, there is no clear-cut, publicly enunciated exclusion of any phenomena: virtually any human, societal, or institutional defect can in principle be brought within its purview. It can be aimed at individuals as well as at institutions and the execution of a wide variety of policies. It can be exceedingly general and grotesquely specific. In short, CSC is both a functioning political institution and a ritual, a pious wish and a debased or diluted practice, an activity of esoteric significance for the political elite and a harmless outlet for the minor grumblings of the masses.

Origins

In order to understand CSC, we must examine the influence of Russian cultural traditions, the political practices and experiences of the Bolsheviks, the ideological conceptions of the Party, and the characteristics of a totalitarian social organization.

We must first note the affinity of CSC with shaming, a time-honored device of social control used especially among Russian peasants. Shaming amounts to the public exposure of the wrongdoer, preferably among his peers. As Gorer noted:

115

> Great Russians rely heavily on public shaming for social control: the *mir* controlled its members by this device. . . . The very unusual aspect of Great Russian character would appear to be the fact that this control by external shame is superimposed on more archaic diffuse guilt.[2]

Such views of Russian cultural traditions and popular predispositions are by no means exceptional. Tomasic reports:

> Lanin, an English writer who closely observed Russian behaviour in the second half of the nineteenth century, found that the sense of guilt was "extremely developed." According to this observer there was not only a tendency to confess one's guilt but there was also on the part of the public an insistence on confession of guilt. . . . Confession of guilt was often accepted in social relations as equal to an eradication of sin and therefore demanded forgiveness. "He who confesses has repented and he who has repented has wiped out his sin" is a Russian folk saying.[3]

These attitudes and traditions—which also help to explain the crucial role confession has played in Soviet court proceedings[4]—were not limited to peasant Russia. A belief in the redeeming qualities of self-abandonment in an embracing community and a relatively underdeveloped notion of privacy were also common among the prerevolutionary intelligentsia. Discussing the radicals of the second half of the nineteenth century, Billington comments on "another ritual of great importance . . . what came to be called even in this period 'self-criticism'—a confession to the circle of moral failings to the sacred cause of progress."[5]

The Bolsheviks rationalized and functionalized these preexisting tendencies and attitudes, harnessing them to the cause of organizational efficiency. Thus, for instance, it is quite likely that the conspiratorial circumstances of early Bolshevik party work contributed to the institutionalization of CSC. For those engaged in illegal political activities, the constant examination and reexamination of their policies is a more pressing need than for those operating under more relaxed conditions. Mistakes for such groups are more dangerous, and CSC in these circumstances can assist in the maintenance of vigilance and discipline.

At the same time, the preoccupation with CSC expresses the basically pessimistic view of human nature entertained and imperfectly suppressed by Lenin and other Soviet leaders. This pessimistic view has been noted by many students of Soviet political thought, particularly Robert V. Daniels, Nathan Leites, Alfred Meyer, and Adam Ulam. The major premise of CSC, as indeed of the entire network of elaborate political controls developed by the Soviet system, is human fallibility. On the one hand, there is the belief, or central premise of Soviet political thought and practice, that unquestionably correct policies exist, and decisions based on them can be reached. On the other hand, there is the fear that these policies and decisions might be subverted in the course of their implementation. The fear of error in the execution rather than in the devising of policies (or in regard to the values which guide these policies) is what has haunted Soviet political leaders. A major task of CSC is to spot and expose mercilessly the sources of error or deviation from the policies devised at the highest level by the infallible elite. Thus CSC is one among several indicators of another unstated yet pervasive assumption of Soviet political life, namely, that things can easily go wrong, and hence the execution of even the best policy requires constant correction and supervision. Therefore, CSC can be viewed also as an expression of the Leninist concept of consciousness—the sharp, penetrating awareness of the nature of the goals set, the appropriateness of the means employed to attain them and of the relationship between the means and the ends, the awareness of the constellation of all political factors in a given situation. CSC is at once a reflection of consciousness and an instrument with which to alert it, to exercise it, an expression of political perfectionism beset by doubt.

Forms

There are two major forms of CSC. The first is CSC in the group setting (or at the interpersonal level) when it is focused on individuals and their personal, political, or productive shortcomings. (In this form, CSC has some affinity with the Chinese practice of thought reform, although the latter is incomparably more systematic, purposeful, and widely used, reflecting not only a shared ideological heritage and commitment to totalitarian methods of government, but also the peculiarities of Chinese cultural tradition and organizational experience.)[6] The second major expression of CSC can be found in the mass media and the press in particular. In this format, CSC tends to be impersonal and focuses more on institutional malfunctioning (especially the various manifestations of red tape) than on individual failings.

At the interpersonal or face-to-face level, CSC takes place typically in two settings: (*a*) the place of work (or study, or service) and (*b*) the Party or Komsomol organization. In both settings, the gathering is a public one insofar as members of the collective in question are concerned. Group participation has great importance for several reasons. In the first place, it is useful to have the official values and policies from which a particular person has deviated reasserted and reaffirmed in the physical presence of many. This is what happens in the process of CSC when it is clarified *what* rules, norms, or values were violated by the person criticized and *why* his offense was repugnant to those who uphold the norms, rules, and values in question. (The principles underlying this procedure exemplify Durkheim's propositions on social solidarity and the functions of the collective reprimand of the offender designed to deepen that solidarity.)

Regarding the actual procedures, either the criticism of a particular member of the collective is initiated by someone in a position of authority or the task might be delegated by prearrangement to an ordinary, rank-and-file member of the group. After the initial stage-setting crticisms are put forward, those present are expected to join in and discuss or add to the themes and substance of criticism made before them. Finally, the person criticized is duty bound to engage in self-criticism on the basis of the criticism made by his comrades. Almost invariably the signs of humility, repentance, and guilt are demanded from the subject of criticism. Thus, for example, an ex-functionary reports that after he admitted the charges against him "came the summing-up by several speakers. The keynote was the same as before; Linden's statement is an evasion— Linden has not grasped the kernel of the problem. His statement shows his superficiality. It would be premature to believe a statement of this kind."[7] The proceedings, apparently designed to inculcate a sense of guilt, were completely successful in the case cited. Linden (i.e., Leonhard) was engulfed by feelings of guilt and helplessness, at least for a time. Feelings of guilt and helplessness on similar occasions are also reported by Jerzy Kosinski (see note 11).

In addition to implanting or strengthening feelings of guilt, anxiety, or apprehension, criticism in the group setting serves many didactic purposes. It is a means of exposing people to the Party line in action, as it were, to its most specific application in each given case, and in particular to its relevance to types of behavior (or misbehavior) which in themselves are not violations of any codified rule, norm, or law. This adds greatly to the flexibility of CSC as an instrument of social and behavioral control. Public humiliation and self-humiliation also fulfill warning functions: they illustrate the consequences of deviance and represent a shaming ritual. But perhaps the most important lesson of such sessions is the demonstration of the powerlessness of the individual in the face of the group. CSC in the primary-group context impresses upon the participants the inescapable need to conform and aims at representing the object of CSC as an isolated deviant.

Beyond these objectives, CSC is also a major weapon in the struggle against individualism and privacy: personal feelings, pride, vanity, a sense of dignity or privacy are to be suppressed and nothing is supposed to remain secret ·or private; *nothing is purely personal.* The collective is entitled to unrestrained self-revelation and total openness on the part of the individual. CSC at the interpersonal level can be viewed also as an adjunct to more formal and specialized coercive institutions, designed to broaden popular participation in social control, to enlist the help of the entire society in the struggle against nonconformity. That such is the case is also indicated by the development of the comrades' courts, which combine the characteristics of CSC and court procedures, representing a transitional phenomenon.[8] In theory at least, CSC in the group setting could serve as a totalitarian control mechanism par excellence aimed at the atomization of all nonpolitical or politically undesirable ties and relationships, including personal friendships. The subordination of friendship to communal-civic goals is to be justified by the slogan of "principledness."

> Principledness [printsipial'nost'] is moulded in the highly exacting conditions of criticism and self-criticism, when the relationship between the workers is built on the foundation of communist ideals. Unprincipledness, the flouting of party and national interests appear most often when the Leninist principles of work with the cadres are violated, when the workers approach one another on the basis of friendship, the spirit of fellow countrymen, etc. Then conditions are inevitably created for mutual adulation, mutual forgiveness, fawning and servility.[9]

The institution of group CSC has great potentials as an instrument of character change or improvement. It allows the devotion of meticulous and informal attention to even the most trivial shortcomings of an individual which could not be handled by other means of control or rectification. The shortcomings for which a person can be criticized fall into four broad, overlapping categories.

First, there are the outright, specific violations of the Party line. For example, Leonhard reports being criticized for espousing "the thesis of the separate road to socialism" in 1949, and some Italians in the Comintern school were scolded for "sectarianism" in regard to their postwar policy plans.[10] A more recent example of criticism incurred for ideological shortcomings is provided by the case of a Soviet university student who was accused of wanting "to torpedo [the class discussions] through a Talmudist use of the most variegated statements of the classics of Marxism-Leninism, torn *ad hoc* from the context in which the classics had used them."

> Moreover, B. enjoys pointing out the inconsistencies and contradictions in these statements. . . . In [his] notebook B. gathered perfidiously selected definitions, citations, and comments of the classics. . . . Whenever discussion

started at the seminar Vyacheslav B. cunningly selected from his "arsenal" the quotations which would most acutely undermine the statements of the professor or of other students. That B. was aware of the impropriety of the possession and use of such "collected quotations" is proved by the fact that in lending it to Avraam Z. he asked him not to show it to anyone.[11]

Second, there are shortcomings associated with work and efficiency, including school work. Thus Leonhard recalls the Soviet school he attended in his early teens:

Pupils who got a bad mark or an "admonition" . . . had to "clarify their attitude" in front of the class. . . . If the pupil made any sort of attempt to talk himself out of it, he was sharply interrupted by the keener members of the class: 'It is a disgrace to have got a bad mark, but it is even more contemptible to try to talk yourself out of it.' This was the first step on the ladder of "criticism and self-criticism."[12]

Kosinski describes the case of a factory worker ("top shock-worker at the plant") who was severely criticized for not wanting to join a particular brigade and subsequently was transferred to a remote location for his defiant attitude.[13]

A third important category of shortcomings includes incorrect attitudes toward the collective and manifestations of individualism. Kosinski quotes a Soviet student:

At the meeting the matter of my alleged "segregation in the laboratory from Soviet reality" unexpectedly came up for discussion. Many people spoke on this subject, including my closest friends. . . . They said that I set myself above others and consider myself more able than they. . . . One of the members of the Komsomol Bureau cited a few instances proving that I am inaccessible, that I surround my research work with mystery . . . that I'm courting the personal attention of Professor K. . . . I admitted that my absorption in research work had undoubtedly caused some detachment from the labors of the collective. . . . But it was of no use. The representative of the District Committee described my self-criticism as bogus and superficial, a proof that I still do not understand my mistakes and continue to regard myself as an individual "above the crowd" following solely his own, self-centered goals.[14]

In the fourth category of deficiencies, we find a multitude of characterological defects, moral weaknesses, and flaws which may have no particular political significance. This could include (before official attitudes toward abortion became more tolerant) the request for abortion on the part of an unmarried woman, violations of socialist morality such as undue eagerness for divorce, the imitation of "bourgeois attire," the pursuit of extramarital affairs, and many other transgressions.[15] We might note, however, that in recent years some of the cases cited by Kosinski would probably not have become matters of criticism following a more permissive atmosphere in regard to personal morality and interest in Western clothing and consumer goods.

The second major manifestation of CSC is to be found in the mass media and the press in particular. While CSC in the group setting aims primarily (though not solely) at the correction of the shortcomings of a particular individual, CSC in the press tends to focus more on the deficiencies of institutions and organizations and the shortcomings in the execution of specific policies, usually at the local level. This is not to say that individual officials cannot be criticized in the press, but rather that insofar as they are, the criticism is directed at the more specific failings manifest in their particular administrative-occupational role.

This second form of CSC may be viewed as the stunted counterpart of the institution of political opposition, which, in pluralistic societies, tells the power holders what is wrong with their values, ideologies, and policies and with the consequences of their policies. The Soviet political system does not permit opposition, but it does need some substitute for it, some feedback mechanism, and CSC does fill, to a limited extent, the gap created by the intolerance of dissent and opposition. CSC has become a very modest substitute for the mechanisms provided by opposition parties, legitimate pressure groups, public opinion, and the free press in democratic societies. At this level, CSC is a self-correcting device at the disposal of the leadership, a part of, rather than split off from, the dominant policy making and controlling bodies and institutions.

CSC in the press can and does fulfill some useful functions which are in many ways similar to those of the Western press. These are the fact-finding missions of reporters, the exposures of the negligent, high-handed, or irresponsible officials (at the lower level), of the violations of public interest, and so forth. The major targets of Soviet press criticism are bureaucracy or red tape, wastefulness, poor services, the defects of consumer goods and of their distribution, the passivity or indifference of Soviet officialdom, and, more recently, urban problems and those of the conservation of natural resources. The press typically criticizes localized, compartmentalized shortcomings related to the execution of policies and rarely the policies themselves.

An important function of the press is to provide space for criticisms by the readers, who are encouraged to report the type of shortcomings described previously. In addition to whatever contribution these grass-roots criticisms and complaints make to greater administrative efficiency, they also provide a legitimate outlet for the expression of the frustrations Soviet citizens face in their daily life.[16] Letters from the readers exemplify what is called in the revealing official terminology "criticism from below," and their publication represents one of many official efforts to mobilize the population for the improvement of the system. This criticism from below is often cited among the democratic characteristics of the political order and is virtually equated with popular participation in affairs of state.

While the targets of criticism "from below" and "from above" tend to be similar (waste, red tape, inefficiency associated with individuals as well as institutions), criticism from above does have a wider scope and can, as noted earlier, also signal the beginning of a new or radically changed policy. Sometimes it becomes difficult to disentangle criticism from above and criticism from below, when, for example, a criticism from above (or a new policy) is preceded by a flood of readers' letters in the press which betray the signs of official instigation or preparation. In this manner, the two types of criticism can easily merge and what at first might have appeared to be a spontaneous grass-roots expression of discontent can be transformed into an elaborately stage-managed high-level "campaign" designed to prepare the masses for the introduction of new measures.

Criticism and Self-Criticism and the Party Leadership

It is unrealistic to expect the emergence of genuine criticism in an atmosphere fundamentally hostile to the critical, questioning spirit, which strives to inculcate political conformity as the highest civic virtue. It is particularly naive to expect genuine self-criticism from the higher power holders who are deeply committed both to the design and the execution of their policies.

This, in turn, explains why only *after* a leader of high standing is removed are the floodgates of criticism officially opened (by his successors) and why only then does it become permissible, and at the same time obligatory, to pass critical judgment.

Thus after Khrushchev's removal several of his errors and shortcomings suddenly came to light. It was found that his agricultural policies, including the Virgin Lands Project and his preference for maize, were wrong. It was revealed that his architectural tastes and policies were poor, and the dominance of concrete over brick favored by him came to an end. His favorite sculptor too was attacked. In the field of science, it abruptly transpired that Khrushchev's support of Lysenko was also wrongheaded;

consequently, scientists opposed to him came back into official favor. Khrushchev's military contributions in World War II were seen in a new light, and his talents on the battlefield appeared to be diminished. Not surprisingly, his role in the Party history has also altered, occupying a more modest place than before. Now that he was absent from power, it was no longer a secret that he deserved criticism on account of his educational and consumer policies as well. There were even indications that he was not entirely blameless for certain shortcomings in the toy industry.

That none of these errors of Khrushchev could be discussed while he was in power and in a position to commit them does highlight the limitations of CSC. During Stalin's rule, CSC received no less praise and attention from the Soviet mass media than after his death. Symbolic of the position it then occupied in Soviet life was the article on CSC in the second edition of the *Large Soviet Encyclopedia*.[17] This four-page article contained no less than thirty-eight references to Stalin, including copious quotations from his statements exhorting both the leaders and the led not to shrink from the hallowed duty of CSC. Certainly, CSC, that "mighty instrument of collective self-examination and truth seeking," has not prevented or diminished the cult of personality and the variety of abuses and errors connected with it. To add to the irony, during Khrushchev's tenure of power he too was often quoted reverently for his insights into the issues of CSC.

The explanation of these paradoxes must be sought in the fact that while encouraged in a narrowly defined, localized context, criticism of the Party and its leaders, or any major social institution and policy, has never been permissible, and that the exhortations to practice CSC have always coexisted with the claims of the infallibility and glorification of the Party and its leaders of the moment. Stalin's distinction between the desirable and undesirable (sometimes also called "constructive" and "destructive") forms of CSC is enlightening in this connection:

> A strict distinction must be drawn between this "self-criticism," which is *alien* to us, destructive and anti-Bolshevik, and *our,* Bolshevik self-criticism, the object of which is to promote the Party spirit, to *consolidate* the Soviet regime, to *improve* our constructive work, to *strengthen* our economic cadres, to *arm* the working class.[18]

Yet it would be a mistake, or at any rate only partially correct, to dismiss the entire practice of CSC as a manifestation of Soviet official hypocrisy. The early Bolsheviks as well as the later leaders of the Soviet Union did and do have a desire to learn from their mistakes. While this desire is genuine, the conditions created for doing so are hardly ideal. The problem is to decide at what point a top-level policy becomes erroneous or a failure, to decide who is entitled to say so (and when), and to what degree should such realizations be made public. Here again we confront the paradox of power and self-criticism. At some point, difficult if not impossible to define for outsiders, errors become unforgivable, leading to loss of power and personal disgrace. The crux of the matter is that being in power confers by definition a degree of infallibility which endures exactly as long as the power of the incumbent. This is one of the built-in contradictions of the Soviet practice of CSC at the highest level.

Western Analogies

At the interpersonal level, we find two institutions in the West which betray some similarity to CSC: the confession in the Catholic church and certain forms of psychotherapy, in particular group therapy and psychoanalysis. All these practices, CSC included, resemble each other insofar as they provide, at least potentially, a method to relieve the individual's feelings of guilt and anxiety; they also help in preventing dissatisfaction with one's self from becoming paralyzing or destructive. Each in its own way also strives to provide some moral guidance to the individual. These practices also represent periodic acts of self-purification and have in common a view of human nature that takes sin, moral or psychological weakness, and faltering for granted, yet at the same time presumes a capacity for self-improvement. Confession and CSC also share the goal of instilling humility, breaking pride, and drawing forth unconditional candor. Without moralizing implications, psychotherapy too demands a similar capacity to recognize and confront one's weaknesses without flinching, which in all three institutions is a precondition of improvement.[19]

There are, of course, important differences as well among these three approaches to self-purification. In the first place, CSC is basically a political institution, whereas confession and psychotherapy are not. Second, CSC differs, at any rate from confession, in that it can provide an expression of aggression directed both against the self *and* others. (This, of course, is also feasible in group therapy, even in psychoanalysis.) Third, in contrast to confession and psychoanalysis, CSC involves the group, the collective, rather than just one representative of the belief system (the priest or the analyst). Fourth, CSC, as opposed to confession, does not utilize a codified inventory of misbehavior (sins).

Postscript 1982

There is little evidence to show that criticism and self-criticism is at the present time a widespread practice in most socialist systems, including the Soviet Union. At the same time, it is also possible that we know little of these practices (especially in the group setting) since such sessions are more likely to take place in the more highly politicized sectors of such societies, such as the various Party schools for elite groups with little if any publicity.

On the other hand, more information about the practice of criticism and self-criticism has become available from China.[20] Clearly, the persistence and extent of such practices (especially again in the interpersonal context) is connected with levels of ideological fervor and collectivism prevailing in the societies concerned. China under Mao, for such reasons, provided a fertile ground for these exercises. It may also be argued that the cultural differences to be found among various socialist countries having to do with attitudes toward private and public, or the individual and the group, also exercise considerable influence on how widespread such practices are.

Criticism in the press (directed at shortcomings at the lower or local level) and criticism associated with high-level succession crises (when the new leaders denounce their predecessors) are aspects of the institution which can be found in most socialist countries including those where criticism and self-criticism in the group setting play little part.

Notes

1. *Rules of the Communist Party of the Soviet Union Adopted by the 22nd Congress of the CPSU* (London, 31 Oct. 1961), p. 8.
2. Geoffrey Gorer and J. Rickman, *The People of Great Russia* (New York: W. W. Norton, 1962), p. 137.
3. D. A. Tomasic, *The Impact of Russian Culture on Soviet Communism* (Glencoe, Ill.: Free Press, 1953), p. 98.
4. Nathan Leites and Elsa Bernaut, *The Ritual of Liquidation: The Case of the Moscow Trials* (Glencoe, Ill.: Free Press, 1954).
5. James H. Billington, "The Intelligentsia and the Religion of Humanity," *American Historical Review* no. 4 (1960):810.
6. Robert Jay Lifton, *Thought Reform and the Psychology of Totalism* (New York: W. W. Norton, 1961).
7. Wolgang Leonhard, *Child of the Revolution* (Chicago: Regnery, 1958), p. 248.
8. A. Boiter, "Comradely Justice: How Durable Is It?" *Problems of Communism* no. 2 (1965); Leon Lipson, "Hosts and Pests: The Fight Against Parasites," *Problems of Communism* no. 2 (1965).

9. "Kritika i samokritika—nashe ispytannoe oruzhie" (Criticism and self-criticism—our proven weapons), *Kommunist* no. 1 (1961):81.
10. Leonhard, *Child,* pp. 516, 260.
11. Jerzy Kosinski, *No Third Path* (Garden City, N.Y.: Doubleday, 1962), p. 34. [Originally published under the name *Joseph Novak.*]
12. Leonhard, *Child,* p. 17.
13. Kosinski, *Path,* pp. 40, 47.
14. Ibid., p. 25.
15. Jerzy Kosinski, *The Future Is Ours Comrade: Conversations with the Russians* (Garden City, N.Y.: Doubleday, 1964), pp. 60–62, 64–66, 162–164.
16. Alex Inkeles, *Public Opinion in Soviet Russia* (Cambridge, Mass., 1958).
17. "Bol'shevistkaia kritika i samokritika" (Bolshevik criticism and self-criticism), in the *Large Soviet Encyclopedia* (Moscow, 1950), pp. 515–18.
18. J. Stalin, "Against Vulgarizing the Slogan of Self-Criticism," *Collected Works of Stalin* (Moscow, n.d.), 2:139.
19. For a discussion of the similarities between psychotherapy, religious revivalism, and thought reform, see Jerome D. Frank, *Healing and Persuasion: A Comparative Study of Psychotherapy* (New York, 1963).
20. For example, Bao Ruo Wang, *Prisoner of Mao* (Harmondsworth, England: Penguin, 1976); Martin King Whyte, *Small Groups and Political Rituals* (Berkeley: University of California Press, 1974).

8.
Comparing Socialist Systems: Ends and Results

Concluding questions and reminders about the fundamental objectives of the comparative enterprise may help to refocus and sharpen our basic concerns, which at times become submerged in more narrowly defined preoccupations and specialized interests. The remarks which follow may also supplement the contents of a volume (*Comparative Socialist Systems*, in which this chapter first appeared, and referred to as "the volume") which was, after all, designed to present primarily the methodological issues related to the comparison of socialist societies. Thus in these final comments it might be fruitful to ask once more *why* we compare different societies and why socialist ones in particular.

Some of the answers are among those clichés which happen to be true. Comparison is a basic thought process inseparable from both understanding and evaluation. It takes place constantly in our minds whether or not we are engaged in some social scientific endeavor, explicitly as well as by implication, with and without self-conscious intent. No serious social scientific undertaking can proceed without comparing various aspects of social reality—institutions, processes, events, or entire societies. Nor can theoretical generalizations and propositions be produced without comparison, and the relationship between the unique and the general be examined or established. Comparative studies certainly do not need defense and justification since few social scientists would question their importance. Nevertheless, the actual number of such studies is hardly commensurate with the recognition of their importance. This is especially true for the comparative study of socialist societies.

First of all, we know less about most socialist systems than about nonsocialist ones, especially the capitalist-pluralistic types among them. This is so both because the social sciences have developed more recently in socialist societies and socialist countries tend to be more secretive. The comparative study of socialist societies may be viewed as part of a more general striving for a better understanding of their major defining characteristics.

Comparing and thus better understanding socialist societies offers the additional benefit of a better understanding, appreciation, or more in-

127

formed criticism (as the case may be) of our own Western societies. Thus, for example, by learning more about the advantages and disadvantages of the economic institutions of socialist societies—which, after all, are the major determinants of their being called "socialist"—we can make more reasoned judgments about the efficiency and inefficiency of Western capitalist and mixed economic systems.

Among the socialist systems, the East European ones have exercised a particular attraction for American social scientists in the last decade or so. This has occurred because their development (with some notable exceptions) confirmed to some degree the hopes about the evolution of socialist systems in a direction appealing to Western liberal sensibilities. Some of these countries provided examples of welcome forms of deviation from the Soviet model: experimentation in the economic field, greater freedom of expression, incipient pluralism, and more diversity in domestic policies. Moreover, they also offered a theoretical challenge to Western social scientists since the transformations of their political structures provided evidence of the limited usefulness of the totalitarian model which had prevailed earlier. At the same time, much disagreement remains among scholars pursuing new models and theories as to the most fruitful classification and conceptualization of such systems. This state of affairs is also reflected in the wide variety of terms that are used to describe them and are found in the volume. Mesa-Lago observed the proliferation of such concepts in his essay, which included the following: command, statist, administrative, bureaucratic, centrally planned; mobilization, communal, leftist, orthodox; market socialist, rightist, reformist, decentralized (p. 95). The title of the volume, *Comparative Socialist Systems,* is a reflection of the persisting difficulties of providing a satisfactory label to such countries, since designating them as "socialist" is also open to question.

A closer review of the essays in the volume suggests interesting aspects of the current state of scholarship on socialist systems. Although neither the disciplinary affiliation of the authors nor the particular topics included can be taken as representative of the field as a whole, the patterns revealed by the contents of the volume do reflect certain trends in the scholarship concerned with socialist systems. It must be stressed again that the design of the volume encouraged methodological concerns and interests which, in turn, influenced the selection of the authors, all of whom (except for this writer) are either economists or political scientists. Perhaps it should be no surprise that there were no historians included, given the lesser interest of historians in methodological issues, and that there were no anthropologists, since they generally do not study complex modern societies. Somewhat more surprising, though not altogether startling, is the absence of sociologists (other than this writer) who more often contemplate social systems in toto and occasionally try to compare them. In any event, the combination of interest in socialist systems, comparative studies in general, *and* methodology is certainly not widespread among American sociologists. Thus the preponderance of economists and political scientists among the contributors is probably a fair reflection of the degree of interest social scientists in different disciplines evince in socialist systems and particularly in the methodological problems raised by their comparative study. Such a selective representation of the various disciplines in the comparative study of socialist systems has considerable implications for what we know and hope to learn about them, about the topics investigated or left unexplored, and the questions raised or neglected. This somewhat uneven development of the field of comparative socialist systems is reflected not only in the volume but elsewhere as well. I will return to this issue later.

It is also noteworthy that *outside* the topics related to economics, very few substantive problems or institutions are dealt with. The few included are political liberalization (Korbonski), bureaucracy (Cocks), and political change (Triska and Johnson). The rest of the essays either fall into the group of strictly methodological discussions (mentioned previously) or of economics (i.e., five-year plans, property rights, industrial organization, foreign trade, cybernetics, and automation).

Another difficulty inherent in a volume comparing socialist systems is that there are many of them (thirteen is the figure usually referred to by the contributors) and few scholars can possibly be familiar with all or most of them. This means that actual comparisons will be limited, at any rate in the framework of any single essay. Nobody can discourse knowledgeably on, say, crime, economic controls, or political institutions in the USSR, North Korea, Albania, Yugoslavia, and so forth. In most cases, experts fall into one of three major groups: They are either (1) Sovietologists, (2) Sinologists, or (3) students of one (sometimes more than one) East European country. The handful of scholars who study Albania, North Korea, North Vietnam, or Mongolia hardly merit the designation of "group." Nor is scholarship on Cuba intensively cultivated. Sometimes there is an overlap between specialists on the USSR and some country of Eastern Europe, but there are virtually no experts on both the USSR and China,[1] or on China and Eastern Europe, or on any one of the five "residual" countries mentioned *and* either the USSR or China. For such as well as other reasons, the comparisons are uneven; some of the contributors compare (or make some reference to) all socialist countries, others only to the USSR and Eastern Europe.

Since Eastern Europe features most prominently of the areas discussed in the volume, with four essays explicitly dealing with it and several others devoting large amounts of space to it, perhaps I should comment here on what appears a resurgent interest in the types of socialism manifest in Eastern Europe.[2]

First to be noted is that social scientific interest in Eastern Europe has been largely independent of corresponding interest in the Soviet Union. In the heyday of Soviet area studies, not much was said and written about Eastern Europe; it seems that as the interest in the Soviet system waned some of that interest was transferred to Eastern Europe. The decline in concern with the USSR has been reflected, among other things, in the decrease in financial support for research in the Soviet area, in falling course enrollments, and fewer research projects undertaken. This is somewhat paradoxical on at least two counts. First, such developments took place when Soviet society had become more accessible and Soviet social scientists themselves began to provide more information about their own society, and second, it coincided with Soviet society losing some of its most unappealing, repressive characteristics.

One explanation of the newly found interest in Eastern Europe might be that it has coincided with the loosening Soviet domination of the area (with the exception of Yugoslavia, which has been free of such domination since 1948). While earlier the tight control of and the attendant wholesale transplantation of Soviet institutions to Eastern Europe might have made the countries concerned look like mere replicas of the Soviet Union, since the late 1950s this has no longer been the case. Inasmuch as the East European countries used to be truly satellites of the Soviet Union, with their social and political structures closely modeled on those of the Soviet, they stimulated little interest among researchers who could assume with some justification that whatever they learned about the Soviet Union was readily applicable to East European societies, which therefore did not merit independent study.

By the same token, developments in the last two decades explain the resurgent interest in Eastern Europe, in the East European varieties of socialism. Most importantly, it has become clear that Eastern Europe is more than an undifferentiated appendage of the Soviet Union, even though Soviet influence in the area has not come to an end. To the extent that internal changes in the Soviet Union resulted in less stringent controls over Eastern Europe, the historical differences between the Soviet Union and the countries of Eastern Europe reemerged. A process of limited differentiation began, although the fundamentals of the institutional framework have not become significantly altered. In particular, the principle of Party control over all aspects of life and a foreign policy subservient to the Soviet Union[3] remained stable while certain economic, social, and cultural policies started to diverge from the Soviet model. As a result, Eastern Europe and its constituent parts have become a more interesting entity providing Western social scientists with new opportunities to observe and study the process of deviation from the Soviet model and versions of socialism which were politically and culturally more open and liberal and more experimental in the economic sphere.

Not only have East European systems succeeded in gradually differentiating themselves from their Soviet progenitor to become interesting subjects of study in their own right, but their new appeal—as noted before—has much to do with the fact that the changes were of a liberalizing nature. They have made the countries concerned more attractive for American social scientists by holding out once more the promise of the combination of greater social justice through socialist economic arrangements with some degree of political democracy or pluralism.

Last but not least, the degree of liberalization achieved in Eastern Europe had significant enough consequences in permitting the freedom to conduct social scientific research, both for natives and foreigners, although this has varied considerably from country to country and has also fluctuated somewhat in time. Many American social scientists interested in studying socialist systems turned their attention to Eastern Europe because they wished to cease being "armchair experts" and gain better access to data—a desire that could be more easily gratified in Eastern Europe than in socialist countries elsewhere.

These considerations (applying primarily to the study of Eastern Europe) are among the factors conducive to a perspective on socialist systems which might be called optimistic-evolutionary and is much in evidence in this volume. The changes which have taken place in Eastern Europe and to a lesser extent in the Soviet Union are the best known, most conspicuous, and most promising of a more complex, diversified, and liberal form of socialism. If "socialism with a human face" was a possibility anywhere, Eastern Europe (or some parts of it) might have appeared its most likely location. The liberalizing changes have also coincided with economic development; that is, further industrialization and urbanization, as well as improvement in the educational attainments of the populations concerned. Such a confluence of economic and political change takes us back to the notion of evolutionary optimism that is virtually synonymous with modernization theory. The heart of modernization theory, to which most of the contributors of this volume seem to subscribe, is economic development. Motivated by the generalizing impulse, the contributors are looking more for similarities than differences among socialist systems, and they are most likely to find them in the framework of modernization theory. Of course in the case of Eastern Europe, economic development cannot be treated, not even by the most ardent believer in modernization, as the sole or major determinant of the systems concerned. As the contributors are well aware, Soviet policy and presence are other powerful determinants of the shape of the societies concerned. To be sure, Soviet policy and economic development interact with the more unique, historically derived qualities of each society.

It is the connections between the generalizing impulse and the evolutionary perspective which help explain the otherwise somewhat startling observation of Professor Korbonski—also illustrative of the major thrust of the current social scientific approach toward socialist systems, and East Europe in particular—according to which "the demise of the totalitarian model, accompanied by the growing availability of political, economic and social data, made the traditional distinction between 'communist' and 'non-communist' systems obsolete and redundant" (p. 192). What is implied here is that distinctions between various social-political systems reduce to differences between stages of development.

While the viewpoint quoted (shared by other contributors as well) bespeaks the intention to integrate the study of socialist systems more fully into the study of all political systems (or into what is judged to be the mainstream of Western political science), other authors find the study of socialist systems a useful corrective to the characteristic biases and preconceptions which prevail among many influential American political scientists. Again, East European states in particular provide welcome reminders that political change frequently has its origins in external rather than indigenous "within-system" sources. Thus Triska and Johnson note:

> Political change literature . . . posits political systems as sovereign masters of their own destiny. Earlier Almond, Dankwart Rustow, David Apter, Samuel Huntington, and Ronald Bruner and Gary Brewer are all concerned with political change in political systems as if they had no foreign environment . . . [whereas] the most significant variable in explaining political systems stability and change in East Europe is . . . Soviet security (pp. 277–78).

To the extent that the essays venture into the realm of prediction, their message tends to be optimistic. Interestingly enough, this seems part of a general tendency among American social scientists to be more inclined to optimism in regard to the future of societies other than their own. It applies especially to the future of Soviet and East European societies and is warranted to some extent by the relaxation of the terror which has gripped these regions for a long time. But such optimistic leanings are also influenced by the perspectives of modernization, often permeated by the nineteenth-century belief in progress. The ingredients of this outlook have been familiar enough, especially as applied to the Soviet Union between the late 1950s and the intervention in Czechoslovakia in 1968, which somewhat deflated the hopes of those who envisaged a unilinear change from repressive to tolerant Soviet policies, foreign and domestic. In the modernization approach, change and improvement are inextricably intertwined, change tending to mean change for the better.[4]

Economic development creates pressures for "political development," which is equated with democratization and the growth of pluralistic tendencies. The scheme is not far removed from Marxist economic determinism, though more complex, containing intervening variables between economic development and political democracy. Most importantly, economic development, industrialization in particular, is seen as a basically rational and benevolent process of building on and at the same time multiplying scientific and administrative rationality. The spread of education is both a precondition and a derivative of successful industrialization. Education, regardless of its substantive content, is further assumed to be a rational, liberating, and liberalizing force—that is to say, a modernizing force. It is suggested that an educated population will increasingly press for greater political participation and freedom. (Observers of political participation in socialist countries often fail to ask whether it has any impact on political decision making or not, whether it is a ritual of political mobilization designed to provide symbolic endorsement of elite policies or not.)

Another aspect of industrialization seen as conducive to democratizing trends is found in its contribution to raising the standards of living. People who consume more are more difficult to control, indoctrinate, or mobilize; they become more committed to the status quo, less ideological, less susceptible to demagogic manipulation, more aware of their real versus apparent, or officially alleged, interests—so the argument runs. They have more to lose. (Again, this line of reasoning fails to take adequate account of the disincentive created by such improvements to participation in politics or to the promotion of social-political change. Thus the fear of "rocking the boat" can help to perpetuate an oppressive system.) The structural complexity of a more advanced industrial society is also said to invite a different and more enlightened political approach. Decentralization in the economy becomes imperative for the achievement of greater efficiency and initiative in decision making, and is expected to spread to the political sphere. A highly industrialized society is supposed to be under pressure to maintain or increase contacts with the world outside (since all such societies are becoming more and more interdependent), and this too contributes to the erosion of ideological rigidities, blinders, and suspicions which isolation reinforced earlier. New models of consumption as well as of political freedom become more available and censorship over the mass media becomes more relaxed. Thus industrialization creates not merely structural but also attitudinal changes, and it raises expectations which exert pressures on the leadership to introduce more flexible policies in various realms of life. "Apolitical technocrats" and specialists become increasingly important and their roles and values further dilute the ideological commitments and objectives of such regimes. This may be a brief sketch of the assumptions which underlie evolutionary optimism as applied to the future of socialist societies, a viewpoint which seems most congenial to several contributors to the volume.

Having commented on some of the orientations and specific interests displayed in the collection, I turn now to a brief review of aspects of the socialist societies which have been given little attention there.

We may begin by noting that not much has been said about the core concept tying these societies (and essays) together, namely, "socialism." Few authors paused to ask what the concept means, or, rather, what are its different meanings and usages, in or outside systems which call themselves "socialist." How many transformations has the concept undergone? How many kinds of socialism exist, implemented and imaginary? How far from, or how close to, the concepts of Marx or Lenin are the current usages of the term?

Another major topic that has received hardly any attention is that of legitimacy, the entitlement to rule, the spontaneous popular support enjoyed by or withheld from the systems in question. Correspondingly, little is said about ways of assessing the legitimacy of such systems.

On the whole, it appears that the contributors, or most of them, assume that the regimes in question enjoy substantial legitimacy and the matter, therefore, needs little further exploration. But there may be other reasons too, not peculiar to this volume, which account for the neglect of the topic. First, there is the general difficulty of assessing and measuring legitimacy. Even if scholars could agree on its indicators and measures, the research required for applying them could hardly be carried out in socialist societies. There is sufficient evidence to suggest that socialist regimes do not welcome the questioning, social scientific or otherwise, of their legitimacy and are intolerant of the slightest challenge to it. For the same reason, Western research into the legitimacy of socialist systems is avoided because of the criticism it implies. Investigating and thus questioning the legitimacy of such systems by Western social scientists is likely to be seen as an unfriendly gesture equated with a revival of the cold war spirit. An expressed interest in legitimacy would also undercut other opportunities for research in socialist countries. Finally, it is also possible that the root of Alfred Meyer's hesitation to inquire into the legitimacy of East European socialist systems is shared by others. He wrote a few years ago: "At a time when the legitimacy of power in the leading nation of the Western world [the U.S.] appears to be shaken to its very foundation . . . and the country troubled by deepening cleavages—at such a time it somehow does not seem quite appropriate for an American . . . to inquire into the legitimacy of power in Eastern Europe."[5]

Thus the lack of attention given to the question of legitimacy in socialist systems is far from unusual. While this omission is understandable both in light of the methodological difficulties involved and the more subtle psychological ones alluded to, it remains one of the major gaps in the comparative study of socialist systems. This is regrettable since the study of legitimacy in socialist systems offers a point of departure for a better understanding of the concept in general. I believe that the type of legitimacy socialist systems enjoy has yet to be conceptualized adequately, even though it may apply to many nonsocialist systems as well and may turn out to be the most widespread form of legitimacy. Such legitimacy is born out of the lack of alternatives. It rests on the fact that these systems have endured, that opposition to them has been made institutionally impossible and practically futile, and that traditions of popular participation in government have not been among the historical legacies of the areas and cultures in question. One may propose that socialist regimes (as many others) are legitimate by virtue of resigned acceptance rather than active endorsement on the part of the majorities of the populations involved; that they are neither actively opposed nor supported at the attitudinal or behavioral level. It may also be possible that they are sometimes seen as legitimate not for reasons derived from moral-ethical principles, but because of a popular acceptance of the axiom that might is right, that those who can tenaciously cling to power earned their right to do so—a notion very different from the Western liberal conceptions of what constitutes the legitimation of political power.

Although the investigation and assessment of legitimacy present difficulties in every society, and especially socialist ones—which cannot even allow the questioning of its degree—I would like to suggest that the problem is not totally intractable, and propose a few lines of inquiry that might be followed in comparing the legitimacy of socialist systems.

An obvious point of departure for assessing and measuring legitimacy might be found in the presence or absence of institutionalized opportunities for criticizing, modifying, or altering the political system. If, and only when, such opportunities are available can we begin to assess the degree of support or acceptance any political system enjoys. Fearful and intolerant of criticism, a political system, like an individual, reveals its own profound sense of insecurity. But the intolerance of criticism is not in itself a sufficient proof of illegitimacy that should lead one to conclude that if tolerated, the floodgates of popular hostility would burst open and swamp the system.

If a political system allows itself to be criticized and its structures modified without violence, it will probably also allow more direct investigations of its legitimacy through opinion and attitude surveys, and the population will less likely be intimidated or discouraged from responding to such attempts.

There are other less direct though equally telling indicators of legitimacy. Among them is the size and differentiation of the coercive apparatus. Large and highly differentiated coercive institutions (police forces of various kinds concerned with political attitudes) are suggestive of a flawed sense of legitimacy, of the expectation of dissent, opposition, and subversion—in short, of the forceful questioning of legitimacy. The actual and expected (or potential) contacts between members of society and coercive agencies can be equally revealing, as are the popular conceptions and awareness of their activities. The freedom to travel abroad (or emigrate)—and thereby have the opportunity to "vote with one's feet"—is another useful indicator of the legitimacy and self-confidence of a political system. Measuring levels of intimidation among the population—especially as connected with free expression—might be another of the devices leading to assessments of legitimacy. Such levels could be reflected in political jokes; the use or avoidance of telephones for political conversation; the sharp distinction made between friends, acquaintances, and strangers in regard to such conversations, and the differentiation between public and private places when sensitive topics are broached. Attitudes toward state or public property could provide further clues of the legitimacy of (and the related sense of identification with) the political system. Mass participation in public affairs and the degree of its voluntary or involuntary nature is yet another obvious indicator, although the difficulties of assessing voluntarism are hard to overestimate. Finally, there are the crises attendant to the obvious breakdown of legitimacy: strikes, riots, sabotage, armed rebellions—the whole gamut of political violence directed against the elites in power or the symbols of their power and legitimacy.[6] Mechanisms of political succession and their functioning supply further information about the legitimacy of the elite groups in power.

In concluding this discussion, it should also be pointed out that the legitimacy of socialist (and not only socialist) systems is also connected with the degree to which the preservation of their political power depends on, or has been derived from, external sources. Hence, at times, what may be critical in judging the legitimacy of a political system is not so much its reliance (or potential reliance) on force, but rather the nature of the force involved. Calling in the troops to maintain order is one thing, but calling in those of a neighboring power is quite another. For such reasons one may propose that, for example, no matter how Stalinist the Albanian regime might have remained and how ruthlessly its internal security forces might repress any challenge to its legitimacy, in a crisis it cannot count on Soviet or Chinese or any other intervention to ward off threats to its survival—as opposed to most other regimes of Eastern Europe.

Another set of problems which may usefully supplement discussions of legitimacy are those connected with nationalities and ethnic minorities in socialist systems. It is not hard to discern links between legitimacy and the position of such minorities. The extent to which they are under-represented, or excluded from the political decision-making process, their access to the rewards of their society—all these have considerable bearing on the legitimacy of the system involved. In ethnically homogeneous societies, there is one threat fewer to legitimacy than in those which are heterogeneous and distribute power and material rewards unequally among different ethnic groups.

Although many socialist systems have made considerable efforts to equalize the position of such minorities, the record of their accomplishments has been mixed. Thus few reasonably impartial observers could argue that in the USSR, Romania, or Yugoslavia the nationality problem has been solved once and for all. Future research should also address one of the most critical aspects of the nationality and ethnic problems, namely, that of bias and prejudice, and the extent to which socialist systems, as compared with others, have succeeded in eradicating or controlling such sentiments and attitudes.

Another topic that may be included in future comparative research on socialist systems is that of social problems.[7] It is hardly a secret that socialist systems, like capitalist ones, have an abundance of social problems, including crime, juvenile delinquency, family instability, pollution, various forms of escapist behavior, the neglect of old people, and others. Such problems constitute a dimension that can be applied not only to the comparison of socialist societies with one another, but also with nonsocialist ones. Though the availability of data varies, there is enough for some meaningful comparisons, especially between industrially advanced socialist and nonsocialist societies. Such comparisons could lead to theoretically significant generalizations. Even preliminary attempts in this direction suggest that the most striking similarities between highly industrialized and urbanized socialist and capitalist societies may well be found in the realm of social problems.[8]

At least two other important areas invite comparison and could throw further light on the nature of socialist systems: stratification, and the official and unofficial beliefs. Concerning social stratification, there has been a steady accumulation of data from Eastern Europe and the USSR (following the emergence of sociology as a legitimate discipline) but much less from the other socialist countries. This is a sensitive area of inquiry insofar as it leads to findings calling into question the strides made toward the attainment of socioeconomic equality. For this reason, the available data are far from comprehensive, especially as they pertain to income distribution and access to privilege of a nonmonetary nature (e.g., housing, travel, special shops).

The comparative study of beliefs and values, except those which are official and public, is still more difficult. What people truly believe in is hard to investigate in any society but particularly so in those which adhere to a well-defined and aggressively propagated official belief system, such as the versions of Marxism-Leninism prevailing in socialist societies. Yet a deeper understanding of such systems will be deficient as long as we do not or cannot investigate the genuine and privately held beliefs of their citizens and the relationships of these beliefs to those publicly professed.

Although the volume has not addressed itself to the comparison of socialist societies with nonsocialist ones, it is hard to avoid some final reflections about the strengths and weaknesses of the societies surveyed there compared with those of a capitalist or mixed economy, high levels of pluralism, urbanization, and democratic political institutions. If we take a look at such societies currently wallowing in a wide variety of crises, the socialist ones present an appearance that is at least superficially appealing. First of all, they are, or seem to be, vastly more stable, whatever indicator of stability we take. In the lands of socialism governments rarely change, the police do not have to disperse rioters, workers do not go on strike, heads of state do not get assassinated, prominent citizens do not get kidnapped. Prices of consumer goods and food do not soar (though they may be high to begin with, in relation to earnings). There is no inflation of serious proportions in most socialist countries, although it is risky to make such sweeping statements about countries which range from Yugoslavia to the Soviet Union with significantly different economic structures. While in any objective, measurable sense living conditions in most socialist countries are less favorable than in the group of countries with which they are being contrasted there, deprivations are less keenly felt. This is so because conditions have not rapidly deteriorated but have been more or less stable and in many cases improved over time. In Western societies today, economic difficulties erupt unexpectedly, sowing the seeds of anger, bewilderment, and frustration. The same could apply to the political sphere at some point in the future. Although personal and group freedoms in Western societies have not declined thus far, if they became more restricted, their absence would also be more keenly felt. Again, by contrast, in socialist countries such freedoms have been always more circumscribed; hence their absence has been barely felt, or only by a few. The key factor in regard to all such issues—living standards, personal freedom, and the variety of deprivations people suffer—lies in the realm of expectations, the mainstay of stability. Of course, the relationship between relatively low expectations and stability is circular. Political stability is facilitated by low expectations, but stability, in turn, reinforces low expectations. When people have little reason to believe that change will be for the better, or that they can bring it about, they will be quiescent and passive. The few who are not, usually the dissident intellectuals, are viewed by the majority either as fools or troublemakers or, at best, misguided idealists.

Let us take a closer look at some other factors which, interacting with the low level of expectations, are conducive to stability. Most of the socialist countries do not have a tradition of active or widespread popular participation in government, or local self-government. The countries in question developed and maintained strong and efficient coercive apparatus and made a heavy initial investment in "revolutionary" terror, the lessons of which linger on for generations. In many of the countries, there is a historical legacy of popular fatalism which has not been dispelled by the mobilization of the population for the performance of economic tasks or crash programs or by the rituals of political participation. In fact, the type of participation, or more accurately, pseudo-participation, encouraged and demanded by the leaders of many socialist societies is quite compatible with the traditional passive and fatalistic attitude toward politics present in many of these societies.

The stability of socialist societies is also connected, in more subtle ways, with this tradition of nonparticipation in politics. Such societies, being highly organized, significantly limit the choices individuals have and create a secure if circumscribed context in which personal responsibility for success and failure is more limited than in Western societies.

Fewer choices mean fewer dilemmas and narrower limits on personal achievement—in politics, money making, or social mobility. They also limit the sense of failure. Small gains in living conditions or personal freedom are therefore doubly appreciated; any revolutionary rise in expectations is restrained by the determination of the political elite to hang on to power (and to the means of assuring this). In the case of the smaller nations in areas contiguous to either the Soviet Union or China, the ruling groups, unless they persistently defy the policies of the neighboring big power—can count on such external support should popular discontent emerge forcefully.[9] If expectations are low in the political realm, it is not only because the vast majority are currently deprived of meaningful political participation. This state of affairs can also be accounted for by cumulative exclusion from political activities over generations, by the unpleasant and at times bloody consequences of the attempts to challenge the powers-that-be, and by the resulting pervasive disenchantment with politics that cannot be measured by abstention from voting, as it can in Western societies. This profound disenchantment means that people, including most intellectuals, are not tempted to seek salvation or personal fulfillment through politics, as some significant if small groups do in other parts of the world.

In the final analysis, comparing socialist systems is not fundamentally different from comparing nonsocialist ones and doing so presents problems and rewards similar to those which are generally encountered in comparative studies. To say this is not to belittle such pioneering efforts. Comparing socialist systems is more difficult from a methodological point of view because the study of such systems in general is relatively new (except in regard to the Soviet Union), the data are less abundant, the accumulated theoretical guidance more sparse, and there are few safe assumptions to build on. Yet basically the objectives of the enterprise are the same as those which guide any large-scale comparisons of societies. When we compare socialist societies, we do so because we wish to learn more about the basic patterns and regularities of social systems, find new data for enduring theoretical generalizations, and uncover the ways in which social institutions do or do not hang together and affect (or fail to affect) the lives of people. Through such studies, we also want to learn more about the sources and varieties of social change. More fundamental to all such endeavors is the desire to learn more about the ways in which various collectivities and institutions grapple with human frustration, satisfaction, and misery; about the interaction between social order and personal freedom and the almost endless attempts to meet or evade the endemic problems of scarcity.

Postscript 1982

Since I wrote this chapter, there has been a striking growth in the number of countries claiming to be, and generally regarded as, socialist. Not only has the "socialization" of Indochina been completed (not without some rival "socialists" fighting for control in Cambodia), but Afghanistan too has reluctantly enrolled in the Socialist Commonwealth (as Brezhnev called this political entity in 1968). In Africa, Angola, Ethiopia, and Mozambique joined; in the Middle East, South Yemen became a charter member. In the Western hemisphere, Grenada and Nicaragua are the newcomers to the socialist camp, and efforts are under way to pry El Salvador away from its nonsocialist moorings. For obvious reasons, none of these countries or their characteristics entered into the discussion of socialist systems in the volume of which my essay was a part.

While socialist countries of mixed cultural-historical backgrounds multiplied in various parts of the globe over these eight years, those in Eastern Europe no longer seem to inspire the kinds of hopes to which reference was made in this chapter. The major blow to these hopes occurred during the recent events in Poland (see also pp. 197–200) which once more clearly defined the limits of social-political change in the Soviet bloc countries of Eastern Europe. Thus the "evolutionary optimism" referred to in this chapter is far less in evidence today as far as Eastern Europe is concerned where the military repression of Solidarity (in Poland) is matched by the frozen stability of Czechoslovakia, the severe economic problems of Romania, the stable repression in Albania and Bulgaria, and the precarious survival of a more tolerant paternalism in Hungary, the "gayest barrack in the socialist camp," as the joke has it. Even in Hungary, by far the freest of the countries of Eastern Europe, alienation and social problems have been rampant as illustrated by books such as Haraszti's *Worker in a Worker's State* (1978) and George Konrad's *Caseworker* (1973). In turn, much new light was shed upon inequality and bureaucratization in Eastern Europe by works such as Walter Connor's *Socialism, Politics and Equality* (1979) and Konrad and Szelenyi's study mentioned earlier. While scholarly views of Eastern Europe have on the whole become more sober, a handful of scholars, and preeminently Jerry Hough, have been working with unflagging zeal on the project of redefining the Soviet Union as a pluralistic society with political institutions and practices not significantly different from those found in Western democracies. There have also been attempts to extend such benign perspectives to East Germany.[10]

While the historical changes and additions to the ranks of socialist states could obviously not have been taken into account in my article, the latter does suffer from an overemphasis on the optimistic views of the process of modernization and a neglect of the less sanguine perceptions of it. In particular, reference should have been made to the work of Peter Berger,[11] who weighed and emphasized the costs of modernization under both socialist and nonsocialist systems. Perhaps, as Berger has written about the promise of socialism, many students of socialist societies have come to believe that the benefits of modernization under socialism could be attained without serious costs. We are still in the process of finding out about these costs both in long-established socialist countries and in those which emerged more recently.

Notes

1. Martin Whyte and Bernard Frolic may qualify as students of both China and the USSR although both have increasingly focused their attention on China.
2. There are many expressions of such interest, including a growing number of publications, an increase in scholarly exchanges, the newsletter on sociology in Eastern Europe, etc.
3. Yugoslavia, as always, is an exception to most of these remarks since both its domestic and foreign policy have been largely free of Soviet control since 1948. Romanian foreign policy is another partial exception in that it has achieved a greater degree of independence than other countries of Eastern Europe. Likewise, Albania has excluded herself from the Soviet bloc while retaining rigid Stalinist domestic policies which might not have displeased the "hard liners" in the Soviet leadership.
4. For a recently published empirical study based on extensive survey research which, by and large, reaffirms this association, see Alex Inkeles, *Becoming Modern: Individual Change in Six Developing Countries* (Cambridge: Harvard University Press, 1974).
5. Alfred G. Meyer, "Legitimacy of Power in East Central Europe," in S. Sinanian, I. Deak, and P. Ludz, eds., *Eastern Europe in the 1970s* (New York: Praeger, 1972), pp. 67–68. A decade after Professor Meyer wrote this article his qualms about inquiring into the legitimacy of socialist systems seem to have persisted as has his strong sense of the inadequacies of American society which created the psychological barrier to such inquiries to begin with (see also pp. 73–74).
6. It is worth noting the frequency with which crowds, hostile to a particular political system, burn flags and destroy public buildings, pictures, and statues of political leaders as soon as the opportunity presents itself.
7. I have taken up this issue more recently (pp. 225–31 of this volume).
8. For a comparative discussion of Soviet and American social problems, see pp. 300–373 in Paul Hollander, *Soviet and American Society: A Comparison* (New York: Oxford University Press, 1973; and University of Chicago Press, 1978).

9. This would probably even apply to countries which enjoy greater autonomy and lesser satellite status, e.g., North Korea and North Vietnam. In the totally improbable event of such regimes being threatened by "nonsocialist" forces, it is hard to imagine that China would stand by idly. The corresponding determination of the Soviet Union has of course been demonstrated on a number of occasions: in 1953 in East Germany, in 1956 in Hungary and Poland, and in 1968 in Czechoslovakia. Only Albania would be unprotected by such assistance should domestic discontent threaten the system, in view of its distance from China and the Soviet hostility toward the present regime. Since this chapter was written, the Soviet Union has also assumed considerable responsibility, together with Cuba, for keeping in power socialist regimes in Angola, Afghanistan, Ethiopia, Mozambique, and South Yemen. At the same time, China developed an intensely antagonistic relationship with Vietnam and Cambodia, which is controlled by Vietnam.

10. Norman M. Naimark, "Is It True What They're Saying About East Germany?" *Orbis* (Fall 1979).

11. Peter L. Berger, *The Pyramids of Sacrifice* (New York: Basic Books, 1975); *The Homeless Mind* (with Brigitte Berger and Hansfried Kellner) (New York: Random House, 1973); and "The Socialist Myth," *Public Interest* (Summer 1976).

9.
Family and Feminism
in Soviet Society*

It is for good reason that contemporary radical feminists in the West admire Alexandra Kollontai.[1] The affinity between her views and theirs is unmistakable. Both believed that without a fundamental transformation of the family no breakthrough in human affairs is possible, no true liberation for women or men, no genuine revolutionary overhaul of all social institutions.[2] As most revolutionaries tend to, both Kollontai and contemporary radical feminists exaggerated the interdependence of all social institutions, disallowing for the possibility that not every part of society hangs together as tightly and logically as they dreamed of in their philosophy, and consequently change in one realm does not always bring about radical change across the board. It is not surprising that the revolutionary temper is attracted to such a vision of society. If radical change is desired, it is easier to envision it on the basis of a conception of social order in which the unraveling of one strand inexorably leads to the unraveling of the whole fabric. It is, moreover, distasteful for the committed revolutionary to contemplate relatively static islands or strongholds among social institutions around which social change swirls but which resist it, to whatever degree. By contrast, structural-functional sociologists in the United States take some pleasure in reporting on the relatively unchanging nature of the family, or, at least, its survival. Amerian sociologists of such persuasion are inclined to consider the family less dynamic than other social institutions—a view that bears surprising resemblance to the Soviet discussions of the differential rate of change of different social phenomena (especially consciousness; that is, values and attitudes which lag behind institutional transformations). For example:

> The economic and politial systems are more dynamic than the family, and the economic order is the most dynamic of all in Western society. . . . Economic production being based on science, is subject in the West to the process of rationalization, and the family is not. . . . But the family, like religion, is designed [sic] to afford stability to social life. We may be

interested in a new model of car every year but not in a new model of
family life.[3]

Writing in 1965, Nimkoff might be excused for not anticipating the
developments of the following decade during which several new "models"
of family lives and styles were introduced and given considerable publicity.

In any case, many American sociologists regarded the family as not
only resistant to change but practically indestructible by virtue of its
adaptability, its ability to perform changing functions. Indeed, many
such sociologists regarded the survival of the family in Soviet society
as proof of its indestructibility—a position that was forcefully challenged
by Barrington Moore.[4]

Although the mere survival of the family in Soviet society has little
to do with the issue of its indestructibility, its preservation in forms
displeasing both to early Soviet feminists and contemporary radical
feminists in America is at least thought-provoking. Nor is it without
significance that a revolutionary society, such as the Soviet Union had
once been, produced at a later stage official family policies and values
more conservative than those which prevailed in some of the bourgeois
societies of the West. It is a matter of historical record how the
experimental and revolutionary approaches toward the family, prominent
in the early 1920s, were swept away by the neo-Victorian standards
which emerged in the 1930s. The latter in modified forms persist to the
present, preventing any radical questioning of the family as it exists.
The weight of such conservative official values may provide the major
explanation for the absence of utopian or quasi-utopian alternatives,
either in the context of high-level social engineering or privatized innovation. Not since Strumilin's proposals in the late 1950s[5] to build
"palace communes" and transform child-rearing practices along the line
has any voice been raised in favor of substantially altering the structure
of the Soviet family.

The decline of any fundamental questioning of the family in the Soviet
Union today is all the more remarkable since there had been, as noted
before, a tradition of radical feminism in the early 1920s, highly critical
of the family. It will be interesting to examine further the degree of
resemblance between the concerns of these Soviet feminists and contemporary feminists in the United States—a comparison which may also
contribute to a better understanding of the status of family in the two
societies today.

The critics of the family in both periods and societies regarded the
family, as it has historically existed, as a major obstacle to individual
self-realization, especially for women. They saw it as incorporating and

perpetuating second-class citizenship for women through its oppressive division of labor, or, in modern terms, its sex role stereotyping. They were also critical of the family for isolating its members from larger society in an emotionally exclusive unit and for reflecting in its structure and values the private property relations of capitalist society. In the early Soviet criticisms of the family, there lurked the additional apprehension that unsupervised by the agencies of society—in turn guided by that unique historical entity, the Party—the family could not be trusted with socializing children. By contrast, contemporary Western feminists, often inclined to some degree of anarchism and perhaps more trustful of human nature and its potentials, do not envision entrusting the socialization of children to the state or some of its agencies. They do not trust self-appointed, powerful elites with the inculcation of the "correct" set of values.

Another difference that may be noted between the Soviet feminists of the early 1920s and the American radical feminists of the late 1960s and early 1970s concerns the attitude toward sexual relations with men. The early Soviet advocacy of free love entailed not only the liberation of sex from institutionalized bonds of matrimony but an attitude toward sex that was largely free of the apprehensions frequently expressed by present-day radical feminists who often view sexual relations with men as highly problematic and a major source of the exploitation of women. Such concerns, except in regard to prostitution, did not seem prominent among feminists such as Alexandra Kollontai and her followers.

It is no revelation that the attitudes of the Soviet regime toward the family have undergone significant changes over time. The early, revolutionary questioning of the family and the encouragement of freedom and diversity in personal relations has given way to abhorrence of "so-called free love and disorderly sex life." Under Stalin abortions were outlawed, divorce was made difficult, extramarital sex was frowned upon, and all references to sex were banished from the mass media and the arts.

Trotsky's explanation of these developments still has much to commend it, especially since he did not fall back on the postulate of the indestructibility of the family. Instead he offered economic as well as political explanations for its survival. Thus he observed that "the real resources of the state did not correspond to the plans and intentions of the Communist Party. You cannot 'abolish' the family; you have to replace it." (He was referring here to the need for child care and housekeeping functions.) But there was more to it than lack of funds to build nurseries or communal dining halls. He also wrote: "The most compelling motive of the present cult of the family is undoubtedly the need of the bureaucracy for a stable hierarchy of relations and for the disciplining of youth by means of 40 million points of support for authority and power."[6]

The consolidation of the Soviet political system under Stalin could not have taken place without restoring social order. The implications of the resurgent conservative moral standards of the 1930s were far-reaching. Although a highly authoritarian social system may aspire to do away with the family if viewed as a competing source of socialization, it has certainly no interest in allowing "free love," or less regulated human relationships to take its place. Contrary to some Western notions about the family as a source of resistance to political controls, the family has proved more compatible with totalitarianism than extrafamilial love and the attendant fluidity of human relations would be. It is not impossible that Soviet leaders may have sensed that authoritarianism, rigidity, and uniformity in political relations and institutions are incompatible with the tolerance of freedom, diversity, and mobility in interpersonal relations. It is difficult to maintain a social order in which there is freedom in one sphere (the personal-emotional-sexual) and severe constraints in others, such as the political and economic.[7] The deprivation of freedom proceeds more smoothly if there are no pockets of it left in some areas of life that can provide standards of comparison. Free love and sexual-emotional excesses are also discouraged by totalitarian rulers for more tangible reasons. They make undue alternative demands on the energies and interests of the citizen.[8] By contrast, the family as a rule does not deplete sexual energies; rather it is a framework in which sexual-emotional relations can be better stabilized.[9]

Today, the major concerns of the Soviet regime are the low birth rates and high divorce rates which are seen as undermining the institution of the family, in addition to diminishing the supply of labor. Low birth rates are also undesirable from the standpoint of power politics unfavorably affecting the military might of the USSR in relation to China. The frequently interconnected public discussions on divorce and childless or one-child families reflect a mixture of such pragmatic concerns (i.e., with labor supply and great power status) and apprehension over the increase in family instability, as well as the associated erosion of moral standards and threat to the proper upbringing of children. According to an article in *Pravda,*

> The existence of one-child families lessens the stability of family ties. There is reason to believe that a large number of divorces are to a certain degree connected with the fact that the absence of children or the presence of just one child makes the breakup of the family less complicated both psychologically and socially. In turn, the fragility of marriages creates,

mainly among women, a psychological inclination to have only one child in the family. . . . The one-child system creates a danger of the formation of a consumer attitude toward life.[10]

Soviet social scientists, presumably in response to official encouragement, have marshaled a wide range of arguments against childless or one-child families. They insist that only children turn out spoiled, individualistic, and lacking in social discipline. As long as the Soviet leadership continues making considerable demands on the population, is unwilling to commit itself to a consumer economy, pursues ambitious foreign policy goals, and maintains the largest military establishment in the world (in terms of the combination of manpower and firepower), a disciplined, compliant, and docile population therefore remains desirable. Hence it is important that the family not become the cradle of hedonism, individualism, "consumer attitudes," and unduly high expectations, material or spiritual.

Large and intact families (with both parents living with the children) are also strongly supported because of the well-established correlation between broken families and juvenile delinquency, reported in many Soviet[11] (as well as Western) studies.

It is in the realm of family size and structure that the values of the regime and popular aspirations, notably those of women, collide spectacularly. Authoritative sources repeat tirelessly that "a family of three children is the point at which society's interests and the correctly understood interests of the parents coincide."[12] Couples are urged not to postpone having children since this leads to lower population growth. In the same spirit, Perevedentsev, the leading demographer, cautions against late marriages which, he believes, not only lower birth rates but also contribute to marital instability. "When people marry young," he states, "adaptation to each other is comparatively easy." But most importantly, "A reduction in the average age of grooms and brides at marriage provides a tremendous reserve for increasing the birth rate."[13]

Although there is no evidence that Soviet women engage in the same radical questioning of sex roles many American women do, they have clearly gone on record in rejecting the official demands for larger families, voting with abortions and contraceptives, as it were. One striking survey established "that nearly everyone who opposes the single-child family in theory has only one child in fact, and no intention of having any more." The survey conducted by Moscow University Department of Economics among 5,000 married women aged eighteen to forty found that while 60 percent considered the ideal to have two children, in fact only 18 percent had that number; 36 percent favored three children but only 1 percent actually had that many, and while only 3 percent favored one child, 64 percent had one![14] A woman cited in another article suggested that "she would rather be shot than have three children, as her husband wishes."

In light of such attitudes it is doubtful that, as long as abortion and birth control are available, some of the remedies proposed by the regime will do the trick of raising the birth rate: "Photographs of mothers of many children are nowhere to be seen. Maternity medals and orders are often presented without the proper publicity. School children . . . are never introduced to hero mothers [those with more than ten children—P.H.], to women who have received the Order of Maternal Glory. But after all this is very important—we should constantly instill respect for motherhood and special respect for mothers with large families."[15]

It is noteworthy that when Soviet demographers lament the low birth rates they are actually talking only about the birth rates of one part of the Soviet population (Russians, Belorussians, Ukrainians, and Baltics), passing over the fact that numerous Soviet minorities have far higher birth rates. (Correspondingly, divorce rates are much lower among many ethnic groups.)[16] It is this state of affairs that prompted the American ethnographer, Ethel Dunn, to ask, "Is Perevedentsev afraid of being swamped by Central Asians, Kazakhs, Caucasian peoples, etc.?" Her letter sent to *Literaturnaya gazeta* was never published and its brief published summary made no reference to the question raised. Likewise, Perevedentsev in his lengthy reply totally ignored it. He did, however, respond to her criticism of his suggestion that women should get paid to stay at home and rear children. He proposed that "it is necessary to find means for the optimal combination of the woman's role in the family with all her other roles" (Perevedentsev, *ibid.*). Thus the assumption remains that it is the women who have several roles (work, familial) which are to be reconciled, and that they should be given whatever help is possible. However, no fundamental restructuring of sex roles within the family is envisioned.[17]

It is perhaps a measure of the liberalization of the Soviet system that not only does it refrain from trying to raise birth rates by making birth control as difficult as in the old days, but it also appears to have resigned itself to high divorce rates. Although some of the official and semiofficial commentaries on divorce retain the old-fashioned, moralizing Victorian undertones, the analysis of its causes seems sound and casts doubt on the often simultaneous assertions of the superior durability and strength of the Soviet family over those in bourgeois societies. Kharchev noted, for example, that while the growing prosperity since the end of World War II has strengthened the family, the positive influence is not as direct as had been expected. Life shows that improved conditions and equal rights for both sexes do not automatically strengthen the institution of marriage. There are still considerable numbers of divorces—600,000 per year, compared to 2 million marriages. Many sociologists propose developing a comprehensive program of sex education for young people of all ages aimed at preparing them for marriage and family life. . . . The present inadequate emotional upbringing of young people—for which our schools and press are both responsible—is the basic, underlying cause of divorce. . . . A crucial problem that affects family stability is the conflict between a woman's career and her household duties.[18]

While the faith put into the salutary effects of sex education in stabilizing marriages is questionable, Kharchev is undoubtedly correct in discerning a relationship between the higher standards of living, the career demands of women, and higher divorce rates. To be sure, the conflict between work and home is hardly a recent development. What is probably new is the lesser willingness to accept the wear-and-tear that results from it. On the other hand, the contribution of higher living standards to marital instability is of more recent origin. In the USSR, as elsewhere, more prosperous families are usually also better educated, and better educated families have fewer (or no) children. The latter, according to some Soviet sociologists quoted earlier, makes it easier to break up a marriage.[19] Such people, having a greater sense of autonomy and control over their lives, are also more unwilling to tolerate the frustrations of an unhappy marriage. Heightened expectations combined with the decline of the traditional restraints on divorce contribute to family disintegration, as was also observed by the sociologists I. Kasyukov and A. Mendeleyev:

> People of different cultural and moral levels and of different backgrounds and ways of life mix. They leave behind them traditional controls by the family, by the public opinion of the village street, by relatives. No social or material factors hinder them from marrying.
>
> Young men and women today make greater moral demands on marriage. They seek to embark upon married life at an earlier age . . . and very often the romantic ideas of married life are wrecked upon its prose.[20]

Despite Soviet claims concerning the fundamental differences between the Soviet and Western families, certain aspects of modernization and the expectations they generate contribute significantly to rising divorce rates in the USSR as in the United States. There is also a good deal of similarity between the positive interpretation which both American and Soviet sociologists have, from time to time, put on family disintegration, asserting that it reflects the increased unwillingness of people to accept unhappiness.

Modernization affects the family not only by generating higher expectations associated with better education and material living conditions. It also does so by knocking out from under the family its traditional social supports through social and geographical mobility which erodes the communities and kinship ties that used to provide such support.[21] And, of course, as has been pointed out many times, modernization also reduces the functions of the family by reducing its economic and educational roles. When social and geographical mobility opens up a vast potential marriage market, individual choices and decisions become the major criteria for selection, and the process ceases to be effectively supported by widely shared social values and normative standards. The ideal of "perfect compatibility" that American sociologists designated as a major factor leading to marital disillusionment is doubtless beginning to affect Soviet marriages. Finally, it cannot be overemphasized that modernization entails secularization, the loss of reliance on traditional, taken-for-granted values. On the one hand, as noted before, this deprives people of guidelines in selecting their marriage partners; their choices become either overly emotional and impulsive (romantic) or overly rational (how much does he/she make, how big an apartment does he/she have, does he/she come from a good family, etc.). At the same time, secularization also means that the sources of meaning external to the individual become seriously depleted; personal ties and intimacy, that is, a few select individuals and relationships assume greater importance. Again, the end result is heightened expectations made upon marriage and the family. If one result of modernization, as previously implied, is the growing moral confusion of individuals and their difficulty to find new bases for making important choices, it should not be surprising that people begin to look for rational, sometimes institutional, solutions to personal problems. We are all familiar in American society with the proliferation of dubious experts, the almost endless varieties of counseling and therapy, computer matching, dating bureaus, advice columns in the press, manuals promising the easy, step-by-step conquest of every single personal problem—the enormous paraphernalia of aides and guides our vacillating society has conjured up to provide substitutes for efficient and consistent early socialization. It is more surprising that suggestions have been made, and received with enthusiasm in the Soviet Union, to introduce "electronic matchmakers" (and matrimonial bureaus) to make it easier for people to meet and because many people feel that "a computer could spare us many mistakes."[22] The possibility of computer dating or matchmaking in the Soviet Union (yet to be implemented) reflects the decline of traditional guidelines to mate selection and the urban anonymity of modern mass societies. Perhaps the interest in computer matching is also an indication of the still ascendant admiration Soviet people have for the marvels of technology and science.

The recent Soviet concern with sex education is also noteworthy in the context of modernization. The current discussions of its desirability reflect both the legacy of the official puritanism and a somewhat questionable belief in the perfectibility of personal relationships through organized effort. Some of the current proposals remain permeated by the paternalistic Victorian moral standards of Soviet officialdom. Noting that parents avoid enlightening their children about sexual matters, thus allowing "young people to find out about sex through cynical, dirty, lockerroom conversations," an expert proceeds to condemn standards that guide the behavior of many young people:

> There is no ignoring the fact that some of our young people are under the influence of the theory of "free love" currently in vogue in the West. "We live in a fast-paced age," they proclaim, and "we are going full-speed ahead after everything we can get out of life!" This attitude holds particular appeal for adolescents who are impulsive, inexperienced, rebellious and imitative and who live for the moment. . . . A primary task of sex education is to teach the young person to control his emotions and be modest. If all girls learn self-respect [*sic*], then we will not need to pass a law prohibiting hugging and kissing on the street. . . .
>
> To some of our young people, chastity is as antiquated a notion as modesty. . . . We doctors often see cases where excessive and promiscuous sex at an early age results in partial or complete impotence. . . .[23]

Many articles in the Soviet press these days urge sex education and/or marriage counseling. There is, according to these articles, "a crying need for a broad network of bureaus to provide counseling on the subject" in a "tactful, sensitive, delicate manner." Others insist that the difficulty lies in not acknowledging the psychological differences between men and women. "Doctors cite a wide range of sex differences that give rise to marital difficulties. For one, it is common knowledge [*sic*] that women tend to be emotional and men more rational, that women rely more on intuition and men on logic. Another normal difference is that at certain times women are irritable and supersensitive."[24]

Although, as the preceding indicates, the social forces and values impinging on the Soviet family and the moral standards supporting or subverting it have been varied and often contradictory, it still requires some explanation why there has been no radical questioning of the institution itself, nor a feminist movement that could have provided the vehicle for such criticisms. Let us first review briefly the circumstances which would seem conducive to the rise of such questioning, familiar in the American social setting.

To begin with, as we noted earlier, there had been a Soviet radical feminist tradition that seriously questioned the family in the early 1920s. Although this tradition did not survive, some of its objectives had been accomplished and conditions created which could have further contributed to "raising the consciousness" of Soviet women. If economic independence and access to higher education are essential to the development of feminist values, millions of Soviet women should have become feminists. Despite such accomplishments, peculiar liabilities in the lives of Soviet women have remained. Economic independence and entry into the professions have not been accompanied by a significant redistribution of domestic labor (hence the "two shifts"); nor has household work been sufficiently alleviated by the diffusion of labor-saving devices, convenient shopping, cleaning, laundry, or other supporting services. Child care has not become universally available or its quality satisfactory in many cases. Although these circumstances placed extra burdens on Soviet women, making family life more dificult and potentially less attractive, few women have drawn far-reaching conclusions regarding the institution itself. (On the other hand, it may be significant to note that most divorces are initiated by women.)[25] Three other circumstances might be mentioned conducive to disillusionment with the family by creating difficulties for the maintenance of close family ties: overcrowded housing with the resulting deprivations of privacy; separate job assignments for husbands and wives, leading to prolonged separation; and separate vacations due to the organization of resorts and assignments for vacations through trade unions or the place of work. None of these seemed to have led to disillusionment with an institution, the benefits of which are more difficult to realize under such conditions.

Concurrently, there has been a vast amount of discussion, questioning, and, indeed, frontal attacks on the family in the United States. Some of it is purely theoretical, but other types of criticism are translated into action, manifesting themselves in communal experiments, alternative life-styles, sexual separatism, and so forth. It might be a useful exercise to imagine how Soviet ideologues, social scientists, educated or uneducated women would respond to propositions coming from a prominent American feminist:

> The failure of the Russian Revolution is directly traceable to the failure of its attempts to eliminate the family and sexual repression. . . . Any

initial liberation under current socialism must always revert back to repression, because the family structure is the *source* of psychological, economic and political oppression.

Pregnancy is barbaric.

. . . people have forgotten what history has proven: that "raising" a child is tantamount to retarding his development. The best way to raise a child is to LAY OFF.

In a future, utopian, state of affairs:

Without the incest taboo, adults might return within a few generations to a more natural polymorphous sexuality. . . . Relations with children would include as much genital sex as the child was capable of—probably considerably more than we now believe—. . . . Adult/child and homosexual taboos would disappear. . . .

The revolt against the biological family could bring on the first successful revolution, or what was thought of by the ancients as the Messianic Age.[26]

It is not too difficult to understand why there is no feminist movement in the Soviet Union. There is not one because there are no other movements whose objectives would diverge from the official "definitions of the situation." From the official standpoint, the problems of Soviet women are not serious enough to warrant the emergence of some special interest group, constituency, or movement. As the officials see it, some problems may remain—and prevent women in some areas of life from attaining full equality—but they are being worked out. In any case, a feminist movement or feminist organizations would be politically divisive and ideologically intolerable. The male leadership knows best what is good for women (and for all members of society), and, by definition, there can be no conflict between the interests of men and women. In short, political conditions make it impossible for a feminist movement to exist.[27] (It would be even more difficult to conceive of the existence of a gay liberation movement which emerged in the United States in conjunction with, and possibly stimulated by, the feminist movement of recent times.)

We must also consider the possibility that the rise of a feminist movement in the Soviet Union has also been hindered by some of the policies of the regime favoring women. Certainly, the disappearance of any legally sanctioned discrimination and the equalization of the sexes in many areas of life removed some of the grievances of women.

Next to the official policies, the second major factor accounting for the absence of feminist groups may have to do with the attitude of

Soviet women themselves. Whatever their justified complaints and grievances (which come to light in opinion surveys or the correspondence columns of the press), they have not drawn conclusions similar to those of American radical feminists about their position and the part played by the family in their lives. This, in turn, requires further explanation. One is perhaps the general extinction of truly radical thinking in Soviet society after half a century of successfully enforced conformity to orthodoxy. Under such conditions, it is simply difficult to think of radical alternatives to *any* aspect of social life including the position of women and the family. Moreover, the conservative official thinking about the family and the relations between the sexes has also been reinforced by the remnants of traditional cultural values which originated in a largely peasant society.

There is yet another feature of Soviet society that acts as a brake on the development of utopian thinking of any kind and makes it difficult to entertain radical alternatives to existing social institutions and values. Soviet society, its prevailing values, organization, and political structure is generally uncongenial to the development of high expectations. One of the keys to the success of the Soviet system, and its stability, has been its ability to control expectations; that is, to keep them relatively low. Objective conditions, and political regimentation in particular, help to structure and dampen personal aspirations and expectations. Choices and options are fewer and more clear cut. People do not wonder about their identity, reflect on their personal growth, or ponder self-consciously what to do with their lives. The framework for major choices is established, far more clearly than in the United States. Even if today Soviet people expect more, especially material goods and services, such expectations are usually well defined, limited, and in theory capable of satisfaction. Soviet society has yet to produce large numbers of people (as the United States has) for whom material gratification soured, who despise affluence and consumer goods, and who have embarked on various unconventional ways to find spiritual fulfillment and meaning in life. Nor has Soviet society produced, or taken a tolerant view of, the type of individualism which in the United States is intertwined with high expectations and revolves around concern with the realization of putatively unique human potentials. The high expectations among a segment of the American population, at any rate, may also be related to what might be called the democratization of alienation and anomie. As Andrew Hacker observed:

> The emergence of individuality has changed self conceptions, creating discontents of a sort that were unlikely to occur to men and women of earlier times. Once persuaded that he is an "individual" entitled to realize

his assumed potentialities, a citizen will diagnose himself as suffering quite impressive afflictions. The intensity with which Americans now explore their egos arises from the conviction that even an average personality is a deep and unparalleled mechanism.[28]

Hacker's point is given further plausibility by the frequency with which the terms "self-realization," "self-expression," and "self-fulfillment" feature in American feminist discussions. This is not to suggest that women have been deluded into demanding more of these, but that the demand for them is part and parcel of a more diffuse longing for meaning and fulfillment in life which is related to the general rise of expectations and growth of individualism, and which is not limited to women.

In this context, it is also relevant to remind ourselves that the frontal attacks on the family and the growth of radical feminism in the United States had been closely associated, initially at any rate, with the rise of the radical Left and the counter-culture in the 1960s—both movements representing various types of radical questioning of existing social institutions and values. No such movements, trends, or currents of ideas have arisen in Soviet society that would have similarly facilitated the questioning of the family and the position of women. It should also be noted that while in the United States much of the radical feminist movement (as other radical groups) found their major reservoir of support on the campuses, there is no comparable mass base for dissent in the Soviet Union where university students as a rule are highly conformist and anxious to hang on to the advantages a college degree confers.

There is yet another circumstance which may provide clues to the absence of radical attacks on the family in the Soviet Union. Insofar as the type of family most severely criticized in the United States is that of the middle-class family,[29] these attacks are very much part of the general criticism of middle-class life-styles and values, which intensified in the 1960s (among members and descendants of the middle classes). Such criticism and questioning is not only nonexistent, but also totally foreign to Soviet people who have yet to develop contempt for middle-class aspirations and ways of life centering on privacy, security, emotional exclusiveness, and shared consumption. Indeed, it may not be an exaggeration to suggest that the proverbial, much despised[30] suburban house with the two-car garage and the various gadgets scattered around it, as well as the typical American middle-class leisure-time activities, are not only respectable but represent at this point in time a pinnacle of aspirations for millions of Soviet people. We must remember that Soviet people, and especially women, have yet to face a surfeit of consumer goods, privacy, or leisure. Moreover, the officially fostered forms of communalism, participation in public life, and deprivations of privacy have scarcely contributed to the development of an appetite for communal living experiments or alternatives to the isolation of the nuclear family.

Perhaps it is only a question of time or a question of further "modernization" before there will be a far-reaching reassessment of the family in Soviet society along the lines by now familiar to most of us in the United States. Yet it is hard to avoid feeling that Soviet society in the foreseeable future will not provide a hospitable environment for such criticism. Perhaps, in the final analysis, American society is in some ways more conducive to revolutionary thinking and the radical questioning of established social institutions (changing them is another matter) than Soviet society or most others. If the free circulation of ideas is a prerequisite of social change, the radical transformation of the family is more likely to take place in American than Soviet society.

Postscript 1982

The condition of women in other socialist societies is highly similar to that in the Soviet Union, although birth and divorce rates may (and do) diverge from the Soviet ones and the authorities may seek to keep down rather than raise birth rates (as in China). However, in no socialist country are women members of the highest decision-making bodies (politburo or equivalent; Mrs. Mao was a short-lived exception to this), and they generally cluster at the lower reaches of whatever hierarchy, political, occupational, or organizational, they belong to. The traditional roles of women—child care and household activities— have in all socialist societies been retained with outside work added on. Yet there is little evidence of the development of a feminist consciousness in any socialist society.

It should be noted here that a letter entitled "A Soviet Feminist"[31] reporting the imprisonment of a Soviet feminist and the existence of an underground feminist publication has been among the few recent indications that at least an embryonic or emergent feminist movement exists on the margins of Soviet society in the subcultures of dissent.

Notes

*Presented at a conference on Soviet women at Stanford University, Calif., in 1975.

1. See, for example, "Foreword" by Germaine Greer to Alexandra Kollontai, *Autobiography of a Sexually Emancipated Woman* (New York: Schocken, 1975).

2. Kollontai, however, would not go quite as far as to think in terms of a "sexual class system," "the tapeworm that must be eliminated first by any true revolution" (Shulamit Firestone, *The Dialectics of Sex* [New York: Morrow, 1970], p. 37). Nor was her work informed by preoccupation with man, the oppressor. Yet her writing does reveal some of the same conflicts contemporary radical feminists discuss in angrier tones. For example: "We, the women of the past generation, did not yet understand how to be free . . . our labor power . . . was dissipated in barren emotional experiences. . . . It was in fact an eternal defensive war against the intervention of the male into our ego, a struggle revolving around the problem-complex: work or marriage and love? . . . . We felt enslaved and tried to loosen the love bond. And after the eternally recurring struggle with the beloved man, we finally tore ourselves away and rushed toward freedom" A. Kollontai, *Autobiography,* pp. 7–8.

3. Meyer F. Nimkoff, ed., *Comparative Family Systems* (Boston: Houghton Mifflin, 1965), pp. 33–35; cited in F. Ivan Nye and Felix M. Berardo, *The Family—Its Structure and Interaction* (New York: Macmillan, 1973), p. 625.

4. Barrington Moore, Jr., "Thoughts on the Future of the Family," in his *Political Power and Social Theory* (Cambridge: Harvard Univ. Press, 1958).

5. S. G. Strumilin, "Family and Community in the Society of the Future," *Soviet Review* (Feb. 1961).

6. Leon Trotsky, *The Revolution Betrayed* (New York: Merit, 1965), pp. 145, 153.

7. The same point was made by Alexander Gerschenkron: "The dictators are likely to assume that looseness in matters of sex may loosen behavior in other areas, and in particular may affect the political discipline of the ruled" (*Continuity in History and Other Essays* [Cambridge: Harvard Univ. Press, 1968], p. 306).

8. The Chinese regime under Mao has been quite explicit about this.

9. This paragraph follows closely a discussion by the author in his *Soviet American Society: A Comparison* (New York: Oxford Univ. Press, 1973), pp. 258–62.

10. Prof. D. Valentei, "Problems of Social Life: On Demographic Behavior," trans. in CDSP, 13 Sept. 1972, p. 14.

11. Kharchev, the prominent family sociologist, for example, noted that "children raised by mothers alone are three to four times as likely as children raised by both parents to become involved in crime" ("Today's Family and Its Problems," *Zhurnalist,* trans. in CDSP, 21 March 1973).

12. Prof. B. Urlanis, "Father, Mother and Three Children," *Literaturnaya gazeta,* trans. in CDSP, 27 Dec. 1972, p. 8.

13. V. Perevedentsev, "Time to Get Married," *Soviet Sociology* (Spring 1972), pp. 378, 381.

14. "One, Two or Three?" *Literaturnaya gazeta,* trans. in CDSP, 7 Nov. 1973, p. 14.

15. D. Novoplyansky, "Reflections on Letters: Concerning the Family with Many Children," *Pravda,* trans. in CDSP, 27 Dec. 1972, p. 8.

16. The highest divorce rates prevail among Latvians (4.2 per thousand population) and Russians (3.7), and the lowest among the Tadzhiks, Uzbekhs and Kirgiz (1.1). Cf. *Problemy byta, braka i sem'i* (Vilnius, 1970), p. 115.

17. Although limited in scope and suffering from a lack of commitment to fundamental change, the official concern with the problems of working women is not purely rhetorical. One reflection of such concerns is the large volume of sociological research inspired by the desire to improve their situation. A good example of such research is the conference volume entitled *Dinamika izmeneniia polozheniia zhenshchiny i sem'ia* (Moscow, 1972). The various papers of the volume are addressed to a wide variety of highly specific issues and problems relevant to working women (education, free time, urban-rural differences, access to consumer goods and services, etc.).

18. In the U.S. there were 715,000 divorces in 1970; hence the rates in the two countries are not vastly dissimilar (Nye, *The Family*, p. 566). See also A. Kharchev, "Today's Family and Its Problems," *Zhurnalist*, trans. in CDSP, 21 March 1973, p. 19.

19. A highly relevant finding concerning the relationship between family size and material well-being was reported by William M. Mandel: "The *larger* the apartment space per person, the *fewer* women want a second child! The explanation is that those with larger apartments are the better educated. Their jobs are more interesting, they have wider interests outside work and home, and their notions of child-rearing are more time consuming" (William M. Mandel, *Soviet Women* [Garden City, N.Y.: Doubleday, 1975], p. 235).

20. Quoted in P. Hollander, *Soviet American Society*, pp. 278–79.

21. Factors and processes associated by Soviet sociologists with both modernization and rising divorce rates are very similar to those mentioned by their Western colleagues. See, for example, pp. 116–21 in *Problemy, byta, braka i sem'i*.

22. V. Shiliapentokh, "Acquaintanceships and Weddings," *Soviet Review* (Spring 1972). Manuals designed for popular appeal and advising people about the problems of love, sex, family, and marriage are also beginning to make an appearance in the USSR. A good example is A. Beliavskii and E. Finn, *Liubov'i Kodeks* (Moscow, 1973). The volume is also recommended for Party propagandists, agitators, and members of comrades' courts.

23. Lidia Bogdanovich (Doctor of Medicine), "Notes of a Psychiatrist: Educating the Feelings," *Ogonyok*, trans. in CDSP, 6 Dec. 1972, p. 18.

24. Ada Baskina, "A Little Family Quarrel," *Literaturnaya gazeta*, trans. in CDSP, 23 May 1973, p. 14.

25. Mandel, *Soviet Women*, p. 228.

26. Firestone, *Dialectics*, pp. 212, 198, 91, 240. For a summary of feminist critiques of marriage and the nuclear family, see Jessie Bernard, *Women and the Public Interest* (Chicago/New York, 1971), pp. 252–63. See also Caroline Bird, "The Case Against Marriage," in L. K. Howe, ed., *The Future of the Family* (New York: Simon and Schuster, 1973).

27. This, however, still does not explain why there has been no underground feminist movement similar to the movements or groupings of political dissidents. In theory, at any rate, some Soviet women could have attempted to organize themselves and express their protest in the manner of other dissident groups. The absence of any such known attempt suggests that factors other than the official intolerance of feminist movements are also at work.

28. Andrew Hacker, *The End of the American Era* (New York: Atheneum, 1971), pp. 167–68.
29. See, for example, L. K. Howe, "Introduction," in L. K. Howe, ed., *The Future of the Family* (New York: Simon and Schuster, 1972).
30. By American social critics and their followers, that is.
31. "A Soviet Feminist," letter to the *New York Review of Books,* 25 June 1981.

10.
The Subordination of Literature to Politics: Socialist Realism in a Historical and Comparative Perspective

Was socialist realism a passing aberration or an enduring feature of the politicized cultural life of certain social systems? A quaint episode of twentieth-century literary history or a powerful device of political indoctrination? A chronicle of social change or a guide to the aspirations and values of the political elites who forced it upon the writers? Was it a product of enthusiasm and commitment or an outpouring of literary hacks and opportunists? Did this framework for the politicization of the arts appear in identical format in various countries at different times, or was it shaped by time and circumstance and the cultural setting where it appeared? Is socialist realism a matter of interest to literary historians, political scientists, or sociologists?

Because socialist realism, at least in its self-conscious design and format, first appeared in the early 1930s in the Soviet Union, thereafter spreading to many other countries that were influenced by the Soviet example, there is certainly sufficient historical perspective from which to evaluate this phenomenon. As Sinyavsky noted, socialist realism is by definition a contradiction. If there is socialist realism, why not capitalist or Catholic realism? The attempt to combine realism with political-ideological tendentiousness represents an effort to merge in one theoretical framework disparate elements. Though contradictory to its core, the effort to harness literary creativity to both highly specific and broad political objectives has been attempted many times in the past in socialist countries.

The rulers of thoroughly politicized societies have been determined to use the arts and literature in particular as an arm in the propaganda process in order to solidify their power. Above all, they have sought to use literature in attaining their most ambitious goal—that of the transformation of human beings, within the context of reshaping social and political institutions. A discussion of socialist realism in a comparative context (stimulated by Joe C. Huang's study of Chinese novels since 1949) also raises the question of value judgments, ethnocentrism, and cultural relativity. Although both the critics and the defenders of socialist realism agree that such literature is thoroughly politicized, they obviously diverge in their assessments of its effect and quality. The problem is not merely one of aesthetics but is part of the broader issue of the impact of politics on other realms, such as the arts. In a related fashion, the matter also involves the links between totalitarian politics and literary policy and the contribution of the arts to the enrichment or impoverishment of life.

It is tempting to argue that socialist realism, especially as it was practiced in the Soviet Union and Eastern Europe under Stalin, illustrated the dire consequences that ensued when politics invaded the arts. The literature of that period was characterized not only by tedium, predictable plots, editorializing dialogues, stereotyped characters, and all too obvious and unconvincing ideological messages, but, more importantly, by deliberate and startling misrepresentations and distortions of reality. The command to portray social reality in its "revolutionary development," to produce "forward-looking art," to discern "the seeds of the future in the present," or to seize the "typical" often resulted in the presentation of a world of make-believe—one that was supposed to exist or was supposedly coming into existence according to the ideological prescriptions and visions of the holders of power. Thus the "theory" of socialist realism produced bad literature (and art) not because it was politicized art per se, but because the sources of politicization lay not in the motivation of individual writers, but in the ideological fiat that was forced upon them. Spontaneous political commitment may produce good art. But when writers are instructed in detail how to present idealized versions of reality and are punished if they fail to do so, the results are, as a rule, unsatisfactory. Indeed, even the official critics have never tired of complaining that many of the writers striving to carry out the established literary policies have failed to create appealing, artistically persuasive works and have failed to reconcile the faithful execution of the Party line with artistic accomplishment. As a result, the political message overwhelmed the aesthetic medium. It has proved difficult to preach convincingly through the pages of fiction, let alone to preach under command.

Art (or what is left of art when such attempts are being made) can be and has been subordinated to politics in various ways. As a minimum, the rulers may simply proscribe the intrusion of ideas they consider undesirable and prevent the writers' political ideas from gaining expression. This is simple censorship and is designed to eliminate unorthodox political content from the arts and to keep them safely apolitical. Policies of this type may enhance escapist themes, making literature a vehicle of diversion. Such policies are usually pursued by regimes that wish to neutralize literature but are not inclined to assign it political tasks. What distinguishes socialist realism from this approach is the intention to reeducate the population. Socialist realist literature is not merely purged of unorthodox ideas, it is an active arm of the agitprop apparatus and is designed to contribute to the drastic overhauling of popular values. It is expected in particular to influence behavior in subtle ways by providing models to emulate (or recoil from) in those areas of life that are difficult to bring under adequate institutional control. The latter include personal relationships and the proper balancing of private versus public interests and commitments. More will be said in this chapter about these central aspects of socialist realism.

Before examining the Soviet and Chinese varieties of socialist realism, in connection with the books under review,[1] I would like to suggest that the concept of totalitarianism, which is rarely used these days, remains helpful for a better understanding of the origins and functions of socialist realism. This is worth noting since even when the concept was more widely used, relatively little attention was paid to the extent to which totalitarian political aspirations and ideologies shaped literary policies and products. This is not to say that historical-cultural traditions of literary moralizing and stereotyping did not facilitate the rise of socialist realism, but to note that without the totalitarian ideological impulses and system of political controls, socialist realism could not have become the prevailing doctrine of all artistic activity. It is symbolic, in this regard, that according to the official Soviet account, the very term owes its existence to the personification of totalitarian rule, Stalin.[2] Likewise, it stands to reason that with the relaxation of totalitarian controls over other areas of life following Stalin's death, socialist realism has also waned. At least, it is not enforced in practice, even if it retains its official standing as the only correct approach to the arts. C. Vaughan James's book provides numerous reminders of the latter point, including Brezhnev's exhortations on the subject.

Despite many ideological disagreements between the Soviet and Chinese regimes, both converge in affirming the subordination of art to politics,[3] although the Chinese have been more consistent in enforcing such subordination. Indeed, from the Chinese point of view, the Soviet relaxation of controls is among the repulsive heresies of the Soviet "revisionists." Thus, for example, an official Chinese source detected poisonous pacifism in some Soviet movies of the late 1950s, such as the *Ballad of a Soldier,* whose purpose was "to spread the dread of war and peddle the philosophy of survival" (cited in James, p. 133).

To say that the Chinese regime has been more seriously committed to socialist realism than the Soviet Union because it has not gone through a liberalizing process such as de-Stalinization is not very illluminating. Nor would it be sufficient to suggest that the difference had to do with the persisting totalitarian character of the Chinese system—true as that may be. A more specific explanation may be found in the greater determination of the Chinese leadership to reshape the individual through reeducation (and not just to restructure social institutions), to demand not only external conformity but a change of attitude, and to wage war on privacy accordingly. These policies, in turn, presumably rest on the Chinese official belief (deeper than that of the Soviet or held with more conviction) that purposeful and tenacious manipulation can drastically alter human nature and personality and make it conform to official values. The strict subordination of literature to official controls and its use as a device for reshaping the masses are not the only indications of such beliefs. A whole series of Chinese policies and control mechanisms, which are designed to change attitudes by group pressure, testify to the convictions of the Chinese leadership that human nature is extremely malleable and that radical social transformations cannot be achieved without a corresponding change in personal attitudes and values.

In light of the previous statements, it is particularly interesting to compare Chinese and Soviet literary stereotypes (such as those that prevailed in their purest form under Stalin) because the foremost function of socialist realist literary works is to provide models of behavior for the reader.[4] Since Huang's study provides a detailed description of numerous Chinese novels, plots, and heroes, it is possible to reach at least some impressionistic conclusions about the degree of similarity between the two sets of literary stereotypes.

To begin with, not unlike the Soviet case, Chinese policies dictated the polarization of literary characters and especially the chief protagonists; that is, the characters had to be clearly recognizable personifications of good and evil. The theory of "middle men" of the early 1960s, which was proposed to reduce such polarization, was subsequently criticized by the authorities and declared a heresy.

The "counterrevolutionary" nature of this theory (which tried to justify the literary presentation of ideologically mixed characters) was criticized as follows:

> Should our literature and art focus on the portrayal of positive characters among the workers, peasants and soldiers or on the so-called "neither good nor bad" men in the middle? . . . This is the fundamental question of

the position of writers and artists as well as a fundamental question of the division between the socialist literary line and the anti-socialist literary line. The promotion of "portraying men in the middle" and "intensification of realism" in effect encourages writers not to portray the positive characters, not to praise the revolutionary spirit of the people, and not to inspire the people to progress, but to stress their backwardness and wavering attitude, to publicize or expose their shortcomings, and to lead the people to retreat.[5]

According to Huang, the tendency toward a polarized, hero-villain approach has strong roots in Chinese cultural history and traditional values and is congenial to the mass of readers "brought up in a society where human behavior has always been seen in terms of black and white" (p. 271). Although such traditions explain a predisposition to accept literary stereotypes that many Western readers would find unconvincing, *the content* of vice and virtue has a more current, ideological-political derivation. In the Soviet case too, it has been observed that postrevolutionary literary policies and practices had a continuity—of a debatable extent—with prerevolutionary traditions and outlook (e.g., see James, p. 2). In the Soviet Union as in China, the extent to which literature came to be infused with political criteria can be understood only by grasping the characteristics of the political system that imposed its values on literature, whatever historical traditions may have facilitated this.

A brief comparison of a few attributes of the positive hero in Soviet and Chinese novels heightens the impression of much similarity between the two species of socialist realism. Although the attributes of the Soviet positive hero are familiar enough, at least for specialists, we know much less about such figures in Chinese literature, for obvious reasons (i.e., the language barrier and the paucity of translations). Yet the similarities encountered, as they unfold in Huang's detailed survey, are not altogether startling. Nor, however, can they be taken completely for granted, given the cultural and historical differences between the two societies. The commonality of the two stereotypes derives clearly from the political functions they perform. In particular, the attributes of the positive hero in Soviet novels, found in an earlier study,[6] seem present in the Chinese counterparts. They were the following: Party-mindedness (*partiinost*),[7] patriotism, collectivism, vigilance, propensity to hate (the enemy), activism, love of work, discipline, modesty, optimism, puritanism, selective emotionalism, the propensity to shame, credulousness, instant enthusiasm, lack of spontaneity (or contrived spontaneity), adaptability, and the drive for self-improvement.

Space does not allow a detailed survey of all these similarities but a few may be mentioned, as they appear in Huang's analysis. As one might expect—in view of the intensity of the indoctrination drive—Chinese positive heroes are on the whole even more "positive" than their Soviet counterparts and, if possible, even more politicized. Huang notes that "not a single novel dwells on the private world of the individual." Such heroes excel in subordinating their private lives and selves to the public domain and the political demands made by the regime. Their self-denial and puritanism remind one of Pavel Korchagin, the venerable hero of Soviet socialist realism in Ostrovsky's *The Steel Is Tempered* (a model still upheld by Soviet literary authorities), who gave his whole life, health, and energy to the Cause. For example, Huang quotes the portrayal of a Chinese soldier:

> Ta-yung had a bandage around his head; his face was dark and lean, his cheeks were sunken, his eyes and nostrils full of sand. His black eyebrows had turned yellowish as a result of burning; his eyes seemed larger than ever. Clay and blood stains, burned spots, and bullet holes spread all over his threadbare uniform. The sleeves were burned off from the elbow down, the trousers torn to pieces below knee level. His bare feet, smeared with blood and clay, were so swollen that they appeared thick and large.
>
> He stood stiffly in front of the commanders, his mouth quivering as if he wanted to say something, but his swollen, scorched lips disobeyed him. . . .
>
> There was a certain childlike shyness in Ta-yung's usually brave and confident eyes. . . . He said: "It's nothing. We completed our task of covering the retreat and I was able to bring our soldiers to join the main force. On our way back the enemy attacked us several times and we fought back!" (p. 155).

Huang summarizes the attitude and moral development of another famous positive hero:

> The theme of the novel is essentially the gradual transformation in Ou-yang Hai, which prompts him to make a personal sacrifice on every occasion, even to the point of sacrificing his life. In effect, however, the hero seems so ready to die that he appears looking for just such an opportunity.
>
> Ou-Yang Hai's death is caused by his attempt to push a horse, loaded with a small cannon, out of the rail tracks. In doing this he saves the passengers on the train, his comrades by the roadside, and valuable state property, but he is crushed beneath the massive steel wheels. . . . His wounds are fatal; his life lingers only a short while. He dies on a hospital bed with a calm smile, suggesting he feels that has completed an important task.

The hero's state of mind, before sacrificing his life, is described as follows:

> In that moment of crisis he had only one clear compelling thought: "I must not permit the destruction of people's lives and property. The time has come to die for the ideal of Communism. A true Communist must plunge forward" (pp. 314–15).

Below is a dialogue between a Communist about to be executed and a Kuomintang official in charge of his prisoner:

> "There is a little news I do not wish to conceal," Hsu P'eng-fei smiled viciously as he studied Hsu Yun-feng's confident face. "The Communist victory is already in sight, yet what a pity you can't witness it! What does Mr. Hsu feel, here and now facing his own death?" Hsu Yun-feng was unperturbed, smiling. "This I can tell you without reservation. As an ordinary worker, mistreated and oppressed in the old society, I finally chose the revolutionary road and became a man feared by the reactionaries. Looking back at the road I've traveled, I've only a sense of pride. I'm happy to witness the victory of the proletarians in China. The surge of the revolutionary tide, like the wind blowing away scattered clouds, proves that my ideal coincides with the wish of all the Chinese people. That gives me infinite strength. . . . There can be no higher glory than to link your own life with the ever youthful revolutionary cause of the working class" (pp. 101–102).

The similarities between Chinese and Soviet positive heroes extend beyond their selflessness and self-denial. There is also much emphasis on puritanism in sexual matters. As Huang observes: "A man's sterling character, in a truly Chinese sense, is best tested in his resistance to the temptation of woman" (p. 255). Likewise, he notes that "the idea that the most intimate relationship exists only in the union of man and woman, both body and soul, is most un-Communist" (p. 61).

There are also many similarities between Soviet and Chinese negative heroes. For example, as in the Soviet case, Chinese authors often succeed in presenting their negative characters in more colorful and interesting ways than those who embody virtue. But Chinese authors too had to grapple with the dilemma of strength versus weakness—a problem that political propagandists have to face in portraying the enemy in non-literary sources as well. If the enemy is presented as a "paper tiger," people may not take the threat he represents seriously enough. But if he is presented as very strong, it may have a demoralizing effect. As Huang puts it: "If villains are too powerful or too cunning in their confrontation with heroes, they may appear to overpower or outwit the heroes" (p. 47).

Although the differences between the Soviet and Chinese versions of socialist realism appear less significant than the similarities, a few of them should be noted. Thus it is at least possible that Chinese novels present a less distorted version of reality than the Soviet ones, insofar as social change in China met more popular approval than it did in the Soviet Union and official policies had more popular support there. This, in turn, must have made the task of writers easier because there was less discrepancy between the social-political realities of their society and the political aspirations and literary policies of the leaders. In other words, it might have been less difficult for Chinese writers to idealize the social order than for their Soviet counterparts because the gap between ideal and actual was smaller.[8] Nevertheless, in China the political controls over the work of writers seem to have been more intense (at least in certain periods) than in the Soviet Union and more closely supervised by appropriate groups. For example, the author of the novel cited previously (about the soldier-hero who sacrificed his life),

> was ordered by the leadership of an army stationed in Canton to collect material about Ou-yang Hai's life and to write a novel about the hero's glorious martyrdom. He was transferred to Ou-yang Hai's former company to experience the conditions of the hero's life. . . . In writing the novel, the author used about sixty of more than a hundred stories he heard about Ou-yang Hai. After each draft, he would read the story to the political commissar of Ou-yang Hai's corps and to the men of Ou-yang's squad, to the Party committee of Ou-yang's home county, to the cadres of the commune, and to Ou-yang's relatives and friends (p. 316).

Such activities followed from the theory of "three in one," which meant that "the army leadership decides on the theme, the masses participate as critics, and the author only provides the writing skill" (p. 318). It should be noted that the total output of Chinese writers has been far smaller than that of their Soviet counterparts and has declined even further since the Cultural Revolution. This would suggest that literature has played a somewhat lesser role in the overall propaganda effort in China than in the Soviet Union, perhaps in part because of China's lower literacy rates.

In assessing the Huang and James books, it should be pointed out that they are very different in scope and goals. Huang's objective is "to reconstruct the operation of the Communist system under various circumstances, more or less in chronological sequence" (p. xiii), or to use the novels as sources of information about Chinese society in the Communist period. Given this concern, his discussion of literary policies and theories is limited and more tangential than that of James. By contrast, James intends to make a contribution to a better understanding of Soviet socialist realism by placing it in a historical and political-ideological context and examining in detail Soviet literary policies and pronouncements from the October Revolution to the present. He also presents or summarizes many official Soviet statements on the subject.

The problem which Huang's undertaking faces is common to all attempts to treat literary works as reflections of social reality, but it has been rendered more difficult by the circumstances of the case—primarily the ability of the Chinese power holders to control and manipulate literary output. Sociologists of literature can never make any safe assumptions about the degree of correspondence between social realities and their literary reflection. The sources of distortion are almost endless, ranging from the most intangible ones, such as the writer's personal bias, predisposition, and values, to the crudest, such as external censorship and pressure. The fact that novels are informative about certain social realities is beyond dispute. The extent and nature of such information remain in question, however. Different social-political and literary conditions invite different assumptions about the relationship between society and literature, as different pressures will bear on the writer in different political settings. In his foreword, Huang indicates full awareness of this issue. "The problem seems to be to distinguish . . . the empirical from the normative component, or more plainly, to distinguish reality from propaganda. It is a totally legitimate question, but unfortunately there can be no answer. A fundamental limitation in the study of China is the impossibility of verification" (p. xi).

Despite this awareness, Huang appears to treat the novels at face value, as accurate indicators of the various events, social transformations, and human attitudes depicted. He assumes that the novels surveyed are by and large helpful in reconstructing the social history of the period and says little about the extent to which they may contain deliberate misrepresentations of reality, whether social-political or personal. Although this approach is certainly legitimate and often fruitful—as, for example, when the novels reveal facts that we have no way of knowing from other sources, such as widespread peasant resistance to collectivization (p. 282)—it might have been better to treat the novels primarily as a repository of information about official values, aspirations, ideals, and policies rather than as social history. In highly politicized and controlled societies, one can, as a rule, learn from literature more about the *rulers'* values and attitudes than about any other aspect of social reality. Another shortcoming of the Huang book, more organizational than substantive, is the lack of integration between the discussion of particular novels and the analysis of relevant literary policies. Thus the chronological structure of the book sometimes obscures the relationship between politics and literature, and the novels are at times discussed in an ideological vacuum, as it were. An introduction for each chapter sketching the prevailing literary policies of the period would have been helpful. At the same time, the author accomplished a great deal by providing illuminating summaries and analyses of a large number of Chinese novels, thereby enabling the nonspecialist to learn about Chinese Communist literature and life. Nevertheless, the main problem of the work is hard to overlook. Huang asks at the end of his survey: "If the novels we have studied truthfully reflect life in China, what then has happened in the last half century under communism?" (p. 321). The "if" remains unresolved, and hence the generalizations that follow the question, though plausible, have insufficient evidence to support them.

James's *Soviet Socialist Realism* is a more modest undertaking and is largely free from difficulties of this kind. It is a concise, well-organized examination of the origins and survival of socialist realism and its intimate integration with political objectives and ideologies.

Both volumes serve to remind us that when theories such as socialist realism emerge and predominate in a society, literature becomes a subject of interest less for the literary critic or historian than for the student of society and politics.

Notes

1. C. Vaughan James, *Soviet Socialist Realism—Origins and Theories* (New York: St. Martin's Press, 1974), and Joe C. Huang, *Heroes and Villains in Communist China—The Contemporary Chinese Novel as a Reflection of Life* (New York: Pica Press, 1973).
2. "The commonly alleged origin of the term 'socialist realism' is of some interest, both anecdotal and in view of the importance sometimes attached to it. Throughout the twenties and into the thirties various suggestions have been made: proletarian realism . . . tendentious realism . . . monumental realism . . . communist realism . . . and in October 1932, at a meeting of writers in Gorky's flat, the subject again came up for discussion. Stalin, who was also present, listened for a while and then intervened: 'If the artist is going to depict our life correctly, he cannot fail to observe and point out what is leading it toward socialism. So this will be socialist art. It will be socialist realism' " (Quoted in James, p. 86).
3. Thus it would be hard to imagine how the Chinese could find fault with the following Soviet summary (put forth during the reign of "arch revisionist" Khrushchev). According to this statement, the tasks of art were "to educate [man] in the spirit of collectivism and love of work, socialist internationalism and patriotism, and high moral principles of the new society and the spirit of Marxism-Leninism. . . . We must develop in Soviet man our Communist morality, at the root of which is dedication to Communism and irreconcilable

hostility to its enemies; acknowledgment of social obligations; active participation in working for the common good; voluntary conformity with the
basic rules of communal living; comradely mutual aid, honesty, justice and
intolerance of infringements of social order" (Quoted in James, pp. 94–95).
4. For a discussion of such models in Soviet literature, see ch. 2 of this volume.
5. Editorial Board, "Portraying 'Man in the Middle' is the Literary Proposition
of the Bourgeoisie," *Wen-ipao* (Literary Gazette), Sept. 1964. Quoted in
Huang, p. 272.
6. Hollander, "Models of Behavior."
7. The concept cannot be fully applied to the Chinese case after the Cultural
Revolution, which was, in a sense, anti-Party. It does, however, remain
applicable insofar as it stands for the total politicization of outlook, attitude,
and behavior on the basis of criteria supplied by the supreme leaders, who
may or may not choose to identify themselves closely with the Party.
8. Since Mao's death and from the vantage point of 1983, we may no longer
be so sure of this.

11.
Public and Private in Hungary:
A Travel Report (1979)

My visit to Hungary was neither an exercise in tourism nor sociological fact-finding; it was a melancholy mission of visiting aged and ailing parents. Since I was born in Hungary (which I left in 1956), I carried with me a mixture of sentimentality and detachment: sentimentality because I grew up in Hungary, detachment because I have been away for over twenty years. I walked the streets of Budapest at once as an outsider and insider, stranger and native son, resting my eyes on sights both familiar and exotic. My Hungarian, after a long period of disuse, came alive after about three days, and I regularly "passed" for a resident Hungarian.

I flew from New York to Frankfurt and in Frankfurt transferred to a Hungarian Airlines flight (the plane was Soviet made). Whereas American stewardesses are no longer uniformly young and dazzling, thanks to the liberation of women and some lawsuits, Hungarian Airlines obviously still believes that young and attractive women are to be preferred in such jobs. We were welcomed aboard American style (in Hungarian, English, and German): "Captain Kovacs and his crew . . . etc." "Hungarian Airlines" was painted on the plane in Hungarian and English. (Later, I also noticed in several public places in Budapest that when information was given in one foreign language only, it was in English; if in more than one foreign language, they were English, German, and Russian.)

The first visual impressions on arrival were comforting. Budapest Airport (the biggest in Hungary) is cozy; the luggage was coming off one conveyor belt and about twenty people were waiting for it. Everything is easy to find. The charms of smallness are palpable, especially after the organized chaos of John F. Kennedy Airport.

Traffic in Budapest is quite heavy. I was told that there are 800,000 cars in Hungary (population 10.5 million), and most of them are in Budapest. Supposedly, 300,000 applications for the ownership of private automobiles are pending. The types of cars seen in Budapest reflect both political change and social stratification. When I was growing up, there was a substantial number of American and British cars, virtually all of them official. At present American and British cars can be hardly seen; the only American ones I saw were in front of the U.S. embassy. There are in general very few Western cars with one exception: the big, black Mercedes which has apparently become the official status symbol, that is, for higher officials. I have never seen a greater concentration of them in any capital of Europe or in any American city. Perhaps they are more noticeable in Budapest in the absence of other Western luxury cars. They can be seen even in front of offices of limited importance: for example, the office concerned with Hungarian waterways (not even a ministry). The rest of the cars are Soviet Fiats (said to be of good quality even by Hungarians not given to praising anything originating in the USSR), East German "Trabants" (small, noisy two-cylinder cars), Romanian Renaults (called Dacia), Czech Skodas, and Polish Fiats. In addition to the officials, only some of the private entrepreneurs ("Maszek" in Hungarian) can afford a Mercedes—I was told repeatedly.

The private entrepreneurs are a new, or relatively recent, elite. Their incomes were discussed in tones of hushed reverence. They are shoe-makers, tailors, dressmakers, electricians, plumbers, car mechanics, carpenters, house painters, owners of small grocery stores, and makers of knitwear. Their services meet real needs and they prosper. Working in tiny shops, workshops, or in their own apartments they may earn eight times the amount a beginning engineer or doctor makes, two or three times that of the manager of an important factory or department head in an office. It is hard to know if their good fortunes are being generally resented or not; probably less so than the privileges of the officials. Well-known artists, musicians, performers, writers, and athletes also command large incomes; but this is the general pattern in Communist countries, not something peculiar to Hungary. Peasants are not doing badly either, although agriculture is totally collectivized; their household plots yield enough to sell at high prices in the free markets. The collective farms too are generally more prosperous and productive than in the Soviet Union.

Everyone I met, except my parents, owned one of the small cars mentioned. Also, in every home I visited (about fourteen) there were huge TV sets (Hungarian made), a few of them in color. (Some people expressed astonishment when, upon inquiry, it was disclosed that I do not possess a color TV set in the United States.) In most homes, there were small refrigerators and washing machines, some of them made in Italy or Yugoslavia and automatically assumed to be better than the Hungarian product. Hungary certainly qualifies as a "consumer society," and people consume with relish and without guilt to the best of their financial ability. Hungarian versions of "affluence" are not felt to be empty for those who have experienced them, largely because they are more difficult to attain and because of their novelty. Thus material comforts—including the second home (however small) with a tiny garden, and an occasional trip abroad—manage to provide a fair amount of meaning to life; they are worth striving for. Western products are still revered. In one home, I was startled to see the lady of the house appear in a "Los Angeles Police Department" shirt. In another home, the husband displayed with great pride a Princess telephone he acquired abroad.

Unlike most socialist societies, the network of various catering establishments in Hungary—restaurants, espresso shops, patisseries—is quite remarkable. Even in many villages I noted—on the few short trips I took—restaurants or coffee bars. This is noteworthy because rural areas in Hungary used to be proverbially backward and almost totally lacking in such amenities. Improvements in rural housing, and especially the now widespread use of brick, was also striking. (In the past, peasant homes were made of a type of adobe or mud bricks.) As far as the supply of goods in general is concerned, in Budapest it is reasonably good, but there are the typical mysterious shortages or bottlenecks. For instance, when I was there it was impossible to buy electric toasters and wicks for cigarette lighters, among other things.

(I suggested to various friends and acquaintances that in my estimation the standard of living resembled that in Italy. This proposition elicited unanimous disagreement as they believed that it was lower in Hungary.)

Having become an environmentally conscious American academic who favors public transportation without relying on it, I found the Budapest system of public transportation impressive. There is a comprehensive network of streetcar and bus lines supplemented by the old and new subways. The new one is modern, efficient, and fast; all forms of public transportation are very cheap. Conductors have been eliminated from all streetcars and buses; people either carry season tickets or buy them at tobacco stores and punch them as they get aboard. I found the interaction among people on the streetcars and buses more civilized than it used to be; in the past, public behavior of this type reflected a fierce struggle for survival (to get on or off), a survival-of-the-fittest mentality. People now appeared more polite than I had recalled. Certainly, the politeness of waiters, cabdrivers, and shop assistants was not disinterested, especially since Hungary boasts a tipping economy of allegedly oriental dimensions (even in the hospitals, I was told, nurses are routinely tipped, and doctors too; on the other hand, doctors will also routinely make house calls). But the politeness of many Hungarians may have other explanations as well. For one thing, the language itself is rich in hierarchical and deferential gradations of greeting and address; there are still some relics of the niceties and mannerisms of bygone gentry-feudal Hungary. The manners of the gentry-nobility used to be the models or trend setters. There are also other remnants of their way of life: hunting is said to be a preferred recreation of what people call the Party-aristocracy.

The questions I was most often asked about life in the United States had to do with my housing conditions, rather than income and make of car. But what impressed my interlocutors most was the American idea, and reality, of "options." They were nonplussed, for instance, upon learning that my wife used to be a high school teacher who subsequently switched to law school and became a lawyer. "This sort of thing could not happen here," I was told. "First, the regime discourages, indeed disallows, people from getting more than one degree (there is a word for it: 'degree hoarding'), especially in disparate fields—it is just not economical. Secondly, most people would not entertain such ideas since it is difficult enough to get a higher education in one field. Thirdly, who would support such a woman (or man) who decides, for no other reason than a notion of personal fulfillment or change of interests, to undertake a new course of study?"

There is a profound difference between the Hungarian (East European) and American attitude toward "options." People just don't switch gears abruptly here; they don't change occupations, appearances, identities, ways of life, and places of residence lightly or easily. And, despite high divorce rates, mate selection too is approached in a serious, calculating frame of mind. There is confirmation of this in the personal advertisements (in daily newspapers), all of which are explicitly matrimonial in their objective. Here is a representative sampling:

> College graduate, youthful widow, with nice apartment and pension looking for partner for life [a Hungarian for spouse] who is handsome, over 170 centimeters tall, is a widower and college graduate, up to ages 65–68.

> I am a 60-year-old, youthful, industrious widow with no children, owner of a house with all conveniences [i.e., usually means hot and cold water, electricity and gas] and a garden plot. I would like to meet a man of similar good looks, a skilled worker without any bad habits.

> I am looking forward to a letter from a skilled worker who leads a sober life, who would like to meet, for the purpose of marriage, a 55-year-old, industrious widow without any children. I have financial means, a house with all conveniences, garden. Those of similar material circumstances preferred.

> A 24-year-old, attractive, brunette college graduate, 164 cm tall, looking for a spouse 180 cm tall, warm hearted, correctly behaved, college graduate.

A 168 cm tall, 60 kg weight, 44-year-old attractive blonde woman in a technical line of work with an apartment and telephone would like to meet a good-natured tall, college graduate up to age 53. No adventurers please.

A lady in high position with corresponding financial means and a car would like to meet a tall man of some means, up to 43 years old.

A 165 cm tall, 62-year-old single man with full control of an apartment in Budapest looking for an appropriate lady with a view to marriage. Those interested in music and books preferred.

A 48-year-old planner divorced with no bad habits would like to meet an attractive woman with a nice figure between 38–43 years old, no taller than 165 cm, independent, pleasant, understanding, family-oriented, white collar worker. . . . I would prefer to hear from somebody with an apartment in Budapest.

Mechanical engineer 30 years old, 177 cm tall, wants to meet for marital purposes a definitely good-looking lady or divorcee up to age 30 of some financial means. I have apartment and car.

Handsome, 183 cm tall, 52 years old, healthy, not fat, interested in the arts, sober worker in technical field with his own house and garden (also, car and garage). Looking for independent, buxom lady up to 54 years old, at least 163 cm tall, with her own home.

What is one to make of these ads which are quite typical of those appearing daily in Budapest newspapers? I plead ignorance of the deeper significance of the obsessive concern with height and do not recall similarly pervasive preoccupations in my youth. Perhaps the specification of acceptable heights is just part of a generally sober and meticulous approach to these matters—an approach dominated by the material, marital, and bodily criteria at the expense of the romantic element. Of course, to suggest that Hungarians are unromantic flies in the face of all conventional stereotypes. Yet they seem to be, at least those who advertise. But many are middle-aged or older which makes a difference. Still, one cannot fail to be impressed by the emphasis on the material underpinnings: house, garden, car, apartment, telephone, good job, and financial security—matters no self-respecting male or female advertising in the personal column of the *New York Review of Books* (or similar places) would be caught dead mentioning!

Social position and status are obviously not matters of indifference here. The pool of eligibles is narrowed not only by specifications of height, but also by insisting on a college degree or the possession of some "skill." By contrast, little is said about what would be considered truly personal and important attributes in American culture. A comparison of the Hungarian advertisements with those appearing in American publications speaks volumes of the differences between values and expectations. On the one hand, there is a serious and untroubled concern with matters material and quantifiable; on the other, there are fanciful flights of individualism and fantasies of personal uniqueness and fulfillment.

The attitudes toward marriage (at any rate as reflected in the advertisements) are not the only expressions of a conventional and unromantic approach to morality and the relationship between the sexes. The latter remain, in many respects, characterized by the persistence of traditional "role definitions" barely touched by the stormy social-political changes of the past quarter century. I noted, for instance, that on every occasion when I was invited to dinner (in the homes of professional people aged thirty to forty) wives (who held jobs) did all the housework while their husbands remained seated and conversed unselfconsciously with the guests.

Another illustration of the persistence or possibly even resurgence of conventional moral standards and judgments was provided at a small social gathering when it was discussed in hushed and scandalized tones that a mutual friend of those present revealed himself to be a homosexual in ripe middle age. This was not a celebratory "coming out of the closet" in the recent American style; he was found out as he surreptitiously made a pass at somebody. Again, all those commenting on this story were highly educated people, some of them physicians.

A final illustration of the relative absence of romanticism was provided in a conversation with a woman friend who claimed that adultery was widely practiced but *by itself* rarely destroyed marriages. The idea that marital infidelity per se could be traumatic was quite foreign for her. (I gathered that when housing shortage is a chronic affliction people will not lightly jeopardize their hard-won housing arrangements.)

What of politics? Hungarians I met, from intellectuals to cabdrivers, Party members and nonmembers, remnants of the old upper classes and those of the new one, all exhibited a peculiar blend of pride and resignation with their political circumstances. It is taken for granted that no significant changes can be expected, but in a society where political decisions affect everybody's life even minor changes and adjustments are scrutinized anxiously. My landlady (a housewife of limited educational attainments) asked me, "What do you think of Gromyko's visit with the Pope?" She had read about the visit in the newspapers. People seek to grasp the political significance of events which would not attract interest or comment in the United States. (My trip to Hungary made me realize once more how profoundly apolitical Americans are, even those who think that they are not.) Several times it occurred to me that Marcuse's ideas about the unchangeability of modern industrial society applies far better to places like Hungary (and Eastern Europe as a whole as well as the Soviet Union) than to the United States and Western Europe, societies far more dynamic and unstable than their Eastern European counterparts. Indeed, Hungary comes very close, or perhaps the closest, to Marcuse's model of the affluent, repressively tolerant society of which change has been virtually banished, far closer than any Western society and especially the United States for which such a description had been intended. Thus Hungarians are truly and devotedly materialistic, obsessed with the acquisition of certain consumer goods and leisure-time activities; their government allows them, within limits, to prosper economically and indulge in privatized consumption precisely in order to divert them from politics and to buy at least tacit support for the regime; harsh political repression is absent, but the limits of permissible nonconformity are well known and clear to the population. Dissenters are repeatedly warned before being punished. As long as people mind their own business or "keep their nose clean," they are left alone by the authorities. The regime is truly paternalistic and reasonably permissive by the authoritarian standards of Soviet client states. There is plenty of entertainment, even nightclubs with sexily dressed women performers and chorus girls, lots of restaurants, coffee shops, and taverns; sports are lavishly subsidized by the government. There is much circus and a fair amount of bread. Whatever the objective realities of change and stagnation, people in Hungary acutely perceive a lack of change, whereas in the West change is widely felt and of late increasingly regarded as unwelcome and ominous.

There is certainly no sense of fear or intimidation in the air; the regime is secure and relatively legalistic; Hungarian dissenters were given suspended sentences or exit visas; none is known to be in jail or in Soviet-style psychiatric hospitals. Two minor, but for those familiar with life in Eastern Europe, significant, episodes illustrated for me the relatively relaxed atmosphere. People in Hungary, as in other Eastern European countries, have to notify the police of all changes of address; foreigners too. I arrived on a Friday and remembered to go to the police only on Monday because nobody reminded me to do so. At the district police, a secretary told me regretfully and politely that I was three days late and had to pay a fine of approximately five dollars. (I did so.) On another occasion, I went to the Institute of Party History, interested in the history of my uncle who became a Bolshevik and Soviet citizen after World War I (he was taken prisoner, fighting in the Austro-Hungarian army and disappeared sometime in the 1930s). At the entrance, I expected demands for identification and the presence of some uniformed figure. I was wrong on both counts. I also expected that, as used to be the custom upon entering every office, I would be given a pass stamped with the date and time of day, which would have to be signed and dated by the person I had seen. I was not given any pass and was simply sent up to one of the offices where I was treated politely and given some information.

There is considerable ambivalence on the topic of anti-Semitism, and I found a wide range of opinion among Jewish friends as to its extent and effects. Everybody agreed that there is less of it than in the Soviet Union. Jewish religious organizations function; I heard of elaborate (and costly) Jewish funerals. At the same time, nobody seems to like to be known as being a Jew. It is something people do not talk about and certainly do not joke about. For some, it seems to be a little secret; for others, a bigger and darker one, depending on both the position held and the level of personal paranoia or insecurity.

Attitudes toward the West remain, understandably enough, ambivalent—a blend of admiration, envy, and contempt. A cabdriver in his early twenties finished a string of complaints about material conditions in Hungary by saying (perhaps because he learned that I lived in the United States), "Oh, the West . . . things are different in the West." He had never been out of the country, but for him, as for many other Hungarians, the West is still in some respects a legendary land of promise. At the same time, they think little of the political acumen of Western politicians and nations; indeed, they are inclined to regard them as decadent and feeble. A Party member observed that the United States ceased to behave like a great power and has undermined the global balance of power by abandoning its allies (such as South Vietnam used to be) and by writing off countries in Africa and Asia as obscure and unimportant. Hungarians, unlike Americans, know more geography and will not dismiss the importance of distant countries such as Afghanistan, Angola, Ethiopia, or South Yemen.

Insofar as Hungary is (as the saying goes) "the gayest barrack in the socialist camp," this is also reflected in the quality of political jokes. Always abundant in these parts, they have become, it seemed, less bitter and biting. It is hard to avoid noting that the characteristics of life in Hungary have a great deal to do with the characteristics of Hungarians. This is and has been for a long time a Westward looking nation with a large talent pool, with a sense of uniqueness and cultural pride. I was repeatedly struck by the image of a compact and enduring culture as the meaning of the concept was brought to life through the daily observation of language, manners, jokes, art, music, or cuisine.

The worst thing said about the regime is that it is corrupt and has created great inequalities. But then, nobody expects equality in *any* political system: what some people argued about was the ethical or moral difference between past and present forms of inequality or the degrees of inequality, past and present.

The mainstay of political stability and relative contentment in Hungary today, as it has been for some years, is the feeling among the population that life in Hungary, despite the lopsided power relations, is better than in the Soviet Union, both in regard to the standard of living and the freedom of expression.

Hungarian attitudes toward the individual and society and the deeper assumptions about social forces and personal fulfillment were poignantly revealed in a conversation I had with a writer on the subject of the Reverend Jim Jones and the mass suicides in Guyana. He said that Jim Jones and his numerous facsimiles in the United States would have found few followers in Hungary or anywhere else in Eastern Europe. It was a thought-provoking remark. As we all know, much has been said about the conditions which provide fertile soil in American society for such groups and cults but very little about the opposite set of conditions which deprive such cults of nourishment, of gullible, naïve, and idealistic following. Obviously, in Hungary and the rest of Eastern Europe people do not have the opportunity to engage in an American-style religious-political-therapeutic free-for-all, since the authorities will not permit such dangerous diversions. There are also some less obvious reasons. I think that people in Eastern Europe learned certain lessons their more fortunate American counterparts had less chance to learn. These include the notion that there are no collective (and political) solutions to personal problems and those attempted are not very gratifying in the long run. The more recent varieties of "escaping freedom" (and the associated pursuits of community), whether at the People's Temple, at Synanon, in the late Symbionese Liberation Army or the "Weather" underground collectives (if they still exist), or even with Hell's Angels, may provide bouts of psychic intoxication and release but the side effects of this type of medicine are rather unpleasant.

People in Eastern Europe lost, if they ever had it, the capacity characteristic of many Americans to yearn for paradise on earth; they have become scornful of promises of utopia. Most importantly, they have developed a healthy immunity to the seductions of collectivism—religious, political, or therapeutic—which many Americans have become vulnerable to of late. Erazim Kohak, a Czech observer of American society, noted more than a decade ago something many Americans still find difficult to believe, namely, that "you cannot build Utopia without terror and that before long, terror is all that is left." One is also reminded of the related truism that power corrupts even apparently idealistic and charismatic leaders. These are old-fashioned homilies for Americans who are tormented by social isolation and lack of meaning in their lives and impatient with the often meager fruits of individualism.

East Europeans have been immunized against collectivism by political systems which tried to impose it on them; they have also become apprehensive about concentrations of power, no matter with what intentions and declarations of faith they have been accumulated. They cherish privacy since it is a relatively scarce commodity they cannot take for granted.

Americans in pursuit of utopia and joyful self-obliteration on the bosom of some group may have to learn more about the darker sides of communitarian life. Above all, they have to learn, or relearn, to exercise their powers of discrimination greatly enfeebled since the 1960s. That famous decade, it will be recalled, contributed to the dilution of many important distinctions: between freedom and repression, art and politics, religion and therapy, mental health and mental illness, innocence and crime, learning and entertainment, and many others.

The "Me" decade (as the 1970s are often thought of) was only in part a decade of surging individualism. It was also one in which personal satisfaction was still sought in a variety of ersatz communities, in which people freed of the ("elitist") ballast of critical faculties would follow a Reverend Jones to Guyana not having learned the lesson that life cannot be made instantly meaningful and that the redemptive powers of the collective are limited and transitory.

In Hungary and similar societies, lower expectations guard the sanity of people; common sense has been honed on the edges of historical events; exuberant expectations are held in check by the close contact between personal desire and sociopolitically imposed limits.

Perhaps it boils down to the proverbial greenness of the grass on the other side. Hungarians are fed up with any and all varieties of collectivism since they live in an officially collectivist society. Americans (or many of them) long for community in a highly individualistic society—they pine for what they don't have. Hungarians learned that social solutions to personal problems are unsatisfactory and often oppressive; Americans bereft of authorities would welcome some social-communal answer to personal problems.

Were any of my favorable reactions prompted by some residual Hungarian cultural patriotism? Is it possible that despite all the unpleasant experiences I associate with this country (where I was first mistreated on account of being Jewish and later as the grandson of a former capitalist) there remains, or has reawakened, some prideful identification with its culture, talented people, and difficult historical experiences?

In the final analysis, it is preferable to come to terms with one's native country (even, and perhaps especially, after one has left it), just as it is preferable to come to terms with one's parents, no matter what they were like, objectively speaking. It is indeed a question of identity. A bitter rejection of the place where one grew up is no more beneficial than a bitter rejection of those who brought one up. Thus there are powerful inner pressures to make the best of such an experience of revisiting the past. There is also the irresistible sentimental association of the past with one's youth as well as the desire to revisit the setting of one's youth. Those of us who seek some balance, continuity, and integrity in our lives prefer to pick up the pieces and dust them off, rather than bury or befoul them, and to see how the parts have added up to the whole.

Let me also say, however, that my relatively favorable reactions to Hungary were not merely or predominantly products of the psychological processes which have just been mentioned. Observable conditions, social realities—mediated through the conversations, gestures, facial expressions, and the tones of voice of people of diverse views and dispositions— also contributed to such a more positive image. Hungary has become over the past decade or so a more humane society precisely in proportion to the willingness of its rulers to abandon their ideologically defined quest for regimented social improvements, in proportion to allowing human imperfection, even corruption, to balance dogmatic puritanism. By Soviet (or Maoist, or Cuban) standards, the Hungarian state interferes little in the lives of its citizens and has allowed the emergence of a reasonable balance between the public and the private realm.

This is not a model of socialism to gladden the hearts of those Western intellectuals who continue to yearn for a sense of purpose, community, and direction emanating from some infallible belief system or social organization, and who are still fixated on a form of society in which meaning for personal lives is provided by institutional arrangements— a society they associate rightly or wrongly with some variety of socialism.

The New Socialist Man has not been born and bred in Hungary, but some attributes of the old, nonsocialist man have certainly survived with many of their redeeming imperfections.

12.
How Banal Is Evil?
Solzhenitsyn's Contribution
to the Sociology of Coercion

The late Hannah Arendt popularized the notion that evil in our time has become banal—Eichmann and his associates were ordinary bureaucrats, Germany and the world were full of equally ordinary people who could have done the same job. It was in the nature of the depersonalized modern world that even acts of evil on such a grand scale came to be deprived of any distinction due to bureaucratization, the division of labor, and obedience exacted by hierarchical organizations. Stanley Milgram's experiments further underlined the lesson: obedience to authority—even when it led to the infliction of pain—was more common and more readily forthcoming than had been anticipated; people proved rather resourceful in relinquishing moral scruples and casting off personal responsibility when they could do so by obeying orders.

The ground swell of receptivity and resonance to the messages of Arendt and Milgram is among the most intriguing chapters of contemporary social and intellectual history. With a curious mixture of horror and relish, pundits and the educated public alike embraced the idea that potentially all of us are amoral monsters but, at the same time, monsters without distinction or originality. There was something morbidly fascinating about the combination of almost unimaginable moral outrages (such as the Nazi extermination camps) and the pedestrian, mundane character of the individuals who perpetrated them. There was also a peculiar, almost masochistic pleasure in pointing out that in our times even the most extraordinary atrocities are brought about by such ordinary people, that even evil lost all claim to distinction and succumbed to mass society and what later came to be called faceless bureaucracy. Perhaps some people felt that if it is the lesson of history and experimental psychology that we can inflict suffering under appropriate circumstances without great difficulty, we have reached a new freedom from moral constraints and perplexities. One may suspect that the popularity of Arendt's and Milgram's work was also related, however obscurely, to a latent protest against modernity which brought us technology, bureaucracy,

impersonality, and efficiency in both inculcating obedience and incin-
erating corpses. For those inclined to environmental determinism, the
behavior of Eichmann and of Milgram's subjects provided evidence that
values have little to do with behavior. At last, receptivity to the messages
of Arendt and Milgram should hardly be surprising in an era in which
moral relativism is a leading current.[1]

Such reflections come to mind as one contemplates the more recent
and most impressive addition to the contemporary explorations of moral
outrage: Solzhenitsyn's work as a whole, and more specifically *The Gulag
Archipelago* trilogy, of which volume three is being reviewed here.[2] With
the work of Solzhenitsyn, a different dimension enters into the contemporary preoccupation with inhumanity. Solzhenitsyn is haunted by evil
and has no interest in converting it into more neutral social scientific
categories and concepts which could relieve people of moral responsibility.
A distinctive feature of the Soviet camps—of which Solzhenitsyn was
well aware—was that unlike the Nazi ones, they were by-products of a
gigantic experiment in social engineering, conceived to improve the life
of people in a backward society. They emerged, so to speak, in the
shadow of a belief system (Marxism-Leninism) which still enjoys great
respect in many parts of the world. By contrast, the Nazi program of
extermination was a part or culmination of a hate-filled ideology and a
social-political system which had little good to offer to most categories
of human beings. There were no noble ends to which the Nazi extermination camps could have been considered as regrettable means unless
one accepts the Nazi belief in the superiority of a world which had been
cleansed of Jews and some other groups. Whereas the Soviet system
had impressive goals and its "corrective" labor camps could be viewed
as regrettable necessities (or impure means) redeemed by their laudable
long-range objectives.

Solzhenitsyn's role in bringing to the attention of Western public
opinion the Soviet camp system can hardly be overestimated. Before
his books appeared in Western languages, only specialists were well
informed about the characteristics of the Soviet system of coercion under
Stalin (and after). And yet well before Solzhenitsyn's work appeared
before Western readers (including his early and important *One Day in
the Life of Ivan Denisovitch*), there was abundant information about
Soviet camps and prisons and the social-political conditions which made
them possible, indeed necessary. Solzhenitsyn was certainly more successful, by his artistry as a writer, in bringing to life and making almost
visually vivid,[3] the Soviet system of coercion. Yet his talents alone do
not explain why before him relatively little was known of, and little
indignation provoked by, these matters. The attention Solzhenitsyn's

work has gained has been part of the gradual delegitimation of the Soviet system in the West and its gradual dissociation from the ideals and concepts of socialism. During much of its existence, including its most repressive periods, many Western intellectuals and opinion makers thought of the Soviet system as basically headed in the right direction, whatever imperfections might have been conceded. While it was a matter of debate (taking different turns at different times) whether one should consider it a socialist society, the Soviet Union has persisted in calling itself one, and this counted for something. It has also persisted in legitimating itself by the ideas of Marx, Engels, and Lenin. And even if it was not exactly what Western intellectuals and Marxist scholars considered a pure socialist society, it was certainly not a capitalist society. It did nationalize the means of production; there was no unemployment; no "private incomes"; no millionaires and idle socialites. There was *some* semblance to, or striving for, socialism. It was difficult to associate such a society, even a defective version of socialism, with what came to be known as the Gulag Archipelago.

In discussing the specifics of the Soviet camp system, it is hard to avoid comparison with the Nazi camps as a point of reference, since they are so much better known in the West than the Soviet ones. What then were some of the distinctive characteristics of the Soviet prison camps?

For one thing, they were not designed as extermination camps with special mechanical devices: there were no gas chambers and no crematoria. In theory, confinement to them was temporary (from ten to twenty-five years), and people could survive and then return to society, even more theoretically, as reformed citizens.[4] In fact, more people died in Soviet than in Nazi camps, although the process stretched over a far longer period. Unknown to most people outside the Soviet Union, the camps were not the inventions of Stalin but came into existence while Lenin was still in command, soon after the establishment of the Soviet system— a matter Solzhenitsyn is at great pains to document. The high mortality rates were achieved simply by the poor living conditions: little food, poor shelter and clothing, minimal medical care, overwork, daily humiliations, isolation from family and friends, alien and inhospitable physical surroundings, and the hopelessness of one's condition. The Soviet camps also differed from the Nazi ones in that their inmates were not used as subjects for medical experiments. There were also differences in the selection process—of critical importance for understanding the Soviet principles and practices of coercion. As we know, the prime qualification for being sent to Nazi extermination camps was racial. The Soviet criteria were not so narrow: the status of political unreliability could be both "ascribed" and "achieved" and on a wide variety of grounds, which rarely included any overt action against the government. The Soviet state security apparatus was committed to the elimination of *potential* dissent or opposition. It is for this reason that relatives and co-workers of those accused of political misbehavior were also arrested; that entire ethnic groups were "relocated"; that people who might have been contaminated by some form of contact with politically questionable groups or individuals (foreign or domestic) were also incarcerated.

In *Gulag—Three* Solzhenitsyn pays special attention to the inmates of the so-called special camps (mostly, but not exclusively, political prisoners), to the institution of exile (an adjunct to the camp system since most of those released automatically become exiles), to escapes from and resistance within the camps, and to developments in the more liberal post-Stalin period, up to 1968, when the book was apparently completed. As in the previous volumes, most of the narrative is based on Solzhenitsyn's own experiences and on information provided by other prisoners while he was "inside" and also after his release. As his enterprise became more widely known, both inmates and former inmates provided him with much information, written and verbal. Solzhenitsyn is anxious to show that contrary to widespread impression, there was resistance to the authorities, including several strikes and uprisings in the prison camps, one of them in Kengir (in 1954) lasting for forty days and involving eight thousand prisoners. This and many other events and episodes make one aware of the many gaps in our knowledge of the history of Soviet political violence. Whoever in the United States heard of the riots in Novocherkassk in 1962 and how they were put down? Or about the deportation of "tens of thousands" of Koreans from the Soviet Far East to Kazakhstan as early as 1937—a minor one among such operations—apparently due to the Soviet apprehensions about Japan! Nor is it widely known outside the Soviet Union how much more humane and lenient the treatment of political offenders was under the czars.

The book (as the others in the series) is an overwhelming catalog of horror, pain, deprivation, and humiliation painstakingly assembled and detailed by a writer driven to compile a historical record and to refute official falsehoods and silence of more than half a century.

Solzhenitsyn's work, more than those of most social scientists (including the handful interested in such matters), goes a long way to explain what seems to have mystified many Western observers of totalitarian politics, namely, the part played by coercion and political violence in the maintenance of political power. Repression (contrary to the beliefs of the

1960s) need not be subtle (or "tolerant") to be efficient; indeed the more subtle, the less perceptible it becomes, the more it loses its capacity to intimidate. Unlike its "subtle," haphazard, and inconsistent varieties, harsh, prolonged, reasonably predictable and consistent repression "pays." It "pays" by creating overt conformity, submissiveness to authority, low expectations, and stability.

The Gulag Archipelago was devised to remove the human obstacles from the path of progress. Certainly, contemporary technology and administrative techniques helped in the process, but the impulse to annihilate groups defined as hostile and inferior is as old as the dream of purging society of evil—an aspiration few of us would care to call banal.

Notes

1. These remarks are not intended to suggest that there was universal agreement with the views of these authors. Among the attacks on Arendt, we may recall the article by Norman Podhoretz (in *Commentary*, Sept. 1963). Milgram, in turn, was criticized by several social scientists (as well as some literary critics) ostensibly for the methodology of his experiments but more likely because he was the bearer of bad news about human nature.
2. Alexander I. Solzhenitsyn, *The Gulag Archipelago—Three* (New York, 1978).
3. It is worth noting here that there is barely any photographic record in the West (or anywhere accessible to the public) of Soviet camps in spectacular contrast to the mountains of photos, newsreels, and documentaries available about the Nazi camps. I suggest that the presence or absence of such visual documentation has much to do with different degrees of moral outrage. The same applies to those exiled by the Soviet regime as opposed to exiles under the czars, Lenin included: "Exile in our day has left behind none of those rather jolly group photographs—you know the sort: third from left Ulyanov, second on right Krzhizhanovsky. All well fed, all neatly dressed, knowing neither toil nor want, every last beard tidily trimmed, every single cap of good fur" (p. 383). As Solzhenitsyn pointed out, in our time such group photos would suggest anti-Soviet organization and would lead to arrest.
4. Belief in the redeeming quality of work was conscientiously implemented. In one camp: "All one-legged men were employed on sedentary work: breaking stones . . . or grading firewood. Neither crutches nor even a missing arm was any obstacle to work. . . . One of [Colonel] Chechev's ideas: putting four one-armed men to carry a stretcher (two of them left-armed, two of them right-armed)" (p. 62).

13.
Afghanistan and the Myth of
"The Return" of the Cold War (1980)

It is somewhat embarrassing these days to use the word "myth" in the title when the claim to be engaged in demolishing one myth or another has achieved a suspicious popularity both in the mass media and the social sciences. It has become fashionable and irresistible, instead of just stating one's opinions and beliefs, to present them as devices employed in the long overdue demolition of some myth—that is, someone else's opinions and beliefs.

Having said this, I have my own project of demystification. The myth I would like to discredit has been around for a long time, but its existence has been spectacularly confirmed recently following the Soviet invasion of Afghanistan. The latter, according to a wide variety of politicians, journalists, and academic experts, signified a "return" to or "revival" of the cold war. Obviously, if the events associated with the Soviet attack on Afghanistan point to the "revival" of the cold war, it is widely assumed that it had once been terminated and a happier period had prevailed which is now sadly coming to an end—hence the "return" of the cold war.

I suggest that the belief in the "end" of the cold war and its "return" is an authentic myth and has all the hallmarks of the myth: it cannot be verified by empirical evidence; yet it has come to be taken for granted, it is shared by large numbers of people and it has (had) a comforting quality.

It would greatly improve the conduct of American foreign policy if policy makers and the public were liberated from this myth. I submit that the cold war has never ended and, consequently, events in Afghanistan do not mark its "return" but only its continuation in a somewhat more unpleasant or crude form. The cold war was terminated only in the minds of American politicians, academic specialists, and segments of the public. It "ended" only insofar as the United States ceased to respond to Soviet actions (earlier defined as cold-warlike) on the assumption that the cold war was over; thus there was no need to respond. As far as the Soviet Union was concerned, the cold war never ended, nor did it begin, except as a term of denigration for American attempts to resist Soviet expansion. Everything the Soviet Union had done during the cold war period proper, it has continued to do after its putative termination. Venomous anti-American propaganda, for instance, produced for domestic consumption and to harm American interests and reputation around the globe, has never ceased. Moreover, the Soviet leaders always and explicitly reserved the right to engage in it, proclaiming that there should never be peaceful coexistence in the realm of ideas. Such propaganda included exhortations directed at oil-producing countries to raise prices and restrict supply; it also played a considerable part in the intensification of the Arab-Israeli conflict, and it has also sought to weaken the NATO alliance.

Indeed, the range of expression of Soviet ill will toward the United States has been quite impressive and varied, ranging from verbal abuse to contributing to limited wars or wars by proxy. Overlooking its numerous manifestations has required an uncommon resolve on the part of well-meaning Americans to explain away Soviet hostility as a defense of legitimate interests, a form of rhetoric, a transient expression of insecurity or, at worst, relatively harmless pranks of a big country boisterously throwing its weight around.[1]

The alleged end of the cold war never led to a cessation of the Soviet effort to change the global status quo. Such activities were often defined by Soviet leaders as lending assistance to national liberation movements. They involved, over the years, the arming and training of pro-Soviet guerrillas and, more recently, providing them with combat troops and military support personnel furnished by Soviet satellites such as Cuba and East Germany. Peaceful coexistence, or détente, was from the Soviet point of view a state of affairs—free of the danger of nuclear confrontation with the United States—which allowed the gradual extension of Soviet influence into areas heretofore in the Western sphere. At the same time, the reverse process was categorically ruled out: the "socialist commonwealth" was inviolable and resignation from membership in it was not tolerated, as the Poles, Czechs, Hungarians, and most recently the Afghans have learned.

It was during the golden years of détente that the Soviet Union, with Castro's cooperation, succeeded in converting Cuba into a satellite and military base; it has also brought into the Soviet orbit Angola, Ethiopia, Mozambique, and South Yemen, and in the process acquired military bases in these countries. Soviet influence was consolidated in Indochina and made its appearance in such unlikely places as Grenada in the Caribbean, which recently voted with the USSR on Afghanistan in the United Nations. It was also in this period of relaxed international tensions, or terminated cold war, that the Soviet Union undertook a vast military buildup in every category of weaponry, which yielded many political benefits including the installation of not merely anti-Western but pro-Soviet regimes in the countries mentioned.[2] While Brezhnev radiantly surveyed what he called the new correlation of forces, or the new balance of power favoring the Soviet Union, American policy makers and politicians focused their energy on explaining why such Soviet successes were insignificant or self-defeating for the USSR in the long run.

The myth of the end of the cold war had its major source in the wishes and hopes of Americans tired of living with the tensions and hostilities associated with the *idea* of the cold war. Vietnam and the isolationism it inspired confirmed the myth: apprehension about communism caused involvement in Vietnam, which was a disaster; apprehension about communism had something to do with the cold war too. People jumped to the conclusion that if the Vietcong were no threat to the United States, the Soviet Union could not have been either. It has become conventional wisdom that only the unresolved domestic problems and the flaws of its own social institutions threatened the United States. As long as there was little, if any, willingness to confront and counteract disagreeable Soviet actions, it was preferable to believe that they did not take place—after all, the cold war had ended a long time ago.

Unless Americans and especially American leaders, experts, and opinion makers rid themselves of the illusion that the cold war had once upon a time been brought to an end, the recent pattern of Soviet advances will continue because there will be no coherent, long-term, and clearly defined American policy to deal with it. What is denied cannot be dealt with. The Soviet Union on its part will do everything to foster the illusion that the cold war had once been terminated and will continue to make many Americans uneasy and guilt stricken by accusing them of being cold warriors. Moreover, there will be no Afghanistans for a while and no tanks rolling into Iran or Pakistan—not until Americans calm down and forget about these distant places.[3] It will also take some time to digest Afghanistan, until Western delegations can be invited to inspect a by-then stable and tranquil country, to be greeted by former tribesmen who are now satisfied tractor drivers on collective farms. Then it will again be business as usual: Western businessmen will resume eagerly selling whatever the Soviet Union will pay for; members of the foreign policy establishment will treat us to new explanations of why the Soviet union is basically a status quo power (and how the Afghan events represented a temporary setback for the Soviet doves); radical-liberal intellectuals will isssue renewed warnings against cold warriors and other alarmists ready to divert attention from domestic concerns and from the responsibility of the United States for the ills of the world.

Notes

1. Two recent examples of more realistic views of Soviet global policies may be found in Walter Laqueur, *The Political Psychology of Appeasement* (New Brunswick, N.J.: Transaction Books, 1980), and Theodore Draper, "Rolling Communism Backward," *New Republic*, 7 March 1981.
2. For an analysis of these developments, see Francis Fukuyama, "A New Soviet Strategy," *Commentary*, Oct. 1979.
3. Getting little news of what is happening in Afghanistan greatly facilitates this process. It is hard to be indignant about matters of which we know less and less, of outrages impossible to visualize in the absence of detailed and persuasive (and preferably visual) information and confirmation. The difference between the reluctance of many Americans and especially intellectuals to believe, for example, in Soviet chemical warfare in Afghanistan and Indochina and their contrasting readiness to believe virtually every guerrilla promoted the atrocity story in El Salvador—usually accompanied by footage or pictures of corpses or bones (which, however, by themselves provide little proof of the identity of the wrongdoer)—illustrates both the importance of visual aids for bolstering belief and the power of predisposition.

14.
Poland: Coercion and the Stability
of Marxist One-Party States (1982)

Even at this early date, certain conclusions may and should be drawn from the recent events in Poland and the American reactions to them, before the memory of the premilitary crackdown period totally fades. As may be recalled, for the past year and a half we had ample information from Poland, including almost daily reports on television, all of which suggested that a grass-roots movement of truly mass dimensions—the 10 million member–strong Solidarity movement, reaching across the entire social landscape—has risen and forced the authorities to retreat step-by-step from their illiberal policies. There were innumerable accounts and daily affirmations of an unbreakable national unity, a zeal for reform, of an irresistible movement for democratic social change at every level of society, a movement that was not only vast in scope and impressive in its idealism, but also well organized with its own communication network, national, local, and regional offices, basking in the support and encouragement of the democratic world and the free trade unions abroad. This, in a nutshell, was the Western view of the Polish situation before 13 December 1981.

It is remarkable that despite the close observation and sustained analysis of developments in Poland over the past year and a half, nobody publicly anticipated the present outcome. Observers trying to speculaate about the future of Solidarity and its accomplishments generally fell into two groups. There were those who recognized that the reforms were intolerable from the Soviet point of view and therefore expected "massive" Soviet military intervention against what appeared to be a rock-solid national unity and far-reaching, irreversible social-political change. They believed that only the ruthless application of Soviet military force could put down Solidarity and what it stood for—hence the anxious watch for Soviet troop movements and maneuvers and the counting of how many Soviet divisions it would take to crush the Poles. These pessimists expecting Soviet intervention were probably evenly matched by those who held that despite everything there would be no Soviet tanks rolling into Poland because this would cost too much to the Soviet Union in blood, prestige, and resources; therefore, Polish democratization would persist despite Soviet glowering and the inept efforts of local Party bosses to stem the tide.

As we now know, neither of these two points of view was correct. Polish democratization and Solidarity were abruptly crushed but without the participation of Soviet troops. The inconceivable happened: the Polish security and military forces (Polish KGB and its supporting forces) did the job with dispatch, without wavering or hesitation. Suddenly the whole oppressive state apparatus sprang to life: there were journalists to speak for the martial law regime, judges to send Solidarity leaders to jail, civil servants to implement the new regulations, people willing to serve on committees screening the population for political reliability ("ideological verification") and, above all, a generally cowed population. Solidarity was decapitated by the arrest of thousands of its leaders and activists. The citizens were sternly ordered to obey or else, the few and relatively small pockets of resistance were quickly liquidated, and law and order Soviet style were restored. There were no mass strikes, mass protest, large-scale civil disobedience, waves of sabotage, or resistance. Solidarity, its spirit and achievements, virtually vanished overnight. The enormity of the change and how it was brought about can be truly appreciated only if we persevere in recalling our earlier image of a Solidarity dominated Poland.

How can we explain the monumental misjudgments of Western observers of where Poland was headed? Why, instead of putting down their submachine guns and embracing their fellow Poles, did members of the various security forces carry out their orders so promptly and efficiently? How come the Polish KGB was so consistently left out of all equations as a force to be reckoned with? Why was the new regime so successful in restoring fear, apathy, and docility to the central place they occupy everywhere in the maintenance of the stability of Marxist one-party systems?

Several explanations may be offered. In the first place, Western observers and Americans in particular overestimated the power of Polish nationalism and the social cohesion it created. It was overlooked that Polish national unity did not embrace the estimated quarter million members of the various security forces which remained intact and which were created in the first place for preventing the rise of Solidarity-like movements. It was also forgotten that not only the Soviet Union but such forces too had a vested interest in returning Poland to pre-Solidarity days. It would have been reasonable to expect that these privileged specialists in social control and coercion, many of them trained in and loyal to the Soviet Union, would not watch idly as their authority eroded.

It was the combination of wishing to defend their material and status privileges, the encouragement (or the order) of the Soviet Union, and, I presume, a residual ideological commitment (conveniently legitimating their privileges as guardians of state power) which mobilized them for action.

That the Polish security forces and military were able and willing to put down Solidarity so quickly only seemed impossible or unlikely because of our Western and especially American reluctance to believe that societies can be governed over long periods of time without the consent of the governed. For Americans it seems difficult to grasp how easily a truly professional political police force can snuff out a mass movement by arresting a few thousand of its leaders and intimidating the rest. Contrary to widespread beliefs, it was once more shown that Poles can shoot at Poles, can put them in jail, throw tear gas at them, beat them up, and mistreat them in a variety of ways just like Russians are able and willing to do the same to Russians, Romanians to Romanians, Czechs to Czechs, and so forth. Members of the specialized coercive forces, so carefully built up in Eastern Europe over a long period of time, do not fade away just because they are unpopular or restrained for a while. Indeed, a most ominous lesson of the recent events in Poland may be that each of the East European Soviet client states may now be able to take care of their own dissidents or protest movements without tangible Soviet help—perhaps this was the lesson the Soviet Union learned from Hungary in 1956 and Czechoslovakia in 1968. It has proved unnecessary to involve Soviet troops when the local forces can be relied upon, bolstered by the knowledge that their Soviet mentors will back them all the way if this becomes necessary.

Perhaps there was a time when the part played by coercion in the maintenance of social stability in Marxist one-party dictatorships had been overestimated. We have come a long way from that, and not only with reference to Poland. In recent years, scholars and journalists alike have increasingly tended to believe that coercion played a relatively trivial part in the maintenance of such regimes which instead came to rely more and more on a variety of "carrots," that is, tacit and open understandings with the population, their leaders pragmatically or benignly inclined to share power with emergent pressure and interest groups. To believe that unpopular regimes can be kept in power (or restored to power) primarily by force, or by the power to intimidate, was the height of intellectual unsophistication and a relic of the perspectives of the cold war era.

The military regime in Poland may show the moral bankruptcy of Soviet policies in Eastern Europe—as was also said about the crushing

of the Hungarian Revolution in 1956 and of the invasion of Czechoslovakia in 1968—but it does not show ineptitude or hesitation in meeting
challenges to power and orthodoxy. Political liberalization is not inherent
in the fabric of any society, including Poland. The Soviet empire is not
going to unravel as long as there is sufficient force vested in the KGB
and its East European affiliates to prevent it from happening. Perhaps
future historians may reach the conclusion that the building and em-
placement of such forces in Eastern Europe (and elsewhere) were among
the greatest political successes of the Soviet Union, its most enduring
and effective form of institution building.

15.
Marxist Societies: The Relationship between Theory and Practice

Introduction

If there was ever a suitable occasion for invoking limitations of space as an excuse for incomplete coverage of a topic, writing a chapter on "Marxist societies" must be it. Clearly, there is no way to do justice to such a vast topic in so little space. At best, what can be done is to focus on certain aspects of Marxist societies and to embark on a course of selectivity, both with respect to the societies to be included and the sociological issues covered in such researches. This title (originally supplied to the author) was obviously based on the premise that there is a distinct group of societies which have something in common by virtue of being "Marxist." But what is "Marxist"? One may debate almost endlessly (as has been done before) the true, authentic, or untrue and questionable meanings of "Marxist" and the grounds on which it can be conferred upon societies, social and political movements, or individuals. Who has the authority to make such a momentous decision? As will be seen later, in societies calling themselves Marxist, such authority, as the saying goes, grows out of the barrel of the gun. Those in power can impose or deny this attribute; they define who or what is a Marxist, a pseudo-Marxist, or a non-Marxist. Correspondingly, the most prominent "Marxists" of our times were also among the most powerful political leaders who insisted on being the most outstanding contemporary disciples of Marx, Engels, and Lenin. They include Stalin, Mao, Enver Hoxha, Kim Il Sung, Mathias Rakosi, and others not too frequently mentioned on the pages of the *Annual Review of Sociology*.

I define Marxist societies as those one-party systems which legitimate themselves by reference to some version or variety of Marxism, or, more correctly, Marxism-Leninism, and share a proclaimed intention to apply or implement such ideologies. These societies also have in common either a substantial degree of institutionalized government control over the economy or policies aimed at attaining and expanding such controls. Beyond such similarities, significant differences remain.

Marxist societies range from huge and complex ones, like the Soviet Union and China, to tiny countries like Albania or Grenada, and from highly industrialized countries like East Germany to partially tribal Angola. The present undertaking becomes conceivable only if the number of countries to be surveyed is reduced or if the substantive material pertaining to each country is reduced, or both.

According to the criteria just proposed, Marxist societies include the following (geographically grouped) countries:

1. In Eastern Europe: the USSR, East Germany, Poland, Hungary, Czechoslovakia, Romania, Bulgaria, and Albania;
2. In Asia: China, Mongolia, North Korea, Vietnam, Laos, Cambodia, and Afghanistan;
3. In Africa and the Near East: Angola, Mozambique, Ethiopia, and South Yemen;
4. In Latin America: Cuba, Nicaragua, and Grenada.

Even such a long list is incomplete. There are at least four other African countries of more uncertain Marxist credentials: Benin, Congo-Brazzaville, Guinea-Bissau, and the Malagasy Republic. There may be others elsewhere in the Third World.

No sociologist of even the most voracious comparative interests can master information about so many diverse societies. I decided to focus on three countries and to supplement the discussion with information derived from additional societies. Given my own interests and prior work, the Soviet Union was a clear choice. (See, for example, Hollander 1969, 1978.) I included China as the other major competitor in the world today for the title of a Marxist society. I added Cuba as representative of a Marxist society in the Western hemisphere, although it is more recent in origin, dwarfed demographically by the other two, and arising out of different historical conditions and cultural contexts. Moreover, the significance of Cuba in the world today far exceeds its size as it is a Marxist society which regards its duty to aid actively and militantly other Marxist or soon-to-be Marxist societies in various parts of the world, notably in Africa, the Middle East, and Central America.

Research on Marxist Societies

Looking at the sources of information on Marxist societies and particularly at sociological studies thereof, it turned out (not quite unexpectedly) that American (and other Western) sociologists have published relatively few works on these societies. That Western and American sociologists have shown so little interest in Marxist societies is all the more puzzling since an increasing number of them regard themselves as Marxist. Thus, for example, a recent, extensive survey of the works of Marxist sociologists in the United States (Flacks and Turkel 1978) is distinguished by the absence of any reference to research on Marxist societies or any expression of interest in them. Among the many sources of such indifference one finds the peculiar view of a world still dominated by a "capitalist world economy" (Flacks and Turkel 1978, p. 205) in which the socialist states (or Marxist societies) are somehow marginal and unimportant.

It would be an understatement to say that the study of Marxist societies is lacking "a compelling paradigm" as was said recently of the study of Third World nations (Hermassi 1978, p. 239). Thus the work on this paper led to the discovery, or rediscovery, that the sociology of Marxist societies hardly exists in American sociology, but whatever exists has not been produced by Marxists or, for the most part, sociologists.[1] There is sociological information on Marxist societies, but most of it has been produced by historians, political scientists, economists, and writers of no discernible academic specialty.

That so many sociologists, and in particular the Marxists among them, failed to produce a respectable body of literature about Marxist societies is an interesting riddle for the sociologist of knowledge and an issue of more general significance as it sheds light on the way sociologists choose or avoid topics of research. As I see it, Marxist sociologists have been shying away from Marxist societies in part for the same reason non-Marxist sociologists have not been studying them; that is, they are not particularly interested in societies outside the United States and they have not been trained for comparative or area studies, nor have they been stimulated by their education and environment to take much interest in the world outside the United States (see ch. 21 of this book). Marxist sociologists in particular may be reluctant to study societies claiming to be Marxist since empirical investigations may reveal the hollowness of the claim (that they are Marxist), the difficulty of applying Marxist ideals in any society, or the unanticipated (and unattractive) results of such applications.

The paucity of sociological writings on Marxist societies necessitated reference to nonsociological materials, including those produced by political scientists, historians, anthropologists, and even informants of no scholarly credentials, including former residents of Marxist societies.[2]

The interests and predisposition of American sociologists are not the only factors accounting for the underdeveloped state of research on Marxist societies in American sociology. To begin with, material support for studies of Marxist societies is limited; most funding agencies prefer to finance work pertaining to American society. In addition, sociologists are generally ill equipped for such research because of their training which, especially since the 1960s, has increasingly precluded the acquisition of language skills. At the same time, Marxist societies have not encouraged their study by foreigners, especially field work. Because of these circumstances, empirically minded sociologists have long felt it to be impossible to conduct scientifically respectable studies of such countries. It has been precisely such barriers to field research which restricted the number of Soviet specialists in sociology to a handful and led to the exclusion or reduced number of American social scientists participating in exchanges with the Soviet Union (Byrnes 1969). This state of affairs has also contributed to the reliance on refugees for some of the landmark studies of Soviet society and its political system (Inkeles and Bauer 1959; Bauer, Inkeles, Kluckhohn 1956).

The difficulties of conducting empirical research in Marxist societies are further illustrated by the experiences of Oscar Lewis and his associates who were granted permission to do fieldwork in Cuba but were expelled after a year (Lewis et al. 1977, Foreword; McDowell 1981; and Halperin 1981). Carmelo Mesa-Lago, "the dean of Cuban scholars" (Dominguez 1978, p. x), has not been allowed to reenter Cuba (his native country). He also reported on the misadventures of an American scholar (sympathetic to Cuba) who was arrested as a spy, held incommunicado for prolonged periods of time, and finally expelled (Mesa-Lago 1978, pp. xiii, 110–11, 176). In China, even under the more relaxed atmosphere of the post-Mao period when the government resumed scholarly exchanges, foreign visitors found themselves isolated and hampered in their researches (Reinhold 1981; see also Whyte, Vogel, and Parish 1977, p. 181). A student of Marxist Ethiopia expressed similar concerns about the accessibility of that society to foreign researchers and warned against the "Potemkin village phenomena" (Cohen 1980).

The secretiveness of Marxist societies thus becomes an issue not only with respect to obtaining social scientific information about them. More significantly, it emerges as one of their defining characteristics that helps to explain and underlies their various structural-institutional attributes.

In light of all that has been said so far, the need for a coherent organizing principle for this article appeared unusually pressing. I chose one which seemed appropriate and challenging taking into consideration certain conceptions of the proper intellectual role of the sociologist and the nature and claims of the societies to be looked at. I came to the conclusion that a focus on the relationship between theory and practice will be the most fruitful for the topic on hand, not only because it allows analysis of the claim that these societies are Marxist, but also because it provides an opportunity for engaging in the exercise of critical sociology. Such an examination of the discrepancies between theory and practice, or ideal and actual, represents both a major tradition of sociological inquiry and a central concern of our times (within and outside our profession) as we look for authenticity in the designs of social systems as well as in personal lives.

Marxism as the Source of Elite Inspiration, Political Education, Legitimation, and Institution Building

Before turning to the relationship between theory and practice, we must ask what observable part is played by Marxism in the foundation, legitimation, and functioning of these societies, what specific uses are made of these ideas and how they are presented to the populations concerned.

It may be noted here that all societies calling themselves Marxist also subscribe to the belief, popularized by Lenin, that ideas are weapons. This conviction is obviously associated with the use of Marxism as a legitimating device and source of guidance in institution building and policy making (Leites 1953; Inkeles 1968, pp. 331–42). The importance of these ideas for the political systems concerned is also indicated by their being turned into an official value system, a transformation pioneered by the Soviet regime (Hollander 1978, pp. 190–96, 146–55). A survey of the part played by Marxism in the life of these societies is complicated by the readily observable discrepancies between the theory and the uses to which it has been put (specific instances of which are examined in this chapter). Notwithstanding such discrepancies, it must be stressed that the "flexible" application, or even the distortion or misuse, of a theory does not mean that it is unimportant. On the contrary, the compulsion on the part of Soviet leaders (and to a somewhat lesser extent of leaders in other Marxist societies) to demonstrate that all their policies are rooted in Marxism-Leninism, no matter how outlandish such claims might seem at times, is a striking indication of the importance such leaders attach to these ideas and their legitimating powers (Leites 1953; Feiffer 1969; Ulam 1979). In China too similar phenomena may be observed. For example, the policies associated with both the Cultural Revolution and its subsequent critique by the new leadership were justified with reference to Marxism-Leninism (*Excerpts from Resolution on History of Mao's Contributions and Mistakes*). In turn, Enver Hoxha of Albania criticized not only the Soviet "revisionists" and "deviationists," but also the thought of Mao Tse-Tung for being "anti-Marxist" (Hoxha 1979, pp. 384–453). Such insistence on the relevance of a set of ideas suggests an uncertain sense of legitimacy on the part of the ruling groups.

While this is not the place to assess how successfully Marxism has been used as a legitimating device, it may be noted that, as a rule, the ideas of Marxism are far more fervently embraced (usually by small groups of intellectuals and students) in countries not regarded as Marxist than in those where Marxism has been converted into an official value system, in particular the Soviet Union and Eastern Europe (Kolakoswki 1970; Hollander 1978). The success of Marxism in performing legitimating functions may also be tied to the stages in the development of the putatively Marxist societies. It appears that these ideas are more potent and persuasive in the early revolutionary periods than after the systems concerned have achieved greater coherence and stability. As Adam Ulam put it:

> One may think of Marxism as a "two-stage" ideology. The revolutionary stage drops off after the revolution. The democratic undertones of Marxism are disposed of . . . and the task of construction in spirit and by means antithetical to the revolutionary stage is begun. . . . It comes in a series of realizations . . . that a faithful application of the principles under which the party had been carried to power would, in the postrevolutionary era, hamper and make impossible the construction of socialism (Ulam 1979, pp. 180–81).

In Marxist societies, most of these legitimating functions have been performed in conjunction with the so-called cults of personality (of which more will be said in this chapter). Such cults proclaim a leader to be the repository of all wisdom and insight attendant upon his thorough knowledge, creative interpretation, and application of Marxism-Leninism; his personal power is allegedly inseparable from his reliance on these sanctified doctrines. When insistence on Marxism as a source of legitimation is thus intertwined with the aggrandizement of putatively charismatic leaders—such as Stalin, Mao, Castro, Kim Il Sung, Enver Hoxha, Ho Chi Minh and others—the use of these ideas tends to acquire a distinctly religious flavor. Thus, the legitimation that occurs in conjunction with the use of these ideas appears to owe much of its strength to quasi-religious or spiritual attributes and appeals and not to the rationally persuasive nature of these doctrines and their supposedly scientific explanation of society and history (Kolakowski 1977).

The importance of Marxism in the societies here discussed derives further from providing a philosophy of modernization (and legitimating its costs with greater determination and coherence than capitalism is capable of) and also from its promise to create an ultimately classless society free of scarcities, exploitation, and coercion (Lowenthal 1970;

Berger 1976). More tangibly, Marxism as a source of elite inspiration and motivation has been instrumental in the construction of the political institutions all these societies shared within the framework of a thoroughly centralized one-party system. The latter, a historical innovation of Lenin, has been more widely and successfully adopted around the world than another innovation of the Soviet system: industrialization carried out by the state. Thus inspired, initially at any rate, by the ideals of Marxism, the elites in these countries build political institutions for the purpose of both the rapid economic modernization (including military strengthening) and the implementation of long-range, quasi-utopian objectives. The maximization of decision-making power was a logical and functional corollary of this process. As Lowenthal observed:

> Only regimes inspired by Communist ideology tend to acquire totalitarian powers in the full sense of an institutional monopoly over policy decision, organization, and information by the ruling party, and of the freeing of the state from all legal limitations in the exercise of its tasks. . . . The specific dynamism of the revolution from above requires the extreme concentration of power in specific totalitarian institutions which in turn require the utopian goal and the dynamism of imposed change for their legitimation (Lowenthal 1970, pp. 49, 109).

While for obvious historical reasons, the Soviet Union excelled in the uses of Marxism as the basis for the legitimation of every major policy, in all Marxist societies this system of ideas is said to be the foundation of all foreign and domestic policies, the repository of the guidelines for the conduct of the daily life of the citizen, and the principal source of motivation and inspiration for the elites and leaders. Lenin, of course, was the first leader to claim such inspiration as well as to contribute himself to the enrichment of the theory. All his successors and imitators in and outside the Soviet Union have similarly claimed to be architects and creative developers of Marxism-Leninism in their time and society. Fidel Castro, too, although more an activist than a theoretician, declared in 1961 that "I am a Marxist-Leninist and I will be one until the last day of my life" (Draper 1965, p. 147). His declaration of admiration for Soviet society also rested on perceiving it as an authentic socialist society which embodied the ideals of Marx, Engels, and Lenin (Halperin 1972, pp. 224–54).

The importance of Marxism-Leninism in Marxist societies is reflected not only in the leaders' claim to such personal beliefs and ideological foundations, but also in the enormity of resources and institutional efforts devoted to the dissemination and inculcation of these ideas.

From the earliest days of the Soviet regime (and even before the October Revolution), the Soviet leaders devoted their utmost attention to the political indoctrination of the population, which meant, to a great extent, the dissemination of the ideas (suitably reinterpreted or revised) of Marx, Engels, and Lenin. Indeed, if there was a single policy which the Soviet regime has pursued with remarkable steadfastness, it was the treatment of ideas as weapons, both in the domestic and international realm. There are at least three major institutional expressions of these concerns. First, the entire system of formal education from kindergarten to university is dedicated to the inculcation of Marxism-Leninism in however diluted and selective way (O'Dell 1978; Whyte 1977). Second, part-time adult education continues to expose the population to versions and fragments of the Marxist-Leninist world view as applied to current events. Here special mention must be made of the Party schools (usually boarding) which provide concentrated political instruction, permeated by the prevailing interpretations of Marxism-Leninism. Attendance at such schools has more than symbolic meaning; it is often a prerequisite for advancement in various hierarchies: the Party, the government, industry, the military, KGB, and so forth (Mickiewicz 1967). Party schools function similarly in Cuba (Fagen 1969, pp. 112–13; Dominguez 1978, pp. 336–37). Third, the mass communication media are harnessed to the propagation of Marxism-Leninism and are colored, to say the least, by adopting it as a dominant perspective (G. Hollander 1972; Hazan 1976; Lendvai 1981). In association with the mass media, the arts too, and especially literature, are supposed to espouse the values and propositions embedded in Marxism, particularly in conjunction with the school of socialist realism (Sinyavski 1960; Dunham 1976; and chapters 2 and 10 of this book).

With appropriate modifications, the Chinese regime has also made the study, dissemination, and application to current affairs of Marxism-Leninism one of its central objectives, those exposed to such studies ranging from Party functionaries and responsible officials (Whyte 1974, pp. 58–63) to inmates of prison camps (Bao 1976, pp. 50–52, 258–59; see also Leys 1977, pp. 165–70).

Like other Marxist societies, and possibly more than most, the Cuban regime too has emphasized the dissemination of Marxism-Leninism and its adaptation to everyday use. Such an emphasis on ideological indoctrination was also related to the revolutionary attributes of the system. As an American student of Cuban education put it, "The transformation of Cuban man into revolutionary man is at the heart of Cuban radicalism" (Fagen 1969, p. 2). Thus the early literacy campaigns, in part universalistic and idealistic, may also be viewed as means intended to assure that the entire population could be reached by the printed words of the regime; literacy was to contribute to the "creation of the new man—the altruistic producer who works hard and unreservedly for the good of the whole society rather than . . . for himself and his family." Moreover, "no discipline is free of political content in Cuba" (Nelson 1972, pp. 132, 145). Cuban education on the whole may be compared to that in China during the Cultural Revolution: its purpose is less to impart general knowledge or theoretical illumination than to provide ideological exhortation and the inculcation of practical skills (Bowles 1971; Wald 1978). Characteristically, manual labor is combined with virtually all levels and types of education (a policy toned down and virtually abandoned in the Soviet Union over the years). It is regarded as not only a practical necessity—for example, to help harvest sugarcane, plant trees, or work on urgent construction projects—but also a precondition for the realization of one of the major aspirations of Marxism: the eventual elimination of different ways of life associated with the division of labor between mental and manual. Education is also integrated with the values of collectivism (associated with Marxism-Leninism), that is, the subordination of the individual to the group and society (Bronfenbrenner 1970; Whyte 1977).

The importance of Marxism-Leninism is reflected in its early introduction into the reorganized curriculum of the University of Havana (and other schools) where "every student must take one year of a course entitled 'Dialectical Materialism,' regardless of what he was studying" (Zeitlin 1967, p. 21) and in the system of political education in the Cuban Communist Party which "closely followed the Soviet interpretation of Marxism" (Mesa-Lago 1978, p. 71).

The dissemination of the prevailing interpretations of Marxism is supplemented by restrictions on the circulation of ideas in all Marxist societies (e.g., Lendvai 1981). In Cuba, as in other Marxist societies, such restrictions were also justified by reference to external threats to the regime, and especially ideological subversion. Thus Armando Hart, the minister of culture, said in 1977 that "the ideological struggle between socialism and capitalism had become more acute, and since literature was one of the battlefields, Cuban writers were expected to: prepare for . . . the ideological confrontation, pay greater attention to the party's line . . ." (Mesa-Lago 1978, p. 112). In Cuba, as in other Marxist societies, training in Marxism-Leninism is associated with political reliability and loyalty to the government; such training is systematically provided to elite groups within the society. For example, an elite unit in the Cuban military forces concerned with coastal-border defense consists of "able political cadres whose status symbolizes the 'exemplary socialist soldiers' . . . [who] are experts on Marxist-Leninist theory" (Horowitz 1981, p. 546).

In addition to the institutional resources devoted to the dissemination of Marxism-Leninism for the benefit of their own citizens, major Marxist societies such as the USSR, Cuba, and China devote considerable energy and expense to the education of foreign students in an atmosphere that combines vocational training with immersion in Marxist ideology (e.g., Thomas 1981).

Theory and Practice

The Flowering of the State

It was the great historic promise of Marxism to inspire societies which would not only eliminate economic exploitation and inequality, but also create such social harmony that would remove the necessity of maintaining social order by force—in short, allow the state to "wither away." Not only Marx and Engels but even Lenin believed (up to a point, at any rate) that this was a realistic prospect given the nature of the postcapitalist, socialist society in which the majority of the "former wage slaves" would firmly and enthusiastically support the government and keep the small minority of former exploiters under control even without a specialized coercive apparatus (Lenin n.d.).

It is one of the great ironies of history that the attempt to translate Marxism-Leninism into reality provoked far more human resistance than had been anticipated and consequently far more political violence and coercion than foreseen. Correspondingly, huge, highly specialized and differentiated political police forces came to be established whose major task has been the liquidation or control of those who were or could be suspected of being hostile to the new social system, including many of its putative beneficiaries (Dallin and Breslauer 1970; Barron 1974; Wolin and Slusser 1975; Calzon 1978). Thus an ideology dedicated to the ultimate achievement of a social order without conflict and coercion spawned "a great *surplus of violence*" (Stojanovic 1981, p. 57).

While it has been reasonably well recognized that political violence and coercion have played a crucial part in the establishment and consolidation of most Marxist societies, the part played by coercion in their *maintenance* has been less well understood. Interestingly enough, both prevailing theoretical perspectives in Western sociology, the functionalist and the Marxist, have contributed to this state of affairs, each in its own way. The Parsonians, or the structural-functionalists, while not sympathetic to Marxist regimes, are in general predisposed—all protestations to the contrary—to underestimate the significance of political violence and coercion in the maintenance of social cohesion and stability. By the same token, they stress the role played by consensus, integrative values, and complementary social forces or interest groups. Functionalists recoil from the Marxist or Hobbesian answer to the question of how social order is possible. They believe that for a society to function and survive there must be at least tacit agreements and understandings between the rulers and the ruled, short of the articulate, explicit approval given by fully participant citizenry. Unlike the functionalists, the Marxists have no problem in viewing social order as resting on force and fraud. However, their perspective tends to be limited to capitalist societies. Ready to regard organized violence as the centerpiece of social order and control, they are reluctant to extend this recognition to Marxist societies which are supposedly free of economic exploitation and the associated social conflicts which, in theory, are alone responsible for coercion by the state functioning as "the executive committee" of the exploiters. Thus Marxist scholars, including sociologists, have either paid little attention to the coercive patterns of Marxist societies or tended to minimize their presence.

The Marcusian approach may be viewed as a variant of the Marxist one; it certainly incorporates the proposition that social order does not rest on the consent of the governed, but not necessarily on brute force either. According to Marcuse and his followers, modern industrial societies, but, again, only the capitalist ones among them, have ingenious means at their disposal to secure the cooperation and submission of the masses short of naked coercion. They do so by inculcating a false consciousness and by providing access to certain consumer goods. In particular, contemporary capitalism disarms the masses ideologically with the help of the mass media which divert their attention from the pressing issues of the day and depoliticize their thinking.

In light of these observations, it appears that there is no satisfactory conceptual scheme that helps to grasp the part played by coercion in the "system maintenance" of Marxist societies. Perhaps part of the problem is that certain contemporary forms of coercion perform a peculiar legitimating function. Thus the massive presence and apparent permanence of coercive institutions "legitimate" Marxist societies by making them seem immovable and basically unchangeable, by eliminating the prospect of alternatives. Consequently, people will accept the system and bring their discontent or frustrations under control; most certainly they will not entertain ambitions to change their society. The result is a kind of "legitimacy"—the passive acceptance of the immovable object. Hence Marxist societies, and especially those which have been in existence for several decades, unexpectedly acquire certain attributes of a traditional society: they are accepted because the citizens, living in an environment of which conceptions of alternatives have been carefully removed, cannot conceive of other ways of being governed and regard the system as "natural" (Brzezinski in Cocks et al. 1976, p. 34).[3]

The problems of grasping the nature of coercion in Marxist societies is exemplified by a criticism made of Jorge Dominguez, a student of Cuban politics, who described political participation in Cuba as "non-autonomous." His critic wrote: "How is it that after two decades of educational improvement . . . the same populace that was sufficiently self-mobilizing to overthrow both the Machado and Batista dictatorships has suddenly become a nation of sheep?" (LeoGrande 1981, p. 194).[4] In other words, if Cubans could mobilize to overthrow two pre-Castro dictatorships, they should be just as able to resist or overthrow the current one. The premise of this rhetorical question reflects an apparent inability to differentiate between the nature of political controls in a Marxist one-party system such as Castro's Cuba and those of its right-wing predecessors. Many Western social scientists have failed to recognize that, by and large, the coercive apparatus of Marxist regimes is more efficient and its capacity to control the population far greater than those of their predecessors. The relative invisibility of coercion in established Marxist societies contributes to its underestimation by outside observers. In such societies, coercive institutions are often located in remote places and rarely exposed to outsiders (or natives) unless they are special exhibits (Hollander 1981, pp. 140–60, 335–46). Likewise, political trials receive little publicity except of a selective, didactic kind. Those subjected to coercive measures (former inmates of penal institutions or families of those detained) are not anxious to discuss their experiences since political imprisonment is an enduringly stigmatizing experience. In addition, many coercive sanctions are informal and secretively administered: loss of employment, demotions, transfers to less desirable locations, and re-vocations of residence permits in major cities are quietly dispensed and help to silence public criticism of the regimes concerned.

Castro under Batista and Huber Matos under Castro provide con-trasting examples of how these two systems differ in their coercive policies (see also Calzon 1978). Castro spent two years in jail under fairly comfortable conditions for leading an armed attack on military barracks (Moncada) of the Batista regime, and he was granted amnesty in 1955. On the other hand, Huber Matos, a fellow revolutionary of Castro, was jailed for twenty years by Castro after he expressed verbal disagreement with Castro's policies. While in jail he was mistreated in various ways. Under Batista, it was not difficult to leave Cuba legally, and people trying to leave illegally were not punished. Under Castro, attempted illegal departures are punished and legal exit is severely circumscribed. The Batista regime did not jail writers who did not follow prescribed literary policies, mainly because that government had no literary policies whatsoever. Under Castro, dissenting writers have been severely punished (Ripoll 1979, 1981; Goytisolo 1979).

Such examples of the coercive policies in Marxist societies suggest the general strengthening of the powers of the state—its flowering, not withering. It may be added that the specialized personnel of the coercive bureaucracy are among the least accountable of all state employees and the least subject to legal restraint. State control over all forms of associational life reduces the need for overt violence. Antigovernment demonstrations need not be broken up by the police because demonstrations are generally unthinkable. Groups capable of organizing demonstrations (or other activities disapproved of by the state) have been destroyed (e.g., former political parties, trade unions, associations not under the auspices of the government), and new ones cannot be organized. Thus society is "atomized." Widespread networks of informers—some, like the Committee for the Defense of the Revolution in Cuba, more openly acknowledged than others (Horowitz 1981, p. 676), assist the political police in preventing the rise of antigovernment groups and ways of life. A former citizen of China under Mao described the connections between governmental efficiency in such matters and atomization:

> One reason that the masses are so powerless is because we are so carefully controlled. . . . The police and the public security office know everybody's business and therefore people rarely speak their minds to each other. We do what we are told. The lowest level in the control system is the resident's committee . . . for supervising the daily life of citizens, . . . police station branches in turn supervise the residents' committees and they are under . . . district public security bureaus . . . [which are] under the jurisdiction of the city and provincial public security bureaus. The public security network . . . command[s] our respect and fear. . . . It is easier for Americans to go to the moon than for Chinese to get around the strict residential control system. Another form of local level control is the urban militia. . . . The Party, the army and the public security apparatus control everything. . . . People thus wind up distrusting one another, and those at the top preserve their power (Frolic 1980, pp. 133–34, 137; see also in the Cuban context Fagen 1969, p. 152).

Marxist regimes lavish vast resources on their coercive institutions and especially their specialized police forces entrusted with the uprooting of domestic discontent or social-political criticism. It has been estimated that the Soviet political police, the KGB, has over half a million members (Hollander 1978, pp. 97–98). Such forces include not only plainclothesmen or networks of informers, but also heavily armed, uniformed detachments and, more recently, psychiatrists (Conquest 1968; Bloch and Reddaway 1977; Horowitz 1981, pp. 545–46). An American student of Soviet society commented that the exceptional efficiency of the KGB

> is possible because a single organization [the KGB, or Committee for State Security] has total control over where Russians work and live, as well as what they legally read and publicly say. Ordinarily, the inherent muddle of Soviet bureaucracy might give some measure of delay, if not protection, to potential victims: a decision to dismiss a man from his job, for example, might not be co-ordinated with revocation of his residence permit in a coveted major city. But Russia's most competent and prodigally financed central agency, the KGB, serves as co-ordinator in all matters of this importance (Feiffer 1969, p. 65).

Similar observations were made in Cuba by a former Chilean diplomat of the Allende regime:

> How could room service be so inefficient, with breakfast frequently arriving an hour late, with coffee instead of tea, one cup for two people and three cups for one, the milk jug without milk, with the bread forgotten and the eggs stone cold; while the service of the machine [the secret police, that is], on the other hand, was immaculate and precise, as if in this field the improvisation and lethargy of the tropics and absenteeism did not count (Edwards 1977, p. 90).

The efficiency of the Chinese system of repressing political dissent is attested to in part by the almost total ignorance in the West of the appropriate institutions and procedures until the passing of Mao. Thus distinguished Western intellectuals believed that the Chinese were determined not to repeat the excesses and mistakes of the Soviet Union under Stalin (e.g., Hollander 1981a; Worsley 1975) and accounts suggesting a contrary view (e.g., Labin 1961; Marcuse 1967; Berger 1975; Bao 1976) had a negligible impact on such perceptions. Similarly, little has been known of the "Vietnamese Gulag" (Doan Van Toai 1978) and of the magnitude of the punitive "reeducation program" and coercive resettlement in the "new economic zones," since these operations benefited from discretion and minimum publicity. Given the government monopoly of the mass media and its power to determine what subjects are fit for public discourse in these countries, the part played by coercion in the maintenance of political stability, social cohesion, and popular acquiescence can be minimized. In turn, depriving dissenters and potential dissenters of publicity is an important tool for reducing their effectiveness and undermining their morale and motivation. Few people will choose to defy a political system and suffer for their defiance if such actions will not only fail to dislodge or weaken the system, but the sacrifices entailed will not even be known and appreciated by the rest of the population and especially those similarly disenchanted. Thus it is not surprising that Western audiences have known far more about the identity and activities of the small number of Soviet dissenters than have their fellow countrymen. The same situation exists in China and Cuba except when the regimes concerned decide to make a public example of the wages of dissent and stage public trials for didactic purposes, sometimes featuring the contrite confessions of the "unmasked enemies" of the state.

The effectiveness of coercive policies is further enhanced when governments are able to control population movements both within a given country and across their national boundaries. Marxist regimes make strenuous attempts to introduce such controls as soon as they come to power. Their policies may fluctuate between the total denial of exit to their citizens and the occasional permission for selected groups or individuals to leave. Unauthorized departures legally defined as treason are punishable (Berman 1966; ch. 5 of this book), and large forces of border guards are deployed to prevent such unlawful departures. Marxist societies also frequently build extensive installations along their national borders to supplement the watchfulness of the troops guarding the borders. These controls serve various political functions. Combined with identity cards (internal passports or ration cards which can be redeemed only at one's place of residence) they enable the authorities to keep track of people who must register with the police when not staying at their regular place of residence. In turn, denying exit to the discontented compels, to some degree, adaptation to the system by removing alternatives. The difficulty of slipping across the borders also increases the risks of taking action against the regimes concerned and contrasts with the ease of movement of terrorists in Western countries and across their borders.

Insofar as in Marxist societies the state is the single major (or sometimes the sole) employer, such a concentration of economic power provides a further mechanism of social control and a new range of sanctions. These methods of sociopolitical control were pioneered by the Soviet Union, especially in the post-Stalin period in which loss of employment (or desirable employment), or denial of access to higher education have increasingly become sanctions against nonconformity (e.g., Feiffer 1969).

A high degree of predictability of punitive sanctions for certain transgressions over long periods maximizes conformity on the part of the majority of the population. In addition to the initial "investment in revolutionary terror," Marxist societies are fairly consistent in meting out punishment for certain forms of political deviance, dissent, or nonconformity[5] even when they do not go to such extremes as did the Soviet Union in the 1930s, China during the Cultural Revolution, or Cambodia under Pol Pot.

All attributes of the coercive policies found in Marxist societies suggest the general strengthening of the powers of the state—its luxuriant flowering, not withering. It may be added here that the specialized personnel of the coercive bureaucracies are among the least accountable of all state employees and least subject to legal restraint. Clearly, it is in the realm of coercion and the expansion of the powers of the state that we encounter the most striking discrepancies between Marxist theory and the practice of societies calling themselves Marxist.

The Party and the Leader

All societies professing to be Marxist are led and governed by Communist parties which are putatively guided by the principles of Marxism-Leninism. These parties radically differ from political parties in pluralistic societies (Rigby 1968; Hollander 1978). Three characteristics distinguish them from political parties of the older type and at the same time represent developments unintended and unanticipated by Marxist thought. Communist parties as ruling parties have become highly bureaucratized, turned into repositories of privilege (for their paid functionaries if not all rank-and-file members), and acquired what might be called a metaphysical image of infallibility. Much of what Trotsky said in the 1930s regarding the transformation of the Communist party of the Soviet Union into such a highly bureaucratized organization of vested interest also applies to such parties elsewhere (Trotsky 1965; Djilas 1957). Among the Marxist societies surveyed here, contemporary Cuba is perhaps the most striking example of a political system—along with Mao's China and Stalin's Soviet Union—in which the leader while professing Marxism overshadows the Party and the entire institutional framework in being the major source of legitimation and ultimate authority. Contemplating such developments, Svetozar Stojanovic, the Yugoslav social philosopher, asked:

> How is it that communist parties which *in theory* invoke so persistently the deterministic formula with the "natural laws" and "iron necessity" of the course of history, so often have such a vital dependence *in practice* on their own leadership? There have been few movements in history whose theory has so diminished the role of the greatest individuals in favor of collective actors and impersonal social forces, and in which the role of the leading personalities at crucial junctures has been so fateful (Stojanovic 1981, p. 44).

Why have the power and the cults of such leaders been persistent features of Marxist societies? Why in addition to Stalin, Mao, and Castro have similarly prominent and revered leaders also arisen elsewhere in the Marxist world such as Ho Chi Minh in Vietnam, Kim Il Sung in North Korea, Enver Hoxha in Albania, Tito in Yugoslavia, Rakosi in Hungary, Ceauscescu in Romania (Fischer 1981), Gottwald in Czechoslovakia, and Dimitrov in Bulgaria?

Two explanations may be proposed. One is that most Marxist societies are products of revolutionary upheaval, which entails a disruption of continuity and the elimination of whatever traditional sources and institutional mechanisms of legitimation had been available earlier. Under such conditions, it becomes easier for a single leader with a presence and personality more readily apprehended to become the principal source of authority and legitimation. These leaders may have genuine charisma (like Castro) or strive to create an aura of pseudo-charisma like Stalin and others (Bauer 1953). In rapidly modernizing and partly traditional societies, individual leaders personify the new regime and provide substitutes for both traditional authority figures and traditional religious objects of worship. These developments were particularly clear-cut in the Soviet Union under Stalin and China under Mao as these "cults of personality" merged into the elevation of the leaders to the realm earlier reserved for deities (e.g., Urban 1972). It is easier to exact loyalty and obedience in the name of an exalted leader than in the name of more abstract ideas or institutions (e.g., the Party). In short, the figure of a supreme leader, genuinely or allegedly charismatic, is the most readily available source of social-political cohesion in societies undergoing revolutionary change and unable or unwilling to develop a pluralistic polity in which an electoral system could provide the basis of legitimation.

The second reason for the consolidation of power in the hands of the supreme leader in Marxist societies is probably related to the dynamics of the concentration of political power. As both Trotsky and Stojanovic observed, a process of "reductive transformation" occurs in such societies: "The revolutionary cause of the proletariat is identified with the revolutionary movement, and the movement is identified with the party, which in turn is identified with the victorious faction. The existing leadership always embodies the party's essence" (Stojanovic 1981, p. 122). And often enough the "existing leadership" means one leader whose authority is unchallenged. Such an ultimate centralization of power and authority, while counterproductive in some respects, simplifies decision making in political systems not inclined to give serious consideration either to the desires of the majority or those of various interest groups.[6] And, to the extent that numerous Marxist societies may also be considered totalitarian (Brzezinski 1976; Cranston 1977; Cohn 1980; and ch. 4 of this book) such concentration of power and authority is even more understandable. As the late Bertram Wolfe observed: "the whole dynamics of dictatorship cries out for a dictator, autocracy for an autocrat, militarized command and militarized life for a supreme commander, infallible government for infallible leader . . . a totalitarian state for a Duce, Fuhrer, Vozha" (Wolfe 1956, p. 23).

It should be added that Castro has exercised power with greater informality than many other similarly placed leaders in Marxist societies. Not only has he possessed an authentic charisma[7]—especially during the initial phase of the Cuban Revolution—but he has also been greatly concerned with detail and has often indulged in the habit of personally supervising the functioning of the system. Of Castro it was observed that he is "like a loving, intelligent and autocratic father who, when he has decided what is best for his children, sits them on his lap and asks them gently to express their own wishes." Furthermore, "when they are finished he 'persuades' them precisely why they really want to do what he wants them to do" (Caute 1974, p. 138). In a somewhat similar vein, a French student of Cuba (and especially its agriculture) recalled: "Traveling with Castro I sometimes had the impression that I was visiting Cuba with its owner, who was showing off its fields and pastures, its cows if not its men" (Dumont 1974, p. 57). Likewise, the attention of Kim Il Sung of North Korea extended to advising workers on how to spend their leisure at home, instructing writers, artists, and film makers and discoursing on the economic advantages of specialized rabbit and chicken farms, among many other matters (Kim Il Sung 1971, pp. 250–57, 500–507).

The exaltation of a single leader and the attendant concentration of power and authority in his hands are obviously antithetical to the letter and spirit of Marxism. In Cuba as in other Marxist societies, the more important the leader has been in running and legitimating the system, the more obvious it has become that belief in the social order has not been spontaneously generated by its benefits, the superiority of its institutions, or its sacred doctrinal underpinnings. The great emphasis on the wisdom and talents of the leader has diminished, both by implication and in practice, the initiative of the masses. As has been the case with other leaders in Marxist societies, most notably Mao and Stalin, the growth and institutionalization of Castro's power has been accompanied by the expansion of his claims of competence in areas of life outside politics: "Castro is no longer content with his claims to military and political fame. . . . He has to feel himself recognized as the leader in both scientific research and agricultural practice. He is the man who knows everything . . . the prolonged exercise of power convinced him that he understands every problem better than anybody else." (Dumont 1974, p. 133).

Castro's preeminence is illustrated by his being president of the Council of State and of the Council of Ministers, first secretary of the Cuban Communist party, commander in chief of the armed forces (and General of the Army), as well as chairman of the National Commission for the Implementation of the Economic Management System (Mesa-Lago 1978, pp. 79–80). Such a lopsided distribution of political power characteristic of Marxist societies may well be described by the concept of "political poverty" that can be applied to situations in which "the citizen has no opportunity to exert real influence on the making of fundamental social decisions" (Stojanovic 1981, p. 51). Cuban political institutions since the mid-1970s have increasingly been shaped along Soviet lines. Cuba too developed a small governing party, even more elitist in nature than its Soviet counterpart including only 2 percent of the population (as against 5 percent in the USSR); 32 percent of the articles of the Cuban Constitution come directly from the Soviet Constitution of 1936, and, most remarkably, the Soviet Union is mentioned by name in the preamble to the Cuban Constitution (Mesa-Lago 1978, pp. 72–73). Even the National Assembly, a more symbolic than real source of power, reflects the characteristic inequalities in the distribution of power—more pronounced, it is safe to presume, in the Party hierarchy. Thus in the Assembly

> the typical deputy is male, either an executive, a technician or a military man, above forty years of age, educated and a member of the party. Although workers and peasants make up [at least] two-thirds of the labor force, they are only represented by 31% of the deputies; females constitute about half of the population but have 22% of the deputies; more than 80% of the population are neither members of the PCC [the Communist Party of Cuba] nor the UJC [the Young Communist League] but they are represented by only 3% of the deputies; more than 60% of the population is below thirty years of age but share only 10% of the deputies; and the majority of the population which does not have intermediate and higher education is represented by 12% of the deputies (Mesa-Lago 1978, p. 80).

The growth of the power of both the Party and the leader in Marxist societies indicates problems of legitimation. Although the relative importance of the individual leader and the Party oligarchy varies in Marxist societies, both styles of government are at best elitist and paternalistic, which suggests that their populations either cannot or do not wish to participate in the political process. The concentration of power associated with one-party systems is also closely related to the goals and urgency of modernization. Marxist societies adopt Marxism in part as a guide to modernization and the social transformations associated with it in the hope of speeding up the process and avoiding the costs incurred by its capitalistic version. This, at any rate, is the theory. In any event, it is by now clear that in Marxist modernizing societies "the accumulation of power necessary for modernization [makes] the future of democracy rather bleak" (Huntington 1966, p. 411).

Inequalities, Incentives, and the New Man

Every Marxist political movement seeks power in large measure to introduce more egalitarian patterns in the distribution of material goods, services, social status, and eventually even political power. Such egalitarian values and policies are among the claims to legitimacy and popular appeal of Marxist societies. While the effects of such policies vary, a few generalizations may be made about the emerging or established patterns of social stratification, that is to say, of inequality in Marxist societies.

First, it may be noted that Marxist societies have removed many traditional sources of inequality and have narrowed the range of material privilege and deprivation which had prevailed earlier. In all such societies, for instance, the benefits of inherited wealth and unearned private income have either been completely eliminated or significantly reduced. Public health measures, universal compulsory education, the confiscation of most income producing property, and the abolition of institutionalized sexual and ethnic discrimination are among the measures such societies have taken to decrease disparities in living standards and social status.

Second, in Marxist societies there is an unusually close connection between social position and status on the one hand, and access to political power on the other. To a degree unknown in many societies, the distribution of power and material privilege are integrated. This is symbolized in the significance of belonging to the ruling party, which in every Marxist society functions as a unifier of elites (Aron 1950; Matthews 1972 and 1978; Hollander 1978, pp. 51–54). Correspondingly, in these societies political power legitimates inequalities (to the extent they are acknowledged to exist); the authorities maintain that merit and advantage are in perfect harmony. For this reason, it is possible—insofar as the citizenry accepts these official assertions—that inequality has a peculiarly debilitating effect on large segments of the population since the material and symbolic advantages entailed are not haphazard or arbitrary (as under capitalism), but, according to official doctrine, reflect genuine merit (Konrad and Szelenyi 1979; Connor 1979).

Third, in all Marxist societies (except those which have very recently come into existence) the early egalitarian policies and ideological aspirations have given way to a well-defined system of socioeconomic stratification against the background of an even more unequal distribution of political power. At the same time, the elites have retreated in theory as well from the egalitarian values of Marxism by stressing that groups and individuals within the population will be rewarded not according to their needs, but according to the worth of their contributions to the social system. Political power determines who will rank order these contributions and how the rewards vary. Thus, perhaps for the first time in history, social inequalities were deliberately planned as different wage scales and salaries (and other, nonmonetary rewards) came to be attached to specific occupations and activities.

While the limited commitment of Marxist societies to civil liberties has been reasonably well known—and usually explained by the urgency of their concern with the elimination of material inequalities and the striving for social justice—far less has been known about the rise of new forms of inequality and the peculiarities of social stratification in such systems. In this realm, too, many features of the Soviet system have been duplicated or have reappeared in modified forms.

Thus in no society calling itself Marxist do the differences in monetary income exhaust the range of inequalities or differential rewards. In the Soviet Union, an elaborate system of nonincome privileges has been constructed for various elite groups (the Party apparatus, higher civil servants, KGB and military officers, etc.), which includes the provision of superior housing, resorts, vacation homes, access to special shops, travel privileges, official (and private) cars, special hospitals, child-care facilities, clinics, and privileged admission to institutions of higher learning (Matthews 1978; Sakharov 1975, pp. 25–28). The meticulous calculation and quantification of privilege even extends to gradations in dining room facilities at the place of work and similar differentiation in the military as well.

Such new forms of privilege (in addition to the substantial income differentials) also exist in Cuba which, for a long time, has been viewed by many Westerners as the most egalitarian of all Marxist societies, alongside China during the Cultural Revolution. Cuba, many averred (e.g., Baran 1961) had not only eliminated material poverty, it had also reduced social inequalities to negligible proportions. Rationing was often seen as a sign of equality which made scarcities more palatable by assuring that the basic needs were met equitably. Meanwhile, however, in Cuba as in other Marxist societies (especially the Soviet Union and Eastern Europe), small elites emerged composed of the upper echelons of the Party administration, military, police, and government bureaucracy, as well as highly skilled technical experts. They not only had the lion's share of power, they also consumed more (Nelson 1972, p. 183; Dumont 1974; Karol 1970; Clytus 1970). More recently, it was established that in Cuba "by the early 1970s egalitarianism was losing out . . . [and] the rationing system . . . once . . . an instrument for equality now became a method to benefit the elite . . ." (Dominguez 1978, p. 229). As Stalin had done in the early 1930s in his famous speech denouncing "petty bourgeois egalitarianism" and its devastating effect on motivation (Hollander 1978, pp. 214–16), Castro in the early 1970s defended income differentials and the associated privileges as necessary rewards and incentives (Dominguez 1978, p. 233). In the Cuban army too, there was a threefold differentiation of messes: "one for officers, one for non-commissioned officers and regular servicemen, and one for the temporary recruits" (Nelson 1972, p. 224). A new symbol of status privilege also arose: the imported Alfa Romeo given to members of the elite (Dumont 1974, pp. 58, 127, 128; Horowitz 1981, p. 331).

In China too the official car has acquired a great burden of symbolic significance. This was hardly surprising in a society in which there were some thirty gradations in the bureaucratic hierarchy, each with its well-defined privileges, including gastronomic ones (Leys 1977, pp. 83, 113–19).

While Leys and Whyte reported such privileges in China before Mao's death (Whyte 1975, p. 685), most information of this kind appeared and received wider circulation after 1976. Nonincome privileges were important in China too. A former friend and student of the Chinese regime wrote:

> Inequality . . . was not merely a matter of an eight-grade wage system but of some thirty grades in the hierarchy of payments. It also involved the *privileges* enjoyed by the cadres of the party and the state, which increased as one rose in the hierarchy. Thse privileges involved, for example, the use of a service automobile, more spacious and comfortable housing, and even above a certain level, a villa and access to special shops (for clothes and certain consumer durables such as refrigerators, radios, TV sets, cameras, tape recorders, etc.). At the level of central leadership, these privileges could extend to the possession of several villas, free use of an airplane for personal trips and so on (Bettelheim and Burton 1978, pp. 108–9).[8]

Elaborate gradations of housing privilege and its generous distribution among elite groups have also been confirmed by former Chinese citizens. Elite groups have also used their connections, or what in China is called the "back door" or "Big Back door," to secure various other material and nonmaterial advantages for themselves and their offspring (Frolic 1980, pp. 126–32).

The persistence of inequality in Marxist societies has often been linked to the problem of incentives and the difficulties of developing a new work ethic. The delayed appearance of such an ethic has been the most serious obstacle to the achievement of the ideals incorporated in the writings of Marx and his followers.

The transformation of human beings and the development of the New Man has been the highest aspiration of Marxist societies as has already been noted particularly in the Cuban context (e.g., Fagen 1969). In China under Mao, according to Professor Fairbank, "a far-reaching moral crusade to change the very human Chinese personality in the direction of self-sacrifice and service to others" was taking place (quoted in Hollander 1981, pp. 297–98). Social scientists and other observers alike were deeply impressed by the Chinese effort to remold human beings culminating in the Cultural Revolution (e.g., Committee of Concerned Asian Scholars). Similar aspirations have been reiterated innumerable times in the Soviet Union and Eastern Europe. The transformation of human nature was to be achieved through both the structural changes in the social environment—in particular by making it impossible for individuals to exploit one another economically by nationalizing the means of production—and the systematic and deliberate attempts to mold the human consciousness; that is to say, social values, beliefs, and norms. As noted earlier, education broadly defined was designated to achieve these goals, in conjunction with political propaganda disseminated by the mass media and the politicized literature and arts. In Soviet society, as in others committed to the policies of developing the New Man, socialist realist literary works and the ideological instructions issued to writers provide excellent summaries of the official conceptions of the New Man Marxist societies strove to create (Sinyavski 1960; ch. 2 of this book). To be sure, he resembles the ideal human being of the Judeo-Christian morality; he is unselfish, dependable, charitable, altruistic, hardworking, loyal, honest, warm, and kind. However, in placing special emphasis on service to the community or the collective, in favoring the public over private, including familial interest,[9] the socialist-Marxist morality parts company with the Western Judeo-Christian. To be sure, as Castro's statement quoted above suggests, there is not supposed to be any conflict between the private and public spheres, indeed hardly any distinction at all when Communist society arrives.

It was in the attitudes toward work that the socially beneficial character traits of the New Socialist Man were to manifest themselves concretely. These attitudes were to be fundamentally changed or were said to be already in the process of changing. The crux of the change was a new motivation. As Che Guevara put it:

> I am not interested in dry economic socialism. We are fighting against misery, but we are also fighting against alienation. One of the fundamental objectives of Marxism is to remove interest, the factor of individual interest, and gain from men's psychological motivations (Silverman 1971, p. 5).

In a similar spirit Castro said: "We should not use money or wealth to create political awareness. We must use political awareness to create wealth" (Silverman 1971, p. 17). In other words, moral not material incentives were to be used to make people work harder for the good of society.

Similar trends and aspirations were also detected in China under Mao. Peter Worsley, a British sociologist, noted "the Chinese attempt to transform human values and personal relationships at the level of everyday life, to challenge assumptions that certain modes of behavior are naturally 'entailed' under conditions of industrial or city life . . . that some form of class system . . . is inevitable . . . that the attractiveness of material gratifications must, in the end, reassert itself" (Worsley 1975, p. 20).

The attraction of material gratifications has reasserted itself in Marxist societies as each has shifted the emphasis from moral incentives to material ones, or to a mixture of them. In such combinations, the material incentives have usually predominated while the nonmaterial ones have been relegated to symbolic or ritualistic functions. Thus, for instance, in the Soviet Union the government made efforts from time to time to upgrade the prestige and increase the attractiveness of service industries. For example, "An All-Union Rally of Young Workers in Trade and Everyday Services was held in Moscow. The banner of the Young Communist League Central Committee was ceremoniously brought onto the stage, and this was a symbol of the fact that the YCL henceforth regards the vocation of sales clerks, waiters, tailors and shoemakers as among the romantic vocations of our times" (Hollander 1978, p. 213). Such social honors or moral incentives were intended as substitutes for the material ones as the wages of workers in trade and everyday services have remained low and so has, consequently, the prestige of such occupations. By contrast, the Soviet government has lavished considerable material rewards upon those whose work it found truly important: scientists, popular artists and entertainers, writers lending support to the regime, high-ranking officers in the military, police and state security (KGB), high-level Party and government officials, or, more generally speaking, individuals at the upper echelons of their respective occupational hierarchy and of demonstrated political loyalty.

The increasing shift to financial rewards instead of honorific ones has not been the only indication that attitudes toward work have not fundamentally changed in Marxist societies. Even more obvious an indication of the failure to instill a new socialist work ethic has been the reliance on coercion or quasi coercion to induce participation in socially useful labor. All Marxist societies introduced, and perfected to different degrees, a form of labor that was not openly coercive (as the corrective labor camps in the Soviet Union, China, Eastern Europe, and Cuba) nor truly voluntary. It was unpaid labor performed under the pressure of informal sanctions and organized ostracism. Individuals were forced to work on weekends, during vacations, or after hours on top of regular working hours (Nelson 1972, pp. 119–22; Clytus 1970). Laws against "parasitism," "vagrancy," "loafing," or labor indiscipline were other means to make work compulsory. Thus a law passed in Cuba in 1964 "established severe sanctions against workers who failed to produce the amount set by the norms" (Nelson 1972, p. 120). Various forms of dereliction at the workplace were also grounds for a stay at forced labor camps, or the so-called Military Units for Aid to Production (MUAP) (Dominguez 1978; Mesa-Lago 1978). In 1971, a law against loafing was passed based on the premise that "regular daily work was a social duty and one to be unavoidably fulfilled by men from age 17 to 60 who were physically and mentally able to work and women from 17 to 55." Violators were subject to a variety of sanctions including "internment in a rehabilitation institution" and "home arrest while working under the supervision of employees at the delinquent's former work center and of the mass organization near his home" (Nelson 1972, p. 122). The Soviet Union and China had introduced similar measures earlier.

Social Problems

Published research on social problems in Marxist societies is not abundant. There are nonetheless considerable variations with respect to the publicity and social scientific attention such phenomena receive in different Marxist societies. In the Soviet Union and some East European states, far more has been officially revealed about social problems than, say, in China, North Korea, Vietnam, and Cuba. The reticence and carefully controlled publicity Marxist societies bring to the study of social problems are due to ideological constraints. Social problems such as crime, juvenile delinquency, vandalism, alcoholism, drug addiction, mental illness, suicide, family disorganization, ethnic or sexual discrimination, and others are not supposed to exist in Marxist (or socialist) societies

(Connor 1972). Indeed, such problems and the associated antisocial or deviant behavior are officially defined as "survivals" of the past. Attachment to religion is among such survivals, a problem peculiar to Marxist societies which devote significant resources to its eradication or at least containment. (For a study of the relevant Soviet policies, see Powell 1975.) By eliminating the various injustices and contradictions produced by capitalism, social problems were supposed to wither away after the victory of socialism. Such assumptions were spelled out by Lenin as he discussed "excesses," that is to say, what we call today deviant or socially problematic behavior:

> We know that the fundamental social cause of excesses, which consist in the violation of the rules of social intercourse, is the exploitation of the masses, their want and their poverty. With the removal of this chief cause, excesses will inevitably begin to *"wither away"* (Lenin n.d., p. 145).

The basic premise of the quoted, and of much of the Marxist-Leninist theorizing about crime (and other social problems), is that people behave badly in bad societies; that is, in exploitative capitalist societies. In those, such behavior is in part a rational response to poverty and deprivation— and, in part, a consequence of the distortions of character due to the ethos of capitalism, its cash nexus, alienation, and dehumanized social relations. Alcoholism too, for example, can thus be explained as a reflection of the despair of the exploited masses in class societies.

Perhaps the clue to the persistence (and the rise of new) social problems can be found in conditions which turned out to be different from what Lenin had anticipated. The "chief cause" as perceived by Lenin might not have been removed, and there were others he and his followers had not considered. The problem lies in part in identifying state ownership of the means of production with socialism. According to Stojanovic: "It is insupportable to identify state ownership with social ownership and to proceed further in taking this to constitute the basis of socialism. If the entire society (with the exception of the state apparatus) is excluded from the control and disposition of property, then the true character of that property and ownership is concealed and mystified by calling them 'social' " (Stojanovic 1981, pp. 68–69).

The examples to follow will show that while Marxist societies share numerous social problems with non-Marxist ones, they are also afflicted by others which are peculiar to them. Until recently, very little was known about the deficiencies of public health in the Soviet Union, and what was known did not necessarily come from social scientific sources but sometimes from the handful of domestic social critics. Sakharov, for example, revealed that "at the hospitals the patients lie in the corridors. . . . For an ordinary hospital the budget allocates less than one ruble per day per patient for everything . . . conditions are frightful. But for the privileged hospitals the budget allocates up to fifteen rubles per day per patient" (Sakharov 1975, pp. 21–22). Similar contrasts have also been reported from China since the death of Mao (Broyelle and Broyelle 1978, p. 16). More recently, much new evidence has become available about "the health crisis in the USSR," which includes rising death rates and especially infant mortality (Eberstadt 1981).

Even socialist countries such as Hungary—far more prosperous than the Soviet Union and most other Marxist societies—experience serious housing shortages, a social problem peculiar in its severity to Marxist societies including Cuba (Mesa-Lago 1978, pp. 47–48). Two Hungarian sociologists noted that "Hungary shows the symptoms of 'overurbanization' common in the developing countries— lines of beds; men living in cellars and lofts, in woodsheds and sties, in old buses, circus wagons and caves; whole settlements of lean-tos built on the fringes of towns . . . and the price of sublet rooms rising faster than that of any other goods or services" (Konrad and Szelenyi in Field 1976, p. 162).

Crime and delinquency are among the better known social problems in the Soviet Union and Eastern Europe. Probably most of these crimes are directed against property, much of it apparently state or public property, perhaps because, as a former Czech judge remarked, "the state 'had become the owner of more wealth than it could possibly protect' " (Connor in Field 1976, pp. 187, 197). The magnitude of such crimes is reflected in a remark attributed to Khrushchev who supposedly noted that "If people stopped stealing for even a single day, communism could have been built long ago" (Bukovski 1979, p. 189). In both the USSR and Eastern Europe, the majority of delinquents and criminals apparently come from the strata of the population which should have been the prime beneficiaries of the social changes introduced by these regimes: the working classes and their most disadvantaged elements, the less educated and less skilled (Connor in Field 1976, p. 193; Chalidze 1977). More unusual in the Soviet case is the relative freedom of major cities from crime and its greater incidence in smaller provincial cities and new construction sites. This phenomenon is explained by the internal passport and residence permit system which channels newly released prisoners (and potential recidivists) away from large cities (they are refused permission to move there); the superior police protection in big cities is another factor (Shelley 1980).

It is debatable to what extent the social problems associated with criminal and antisocial behavior in these countries are to be explained as responses to the disruptions caused by modernization (and the attendant decline of informal social controls), results of the rise of expectations, or reflections of inadequate living conditions characterized by Sakharov as "a general setting of an exhausting struggle for subsistence among the majority of the population" (Sakharov 1975, p. 12). The same may be said about heavy drinking, the principal among the few forms of escapism available in these societies. The dimensions of this problem have been well documented both within and outside the Soviet Union and Eastern Europe. As far as the USSR is concerned, per capita consumption of alcohol has been steadily rising and significantly exceeds that of pre-revolutionary times. Alcohol abuse in the Soviet Union has also increasingly involved teen-agers and women, and causes enormous economic losses due to accidents, tardiness, and absenteeism at work. Heavy drinking has also been associated with decline in public health (Feiffer 1981; Powell 1983).

While far less is known of crime and delinquency in Cuba than in the Soviet Union and Eastern Europe, its presence has been well established and some of its characteristics are familiar, in particular the association between delinquency, unstable or broken homes, low socioeconomic background, truancy, and low educational attainments (Horowitz 1981, pp. 256–59). Moreover, despite impressive allocation of resources to education, high dropout rates have been found in Cuba, with 12 percent of the total student population neither studying nor working and a percentage of dropouts dramatically increasing with age (Mesa-Lago 1978, p. 102; Nelson 1972, pp. 140–44). In recognition of the seriousness of the crime problem and its dual association with the young and lax discipline of labor, the age of legal liability was lowered to sixteen and "tough sanctions (up to life) were introduced for crimes against the national economy, abnormal sexual behavior and other offenses" (Mesa-Lago 1978, p. 105). Antisocial behavior associated with labor indiscipline emerged as a serious social problem in Cuba and prompted strict responses from the government, reflected in the 1971 law on "loafing" and also in the 1976 Constitution which "reserves to the party and to the state full discretion to limit individual rights" (Dominguez 1978, pp. 251–52). In Cuba as in other Marxist societies, elaborate files follow the worker from one place of employment to another (Nelson 1972, pp. 120, 121–24; see also Bernardo in Horowitz 1981). More specifically:

> Each worker . . . has to have an identification card to get a job and a file with a complete record of his merits and "demerits" (faults). The merits include . . . voluntary (unpaid) labor in the sugar crop; overfulfillment of

work quotas; overtime work without pay . . . a high level of political consciousness. . . . The file also registers any sanctions applied to the worker by civil, military, revolutionary, and other people's courts (Mesa-Lago 1978, pp. 94–95).

Only since the death of Mao have Western social scientists and the public at large begun to have more substantial information about social problems in socialist China. They included the disastrous economic consequences of the Cultural Revolution, rising juvenile crime, defects in new housing programs, air, water, and land pollution, as well as official corruption, favoritism, and embezzlement (on some of these issues see Eberstadt 1979a and 1979b). The problems of rural areas in China, and especially those associated with the motivation of agricultural workers, turned out to be quite similar to those found earlier in the Soviet Union and Eastern Europe. Chinese peasants, like their Soviet counterparts, were more interested in working their private plots than those belonging to the agricultural collectives. They too produced proportionately far more food on a fraction of all arable land, exactly as was the case in the Soviet Union. For example, 25 percent of noncereal products were produced on 5 percent of all cultivated land (Broyelle and Broyelle 1978, p. 15). In Vietnam, too, collectivization of the land had an "adverse impact" and led, like similar campaigns in the Soviet Union in the early 1930s, to "Villagers slaughter[ing] their buffalo and oxen rather than have them confiscated, thereby losing draft animals and fertilizers" (Karnow 1981, p. 12). Due to such (and other forms of) economic mismanagement and the burden of maintaining an army of over a million troops the Vietnamese "people are poorer now than they were during the war." Recently, the government decided to allow greater freedom for private enterprise in the hope of improving the production of many goods and services which can now be sold at free market prices (Shawcross 1981, pp. 62, 63). Such and other revelations in the years since Mao's death and the unification of Vietnam lend plausibility to Peter Berger's suggestion applicable to many societies in the Third World including the Marxist ones: "Perhaps Third World dictatorships only appear to solve the problems of development because they control our information about these problems" (quoted in Hollander 1981, p. 325).

Those touched on thus far do not exhaust the range of social problems in Marxist societies. There also exist discrimination against women (Lapidus 1978; Jancar 1978), ethnic tension and discrimination (Hollander 1978, pp. 341–49; Azrael 1978; Gitelman 1981), and problems centered upon family instability or disorganization (Geiger 1968; Atkinson, Dallin, Lapidus 1977). Marxist societies also have environmental problems (see, for example, Goldman 1972), a pervasive bureaucratization of daily life, and alienation from work socialist style (Konrad 1973; and Haraszti 1978).

Finally, most Marxist societies have one social problem which does not have a counterpart in Western capitalist-pluralist societies: the presence of large groups of people intent on leaving such societies whenever the opportunity presents itself. They included Soviet refugees during World War II; Hungarians after the 1956 revolution; Czechs in 1968; the boat people of Indochina since the mid-1970s; Cubans intermittently since the revolution in 1958 whenever exit was possible; the Chinese making their way to Hong Kong at various times; the East Germans before the Berlin Wall went up; and, most recently, the Afghans. It should be noted that in addition to these massive migrations there has been a trickle of dangerous and illegal departures from all Marxist societies throughout their existence.

Such mass migrations have been socially problematic for the regimes concerned for several reasons. First, there is the symbolic issue, the spectacle of people "voting with their feet," abandoning countries which have prided themselves in creating the historically most advanced and equitable social conditions ever known. Second, the outflow of population, the loss of manpower, and especially of valuable segments of the labor force, is undesirable from the economic point of view. Third, the possibility for discontented segments of the population to emigrate weakens political stability by opening up alternatives rather than compelling adjustment to circumstances which cannot be altered.

The history of Marxist societies is the history of large population movements: voluntary when the borders open up, or their controls can be breached; involuntary when they occur inside the countries and involve the resettlement or dispersal of parts of the population from one part of the country to another, from urban to rural areas, for political, military, or economic reasons (for example, Nekrich 1978). No Marxist society, with the possible exception of Yugoslavia, has ever allowed its citizens to emigrate without punitive restrictions, such as the loss of employment or housing upon application for an exit visa and the prohibition against taking anything but minimal personal property. Moreover, it appears that whereas during the establishment of these societies those inclined to emigrate came primarily from the middle or upper classes, with the passage of time both the socioeconomic and generational composition of these groups have changed. Thus, for example, twelve years after the Cuban Revolution, it was observed that "almost all those emigrating today are from among the poorer classes . . . the very people in whose name the revolution was made" (Horowitz 1981, p. 309). The same phenomenon was also observed with reference to the most recent wave of Cuban refugees—those who came by boat in 1980 (Horowitz 1981; and Hollander 1981, pp. 233–34).

The growing realization that social problems exist in Marxist societies may be taken as proof of the triumphant march of "convergence" earlier thought to herald the confluence of the economic and political structures of Western pluralistic and "Eastern" socialist, state-controlled societies. As time goes by, it appears that what converge most readily are neither the institutional structures nor the loftiest accomplishments of these disparate social systems but their problems and difficulties. It is fairly clear by now that socialist societies have not been more successful than Western ones in controlling their social problems, although they seem less hesitant in devising and applying policies to that end (Solomon 1978). Yet, in all fairness, one should not blame Marxist societies for the failure to eradicate social problems. Many basic sources of social problems, and especially those associated with antisocial and escapist behavior, are endemic to most societies, contemporary and past. Apparently, the typical attributes of Marxist societies, such as the state control over the means of production, one-party rule, and the repetition of watered-down versions of Marxism-Leninism, have not increased greatly the fund of human contentment, the capacity for self-control of the bored and frustrated, reduced interpersonal tensions and conflicts, or improved the ability of human beings to adjust their aspirations to their opportunities.

In Marxist societies (as in non-Marxist ones), the tension between ideal and actual, or between theory and practice, will remain troublesome—and the more so, the more the political authorities dangle the promises of "theory" in front of their citizens, purportedly structuring their societies according to the guidelines of a theory which was conceived over a century ago and has made few claims to apply to parts of the world we now call underdeveloped.

Notes

1. A partial exception to this generalization is Soviet society which attracted more sociological interest over the past three decades. Nevertheless, American sociologists specializing in Soviet affairs remain a handful who would barely fill a seminar room.
2. Of such sources it was said in the Chinese context: "Gradually I realized that the stories these refugees had to tell were richer and more vivid than any other data source. . . . I was struck by the fact that they were teaching me more about Chinese life and politics than I was learning in Peking" (Frolic 1980, p. 2). The issue of using such informants has also been dealt

with in Inkeles and Bauer 1959. Since social scientists rarely reject or regard with suspicion the information provided by disaffected members of their own society (e.g., the poor, the unemployed, ethnic minorities, inmates of prisons, juvenile delinquents, dropouts, residents of counter-cultural communes, political activists, etc.), the same courtesy may be extended to disaffected groups in other societies whose alienation is signaled by their departure. It may also be noted that most American sociologists do not devalue or dismiss the work of those of their colleagues who are highly critical of the society they live in. By the same token, being critical of the society left behind need not disqualify informants from other countries. As for sociologists, such critical attitudes have been regarded as an essential part of their intellectual equipment. Or, as I put it elsewhere: "Alienation in the American context is seen by and large as a wholesome quality and a veritable prerequisite of insight and authenticity" (Hollander 1978, p. xv). For a further discussion of the information refugees provide, see Whyte 1974, pp. 242–47 and London 1975.

3. While the people of Poland managed to develop such alternative conceptions in 1980–81 during the short-lived era of the Solidarity movement, the military crackdown of December 1981 drove home the lesson that such alternatives are illegitimate and intolerable.

4. A question reminiscent of Upton Sinclair's disbelief that those who confessed in the Soviet Purges in the 1930s could have done so involuntarily: "These men had withstood the worst of what the Czar's police could do. . . . My belief is that the Bolsheviks would have let the GPU agents tear them to pieces shred by shred before they would have confessed to actions which they had not committed" (Hollander 1981, pp. 161–62).

5. Thus, for example, "Cuba's rate of political imprisonment is well above that of other authoritarian Latin American governments. In 1974, after fifteen years of revolutionary rule, Cuba had no fewer than forty political prisoners for every 100,000 people in its population; in December 1975, barely two years after the start of military rule, Chile (according to opposition sources) had no more than forty-seven political prisoners per 100,000 population" (Dominguez 1978, pp. 253–54).

6. Or, as Che Guevara poetically expressed such reluctance: "Our vanguard revolutionaries . . . cannot descend, with small doses of daily affection, to the terrain where ordinary men put their love into practice" (Guevara in Silverman 1971, p. 352).

7. Or as Norman Mailer put it: "It was as if the ghost of Cortés had appeared in our century riding Zapata's white horse. You [Castro] were the first and greatest hero to appear in the world since the Second War" (Hollander 1981a, p. 236).

8. Thus it was also reported that "Teng Hsiao-ping does not hesitate to have friends of his with whom he wants to play bridge brought to Peking by airplane" (Bettelheim and Burton 1978, p. 127).

9. Castro said: "In a Communist society, man will have succeeded in achieving just as much understanding, closeness and brotherhood as he has on occasion achieved within the narrow circle of his own family. To live in Communist society is to live without selfishness, to live among the people and with the people, as if every one of our fellow citizens were really our dearest brother" (quoted in Fagen 1969, p. 139).

References

Aron, R. 1950. "Social Structure and the Ruling Class." *British Journal of Sociology* (June).

Atkinson, D., Dallin, A., Lapidus, G., eds. 1977. *Women in Russia.* Stanford: Stanford Univ. Press.

Azrael, J. R., ed. 1978. *Soviet Nationality Politics and Practices.* N.Y.: Praeger.

Bao, Ruo Wang. 1976. *Prisoner of Mao.* Harmondsworth, U.K.: Penguin.

Baran, P. 1961. *Reflection on the Cuban Revolution.* N.Y.: Monthly Review Press.

Barron, J. 1974. *KGB: The Secret Work of Soviet Secret Agents.* N.Y.: E. P. Dutton.

Bauer, R. 1953. "The Pseudo-charismatic Leader in Soviet Society." *Problems of Communism* (June-July).

Bauer, R., Inkeles, A., Kluckhorn, C. 1956. *How the Soviet System Works.* Cambridge, Mass.: Harvard Univ. Press.

Berger, P. L. 1975. *The Pyramids of Sacrifice: Political Ethics and Social Change.* N.Y.: Basic Books.

————. 1976. "The Socialist Myth." *Public Interest* (Summer).

Berman, H. J., ed. 1966. *Soviet Criminal Law and Procedure—The RSFSR Codes.* Cambridge, Mass.: Harvard Univ. Press.

Bettelheim, C., Burton, N. 1978. *China Since Mao.* N.Y.: Monthly Review Press.

Bloch, S., Reddaway, P. 1977. *Psychiatric Terror: How Soviet Psychiatry Is Used to Suppress Dissent.* N.Y.: Basic Books.

Bowles, S. 1971. "Cuban Education and Revolutionary Ideology." *Harvard Educational Review* 41(4).

Bronfenbrenner, U. 1970. *Two Worlds of Childhood: U.S. and U.S.S.R.* N.Y.: Russell Sage Foundation.

Broyelle, C., Broyelle, J. 1978. "Everyday life in the People's Republic." *Quadrant* (November [Sydney, Australia]).

Brzezinski, Z. 1976. "Soviet Politics: From the Future to the Past?" In *The Dynamics of Soviet Politics,* ed. P. Cocks, R. V. Daniels, N. W. Heer. Cambridge, Mass.: Harvard Univ. Press.

Bukovsky, V. 1979. *To Build a Castle: My Life as a Dissenter.* N.Y.: Viking.

Byrnes, R. F. 1969. "American Scholars in Russia Soon Learn about the KGB." *N.Y. Times Magazine* (November 16).

Calzon, F. 1978. "Repression and Political Prisoners." In *Castro's Cuba in the 1970s,* ed. Lester A. Sobel. N.Y.: Facts on File, Inc.

Caute, D. 1974. *Cuba, Yes?* London: Secker & Warburg.

Chalidze, V. 1977. *Criminal Russia: Essays on Crime in the Soviet Union.* N.Y.: Random House.

Clytus, J. 1970. *Black Man in Red Cuba.* Coral Gables, Fla.: Univ. of Miami Press.

Cohen, J. M. 1980. "Analyzing the Ethiopian Revolution: A Cautionary Tale." *Journal of Modern African Studies* 18(4).

Cohn, W. 1980. "Perspectives on Communist Totalitarianism." *Problems of Communism* 29:68–73.

Committee of Concerned Asian Scholars. 1972. *China! Inside the People's Republic.* N.Y.: Bantam Books.

Connor, W. D. 1972. *Deviance in Soviet Society: Crime, Delinquency, and Alcoholism.* N.Y.: Columbia Univ. Press.

────── . 1976. See Field 1976.

────── . 1979. *Socialism, Politics and Equality: Hierarchy and Change in Eastern Europe and the USSR.* N.Y.: Columbia Univ. Press.

Conquest, R. 1968. *The Great Terror.* N.Y.: Macmillan.

Cranston, M. 1977. "Should We Cease to Speak of Totalitarianism?" *Survey* (Summer).

Dallin, A., Breslauer, G. W. 1970. *Political Terror in Communist Systems.* Stanford: Stanford Univ. Press.

Djilas, M. 1957. *The New Class.* N.Y.: Praeger.

Doan, Van Toai. 1978. "Former Vietnamese Captive Describes Life-and Death-in Saigon Prison." *Washington Post* (December 20).

Dominguez, J. I. 1978. *Cuba: Order and Revolution.* Cambridge, Mass.: Harvard Univ. Press.

Draper, T. 1965. *Castroism: Theory and Practice.* N.Y.: Praeger.

Dumont, R. 1974. *Is Cuba Socialist?* N.Y.: Viking Press.

Dunham, V. 1976. *In Stalin's Time: Middle Class Values in Soviet Fiction.* Cambridge, Mass.: Cambridge Univ. Press.

Eberstadt, N. 1979a. "Has China Failed?" *N.Y. Review of Books* (April 5).

────── . 1979b. "China: How Much Success?" *N.Y. Review of Books* (May 3).

────── . 1981. "The Health Crisis in the USSR." *N.Y. Review of Books* (February 19).

Edwards, J. 1977. *Persona Non Grata.* London: Bodley Head.

Fagen, R. 1969. *Transformation of the Political Culture of Cuba.* Stanford: Stanford Univ. Press.

Feiffer, G. (An observer) 1969. *Message from Moscow.* N.Y.: Random House.

────── . 1981. "Russian Disorders." *Harper's Magazine* (February).

Field, M. G., ed. 1976. *Social Consequences of Modernization in Communist Societies.* Baltimore: Johns Hopkins Univ. Press.

Fischer, M. E. 1981. "Idol or Leader? The Origins and Future of the Ceauscescu Cult." In *Romania in the 1980's,* ed. D. N. Nelson. Boulder, Colo.: Westview Press.

Flacks, R., Turkel, G. 1978. "Radical Sociology." *Annual Review of Sociology* 4:193–238.

Frolic, B. 1980. *Mao's People.* Cambridge, Mass.: Harvard Univ. Press.

Geiger, K. 1968. *The Family in Soviet Russia.* Cambridge, Mass.: Harvard Univ. Press.

Gitelman, Z. 1981. "Ethnocentrism and Popular Perceptions of Ethnic Relations in the USSR." Paper presented at the Annual Meeting of American Association for Advancement of Slavic Studies.

Goldman, M. I. 1972. *The Spoils of Progress.* Cambridge, Mass.: M.I.T. Press.

Goytisolo, J. 1979. "Twenty Years of Castro's Revolution." *N.Y. Review of Books* (March 22).

Halperin, M. 1972. *Rise and Decline of Castro.* Berkeley: Univ. of Calif. Press.

────── . 1981. *The Taming of Castro.* Berkeley: Univ. of Calif. Press.

Haraszti, M. 1978. *Worker in a Worker's State.* N.Y.: Universe Books.

Hazan, B. A. 1976. *Soviet Propaganda.* New Brunswick, N.J.: Transaction Books.

Hermassi, E. 1978. "Changing Patterns in Research on the Third World." *Annual Review of Sociology* 4:239–57.

Hollander, G. D. 1972. *Soviet Political Indoctrination: Developments in Mass Media and Propaganda Since Stalin.* N.Y.: Praeger.

Hollander, P., ed. 1969. *American and Soviet Society: A Reader in Comparative Sociology and Perception.* Englewood Cliffs, N.J.: Prentice-Hall.

Hollander, P. 1978. *Soviet and American Society: A Comparison.* Chicago: Chicago Univ. Press.

————. 1981. *Political Pilgrims: Travels of Western Intellectuals to the Soviet Union, China, and Cuba.* N.Y.: Oxford Univ. Press.

Horowitz, I. L., ed. 1981. *Cuban Communism.* New Brunswick, N.J.: Transaction Books.

Hoxha, E. 1979. *Imperialism and Revolution.* Tirana.

Huntington, S. P. 1966. "Political Modernization: Europe vs. America." *World Politics* (April).

Inkeles, A., Bauer, R. 1959. *The Soviet Citizen: Daily Life in a Totalitarian Society.* Cambridge, Mass.: Harvard Univ. Press.

Inkeles, A. 1968. *Social Change in Soviet Russia.* Cambridge, Mass.: Harvard Univ. Press.

Jancar, B. W. 1978. *Women Under Communism.* Baltimore/London: Johns Hopkins Univ. Press.

Karnow, S. 1981. "Hanoi—The Problems of Peace." *The Atlantic* (August).

Karol, K. S. 1970. *Guerillas in Power: The Course of the Cuban Revolution.* N.Y.: Hill and Wang.

Kim Il Sung. 1971. *Selected Works,* vol. III. Pyongyang: Foreign Language Publishing House.

Kolakowski, L. 1970. "The Fate of Marxism in Eastern Europe." *Slavic Review* 29.

————. 1977. "Marxism—A Summing-up." *Survey* (Summer).

Konrad, G. 1973. *The Caseworker.* N.Y.: Harcourt Brace Jovanovich.

Konrad, G., Szelenyi, I. 1979. *The Intellectuals on the Road to Class Power.* N.Y.: Harcourt Brace Jovanovich.

Labin, S. 1961. *The Anthill.* N.Y.: Praeger.

Lapidus, G. 1978. *Women in Soviet Society: Equality, Development and Social Change.* Berkeley: Univ. of Calif. Press.

Leites, N. 1953. *The Study of Bolshevism.* Glencoe, Ill.: Free Press.

Lendvai, P. 1981. *The Bureaucracy of Truth: How Communist Governments Manage the News.* Boulder, Colo.: Westview Press.

Lenin, V. I., n.d. *The State and Revolution.* Moscow: Foreign Languages Publishing House.

LeoGrande, W. M. 1981. Two Decades of Socialism in Cuba. *Latin American Research Review* 16(1).

Lewis, O., Lewis, R. M., Rigdon, S. M. 1977. *Four Men: An Oral History of Contemporary Cuba.* Urbana, Ill.: Univ. of Illinois Press.

Leys, S. 1977. *Chinese Shadows.* N.Y.: Viking.

London, Ivan D. 1975. "Interviewing in Sinology: Observations on Methods and Fundamental Concepts." *Psychological Reports* 36:683–91.

Lowenthal, R. 1970. "Development vs. Utopia in Communist Policy." In *Change in Communist Systems,* ed. C. Johnson. Stanford: Stanford Univ. Press.

Marcuse, J. 1967. *The Peking Papers.* N.Y.: Dutton.

Matthews, M. 1972. *Class and Society in Soviet Russia.* N.Y.: Walker.

————. 1978. *Privilege in the Soviet Union: A Study of Elite Life-Styles Under Communism.* London: Allen and Unwin.

McDowell, E. 1981. "Did Castro Double-cross Oscar Lewis?" *N.Y. Times* (October 26).

Mesa-Lago, C. 1978. *Cuba in the 1970s: Pragmatism and Institutionalization.* Albuquerque, N.Mex.: Univ. of New Mexico Press.

Mickiewicz, E. 1967. *Soviet Political Schools.* N.H: Yale Univ. Press.

Nekrich, A. 1978. *The Punished People.* N.Y.: W. W. Norton.

Nelson, L. 1972. *Cuba—The Measure of the Revolution.* Minneapolis: Univ. of Minnesota Press.

O'Dell, F. A. 1978. *Socialisation Through Children's Literature: The Soviet Example.* N.Y./London: Cambridge Univ. Press.

Powell, D. E. 1975. *Antireligious Propaganda in the Soviet Union.* Cambridge: M.I.T. Press.

————. 1983. "Drinking and Problem-Drinking in the Soviet Union." Cambridge, Mass. (Unpublished.)

Reinhold, R. 1981. "Peking Hampering Scholars from U.S." *N.Y. Times* (August 16).

"Resolution on History of Mao's Contributions and Mistakes." 1981 [excerpts]. *N.Y. Times* (July 1).

Rigby, T. H. 1968. *Communist Party Membership in the USSR, 1917–1967.* Princeton: Princeton Univ. Press.

Ripoll, C. 1979. "Dissent in Cuba." *N.Y. Times Book Review* (November 11).

Ripoll, C. 1981. "The Cuban Scene: Censors and Dissenters." *Partisan Review* 48(4):574–87.

Sakharov, A. 1975. *My Country and the World.* N.Y.: Vintage Books.

Shawcross, W. 1981. "In a Grim Country." *N.Y. Review of Books* (September 24).

Shelley, L. 1980. "The Geography of Soviet Criminality." *American Sociological Review* 45 (February).

Silverman, B., ed. 1971. *Man and Socialism in Cuba: The Great Debate.* N.Y.: Atheneum.

Sinyavski, A. 1960. *On Socialist Realism.* N.Y.: Pantheon Books.

Solomon, P. H., Jr. 1978. *Soviet Criminologists and Criminal Policy.* N.Y.: Columbia Univ. Press.

Stojanovic, S. 1981. *In Search of Democracy in Socialism.* Buffalo, N.Y.: Prometheus Books.

Thomas, J. 1981. "Cuba's School for Exporting Marxism." *The New York Times Magazine* (October 4).

Trotsky, L. 1965. *The Revolution Betrayed.* N.Y.: Merit Publishers.

Ulam, A. B. 1979. *The Unfinished Revolution.* Boulder, Colo.: Westview Press.

Urban, G., ed. 1972. *The Miracles of Chairman Mao: A Compendium of Devotional Literature 1966–1970.* Los Angeles: Nash.

Wald, K. 1978. *Children of Che: Childcare and Education in Cuba.* Palo Alto, Calif.: Ramparts Press.

Whyte, M. K. 1974. *Small Groups and Political Rituals in China.* Berkeley: Univ. of Calif. Press.

————. 1975. "Inequality and Stratification in China." *China Quarterly* 64:684–711.

————. 1977. "Child Socialization in the Soviet Union and China." *Studies in Comparative Communism* 10(3).

Whyte, M. K., Vogel, E. F., Parish, W. L., Jr. 1977. "Social Structure of World Regions: Mainland China." *Annual Review of Sociology* 3:179–207.

Wolfe, B. D. 1956. *Communist Totalitarianism.* Boston: Beacon Press.

Wolin, S., Slusser, R. M. 1975. *The Soviet Secret Police.* Westport, Conn.: Greenwood Press.

Worsley, P. 1975. *Inside China.* Totawa, N.J.: Rowman and Littlefield.

Zeitlin, M. 1967. *Revolutionary Politics and the Cuban Working Class.* Princeton: Princeton Univ. Press.

Part II
CONTRASTS

16.
Sociology, Selective Determinism, and the Rise of Expectations

While many complaints have been made about the inadequate impact of sociology on American society (as well as some exaggerated claims about its powers, benevolent or diabolical), one manifestation of its influence has been given little attention. It is the spread of some basic premises of the discipline, in particular the belief in the social-cultural determination of personal life, which have deeply penetrated popular thinking in the 1960s. That sociologists, in their professional roles, subscribe to some form or degree of such determinism is no revelation.[1] It could not be otherwise. Sociology stresses the social over the personal, the group rather than the individual, social forces over personal motives, the patterned instead of the unique, and the determined rather than the undetermined aspects of social existence. Not only does such an orientation follow from the most obvious and fundamental premises of the discipline, it is also intimately related to the liberal political values and social consciousness of most sociologists.[2] One channel through which such ideas and orientations have filtered through to the general public is college education. Several generations of college-educated Americans have been exposed to them, not only because of the absolute growth in the numbers of those who attend college, but also because of the popularity of sociology courses.

In the 1960s, such general themes of sociology became increasingly merged with those of social criticism and with the growth of highly *personal* expectations and not only of social, racial, and sexual justice, the redistribution of wealth, or institutional reform, but also of personal happiness, fulfillment, and self-realization. Peculiarly and paradoxically, such desires came to be fused with an unusually explicit and intense emphasis on sociological determinism—with the claim that the individual has become less and less in control of his fate, less and less responsible for his happiness or unhappiness. Correspondingly, the latter came to be seen as increasingly dependent on society, on social institutions and forces.

These attitudes are well illustrated by the remarks of members of a radical group intensely alienated from and critical of American society.

While individual misery and deprivation have often and justly been blamed on social institutions, the derivation of highly personal problems and attitudes from the defects of society was usually absent from the utterances of revolutionaries of other periods. It is hard to imagine Robespierre, Bakunin, Lenin, or Trotsky voicing sentiments such as the following:

> I am all fucked up. Too many problems that I have to deal with. I am amazingly selfish . . . [because] that's certainly how we are taught in a capitalist society, and I am a child of capitalism.
>
> Venceremos brigade shows the extent . . . to which this country's system of values prevents us from achieving our revolutionary goals. [Comment made with reference to extreme individualism, "ego-tripping," lax work discipline, etc., observed among members of the Brigade—P.H.]
>
> I am beginning to understand how very thin is the line between neurosis and oppression, and consequently how in the most profound way the solution to what formerly seemed our most personal problems is deeply political.
>
> I can fight the system because I truly hate it. I hate how it has warped the people of our country. How it tries to warp me and everyone it can.
>
> Amerika does a lot of ugly things to people. It puts walls between them.[3]

A recent letter to the *New York Times* exemplifies another variant of the same tendency:

> Listening to the stories behind each hijacker . . . points to a recurrent theme of frustration: to the hijacker the hijacking seems to represent a last, desperate effort for personal integrity in times that make this basic human feeling so hard to realize. It saddens me to hear these frightened, despondent men sentenced to more of the same despondency for 20 years. Perhaps an understanding of the man behind the act will calm our outrage in the hope that a potential hijacker can feel that the people of this nation empathize with him and with his economic and personal frustration and despondency.[4]

Gwynn Nettler commented on the same phenomenon (and the contribution of the social sciences to it) in another context, that of modern morality:

> The moral movement that is shifting the burden of responsibility is represented by . . . *the death of traditional justifications.* . . . The new mythology sees entities called the Establishment, the Power Structure, Society (with capital S) and, of course, the System as the origin of goods and evils, of the causes of our conduct, and hence, as "responsible" to

and for us. The logic that attributes blame to the System reduces the responsibility of the individual enmeshed in it. . . .

The demise of traditional justifications and the birth of new ones have been assisted by the burgeoning of the behavioral sciences. . . . The behavioral sciences have helped shift the load of responsibility from individuals to environments. Their message allocates responsibility for conduct to causes beyond the control of the actor. He is seen as a *product* . . . interacting with his rearing (which he could not have arranged) and realized through the opportunities provided or denied to him by his place in a "social structure" in which, without election, he found himself. . . . Modern morality attributes behavior to circumstance; it thereby converts sin to sickness and erases fault. Its working hypothesis is that, if behavior is caused, its agent is not culpable.[5]

It could, of course, be argued that the popular themes of social determinism were not taken from sociology, but are of an ideological and political derivation. This possibility is suggested by the fact that the popular social determinism of our days is not consistent but selective. In general, it proposes (or implies) that only the behavior of "underdogs" is socially determined, that only people assigned to such groups are not in full control of their lives and behavior; only the lower strata are cast into certain roles by more powerful social forces, groups, or agencies, or are equally helpless victims of expectations or "labeling."

It is debatable how one defines underdog groups or individuals, or what constitutes being underprivileged, deprived, or powerless. Power and powerlessness are not one-dimensional (e.g., student radicals may not be able to change American foreign policy, but they can easily bring to a halt, disrupt, or alter the operations of large universities). Still, one could reach agreement on the definition of some important underdog categories, such as the poor. We would, however, still have to face the question of whether or not the social-cultural determination of behavior operates only among the underprivileged and, if so, how systematically or uniformly. Or to put it differently: is the lack of opportunity (and what type of opportunity?) the only form of social determination that reduces responsibility for one's behavior? It could certainly be argued, as Marx did (though it is rarely done today), that if members of the more powerful or privileged groups are also "products" of their environment, then their choices too are limited and hence their moral accountability.[6]

Today, sociological determinism is generously but selectively applied to excuse, mitigate, or condemn different forms of behavior, or even the same behavior on the part of different people or groups. There is, for example, an increasing tendency among people of liberal persuasion to view convicted criminals as victims of the system (sometimes even as political prisoners), or extend a measure of sympathy and understanding to those who undertake politically motivated bombings or attacks on policemen. Such acts are sometimes seen as reflections of a deep frustration with an unresponsive political system that allows little if any choice. At the same time, social determinism (sympathetically applied to those who are perceived to be the underdogs) becomes suspended when judging the behavior of other groups such as the military brass, FBI agents, policemen, politicians, corporation executives, Southern "rednecks," or Northern construction workers. In short, the bad guys have a choice but the good ones don't. Moral indignation presupposes choice on the part of those who provoke our indignation.[7] A plausible victim-aggressor scheme needs a device such as selective social determinism that relieves some groups of responsibility for their actions but not others. It remains an interesting and little studied question as to what circumstances of life actually deprive people of making a choice, or limit their responsibility, and in what situations. There is, however, general agreement that great poverty and little or no education are among such factors. This, however, does not mean that they are the only ones.

Whatever the basis of such claims—and they may be perfectly valid—the fact being stressed here is that more and more groups, and especially the most alienated, among *both* the privileged and underprivileged, resort to a form of sociological determinism that reduces (or eliminates) responsibility for their behavior and dissatisfaction with their circumstances of life. It is also apparent that sociology can be used, and is being relied upon, to support this endeavor, even if its principal motives are to be found in the political-ideological realm.

It is noteworthy that a strong sense of the social-cultural determination of personal lives is so often linked to a far from fatalistic attitude toward the social determination observed and decried. Within the same ideology we find both an allegation that society, or its institutions, impose suffering and frustration upon the individual in a determinate manner and, at the same time, a growing intolerance of these very frustrations and a generally rising level of expectations for improvement. According to those who simultaneously espouse determinist and antifatalistic views, the determinism that is operant in the world of the unfortunate victims of institutional arrangements does not imply any limitations on the possibilities of realizing, through human action, the most difficult aspirations and expectations for material prosperity and personal fulfillment. Observing such contradictory attitudes does not imply a viewpoint which would either deny the (limited) problem-solving capabilities of sociology or the obvious fact that there are connections between the personal and social realm, between what C. Wright Mills called "personal troubles" and "public issues." The difficulty lies both in assessing the precise nature of such connections and in arriving at a satisfactory moral position for the sociologist who must live with the uncomfortable knowledge that the social world and individual lives are neither totally determined nor wholly undetermined.

What we now see is an extravagant emphasis on the freedom of the social sciences to transcend any determinate limitations on human conduct; we are told that sociology must help remake the world and even provide meaning for the lives of individuals. This expectation, which is manifest in the growing radicalization of sociology (and of the social sciences in general), is not merely a reflection of the spread of political protest and activism around the campuses or of the mood of social criticism among many intellectuals that has taken root and intensified since the mid-1960s. It is more deeply rooted in a massive rise in the level of expectations—no longer only or predominantly material, but also psychic and philosophical. It is part of the accelerating quest for meaning in life and the rising expectations that such a quest can and ought to be successful. It is another side of the well-worn coin of anomie described recently by Gagnon and Simon:

> Affluence generates a kind of anomie all its own. The ease and abundance with which certain goals are achieved trivialize the goals. One response to the anomie of affluence, as seen long ago by Durkheim, is a quest for new, more intense experience. Something of this phenomenon can be seen in the pursuit of drug experience by many middle class young people.[8]

A reflection of rising expectations and of the pressures put upon sociology (and the other social sciences) "to deliver" can also be detected in the renewed questioning of the scientific status and claims of sociology. To be sure, this questioning and the related debates are not new; the humanistic tradition and focus in sociology is venerable and long-standing, as is the related fear of the impact of dehumanizing and depersonalizing techniques and methods. (We are all familiar with the scornful label of "technician" juxtaposed to the proud title of "intellectual.") What is perhaps new is the ideological fervor with which even attempts at objectivity are denounced in the name of strong value commitments.

The current questioning of the functions, status, and achievements of sociology is more intense, more widespread, and more explicitly tied to social protest than before. Cries of despair, such as the following, are becoming so commonplace as to no longer be shocking:

Something is dreadfully wrong with contemporary sociology.[9] While the usual indexes of professional success . . . show a marked increase and proliferation, a malaise of undefined proportions still stalks the discipline.[10]

Less common but even more revealing are impassioned attacks such as the following:

Sociologists stand guard in the garrison and report to its masters on the movements of the occupied populace. . . . Sociology has risen to its present prosperity and eminence on the blood and bones of the poor and oppressed; it owes its prestige in this society to its putative ability to give information and advice to the ruling class of this society about ways and means to keep the people down.[11]

Comments such as these reflect more than impatience with the slow progress of the discipline, or its failure to provide significant findings about society or to display powers of prediction; even more than disillusionment with its alleged lack of social criticism. Such outbursts exemplify an attitude of ideological engulfment—anger over the defects of American society displaced in effect upon sociology. If Mr. Nicolaus and his sympathizers had their way, sociology would become a vehicle of political protest and partisanship and a new form of rhetoric which, expressive as it may be, would do little to alleviate the evils of American society or make us understand them better. (It may be noted that the attribution of evil is not only psychologically satisfactory, but also offers a shortcut, or substitute, for analysis and explanation; evil is self-explanatory, and its attribution or discovery removes the need for qualified assessments, for the recognition of complexity or unintended consequences which might dilute or defuse indignation.)

The radical approach also entails a curious mixture of optimism and pessimism: despair over the present cannot turn into anger without some underlying optimism about alternatives in a fundamentally improved future; without such optimism it could not be urged that sociology become totally committed to and instrumental in bringing about social change. The radical critique of the status quo implies a belief in the far-reaching perfectibility of social institutions (and human beings); otherwise, it would have no basis for denouncing those uncommitted, or insufficiently committed, to such changes. As Lewis Killian observed:

Radical sociologists who look forward to a revolution in which not only the evils of the existing system will be swept away but evil itself will be diminished or abolished are in their way as optimistic as "liberal" theorists who conclude that the system can and will endure if it is only reformed.[12]

Another expression of the same phenomenon is a revulsion from specialization and the quest for becoming interdisciplinary—a trend that may also have significant implications for the future of the discipline. Thus the desire for "wholeness" at the personal level manifests itself on the scholarly level by impatience with disciplinary boundaries, just as a more general rejection of fragmentation and specialization often leads to the rejection of social, or role, differentiation of any kind. In the final analysis, sociology, as a field of learning with a relatively well defined entity, may be eroded if such tendencies reach fruition.

In this context, it should also be noted that advocates of special group interests—e.g., those promoting Black Studies, Ethnic Studies, Women's Studies and Radical Studies—have little concern with or interest in disciplinary or even intellectual autonomy;[13] such studies are, as a rule, frankly politicized and find it difficult to comprehend the usefulness of such conceptions.

The emergence of a new set of expectations is further reflected in the occasional teaching of sociology (and psychology) in the sensitivity-training format, also directly related to the attempt to utilize these disciplines as personal or group problem-solving devices.

Hence it is not altogether impossible that sociology as a discipline (already fragmented by its current subfields) might wither away, becoming further fragmented along ideological lines or absorbed into specific problem areas, such as urban or ethnic studies. Developments sketched here mirror the ideological polarization of American society as a whole and the politicization of academic life in particular.

It is hard to be sanguine about the ability of sociology to make a dent on the contradictory and diverse demands made upon it. It is a discipline which (in some of its current interpretations and uses) subscribes to social determinism in regard to some groups and wide margins of moral choice and responsibility for others. It is assumed to be a vehicle of social change (gradual or revolutionary, depending on who makes the assumption) which contributes to the rise of expectations (material as well as nonmaterial), but it has little to offer when the expectations raised founder in anomie, and people cry out for new sources of social cohesion, solidarity, and personal values. If used without flinching, sociology mercilessly relativizes all beliefs and values at a time when despite certain forms of debunking or demythologizing, multitudes of middle-class Americans long for sustaining beliefs.

Can sociology be all things to all people? Can it simultaneously raise and control expectations, subvert and support ideologies? Can it be used by protectors *and* critics of the status quo alike—expose one set of illusions while creating hunger for others? Can it be both a scientific discipline and a tool of radical social change?

It is perhaps unfortunate for the development of sociology that its popularity and high levels of institutionalization coincide with a period in American history when the consequences of secularization long in the making are the most painfully felt, especially by intellectuals and those with humanistic interests and ideals in the population at large. Sociology (and other social sciences), if honestly pursued, cannot but conclude with the dispiriting finding that, as Isaiah Berlin noted, not all highly valued ends are compatible or, as observed by Merton, that highly valued things often lead to and generate other things we devalue and wish to escape from. In other words, among the patterns the social sciences uncover is one that suggests that scarcities rule our lives and that human existence is framed by limitations of every kind[14]—a proposition incompatible with the current rise of expectations and abhorred by those groping for more intense meanings and fulfillment in life today. And yet these are precisely the kinds of expectations which are being projected on the social sciences and sociology in particular.

No matter how often sociologists tell one another, their students, or segments of the larger public that values cannot be derived from facts (even if we find out what the facts are and agree upon them), the hope lingers on that those who know more of certain things are wiser. Or, more specifically, the belief persists that since sociologists are, at least in theory, better informed on important human and social problems that concern everybody, they may—and should—have better answers and better access to values, or be more qualified to formulate social policy, which after all represents an application of (somebody's) values. Yet, as Duncan McRae, Jr., points out:

> The dominant concepts of sociology seem singularly inadequate for a general value system acceptable today. Social order and functional analysis point to precisely the opposite values from those that many younger sociologists wish to realize. . . . In response they have proposed more emphasis on other concepts . . . : conflict, violence, power and revolution. But . . . these concepts are also inadequate valuative bases: they deal with means, not ends. To favor revolution and oppose power is a temporary stance at best, for one is driven to ask: Revolution for what?[15]

It is more than likely that demands will mount in all the societies where sociology is widely practiced. Sociologists will be asked to be helpful in relation to a large variety of social problems, including those reflecting anomie, or the crisis of values. As bewildered individuals in search of an identity, and the alleviation of a wide range of personal problems, turn to psychiatrists, therapy groups, or political movements—groups of people turn to sociology for more than a dispassionate diagnosis of the pervasive sense of malaise, meaninglessness, and confusion. In most secular, urban societies expectations will continue to grow—both material and meaning-seeking—but it is difficult to see what social forces may gather to satisfy them.

Postscript 1982

This chapter, as most of the other pieces found in the second part of this volume, touch on or explore some facet of alienation among intellectuals (and other groups) in American society. As such it also sheds some light, if only by implication, upon the persisting susceptibility to the ideals associated with socialism.

Since the article was written, there has been one notable development in American and Western European sociology: the rise and penetration of Marxist perspectives and the new focus and content they have given to the sentiments and attitudes of alienation discussed previously. Thus estrangement has moved from the street, so to speak, from protest, riot, and demonstration, to the classroom and the pages of academic journals. Marxism in some form or another has achieved a new respectability and influence in the social sciences, and sociology in particular.[16] This development has in no way diminished the selective uses of social determinism I had discussed in my article. It seems plausible that the revival of Marxism in Western societies (as opposed to the total indifference toward it in societies which legitimate themselves by its ideals) has more to do with its use as a fuel or component of estrangement and social criticism than its intrinsic problem-solving power or theoretical illumination.[17]

One final comment. The rise of expectations has been arrested or at least reduced in the course of the late 1970s and early 1980s due to the newly arisen domestic economic difficulties. Since these economic hardships followed long periods of material prosperity, they are unlikely to create the kind of stability of expectations and concomitant resignation that prevail in societies where expectations are generally low and fluctuate little. Thus, perhaps paradoxically, in American society at any rate, both prolonged affluence such as peaked in the 1960s and occasional economic hard times intensify estrangement and social criticism.

Notes

1. However, in their nonprofessional roles they give no more evidence of adherence to such beliefs than most other segments of the population.

Paradoxically, one only finds evidence of such "beliefs" among groups who are totally unaware of the existence of these concepts but nonetheless behave as if they subscribed to them; that is, the most impoverished, downtrodden, and apathetic groups. Berlin's comments on the more general aspects of this phenomenon are applicable to sociologists: "Men evidently find it perfectly possible to subscribe to determinism in the[ir] study and disregard it in their lives. Fatalism has not bred passivity in Moslems, nor has determinism sapped the vigor of Calvinists or Marxists." He also noted that "whether or not determinism is true . . . it seems clear that the acceptance of it does not in fact color the ordinary thoughts of the majority of human beings, including historians, nor even those of natural scientists outside the laboratory. For if it did, the language of believers would reflect this fact" (Isaiah Berlin, *Four Essays on Liberty* [New York: Oxford University Press, 1969] p. 69).

2. S. M. Lipset and E. C. Ladd, "The Politics of American Sociologists," *American Journal of Sociology* 78 (July 1972): 67–104; and W. R. Gove, "Should the Sociology Profession Take Moral Stands on Political Issues?" *American Sociologist* 3 (Aug. 1970): 221–23.

3. *Venceremos Brigade* (New York: Simon and Schuster, 1971), pp. 16, 392, 388, 373.

4. *New York Times*, 16 July 1972.

5. G. Nettler, "Shifting the Load," *American Behavioral Scientist* (Jan.–Feb. 1972): 372–73.

6. For example, being born in a military family where the son is expected to follow the father's career and being deprived of access to more liberal viewpoints represents a limitation on opportunities for self-realization. To be sure, a person may even under such conditions evade the pressures of his environment and choose a nonmilitary occupation, or become a humane and liberal military officer. The same can be said of the proverbial slum child, born in a poverty stricken, broken family surrounded by criminals, drug addicts, prostitutes, and school dropouts, without becoming one himself. One may also consider the behavior of some of the Watergate conspirators highly determined: Were they not "products" of the cold war period, exposed during their formative years to anti-Communist hysteria, parents with right-wing beliefs, growing up in Southern California in an ethos of public relations and manipulative advertising?

7. Or again, as Berlin has written: "To blame or praise individuals or groups of individuals for acting rightly or wrongly . . . entails a suggestion that they are in some sense genuinely free to choose betweeen alternatives . . ." while on the other hand, ". . . one cannot complain of what cannot be otherwise." For the consistent determinist "praise and blame are functions of ignorance; we are what we are, like stones and trees, like bees and beavers, and if it is irrational to blame or demand justice from things or animals, climates or soils or wild beasts when they cause us pain, it is no less irrational to blame the no less determined characters or acts of men" (Isaiah Berlin, *Four Essays on Liberty*, pp. 51, 105, 59–60).

8. J. H. Gagnon and W. Simon, eds., *The Sexual Scene* (New York: Aldine, 1970), p. 19.

9. Meaning American sociology, since the article quoted made no reference to sociology in other countries.

10. H. Gamberg, "Science and Scientism: The State of Sociology" *American Sociologist* 2 (May 1969): 111.
11. M. Nicolaus, "Remarks at ASA Convention," *American Sociologist* 2 (May 1969): 155.
12. L. Killian, "Optimism and Pessimism in Sociological Analysis," *American Sociologist* 4 (Nov. 1971): 281.
13. It is paradoxical that sociologists in societies where the discipline is explicitly subordinated to public policy and political values are desirous of greater autonomy (e.g., in the USSR and Eastern Europe, veiled as the expression of such desires might be), while the autonomy of sociology in the United States and other Western societies is often denied or disparaged or rejected altogether by those who wish to subordinate it to programs of social transformation or revolutionary change.
14. Including such limitations as the "imperatives of order, of continuity and of triviality," as observed by Peter Berger. That, as he points out, "sociology is conservative in its implications for the institutional order" is the most intriguing paradox in view of the values and beliefs of so many who are attracted to sociology precisely because of their desire for rapid and radical social change (P. Berger, "Sociology and Freedom," *American Sociologist* 6 [Feb. 1971]: 3). See also Edward Shils, "Plenitude and Scarcity," *Encounter*, May 1969.
15. D. McRae, Jr., "A Dilemma of Sociology: Science Vs. Policy" *American Sociologist* 6 (June 1971): 5, 6.
16. The continued or renewed appeals of Marxism are also discussed in other essays in this volume (See pp. 318–19, 326–27).
17. See also Leszek Kolakowski, "Marxism—A Summing-up," *Survey* (Summer 1977).

17.
The Ideological Pilgrim—
Looking for Utopia, Then and Now

It is surely no secret today that many of the distinguished Western intellectuals who visited the Soviet Union in the 1930s fell short of grasping the true nature of Soviet society. Their predispositions, combined with the special efforts of their hosts, resulted in grotesque misjudgments which are no longer matters of dispute. We have learned since, as did most of the visitors themselves, that the Soviet Union was not a very happy land in the 1930s.

Today, as a rule, Western intellectuals who hope to find a social system superior to, or more promising than, their own no longer go on pilgrimages to the Soviet Union. If they go there they do so in a more critical frame of mind, aware of the basic shortcomings of the society they are visiting. At the same time, a new generation of intellectuals has set out (since the late 1950s) on new voyages of discovery. Their destinations were: Cuba, China, and North Vietnam.

Their motives were as varied as their personalities, occupations, levels of accomplishment, and renown in their own societies. Yet they also had enough in common to be analyzed as one group. They were all ready, in some degree of eagerness or desperation, to be favorably impressed by the countries to be visited. This does not mean that all came back favorably impressed, or that all of them praised without reservations what they had seen. Nevertheless, most of the accounts from all three countries are generally positive and bear an astonishing resemblance to the reports of the earlier generation of visitors to the Soviet Union. Even without the rash assumption that "history is repeating itself," there are enough similarities, and enough of a pattern, in these eyewitness accounts to sustain the possibility that the similarities may have as much to do with the attitudes and perceptions of the visitors as with the sights and conditions actually observed.

If indeed many similarities can be noted in such travel writings, there are the following possibilities to account for them. The countries and their institutions observed were highly similar. The backgrounds, social position, and ideological leanings of these Western intellectuals had enough in common to produce similar perceptions of dissimilar realities. It was the nature of Western societies that predisposed them to a shared susceptibility to the appeals of new societies. Finally, it is also possible that in all four countries in both periods the visitors were exposed to the same refined techniques of hospitality (or, perhaps, the same manipulation of experience) which, despite different historical and social conditions, produced similar impressions. Until we know as much about present-day social institutions and life in Cuba, China, and North Vietnam as we know of the Soviet Union under Stalin, the question of *how* inaccurate recent reports have been compared with those written earlier about the Soviet Union must inevitably be left open.

It would be wrong to suggest that *all* the travelers I will be considering here were "utopia seekers." They represent rather a range of attitudes which does include a quest for utopia as well as milder degrees of favorable predisposition and susceptibility toward the utopian aspects of the new societies. Not all the travelers set out to find some approximation of their ideals and longings. Many of them went on their tours out of "sheer curiosity" or because they felt that it was "important" that they themselves assess the nature of these societies often seen as misrepresented or slandered in the mass media of their own countries. Others embarked on these journeys because of certain concerns and interests. They wanted to know how particular problems unresolved in their own societies were handled, from race relations to public health, from day-care centers to industrialization, from prison reform to state support of the arts. Thus while some visitors projected the most extravagant hopes on the countries visited, envisioning a totally new way of life and a radical break with all the imperfections of the past and of organized social life, others focused on more tangible and specific accomplishments: on new forms of economic organization or administrative techniques, on more rational (or seemingly more rational) solutions to age-old problems. Yet enough of them may be described as "ideological pilgrims," and it is this group which will be my major focus.

Participants in the ideological pilgrimages can be classified in terms of the metaphor of the Romantic Lover or the Religious Pilgrim. The Ideological Pilgrim, like the religious one, visits the holy places of his secular religion. It may be Lenin's tomb (a literal parallel), the walls of the Kremlin, the "heart of socialism" (as Moscow used to be considered), a commune in China, the sugarcane harvest in Cuba, a school for reformed prostitutes, a model prison, a new factory, a folk-dance festival, a political mass rally—or any other setting, event, or situation in the countries he visits which symbolizes the realization of his dreams and values. After the pilgrimage, he returns spiritually refreshed. Back in his homeland, he continues to revere the beliefs and symbols associated with holy places visited.

In turn, the ideological pilgrim resembles the Romantic Lover in that his passions are fueled by the unattainability of the love-object. The Lover in the Western world, as Denis de Rougemont once demonstrated, has always needed carefully retained obstacles to the fulfillment of his longing. He knows that he will not live in the society he admires but will return to the comforts and boredom of the one which he despises. George Bernard Shaw spoke for many such travelers when he said, embarking on his return trip from the Soviet Union in 1931: "Tomorrow I leave this land of hope and return to our Western countries of despair." Although such a traveling intellectual seeks to immerse himself in the setting of his ideals, he will not become part of it. Distance remains, and it helps to conserve the dreams. Usually he knows neither the language nor the unappealing features of the country visited. He is shielded by his hosts from a close embrace with the object of his affections. Mysteries will persist although he may succeed in convincing himself that he knows all that is to be known. Both the institutions and individuals representing the longed-for social order remain only partially and poorly known. He can continue the idealization and projection of his deepest desires.

The persistence of this phenomenon is at present illustrated by the attractions of China. In the wake of the recent reestablishment of American contacts with her, there has been a resurgence of interest in that country on the part of both the American public and large segments of the Western intellectual community. Startling transformations of the image of China are taking place. We are witnessing a rare moment in history when one set of stereotypes is being abruptly replaced by another.

Those who have always been favorably inclined toward Communist China speak out with a new pride and forcefulness. The benefit of doubters is confirmed in their lurking sympathies; the critics are beginning to feel uncomfortable. The trickle of highly selected Western visitors, journalists, sympathetic academics, businessmen, and assorted VIPs is likely to become a sizable rivulet. More and more intellectuals will be taking their turn on the ideological pilgrimage to China; the number of similarly disposed visitors to Cuba and North Vietnam is declining.

Many times in European (and American) history such attitudes have intensified in times of crisis. Dissatisfaction with existing social arrangements and institutions has always prompted a quest for alternatives. The more recent twentieth-century journeys to new societies may well fit into a broader, long-standing, historical pattern. This, as I will try to show, is most strikingly demonstrated in one recurring theme in the accounts of both sets of travelers. It is the theme of Simplicity, Community, and Authenticity allegedly found among the peoples of the new societies. As Henri Baudet has put it: "The natural goodness that developed so harmoniously in others formed a striking contrast to our errors and corruption."[1]

The countries most likely to be idealized in this century have had to meet certain requirements. In particular, they had to be (1) distant; (2) scarcely known; (3) hostile to the United States (and one or two selected West European nations); (4) seemingly dedicated to some set of utopian goals; (5) the claimants of a Marxist ideological legacy. The fifth element is noteworthy because it draws attention to the continuity of some form of "leftism" among groups of Western intellectuals. Finally, among the sources of attraction we also find (6) the Underdog image. All of these countries tend to be viewed (at the time of the visit) as Victims—victims of history, of backwardness, and (more importantly) of the West. Correspondingly, the appeals of the Soviet Union faded by the mid-1950s, in part because it became difficult to cast her in the role of "the underdog" when she emerged as the second major military and industrial "superpower" of the world.

Estrangement from one's own society and susceptibility to the attractions of another land are closely related. The late 1920s and early 1930s of the depression-ridden United States and Western Europe offer a good example from the recent past. Then, as now, intellectuals were in the grip of a "crisis of confidence" concerning their own society. The Soviet case offered a hopeful alternative to the economic and social chaos of the period. Today, in the United States and Western Europe, the emptiness of second- (or third-) generation affluence and the growth of various complex social problems are among the factors which contribute to the admiration of societies which seem to exude a "sense of purpose" and appear to have provided "meaning" for the lives of their citizens. Social criticism must rest on a vision of new alternatives, radical departures, hopeful beginnings, or inspiring models.

In both periods, many intellectuals were searching for a type of social order which they could enthusiastically endorse and contrast with the dispiriting state of affairs in their own countries. To contrast the two periods is of additional interest since the two groups of intellectuals who made the visits have been, for the most part, of different generations and political persuasions. The most obvious difference is, as I have suggested, that by the 1960s alienated Western intellectuals were no longer looking to the Soviet Union for inspiration; nor were they adherents, members, or "fellow travelers" of the Communist parties of their countries.

Thus the difference between the two groups is also the difference between the Old and the New Left.

If some degree of estrangement from one's own society precedes the projection of hope on to others, what exactly did intellectuals (and especially those going on expectant visits to the countries mentioned) dislike most about their own, their native land?

The basic theme beneath all the specific complaints associated with the attitude of "alienation" is that society, through some (or most, or all) of its major institutions, unjustly and unnecessarily blocks people from self-realization. That the fulfillment of the true self remains a vaguely defined concept has no bearing on the intensity with which this form of criticism is felt and formulated. It is easy enough to define and comprehend "self-realization" when it refers to access to such self-evident necessities as adequate food, shelter, clothing, and medical care which are insufficiently provided even in many prosperous Western societies. Hence concern over Poverty as a major obstacle to self-realization is one of the common themes displayed in the writings of alienated intellectuals in both periods. Indignation over poverty leads to the more general criticism of inequality (which transcends unequal income distribution and inequality of opportunities of various kinds).

Alienated intellectuals in Western capitalist societies also deplore the poisonous effect of the "pursuit of money," the "crass commercialism" permeating society, and the related impoverishment of the aesthetic-spiritual sides of life. In short, the critique of the pervasiveness of the "cash nexus" has been, since the Communist Manifesto (1848), a principal component of the social criticism mounted by Western intellectuals. Not surprisingly, it was among the appeals of the new societies that they were (or seemed to be) free of the preoccupation with money: ". . . for the first time in my life I was sharing the breath of a great city with a folk which has not fouled the air by perpetual forced incense to the cult of money."[2] This was the joyous observation of an American writer, Waldo Frank, in his Dawn of Russia, upon his arrival in Leningrad in 1932.

Broadly speaking. alienated intellectuals in both periods have been critical of what in the received phrase of today is called the "quality of life." The hallmark of this critique has been a concern with the distortion and erosion of spiritual values, the loss of individuality and critical spirit, and the bondage of the masses. It has also focused on the insidiously corrupting influences emanating from an affluent industrial-consumer society and the more refined but more deadly manipulations to which people of such societies are subjected. This is how Norman Mailer registered (in 1963) the defects of American society, contrasting it with Cuba:

> In Cuba hatred runs over into the love of blood; in America all too few blows are struck into the flesh. We kill the spirit here, we are experts at that. We use psychic bullets and kill each other cell by cell.
>
> We have had a tyranny here . . . a tyranny one breathed but could not define; it was felt as no more than a slow deadening of the best of our possibilities, a tension we could not name which was the sum of our frustrations. . . . In silence we gave you [Castro] our support . . . [for] you were giving us psychic ammunition, you were aiding us in that desperate silent struggle we have been fighting with sick dead hearts against the cold insidious cancer of the power that governs us.[3]

A further component of alienation, felt with special intensity by American and European intellectuals, is apprehension about Technology and its misuses. Here we have a revival of another long-standing fear haunting the literati for a century, the nightmarish vision of Man against the Machine and the impersonality associated with the latter. For Susan Sontag, "what's most ugly about America [is] the principle of "will," the self-righteous taste for violence, the insensate prestige of technological solutions to human problems."[4]

Although Vietnam, poverty, and racial discrimination supplied the major components of the critique of American society in the 1960s, beyond and beneath it lurked other sentiments, other sources of despair, as Mailer's remarks have suggested. What many of the critics detested most about American society was what they believed it had done to people, to personal relationships, the capacity for love, trust, and a sense of community. In this vision, American people have become "fragmented," sapped of the capacity for strong and authentic feeling, cogs in a dehumanized "System." Such sentiments are readily and frequently voiced by present-day American social critics:

> I can fight the system because I truly hate it. I hate how it has warped the people of our country. How it tries to warp me and everyone it can.
>
> Not long ago I was in pieces. All the experiences of my life had conspired to fragment my understanding. . . . I suffered from the prime American problem: middle class consciousness, the inability to feel.
>
> We had all been taught to relate to people in their social roles. . . . In Cuba this was not the case.[5]

Nor was it the case in China or in North Vietnam:

The atmosphere in which the Chinese worker lives seems to be a healthy one, a place where a worker can grow and develop into a well-rounded, complete person.[6]

There possibly is no place in America where people feel "community" as much as in this Vietnamese village.[7]

The feeling that something was fundamentally wrong with Western societies, that their failings transcended the more specific and easily identifiable ills (such as poverty, unemployment, or racial discrimination), although especially intense in the 1960s, was also discernible in the 1930s. There was, in many instances, a similar sense of the fundamental flaws and aimlessness of the societies the travelers came from. Thus Feuchtwanger wrote:

I came to the Soviet Union from countries where complaints are the general rule and whose inhabitants, discontented with both their physical and spiritual conditions, crave change. . . . The air which one breathes in the West is stale and foul. In the Western civilization there is no longer clarity and resolution. . . . One breathes again when one comes from this oppressive atmosphere of a counterfeit democracy and hypocritical humanism into the invigorating atmosphere of the Soviet Union.[8]

As George Bernard Shaw felt:

The bourgeoisie is rotten. The army is rotten. The monarchies are rotten. Above all parliamentary institutions are rotten.[9]

Corliss and Margaret Lamont perceived the contrast in these terms:

The direction in the Soviet, from both the material and cultural standpoints, seems steadily and on the whole upward, and the problems those of growth. Elsewhere in the world the direction seems downward and the problems those of decay. In other words the many stresses and strains still existent in Russia are justified in the light of the great goal ahead. The masses of the people are making what may be called *constructive* sacrifices, with a splendid purpose held consciously and continuously in mind.[10]

Once the facts of intense alienation are established it is comparatively easy to understand why, and how, sympathy toward certain other societies develops. It is of particular importance that these other societies—their spokesmen and mass media—reproach American society (or other Western societies) for almost exactly the same defects the estranged intellectual feels so strongly about. Kindred voices are raised (or so it seems) denouncing: racism; unemployment; capitalistic greed; wastefulness; irrational economic arrangements and the misuse of resources; the expenditure on the military; the impoverishment of human relationships; the decline of meaningful values; the lack of community; and the vulgar noises of advertising. How could an intellectual resist a sense of affinity with, and sympathy toward, those who evidently share his values, likes, and dislikes?

The alienated intellectual is favorably disposed toward these "new societies" in order to avoid the despair that comes from the lack of alternatives. He must believe that better social arrangements are possible and must be able to point, at least tentatively, to such arrangements to make his social criticism more meaningful. The worse one's own society appears, the more alluring and promising others become, especially from a distance or through the haze of a conducted tour that minimizes the possibility of disillusioning experiences intruding on the visitor. For the intensely alienated intellectual to admit that other social systems are "just as bad" as the one he knows best, or that they represent no significant improvement over his own, would dilute his moral outrage directed at his society. If social injustice is endemic and discernible even in "new" revolutionary societies, it becomes difficult to sustain the impassioned criticism of one's own. But when particular defects of society are viewed as easily remediable, and if some societies can be found to illustrate this, a new and vastly improved basis for the critique of one's own society is created. It is this need for new, fresh alternatives which explains why attachment to the Soviet model was relinquished with the passage of time.[11]

After fifty years, not only has there been an impressive accumulation of data concerning the nature of Soviet society and the extent to which it has departed from its revolutionary origins and ideals, but there have also emerged new, "more authentic" revolutionary societies (such as Cuba, China, and North Vietnam) which could absorb the types of sentiments and sympathies which had earlier been reserved for the Soviet Union.

An inventory of the appeals of the "new societies" might begin with their accomplishments in reducing economic backwardness and other liabilities of the past.

Julian Huxley noted, for example, that in Siberia

> cities spring up almost overnight, called into being out of barren steppes at the behest of central authority, all in due relation with the natural resources of the region and the planned lines of communication and electrification.[12]

For Huxley, as for many others, the Soviet Union of the 1930s was "an enormous experiment" based "on reason alone" (in the words of Lion Feuchtwanger). The gigantic social-economic transformations observed and praised were inseparable from a rational and energetic application and organization of work. Western visitors of both periods repeatedly expressed amazement at both the scale and intensity of the work being accomplished, and the "new meaning" it held for those performing it. Waldo Frank wrote:

> Here are happy workers, because they are whole men and women. . . . Dream, thought, love collaborate in the tedious business of making electric parts . . . he [a Russian worker] was closer to the artist than to the Western factory worker. His eyes burned with an ascetic flame . . . he might have been a saintly artisan in some medieval convent (*Dawn in Russia*).

Tom Hayden and Staughton Lynd, stopping in China (en route to North Vietnam), caught glimpses of the dedication to work:

> Everywhere is the pulse of purposeful activity. Walking before breakfast one day we passed a group of women energetically singing before starting a day's work . . . progress is everywhere. Millions of Chinese are involved in its creation. In Peking we saw thousands of people digging a canal while music blared from outdoor loudspeakers (*The Other Side*).

The visible transformation of the landscape, the sight of new cities, industrial plants, flood-control projects, bridges, newly cultivated lands— all these offered tangible and indisputable proof of the Great Change taking place. Equally impressive were the new or reconstructed social institutions the visitors saw.

The visitors in both periods were keenly interested in improvements in educational institutions and the spread of knowledge to the masses. Such improvements held a strong appeal because of their close association with equality and because they were linked to the vision of bringing to the surface the hidden potentialities of man. Corliss and Margaret Lamont's enthusiasm was widely shared among the visitors of both periods:

> In whatever museum we enter in Leningrad we run across workers' tour groups thirstily drinking in the knowledge which is offered them by guides especially trained for the purpose. . . . If you glance at their faces you find that they are all alike in having an eager, awakened look (*Russia Day by Day*).

Discussing the Hanoi Museum of Art, Father Berrigan was moved by "a people, who in the midst of a rain of death conceive and push to fruition a museum of art."[13] Jean-Paul Sartre reported that in Cuba "most of the old army barracks have been converted into schools."[14] Discussing the cultural policies of the Chinese regime, Simone de Beauvoir wrote: "The Chinese government is aware of its duty to serve the entire nation; it considers truth its soundest ally."[15] Ella Winter was impressed by the educational role of the Soviet press:

> What they print is directed towards making an active, conscientious, responsible human being. Journalism in Russia, like all other means of communication, is dedicated in the fullest sense of the word, to the education of all people.[16]

Another form of education (or reeducation) which made a deep impression was discovered in the prison system. Here was an example of both the "new humanism" displayed by these societies and their rational, ingenious problem-solving capacity. Replacing the odious spirit of punishment were "humane prisons" oriented toward the rehabilitation of wrongdoers. This is how the philosophical foundations of the new approach to crime were perceived by an early visitor to the Soviet Union:

> Crime according to Soviet law . . . is always the result of faulty social organization and bad environment. The word punishment is not approved of: it has been replaced by the phrase: "measures of social defense." . . . Sentences are short and once the sentence has been served the miscreant is readmitted into everyday life with no . . . scar of shame, no brand of having been a "convict." . . . Soviet criminology seems to assume that the "criminal" is not a criminal. He is not to be treated as an outcast. . . . He is an "unfortunate," sick, weak or maladjusted and must be trained to become . . . a functioning member of society.[17]

George Bernard Shaw, inspecting a Soviet prison for women, opined that "none of the women would have been better off as innocent persons earning their living in an English factory," and found being in a Soviet prison a "privilege" compared with those in capitalist countries. Visitors to Chinese prisons were similarly impressed. For example, while Simone de Beauvoir pointed out that the prison she had visited was "not a model prison," it had, among many others, these appealing features:

> The prison is in the depth of a kind of park; two soldiers are on duty at the outer gate; but once you are inside it you see no wardens, no guards, no guides, only un-uniformed and . . . unarmed overseers. They exercise

the function of foremen and political and cultural instructors (*The Long March*).

The appeal of specific institutions (farms, factories, schools, clinics, or model prisons) converged on the overarching accomplishment of social equality, or at least the great strides taken in its direction. For Julian Huxley the result was seen as

> a system in which the results of work go primarily to raising the level of general well-being instead of largely seeping away into private channels (*A Scientist Among the Soviets*).

Even more pronounced were the results in China: "What is most striking about the tranquil and gay crowd at one's side," wrote Simone de Beauvoir,

> is its homogeneity. Men are not all of the same station in China but Peking offers a perfect image of a classless society. Impossible to tell an intellectual from a worker . . . nobody is arrogant here, nobody is grabby, nobody feels himself above or below anybody else (*The Long March*).

Similar attitudes dominate the accounts of the visitors to Cuba:

> There is so little condescension here. That is the most beautiful thing. Every man, no matter what he is doing, is contributing. Every man and woman, and Fidel brings this out constantly, is just as important as he, Fidel is (*Venceremos Brigade*).

The appeal of the Leaders was as powerful as that of the newly dignified Masses. They were perceived as honest, modest (though immensely able), dedicated, and hardworking men, all preoccupied with the Public Good. Feuchtwanger considered Stalin "the most unpretentious" of all the men known to him who ever held power; the Soviet leaders in general were "as good as their word . . . ready to receive criticism and exchange frankness for frankness."

Simone de Beauvoir commented on the impressive characteristics of the Chinese leaders as she observed them at a reception:

> Chou En-lai moves amid the guests, exchanging words, shaking hands; then similarly at ease Mao Tse-tung, by himself, with quiet unostentation makes the rounds of the tables. What is so winning about these Chinese leaders is that not one of them plays a part; they are dressed like anybody else . . . their faces . . . are just faces, plainly and wholly human. Never before have I seen official dignitaries whom their position did not hold

some distance apart from the rest of the crowd . . . their visage manifests an uncommon personality . . . they inspire . . . respect (*The Long March*).

As for Father Daniel Berrigan, he was reminded by Ho Chi-Minh of Jesus and his sufferings.

For Jean-Paul Sartre, Castro and his comrades exerted an even deeper fascination, conjuring up visions of the triumph of mind over the body, spirit over the flesh. This is how Sartre described a visit to Che Guevara's office at midnight:

> I heard the door close behind my back and I lost both the memory of my old fatigue and any notion of the hour. Among these fully awake men, at the height of their powers, sleeping doesn't seem like a natural need, just a routine of which they had more or less freed themselves. . . . They have all excluded the routine alternation of lunch and dinner from their daily program.
>
> . . . of all these night watchmen, Castro is the most wide-awake. Of all these fasting people, Castro can eat the most and fast the longest . . . [for they] exercise a veritable dictatorship over their own needs . . . [they] roll back the limits of the possible (*Sartre on Cuba*).

Powerful and heroic Renaissance men, rolling back the limits of the possible, exercising iron-willed command of body and mind, tirelessly reshaping their society—such was the vision of these leaders that many Western intellectuals like Sartre were ready to embrace. They were touched by the heroic dimension not only in the lives of the Leaders, but also in the newly meaningful and dramatic aspects of everyday life of the Masses, from which the humdrum, prosaic elements seemed to have vanished.

Reading through these accounts (and many others I have not cited here) the reader is left with the impression that the major appeals of the new societies cannot be reduced to better schools, higher living standards, improvements in public health, or even to the apparent realization of the ideals of the Enlightenment (as was recently argued in a study of Communist fellow travelers by David Caute).[18] What is involved transcends the economic and even the political realm. Only if the meaning of "political" is stretched to encompass concerns with community, identity, self-realization, authenticity, and meaning in life, only then can we properly define these appeals as political. Many of the visitors were most impressed by the virtuous peoples of these lands: their good nature, innocence, candor, openness, honesty, and simplicity. These attractions were especially notable for complicated people coming from complex societies. As Barbara Wootton put it recently in *Encounter* (June 1973):

> To anyone coming from a world which threatens to strangle itself in its own complications it is the apparent simplicity of Chinese life which makes an irresistible appeal.

Upon his arrival in a Russian village Waldo Frank found

> a homogeneous world: man and animal and fruit, air and wood and earth, were a single substance whose parts slowly vibrated round its core—the sun.
>
> . . . I stood in the village mud and sensed the organic rhythm of this telluric world—the pulse of earth and beast and man together. The peasant, the unsophisticated toiler, has a self knowledge, humble but authentic. This our Western culture has merely covered and destroyed with a patina of lies. And that is why there is more hope in the uncultured workers of all races (*Dawn in Russia*).

It is the vision of and fascination with "wholeness" that dominates:

> There are no separate things in Russia, no separate persons . . . every person is in full flowing action with the folk about him. Therefore he is vital—with the whole vitality of Russia.

Several decades later it is, again, the attribute of wholeness that affects most deeply another pilgrim (Susan Sontag), this time to North Vietnam:

> In Viet Nam one is confronted by whole people possessed by a belief in what Lawrence called "the subtle, lifelong validity of the heroic impulse."

And again, like the Russian peasants, their appealing qualities were enhanced by the primitive material conditions surrounding them: "We see charming, dignified people living amid bleak material scarcity." Miss Sontag found North Vietnamese men "extraordinary human beings," free of "the phenomenon of existential agony, of alienation." Lynd and Hayden regarded the Vietnamese they encountered as "the gentlest people we had ever known" and were "struck by [their] grace, variety and established identity."

The qualities of the people and the sense of community that prevailed among them were seen as closely related. The escape from a deeply felt social isolation has been the most powerful attraction that the "new societies" exert. Of all the accounts I have read, those by members of the "Venceremos Brigade" provide the most striking example of this ecstatic submersion in the group:

> At the end of their performance, the entire crowd of us—performers, the directors of the camp, all the compañeros—surged out in a happy, dancing, hugging, silly, singing herd with this tremendous, overwhelming group energy. We stamped and yelled and improvised our way around the entire camp, people banging on all kinds of things: empty wooden boxes, drums, spoons, bottles, anything.
>
> Here people are high on their lives all the time. A group called *Los Bravos* charged in from back, parting the crowd, sounds of deep drum, a bell, a guitar, and sticks, charging deep rhythm. Everyone went wild. . . . An actual physical force seemed to surge through the room, men dancing with men, women with women, everyone's hands on everyone else's shoulders, a huge snake line forming and chugging around the hall: lawyers, translators, drivers, cane cutters, students, waiters, an absolute frenzy of brotherhood and excitement. . . .
>
> The Cubans are like superthyroid freaks; the men will make music and dance and screw around at the drop of a hat.
>
> At lunchtime . . . the whole crowd spilled out onto the lawn, falling down sweaty, screaming at the top of their lungs, rolling down the hill. . . . That much unadulterated emotional give is almost unbearable. I begin to really conceive of being part of a current, that in the process of a revolution you are both very important and very small; we're talking about something bigger than all of us, and that is the transformation of an entire people, the liberation of that kind of energy we saw this evening, the beginning of building the new man. . . . High on the people! Woooiiieeeeeeee!!

The visitors also found much to approve of in regard to the position of intellectuals in the countries visited. To begin with, the Leaders themselves had discernible intellectual leanings: Mao and Ho (the poets), Stalin (the voracious reader deeply concerned with theory and linguistics), Castro and Guevara (thinkers and doers)—each had attributes intellectuals could admire and identify with. They also had power to implement their ideas—which Western intellectuals did not have, as a rule. The local intellectuals were taken seriously by the leaders who held that "ideas are weapons." They also seemed "well integrated" in their society, not living on its margins as ignored eccentrics. There were also attractively tangible forms of recognition. The visitors often observed that the material circumstances of artists and intellectuals were commensurate with their importance in their society. Feuchtwanger wrote:

> They are appreciated, encouraged and even pampered by the state both with prestige and large incomes. . . . The books of favourite authors . . . are

printed in editions of a size which makes the foreign publisher gasp (*Moscow 1937*).

In China, de Beauvoir noted:

> By and large Chinese writers have never enjoyed such material prosperity . . . author's royalties being 10 to 15% earnings may be very high. . . . If moreover a writer wishes to travel, to undertake research, if he needs spare time for study or creative work, if he needs medical care or rest, all sorts of facilities are at his disposal. This preferential service is paid for: in China whoever receives must give; the writer is expected to render *service* (*The Long March*).

Even when the visitors caught glimpses of certain limitations of intellectual freedom they often felt that such restricitons were only a temporary necessity and a relatively small price to be paid for "effective participation in a new social order," for "escaping social isolation," for gaining a "new sense of community," and for finding life generally pulsating with purpose and meaning.

In the final analysis, the many appeals of the New Societies coalesce around two major themes. One is that of Social Justice and its many components—economic, political, and cultural. The second theme is more elusive but probably more important. It comprises the achievement of or striving for "Wholeness," the sense of Identity and Community. Such appeals mirror a *malaise* which goes beyond and beneath dissatisfaction with specific political arrangements, with the defects of capitalism and the particulars of social inequality. They derive from "civilization and its discontents." Some are endemic, while others intensify in an increasingly secular society that can no longer either legitimate the curbing of individualistic impulses and fantasies, nor can it offer fulfilling social myths and values which could divert attention from the growing preoccupation with the self. Behind the metaphors of Wholeness, Identity, and Community lies the craving for a universe, or at least a social world, that makes sense, that has meaning and direction.

Such a craving is no less pronounced among intellectuals than among "ordinary" people. Of late it appears that the former find it less tolerable to live in a world of "disenchantment" from which "the ultimate and sublime values have retreated"—as Max Weber once characterized the corrosive process of secularization. It is one of the paradoxes of our times that intellectuals, once the vanguard of the process of secularization, seem to have become its victims, unwilling to come to terms with an existence that offers no old or new versions of "enchantment."

How does the organization of the Ideological Pilgrimages influence the perceptions and judgments of the travelers? Here, again, the crucial part played by predispositions must be stressed. No matter what the most expansive of hosts arranged, his efforts might well have been completely unsuccessful without the favorable predispositions of the visitors. This, however, does not mean that the techniques of hospitality—the special, organized circumstances under which the tours took place—can be dismissed as unimportant.

Let me note, to begin with, that most of the visitors discussed here did not speak the language of the country visited. Hence they were largely limited to communication through interpreters. (Brief encounters with those speaking the language of the visitors did occur; but rarely were they chance occurrences.) In most cases, they traveled in groups and were escorted by guide-interpreters; even when they were not in groups, guides were assigned to them. As a rule, the visitors had never been in the country before and, generally speaking (though with some notable exceptions), their knowledge of the country was not extensive. People who had given indications of a critical attitude toward the countries in question were not invited or encouraged to go on such trips.

The techniques used to create favorable impressions were of two types. The first had to do with the treatment of the visitor, his personal comfort and welfare, and the measures taken to make him feel important, well liked, and appreciated. All such measures had the objective of making it psychologically difficult to develop or express negative feelings toward those who were so kind and friendly to him and toward the society they represented.

The second consists of the selective presentation of reality, the highly organized and planned nature of the trips. The probability of acquiring positive impressions is vastly enhanced when the visitor is systematically and purposefully exposed to the attractive aspects of a country: good food and accommodations; comfortable travel; politeness at every turn; and pleasant, interesting, or inspiring sights.

Both techniques are greatly facilitated by the centralized nature of the societies in question: by the governmental control of such resources as accommodations, travel, tourism, the mass media, and cultural life. "Ordinary citizens," in turn, are fully aware of the importance of foreign visitors and of the role and authority of the guides and interpreters escorting them—a circumstance that greatly reduces spontaneous exchanges between them and those so escorted.

The "most favored" treatment of distinguished visitors starts at the very beginning of their journey. After George Bernard Shaw's special sleeping car crossed the border at the station, the guide formally introduced him to two waitresses [of the railroad restaurant] who were longing to meet the great Bernard Shaw. By an extraordinary coincidence they were intimately acquainted with his works. GBS was sufficiently moved by this remarkable evidence of Russian literacy to express the opinion that waitresses in England were not so well read as their Soviet sisters (*The Rationalization of Russia*).

Although not every visitor was given such honors, even figures of lesser importance received the kind of treatment they could not expect in their own society (certainly not on the part of the government). The Lamonts, for example, were met at the Leningrad railroad station by a "brand new Lincoln-Eight." On the arrival of Lord and Lady Boyd Orr: "Hardly had the door of the plane opened than a blue uniformed figure was bounding toward us. . . . [He] beamed and thrust a bouquet into my hands and another into my wife's. 'We have a car.' " Accommodations also turned out to be most satisfactory. it was a "fine hotel, six stories high, with lifts, marble entrance floors and a bathroom to every bedroom." The very same night an impressive dinner awaited the visitors. "It was our introduction to Chinese feasts, and thirty officials, most of them from the Ministry of Foreign Trade, helped to induct us. Tiny cups of warm wine for toasts . . . the intricacies of Peking duck . . . soup at the end of the meal. . . . We rose from the meal lighter in heart, for there was Dr. Chi Chaoting . . . suggesting that, if we were willing, he might find time to accompany us for part of our travel. We could not have asked for more."[19]

In turn, Lynd and Hayden upon their arrival in Hanoi were confronted with the irresistible charm of "little girls dressed in colourful uniforms approaching us hesitantly, with flowers and salutes"—while for Father Berrigan "the loveliest fact of all was the most elusive and insignificant; we had been received with flowers."

Accommodation was rarely less than excellent. Simone de Beauvoir records her own experience:

My room . . . was immense: all to myself I had two brass double beds, covered with a bright pink silk. . . . I had a mirrored wardrobe, a desk complete with everything I needed for writing, a vanity table, a couch, armchairs, a low coffee-table, two night-tables, a radio; on the bedside rug were a pair of bedroom slippers; cigarettes and fruits were placed every day on another table (*The Long March*).

Lavish hospitality in Cuba (for members of an International Cultural Congress) included:

the free, all-in, luxurious hotel life for the delegates . . . four enormous nightclub dining-rooms to choose from, an international cuisine (changed daily), free laundry service, free telephone . . . free taxi-cabs and Congress cars and buses, free (three) daily papers and weekend magazines in three languages, and free entry to the city's theatres and exhibitions . . . added to all that my return air ticket, plus my overweight was also paid when leaving Cuba. Too much, much too much to accept.[20]

Visitors to each of the four countries have also reported the receipt of a wide variety of gifts, ranging from the collected writings of Ho Chi-Minh to records, cigars, caviar, wine, cigarettes, bottles of rum, and various other items.

Attention to their welfare and comfort also manifested itself in the provision of superior means of transportation (chauffeured limousines, first-class railroad compartments, planes and helicopters), even when such means of transportation were scarce.

The visitors were notably well fed even at times when food shortages existed in the countries they toured, such as the USSR in the 1930s or North Vietnam in the late 1960s (and to a lesser extent, also in Cuba and China). That food was of some importance is also suggested by the many references to its quality, quantity, and variety in most of the travel reports.

Examples of this kind could be multiplied, but surely there is no need for this. Few would deny that the visitors were well treated and that the hosts were anxious to make a favorable impression. What I suspect would be less readily agreed upon is the result of such attentions. Most visitors would argue that they were not blinded by all or any of the forms of hospitality; nor could it be proven that such was the case. The fact remains, nevertheless, that the hosts were intent on producing favorable impressions on the visitors, and that in most instances they did depart with such impressions as reflected in their written accounts.

I must stress once more that the details of hospitality are not significant in themselves but in their totality. Warm, friendly reception, comfortable accommodations, pleasant travel arrangements, fine food, interesting sights, interviews with important and busy political figures—all add up to a set of impressions and experiences calculated to make the visitor feel in some measure receptive to the Message his hosts intend to convey to him. Given the combination of personal flattery, the provision of material comforts, and carefully screened sights and personal encounters, it would have been peculiar indeed if the visitors had not left the countries in question with their favorable dispositions strengthened and with a new accumulation of enthusiastic judgments and observations.

Several clearly defined patterns of selective exposure to reality emerge from the travel reports. In many instances, the visitors themselves were fully aware of, and at times uncomfortable with, the manner in which their tours were organized. They did not, however, consider this a real threat to the authenticity of the experiences gained. Compare a few descriptions of such patterns.

> In each visit to a commune, hospital, factory, housing area or other unit, there was a basic pattern. We would arrive, chat for a few minutes, and then be shown into a room for a short briefing. Inevitably there were glasses of hot tea, cool, damp towels for freshening our faces, and packs of cigarettes. These sessions were usually conducted by a "responsible person," that is, some sort of leader of the area we had come to see. After his or her talk, we asked questions for a while, and then were given a tour of the area. . . . We never saw anything to indicate that our briefings had not given a very good representation of the situation (*China! Inside the People's Republic*).

Evidently, such patterns changed little over time in China since, while the aforementioned was observed in 1971, the following dates from the mid-1950s:

> No matter what factory, school, village anywhere from Peking to Canton, the ritual would never vary an iota. You enter a large room whose walls are covered with red banners bearing gold inscriptions; these are tokens of satisfaction conferred by the government, or messages of friendship or various commemorative diplomas. You sit down on a sofa . . . before a low table loaded with cigarettes and cups which an attendant keeps at all times brimful of green tea. . . . Some person of rank, a cadre, sets forth the situation. Next you inspect the premises. After that, it is back to the seats for more tea-drinking and question period (*The Long March*).

Susan Sontag wrote of her experiences in North Vietnam:

> We are truly seeing and doing a great deal: at least one visit or meeting is planned for every morning and afternoon, and often in the evening as well. . . . We are in the hands of skilled bureaucrats specializing in relations with foreigners. . . . Everybody here seems to talk in the same style and to have the same things to say. This impression is reinforced by the exact repetition of the ritual of hospitality at each place we visit.

She complained about

> the constraint of being reduced to the status of a child: scheduled, led about, explained to, fussed over, pampered, kept under benign surveillance.

> Not only a child individually, but even more exasperating, one of a group
> of children (*Trip to Hanoi*).

Hebert and Trudeau also experienced the technique of being shielded
from private contacts with the citizens. In one instance, their conversation
with a French-speaking priest was obstructed; in another, they were not
allowed an unsupervised meeting with an English-speaking Chinese
journalist. They concluded:

> We could ask almost anything of our Chinese hosts, and they actually
> refused us nothing—except to talk to a Chinese without a witness.[21]

Occasionally, the selective presentation of reality involved more than
shielding the visitor from random or disapproved contacts and experiences. At times, "reality" was restructured. For example, when Henry
Wallace and Owen Lattimore visited Magadan, one of the notorious
forced labor camps in the Soviet Union, in 1944:

> All prisoners in the area were kept in their huts. Watch towers were
> demolished. Various other deceptions were undertaken. . . . Wallace was
> shown a farm, the best in the area: fake girl swine herds, who were in
> fact NKVD [political police] office staff, replaced the prisoners for the
> occasion. All the goods that could be scraped up in the neighborhood were
> put in the shop windows, and so on.[22]

A highly unusual "inside" account of the use of such techniques
(provided by a former Chinese guide assigned to foreigners) offers yet
another perspective on the scope and intricacy of these operations. Many
of its details are borne out, indirectly, by the accounts of some visitors
and their particular experiences.

> In Shanghai, as in other selected cities, the Communists organized a special
> Committee for Reception of Visitors. . . . It employed a large number of
> college graduates as interpreters and receptionists, whose qualifications were,
> in order of importance: (1) membership in the Communist Party or Young
> Communist League, wholehearted devotion to socialism and political al-
> ertness; (2) good presence and manners; (3) knowledge of at least one
> foreign language. After they were engaged, they attended frequent political
> lessons. . . . They had to go early in the morning to receive instructions
> from the reception committee; each night, after saying goodnight to the
> visitors . . . they had to submit a written and verbal report to the Committee
> and discuss any problems which might have arisen during the day, such
> as unsympathetic attitudes or questions by the foreigners or clumsy be-
> haviour by any Chinese.

The selection of sights to be shown was predetermined:

> First, the Party selected certain cities where the travellers could "freely choose" to go: Canton, Shanghai, Hankow, Tientsin, Hangchow, Mukden, Changchun and Peking. . . . In these cities the best hotels were chosen for official guest-houses. . . . Local people entered these premises only by special permits. First-class attendants, cooks, hair-dressers, and beauty specialists were employed after careful scrutiny and approval by the Security Bureau. Top quality consumer goods such as tea, silk, brocade, and works of art unavailable in the open market were sold to visitors at ridiculously low prices. . . . Buddhists or persons interested in religious freedom would be taken to Shanghai's beautiful Yu Fe or Bubbling Well Temple. There the monks would earnestly inform visitors that before the Communists came the temple buildings had been in a very dilapidated state. . . . Since the Communist take-over, they would say, the Government had spent a great deal of money on renovations. . . . What the monks never mentioned was that more than 90 per cent of Shanghai's Buddhist clergy had already left priestly for worldly lives because of Communist persecution.

Person-to-person meetings were arranged with equal care.

> To meet the requests of overseas "friends" for contact with private Chinese individuals, the Reception Committee made arrangements for visitors to call on people in every walk of life, to have a meal or cup of tea and chat with them. These model homes of scholars, factory workers, peasants and capitalists were the show windows of socialism.[23]

Only in regard to the Soviet Union of the Stalin period has it been clearly established that the visitors were deceived, if not always by staged events or settings, then by the overall image of Soviet life conveyed to them. The Soviet case, at any rate, has proven that "being on the spot" or "seeing things for oneself" is not a guarantee or sufficient condition for the accurate assessment of the nature of a society. This is, I think, worth stressing since, in general, a major factor which influences the perception of the travelers (and the sweeping conclusions drawn from what they have seen) is that they were provided with a representative or characteristic sampling of the social institutions and aspects of life in the countries visited. The idea that they have been exposed to carefully selected sights, groups, or individuals might (and often did) cross their minds, but they usually brushed off this possibility. Thus they could proceed freely to generalize about life in these countries on the basis of isolated experiences and brief encounters.

Although there are many similarities between the techniques of hospitality used in all four societies in both periods, this in itself does not and cannot prove that visitors to China, Cuba, and North Vietnam were also deceived. If this were the case, it would mean that broader social realities in these three countries diverged as extensively from what the visitors had seen as was the case in the Soviet Union. Thus far, we do not know *how great* a gap there was between the selected exposures and all that the visitors had no opportunity to see—although I submit that there are numerous enough similarities between the two sets of travels to suggest such a possibility.

In the final analysis, we must look to the nature of Western societies to find the major clues for a better understanding of both the estrangement and the utopian impulses among Western intellectuals.

What, traditionally, has been the social role of intellectuals and especially the intelligentsia's conception of its social role?

For at least a century, leading Western intellectuals conceived of themselves as Outsiders and Critics (especially in the United States), deprived of appropriate recognition, rewards, and power. Although objective social conditions have significantly changed—resulting from the expansion of higher education, the growth of the mass media, and increased governmental reliance on the skills of intellectuals—these perceptions and attitudes have persisted. Intellectuals remained estranged from and critical of the ethos of bourgeois-capitalist society, its preoccupation with commerce, business, material success, social status, and competitiveness.

Second, intellectuals, like the rest of the populations in these societies, have experienced the psychological difficulties of living in large-scale, complex, mobile, and bureaucratized urban societies in which the level of social isolation and impersonality has significantly risen. Such weakened social ties have been especially strongly felt by intellectuals for a variety of reasons. These probably include their greater mobility and higher expectations; propensity toward certain forms of abstract thinking, idealism, and concern with social justice; their iconoclastic or critical dispositions; the desire for creative self-fulfillment; and high levels of personal aspirations geared to nonmaterial goals.

Third, Western societies of the last decades (and Western intellectuals in particular) have been increasingly affected by the century-old process of secularization. Its most shattering results have been felt in the last decades. Intellectuals proved especially liable to seek escape from the vacuum of secularization, to search for a new faith in politics, in "secular religions," in the promise of gigantic social transformations, in new hopes for "community," and in new visions of limitless personal fulfillment.

Fourth, the relatively privileged and leisured condition of many intellectuals might also be contributing to the state of mind I have been sketching here. The systematic generation and articulation of dissatisfaction and frustration—and the nurture and elaboration of ideals and alternatives—require time and freedom from pressing material needs and time-consuming routines.

In the context of their times, the Ideological Pilgrimages are among the many incidents of human history which illustrate the results of an intense confrontation between despair and hope. It is this confrontation which, in an appropriate setting, brings about the transformation of the tough-minded social critic into an affirming enthusiast, the defiant individualist into the admirer of collectivism, and the faithless pessimist into a confident and true believer.

Distant and poorly known societies which differ deeply from those that socially conscious Western intellectuals inhabit will continue to exert an attraction (transient though it may be) as long as dramatic enough contrasts remain between the all-too-familiar setting of frustrated longings and the promise of their gratification in faraway places. The lands upon which such hopes are projected may change over time, but the basic pattern of an Ideological Pilgrim who moves from estrangement to affirmation persists.

Postscript 1982

This essay was the forerunner of the book-length study I published in 1981 under the title *Political Pilgrims—Travels of Western Intellectuals to the Soviet Union, China and Cuba.*

Today, close to a decade after the original article appeared, the issues dealt with remain somewhat discouragingly alive and relevant. To be sure, the same countries may no longer be idealized. In particular, the Soviet Union has for decades been discarded by Western intellectuals as an object of political affection. China too since the death of Mao has lost much of its appeal—a development due in part to new information becoming available, the rapprochement between China and the United States (which reduced China's revolutionary credentials as a staunch opponent of the evils symbolized by American society), China acting as a big power in its border war with Vietnam (the latter now more conveniently fitting into the role of underdog than its populous adversary) and, lastly, the modest reforms and pragmatic policies of the post-Mao leadership have also helped to dull the image of China in the eyes of those who thrilled to the drama of the Cultural Revolution. Cuba's attractions have not faded so significantly among Western intellectuals (waiting for a system that will usher in authentic socialism), due presumably to the durability of its revolutionary and still somewhat charismatic leader, Fidel Castro. Remarkably enough, such benefits of doubt still extended to Cuba survived the outflow of about a million Cubans (including the most recent, 1980 "boat people"), the dispatch of Cuban expeditionary forces to Africa propping up unpopular dictatorships, Cuba's almost total subservience to the global policies of the Soviet Union, and evidence of the brutality of the regime exemplified by the imprisonment of the crippled poet Armando Valladares, among others.[24]

It appears that today the political affections of Western intellectuals estranged from their own societies are more widely dispersed. For one thing, the undifferentiated entity called "the Third World" continues to attract a certain vague reverence mainly because it is viewed, by these intellectuals, as a victim of the West, that is, their own societies. The Third World also commands approval because of its (largely rhetorical) confrontation with the West. Yet, on the whole, these diffuse political sympathies are lacking in the degree and type of intensity that had characterized past devotion to the Soviet Union and China, or to Cuba during its more authentic revolutionary periods.

Besides the generalized and somewhat shallow reverence for the Third World, Angola and Mozambique in Africa, Nicaragua and the guerrillas in El Salvador emerged as the prime foci of current political devotions and objects of wishful idealization. The guerrillas of El Salvador are all the more appealing since they still represent the revolutionary promise and possibility short of fulfillment and untarnished by contact with the reality of established power. As far as Nicaragua is concerned, it has become (as I have written over two years ago) "an especially strong contender in the marketplace of revolutionary promise and purity." Thus, for example, Ramsey Clark (who in 1974 could detect no internal conflict in North Vietnam and felt "a unity of spirit" during his visit) reported from Nicaragua: "You will not find a revolutionary movement in our epoch in which there has been such a high commitment to human rights."[25] Other sympathetic observers eagerly rationalized the reluctance of the new rulers of Nicaragua to hold elections,[26] while a veteran admirer of Cuba, Saul Landau, helped to prepare a laudatory television program on public television about it.[27] Not only have American intellectuals and students rallied to this latest embodiment of revolutionary promise, but "Managua today is being occupied by a fresh-faced army of backpacking youth in shorts and hiking boots. They are left-wing students on holiday from Europe, here to see the revolution firsthand."[28] A *New York Times* reporter entitled his sympathetic article "Nicaragua's Revolution Breaks the Mold."[29]

Both the guerrillas of El Salvador and their victorious cousins in Nicaragua rekindled memories, images, and associations of Vietnam. Like the Vietcong, the Central American guerrillas were seen as heroic, popular, altruistic; idealists of the highest order, fighting evil, corrupt, and unpopular regimes. There were certainly parallels with Vietnam, although not necessarily those the supporters of the Salvadoran guerrillas perceived and stressed. In the 1960s as in the early 1980s, the protest against United States involvement stemmed not primarily from aversion to the United States getting "bogged down" in a distant part of the world "where we had not business to be" (after all, El Salvador was a good deal closer than Indochina, the number and strength of guerrillas far smaller, and the military problems more manageable), but from sympathy toward the guerrillas. Their supporters, as those of the Vietcong, wanted them to win. In the early 1980s as in the late 1960s, almost any movement or regime opposed to American foreign policy and influence was regarded with warmth and support by the estranged intellectuals, including not only Nicaragua and the Salvadoran guerrillas but also Iran under Khomeini and the PLO.

There were also parallels in the media coverage of the guerrillas of Central America and those of Indochina. In both cases, they were treated sympathetically. Generous publicity was given to the atrocities committed by the forces opposing them, but meager was the information provided about the guerrilla atrocities. More recently as in the past, claims of foreign assistance were dismissed and ridiculed. The guerrillas in Central America were entirely independent; Cuban or Soviet help was nonexistent and merely a State Department invention just as North Vietnamese help of the Vietcong (and Soviet and Chinese help of North Vietnam) used to be dismissed or relegated to insignificance.

Whatever the exact nature and extent of such similarities, the major continuities in the history of political pilgrimages, including their most recent manifestations, are to be found not in the usually transient sympathy toward particular countries or political movements abroad, but in the persistence of estrangement which inspires the pilgrimages in the first place. Of late, it may be argued, alienation has again intensified in the United States due to the Republican administration and its various domestic and foreign policies. One may also explain, at least in part, the recent upsurge of the antinuclear movement (or nuclear freeze movement) as a protest against the policies and values of the Reagan administration as much as a protest against the dangers of nuclear war per se. Alienation from the prevailing social order is also reflected in the ultimate assumptions of many adherents of the new antinuclear movement, that is, in the revival of the "better red than dead" sentiment, or survival at any cost and the attendant indifference to the preservation of characteristic Western institutions and values, including political and cultural pluralism. The corollary of the mistrust the freeze adherents display toward their own society and especially the United States is the benign, benefit-of-the-doubt attitude shown toward the Soviet Union which many protestors seem to regard as more sincere about disarmament and less threatening despite all its nuclear and conventional armaments. Western European disarmament movements in particular have shown hardly any apprehension about the Soviet medium-range missiles already installed and aimed at their countries while rising to a fever pitch of concern about the American missiles yet to be introduced into the area.[30]

Thus I am suggesting that just as the Vietnam antiwar movement tapped preexisting or latent reservoirs of alienation and social criticism, the protest against United States aid to the Salvadoran regime (even under its moderate Christian democratic leader, Duarte) and the protest against primarily Western nuclear arms stem from similar sources.

There have been similarities and continuities not only between the general predispositions and attitudes of estrangement behind the pilgrimages, but also between the specifics of the visits, their organization, and, sometimes, impact as well. In other words, political tourism still flourishes and its organizers still anticipate results. Guardian Tours of New York (associated with the radical weekly the *Guardian*) organizes tours to Cuba, Vietnam, Grenada, and Nicaragua, which from their published descriptions fit exactly into the patterns I had discussed in the 1973 article and the volume that followed eight years later.[31] *Nation* magazine co-sponsored tours to the USSR which offered the traveler the opportunity to: "Find out for yourself what's going on in the Soviet Union . . . nightly dialogue with leading Soviet and American experts . . . relax in comfort and fellowship . . . folk dancing . . . cultural films, recreational games . . . visit Lenin's birthplace."[32] Trips to Cuba promoted for the benefit of college students promised: "Cuba trip allows one to see for self" and offered to combine the joys of the Caribbean with visits to the Museum of the Literacy Campaign and meeting with African students on the Isle of Youth.[33]

The most remarkable recent example of the manipulation of the visitor's experience, yielding particularly rich results for the hosts, was provided by the visit of the Reverend Billy Graham to the Soviet Union in May 1982. His visit offers a number of striking similarities to those of a long line of clergymen, intellectuals, and politicians who made brief forays into the USSR either for idealistic motives or with pragmatic political purpose in mind. Like others before him, Billy Graham appeared to be under the impression that whatever his hosts' intention in using him for their purposes, he too used them for his own. ("I know I may be used for propaganda . . . but I believe my propaganda—the gospel of Christ—is stronger.") In the same spirit he also observed with satisfaction, upon his return, that while the visit created controversy, it "helped increase the size of the crowds" in the United States. And, as had been so often the case, his compliant attiitude toward the Soviet government was also motivated by the desire to return; that is, "his aides said the evangelist was circumspect in the hope of returning to the Soviet Union someday."[34]

The most striking (and perhaps the only major) difference between the visits and statements of the dignitaries of the past and those of the Reverend Billy Graham is that those lending themselves to Soviet propaganda in the past usually arrived in the USSR with markedly favorable predisposition (like, for example, Hewlett Johnson, the Dean of Canterbury, or Sherwood Eddy, the American Protestant leader among the clergymen) rather than with the anti-Communist credentials of Billy Graham.

The major similarity between Billy Graham's statements and those of past luminaries has been the total lack of restraint in generalizing from pitifully limited and highly manipulated experience (Billy Graham had seen "no evidence of religious repression," expecting perhaps to be taken on a tour of prison camps where Baptists are held?), not unlike George Bernard Shaw who had seen no evidence of food shortages in 1931 in the first-class restaurant he was taken to by his considerate hosts. There is special poignancy in this parallel since Billy Graham also commented in a similar spirit on the provisions he had received in the Soviet Union: "The meals I had are among the best I have ever eaten." "In the United States you have to be a millionaire to have caviar, but I had caviar with almost every meal."[35]

The remark suggests yet another similarity in the pattern of response to the VIP treatment, past and present. Evidently, the techniques of hospitality (including the regular and ample supply of caviar and other high quality provisions) work in many if not all cases. The Reverend was clearly impressed by being treated as a major dignitary and respected guest, and presumably those daily portions of caviar also contributed to the favorable impressions he so readily shared with his hosts and the world outside. Most importantly, he was eager to associate himself without reservation with the blatantly one-sided "peace" propaganda campaign conducted by the Soviet Union. His hosts also succeeded in inducing him to exonerate the Soviet regime of any antireligious policy or offense. Not only that, but he even made favorable comparisons between religious freedom that is permitted in the United States and the USSR.[36] These were remarkable accomplishments on the part of the Soviet hosts, especially since Billy Graham, being a Baptist, might have been particularly concerned with, or at least interested in, the fate of the same religious group in the USSR which suffered most severely in recent years. But, as others before him, "he is [his aide said] keen not to upset his chances of returning."[37]

In the final analysis, it is hard to decide exactly what blend of ignorance, vanity, opportunism, and willful denial of reality produced the attitudes and embarrassingly uninformed statements which made this visit of the Reverend Billy Graham so memorable and discouraging, especially for those who entertained illusions about his intelligence or integrity.

The most recent examples of political pilgrimages testify to the persistence of a phenomenon that rests in part on idealism, ignorance, and opportunism (as far as the pilgrims are concerned), and on shrewd political calculation as far as their hosts are. While the settings may and will vary, the pilgrimages are going to recur as long as Western societies create enough discontent to motivate certain individuals to undertake a search for alternatives and as long as highly regimented societies are capable of putting on display groups, institutions, and policies which such Western visitors find appealing.

Notes

1. Henri Baudet, *Paradise on Earth—Some Thoughts on the Images of Non-European Man* (New Haven: Yale Univ. Press, 1965), p. 51.
2. Waldo Frank, *Dawn in Russia* (New York: Scribner, 1932), p. 22.
3. Norman Mailer, *Presidential Papers* (New York: Putnam, 1963), pp. 69–70.
4. Susan Sontag, *Trip to Hanoi* (New York: Farrar, Straus and Giroux, 1968), p. 40.
5. Carol Brightman and Sandra Levinson, eds., *Venceremos Brigade: The Experiences of American Radicals Who Shared the Life, the Work and the Revolution of the Cuban People* (New York: Simon and Schuster, 1971), pp. 388, 373, 311.
6. Committee of Concerned Asian Scholars, *China! Inside the People's Republic* (New York: Bantam, 1972), p. 194.
7. Staughton Lynd and Tom Hayden, *The Other Side* (New York: New American Library, 1966), p. 71.
8. Lion Feuchtwanger, *Moscow 1937* (London: Golancz, 1937), pp. 3, 149, 150.
9. George Bernard Shaw, *The Rationalization of Russia* (1931; reprint ed., Bloomington, Ind.: Indiana Univ. Press, 1964), p. 102.
10. Corliss and Margaret Lamont, *Russia Day by Day* (New York: Covici, 1933), pp. 257–58.
11. There is yet another option for alienated intellectuals who learned the lessons of history and are reluctant to project their hopes on existing alternatives. This option is to idealize abortive revolutions or social movements which were not given a chance to go stale or oppressive. A recent example is the French student rebellion of 1968 which an American social critic viewed as "the most significant event in Western politics in a generation" (Norman

Birnbaum, *The Crisis of Industrial Society* (New York: Oxford Univ. Press, 1969), p. viii.

12. Julian Huxley, *A Scientist Among the Soviets* (New York: Harper and Row, 1932), p. 77.

13. Father Daniel Berrigan, *Night Flight to Hanoi* (New York: Macmillan, 1968), pp. 45–46.

14. Jean-Paul Sartre, *Sartre on Cuba* (New York: Ballantine, 1961), p. 118.

15. Simone de Beauvoir, *The Long March* (Cleveland and New York: The World Publishing Co., 1958), p. 228.

16. Ella Winter, *I Saw the Russian People* (Boston: Little, Brown and Co., 1945), p. 119.

17. Ella Winter, *Red Virtue* (New York: Harcourt Brace Jovanovich, 1933), p. 206.

18. David Caute, *The Fellow-Travellers* (New York: Macmillan, 1973).

19. Lord Boyd Orr and Peter Townsend, *What is Happening in China?* (Garden City, N.Y.: Doubleday, 1959), pp. 32–35.

20. Andrew Salkey, *Havana Journey* (Harmondsworth, England: Penguin, 1971), p. 25.

21. J. Hebert and Pierre Elliott Trudeau, *Two Innocents in Red China* (New York: Oxford Univ. Press, 1968), p. 108.

22. Robert Conquest, *The Great Terror* (New York: Macmillan, 1968), p. 354.

23. Robert Loh, "Setting the Stage for Foreigners," *Atlantic Monthly*, Dec. 1959, pp. 80–82.

24. Carlos Ripoll, "Poet Endures—Imprisoned, Crippled," *Miami Herald,* 16 Nov. 1980. Many of the points made in the rest of the postscript follows closely parts of the preface to the paperback edition of *Political Pilgrim* (New York: Harper and Row, 1983).

25. Quoted in *Political Pilgrims*, p. 271; his statement on Nicaragua was quoted in George F. Will, "Again, the Fact Finders," *Newsweek*, 1 March 1982.

26. As, for example, in Eldon Kenworthy, "Troubled Nicaragua," *New York Times*, 18 Feb. 1982: Op-Ed. Page.

27. *Contentions* (April–May 1982), p. 2; see also "Nicaragua Film on PBS Is Called 'Propaganda,' " *New York Times*, 9 April 1982. For a publication (coming out of Berkeley) devoted to the praise of Marxist-Leninist Nicaragua, see *Nicaraguan Perspectives* (e.g., Fall 1981). Since the editors thanked the "Community Project Office of the University of California at Berkeley for the support and encouragement of this project," it may be presumed that once more, as with the program on public television, the taxpayers' money was channeled into pro-Nicaraguan propaganda.

28. Warren Hoge, "Nicaraguan Scene: Fiery Slogans, Designer Jeans," *New York Times*, 6 Jan. 1982.

29. Warren Hoge, "Nicaragua's Revolution Breaks the Mold," *New York Times*, 30 Dec. 1981.

30. Vladimir Bukovsky, "The Peace Movement and the Soviet Union," *Commentary*, May 1982.

31. "New Destinations," *New York Times*, Travel Section, 21 Sept. 1981.

32. "Washington Diarist," *New Republic*, 31 March 1982.

33. "Cuba Trip Allows One to See For Self," *Massachusetts Daily Collegian*, 9 March 1982.

34. "Mission in Moscow," *New York Times*, 17 May 1982; "Graham Says Soviet Trip Increased His Crowds," *New York Times*, 28 May 1982; "Graham Preaches at Church in Moscow," *New York Times*, 10 May 1982.
35. "Graham Offers Positive View of Religion in Soviet," *New York Times*, 13 May 1982; see also "Billy Graham Rebuffs Criticism of Soviet Trip," *New York Times*, 18 May 1982; and "Billy Graham, Back Home, Defends Remarks," *New York Times*, 20 May 1982.
36. See *New York Times*, 18 May 1982.
37. *New York Times*, 10 May 1982.

18.
American Society
and Soviet Power

In this chapter I shall focus on the influence exerted by the internal characteristics of American and Soviet society respectively, on their relations with one another, and more generally, on their foreign policy. I will be looking at some of the social forces and processes which less obtrusively, more indirectly shape participation in international affairs. I will also try to envisage the future relations of these two countries (and by implication, the others grouped around them) by extrapolating from their respective domestic conditions. Most attention will be paid to some of the properties of American society today which encourage the global ascendancy of Soviet power and influence.

Let me start with a simple prediction. If "good" relations between the USSR and the United States mean the avoidance of nuclear or conventional war accompanied by trade, cultural relations, and scientific exchanges—then one might project continued "good" relations between East and West, or their major and most powerful representatives. Moreover, nothing precludes the indefinite continuation of such relations as long as the United States is willing to get out of the way of the Soviet Union, so to speak, and avoid confrontation. In other words, Soviet-American relations will remain free of significant friction provided the United States will continue to scale down its international commitments, redefine its national interests, rationalize the ascendancy of Soviet military power and influence, dismiss Soviet initiatives in various parts of the world as insignificant, and *even redefine what constitutes the expansion of Soviet power.* All these processes are much in evidence. In short, as long as the contraction of American power and influence around the globe continues, Soviet-American relations will remain cordial; should the United States attempt to arrest or reverse this process they will become strained. Hence I foresee the continuation of détente accompanied by the shrinking of areas under American influence, that is to say, areas where some degree of political and cultural pluralism or political democracy can survive or might have a chance to develop. As a corollary, I also foresee the continued rise of Soviet confidence and activism following on the heels of declining American confidence, assertiveness, and involvement in international affairs.[1] A graphic, quantitative illustration of these inverse but functionally related processes can be found in the growing number of Soviet military bases, port and airport facilities all over the world, paralleled by the loss of similar facilities on the part of the United States during the past decade. The contrasting trends are quite dramatic.

I am, of course, not prepared to predict what exact forms the coordinated process of increasing Soviet assertiveness and the declining American one will take. It will presumably include further withdrawals of American military forces from various parts of the world (Thailand may be followed by the Philippines and South Korea); the growing reluctance of the United States to aid pro-Western movements or regimes (as in Angola);[2] and the corresponding emboldened Soviet resolve to aid other movements and regimes, with or without the military forces of nations allied to the Soviet Union (as was the case with the use of Cuban troops in Angola). Soviet-East German pressure on Berlin may also revive, and there have already been some signs of such a revival. One can also anticipate increasingly shrill and menacing Soviet rhetoric at times when the United States might intervene to help pro-Western movements or regimes and feeble American responses even at the verbal level. It can also be expected that the Soviet Union will continue to take the initiative in the United Nations and various other international gatherings sponsoring or supporting hosts of anti-American resolutions, "exposing United States imperialism," and reaping not inconsiderable propaganda benefits. It is also highly probable that the United States will continue its policy of not presenting its case forcefully to either world or domestic public opinion. In particular, American spokesmen will continue avoiding critical references to the Soviet Union in the interests of détente, a gesture that has gone unreciprocated for many years. Perhaps in the end, former Senator Fulbright's proposal to close down U.S.-supported radio stations critical of the Soviet Union, without getting anything in return will be accepted in order "to reduce international tension."

Assuming that my perception of growing Soviet assertiveness and declining American global influence is essentially correct (and could be supported by far more evidence and argument than produced above), the next step is to offer some explanation of these trends.

What is it in American society today that creates pressures for the development of an isolationist foreign policy in general and the appeasement of the Soviet Union in particular? Why is it that American foreign policy makers, politicians, intellectuals, businessmen, and public opinion at large considered the Soviet Union far more threatening at a time (roughly between 1947 and 1956) when it was a good deal weaker and in many ways more cautious than today? The multiple ramifications of American involvement and failure in Vietnam provide the most obvious and most frequently proposed answer to these questions. But Vietnam in itself, and without regard to other circumstances, cannot account for the phenomena being discussed here.

I think the most fundamental reasons for the gradual American retreat from the international arena are to be found in the declining number of Americans (especially among those of various elite groups) who believe that the values and institutions of American society are worth defending or promoting in other parts of the world. This is what other authors have referred to as the crisis of confidence, failure of nerve, the malaise of the 1960s, the "greening" of American foreign policy, decadence, and alienation. All these terms add up to one thing: a highly unfavorable collective self-image held by a significant portion of Americans. Such collective self-images are quite consequential in international affairs. It matters when large numbers of people in any given society believe that their country has little to offer to the world, that it has few if any values, institutions, or policies worthy of emulation, promotion, or defense. A significant and vocal minority, mostly among the better-educated youth, intellectuals, and academics in the humanities and social sciences, alongside some of the guilty rich genuinely believe that the United States is a uniquely evil or immoral society. They welcome the advances of any country, movement, or system made at the expense of American power or influence. This bitterly hostile minority may be small, but it is not without influence. Its views have percolated far and wide and even if they have not been totally accepted, they have succeeded in neutralizing more favorable assessments of and attitudes toward American society.[3]

The negative attitudes toward American society as sketched above, are associated with a combination of individualism, hedonism, and a self-conscious pursuit of "self-fulfillment." More specific expressions of these attitudes range from "consumerism" to preoccupation with mysticism, religious cults, and various forms of psychotherapy. Such concerns are obviously incompatible with any policy that may require some degree of deprivation or deferred gratification. There is an unwillingness to subordinate personal interests to any social or collective purpose, which could incapacitate a country both in the conduct of foreign affairs and domestic policies. Andrew Hacker remarked that "the inflation of 200 million egos . . . carries political consequences. A society so inordinately attached to personal pursuits cannot be expected to renounce them simply because social survival demands such an adjustment."[4]

A further explanation of current American attitudes toward international affairs can be found, somewhat paradoxically, in the level of security, which, despite all protestations to the contrary, most Americans have attained. A majority of Americans find it hard, if not totally impossible, to imagine that their ways of life could be threatened, or significantly altered, by political events and especially those which originate abroad. The idea that the actions of some foreign power in some distant part of the world might have some tangible effect on an American's life is as bizarre and inconceivable for the Midwestern farmer as it is for the liberal East Coast academic or California dropout. This profound sense of security has often been connected with the American historical experience which excluded foreign invasions, occupations, enemy bombardments, or battles fought on American soil since the Civil War. Efficient police states, particularly the Soviet Union and those modeled after it,[5] and their impact on the lives of their citizens, remain hazy abstractions for most Americans. I believe that neither the cold war nor its alleged end (with the attendant increase in the flow of information) has made much of a dent on this kind of deep ignorance and incomprehension of the social-political arrangements which prevail in Communist societies. It could, of course, be argued that the conduct of foreign policy has little to do with the level of information possessed by the citizens about the international setting and its major protagonists. After all, few would argue that the Soviet public is well informed about the United States or Western Europe and that Soviet foreign policy is anchored in a popular understanding of the Western world. For better or worse, public opinion in the United States does have a considerable impact on foreign policy; therefore, it matters what people believe, or know, or do not know.

High expectations directed at their own society also contribute to the trends outlined here. Many educated and idealistic Americans feel strongly that their country should retreat from the international arena until it has attained a much higher level of social justice at home and has solved its social problems. (This is what Nathan Glazer called the "clean hand argument" in a recent article.) For Americans of this persuasion, any policy or action designed to uphold political pluralism and the values associated with it in other parts of the world is totally hypocritical. Interestingly enough, while these Americans expect a great deal of their own country, they are extremely tolerant of the vices of countries hostile toward their own, provided that these countries claim to adhere to some form of socialism. Such attitudes range from benevolent neutrality, and giving the benefit of doubt, to active sympathy toward the Soviet bloc countries and, even more so, the Third World. Incipient distaste for political repression can instantaneously be neutralized by any professed intent on the part of these countries to pursue egalitarian social policies.

The contributions made to the current state of American foreign policy stem from many diverse sources and sectors of society. If much of what I have said so far applies primarily to a loosely defined left-liberal-intellectual middle-class contingent, Wall Street and its "lackeys" play a part of their own. Increasingly, American businessmen and corporations are showing that they are intent on doing business with anybody, that is, any country or political system as long as a reasonable profit can be anticipated. If in the past such a disposition often led to the covert or open support of stable right-wing dictatorships which provided a favorable climate for investment, today, identical attitudes emerge toward stable left-wing dictatorships which provide new and secure opportunities for trade and business. (The veritable romance of Mr. Kendall of the Pepsi Corporation with the Soviet Union, and Brezhnev in particular, is a good example of this trend.) The alacrity with which Gulf Oil Company established good working relations with the pro-Cuban and pro-Soviet regime in Angola is another example. The devotion of the oil lobby to a wide range of antidemocratic Arab regimes is further indication of business before politics and ideology. Marx was wrong: capitalists are not class-conscious, they are often politically illiterate. Lenin had a better idea conveyed in his famous remark about the willingness of capitalists to sell the rope. . . .

A more vigorous foreign policy, a more perceptive assessment of Soviet motives and actions, is further hindered by the unfortunate circumstance that in recent American history much of the most vocal opposition to Soviet expansionism and Soviet-supported or inspired dictatorships has come from the less educated, less intelligent, domestically illiberal segments of the American population and political leadership. How could American liberals take seriously the Soviet threat, now or in the past, if by doing so they became the strange bedfellows of some of the most reactionary politicians or fundamentalist eccentrics of the political spectrum? The problem is not new, but it persists tenaciously. If it was Richard Nixon who accused Alger Hiss, the latter must be innocent. If Senator Stennis of Mississippi pushes for a bigger military budget, then the Soviet threat must be fake. It has been a disturbing aspect of recent American history and domestic politics that many of those who have taken the threat of Soviet global ascendancy the most seriously belong to the less attractive groups of the political spectrum.

Could the elusive American national character have anything to do with the present problems and flaws of American foreign policy? I think it may, especially in combination with the other factors discussed previously. Already de Tocqueville has observed how much Americans want to be loved, that they excel in the desire to please and to be popular, that they find disapproval unusually painful and hostility more difficult to face than many other nations and nationalities. Correspondingly, it is highly uncongenial for most Americans to believe that hostile attitudes between nations may be sustained for years or decades. They find it hard to live with such tensions, and a strong desire builds up over time to redefine the situation. In foreign as in personal relations, Americans try to convince themselves that if they do the right thing (e.g., exchange scholars, refrain from criticizing the other party), sooner or later they will overcome unfriendliness. I never cease to be impressed by the extent to which Americans can be affected by both hostile and friendly gestures. Highly trained, competent academics no less than hard-nosed business executives are capable of believing that the key to Soviet conduct may be found in after-dinner convivialities lubricated by drink and jokes, that those who smile cannot be threatening, and that international conflicts can be ironed out through face-to-face communications.[6] Correspondingly, many Americans are bewildered and pained by hostility (again, more so than people of other countries) and tend to search their souls for the reason why such sentiments are directed at them. Richard Pipes said most perceptively that

> a strong residue of Protestant ethic causes Americans to regard all hostility to them as being at least in some measure brought about by their own faults. . . . It is quite possible to exploit this tendency to self-accusation by setting into motion a steady barrage of hostile actions accompanied by expressions of hatred. The natural reaction of the victims, if they are Americans, can be and often is, bewilderment, followed by guilt. Thus is created an atmosphere conducive to concessions whose purpose is to propitiate the allegedly injured party.[7]

To be sure, these attitudes coexist with many others which are often contradictory; nor am I suggesting that they are evenly distributed in the population. On the contrary, they are concentrated among those who matter more: people with power, influence, education, access to the media, as well as those who show a greater (if selective) concern with public affairs.

I would also like to say something about ways in which the attitudes described in this article are translated into political behavior. Two major mechanisms come into play: wishful thinking and projection. Wishful thinking regarding Soviet foreign (or, for that matter, domestic) policy has been with us for a long time. Its major theme is the denial or the playing down of Soviet aggression when it occurs and the questioning of aggressive intent when it can be inferred from ideology or policy statement. For the wishful thinker, Soviet statements are accepted at their face value when they convey benevolent intentions, but they are disbelieved when belligerent. In the latter case, they are viewed as "rhetoric" masking peaceful attitudes or dismissed as ideological window dressing proffered for the benefit of a few aged "diehards" left over from the Stalin era. It is understandable why so many American journalists, social scientists, and politicians have been at such pains to deny or dispute the ideological underpinnings of Soviet policy. Should they be taken more seriously, they would make a most significant contribution to the understanding and appreciation of Soviet expansionism—the very phenomenon the same groups wish to deny. The more serious Soviet leaders are about their ideology, the more menacing they become and the less they resemble that team of pragmatic-technocratic-managerial types wishful Americans have been trying to conjure up for decades. Even a perception of the Soviet Union as merely obeying the dictates and dynamics of great power status and inexorably filling in the gaps left by another, retreating great power is more comforting than the image of a system propelled by any degree of messianic urge, intent on spreading the true belief and the institutions supporting it.

Wishful thinking also means that insofar as Soviet expansionism is acknowledged, it is viewed as limited in its objectives, capable of satisfaction (or appeasement), and a mere continuation of the age-old Russian quest for security.

Projection, closely related to wishful thinking, comes into play as Soviet leaders and policies are cast into shapes familiar to and deriving from the American experience. Thus they have their hard liners as we have ours; their military lobbies for a bigger slice of the pie just like ours; their leaders must be responsive to a public that demands more consumer goods and has no stomach for military adventures; their leaders no more believe in their ideological pronouncements than the average American politician making a Fourth of July speech; they are just as interested in the balance of power, global stability, and status quo as we are, and so forth.

Although I believe that the current global retreat of the United States is more significantly determined by conditions existing in American than in Soviet society, I would also like to make a few comments about Soviet social-political conditions which faciliate the present global ascendancy of Soviet power. There are numerous aspects of the Soviet social order and Soviet-Russian political tradition which are helpful for the conduct of a vigorous, expansionist foreign policy.

To begin with, public opinion plays no part in the formulation, implementation, or influencing of foreign policy. Fatalism, apathy, passivity, and apolitical attitudes among the vast majority of Soviet people (in addition to the decision-making structures of the system) provide the leadership with a virtually free hand. Soviet people have been traditionally uninvolved in politics and especially foreign affairs which are totally removed from their purview. This well-established pattern of nonparticipation (or pseudo-participation when, for example, Soviet collective farmers fervently demand that the president of Sudan commute the death sentences of local Communist party leaders accused of conspiracy) greatly increases the flexibility of Soviet foreign policy makers.

There is also an element of traditional patriotism which allows the Soviet masses to derive some satisfaction from the growing strength of their country that has hardly any counterpart today in the United States. For large numbers of Soviet people, the external successes of the regime may help to legitimate in some measure its domestic policies and provide some compensation for the material deprivations experienced. If people in Cuba or Angola or Iraq seem to opt for "socialism" of some sort and allegedly look to the Soviet Union for aid and inspiration, then the average Soviet citizen's acceptance of his political system is enhanced. Even the better educated must feel that "we are doing *something* right" if Soviet influence is waxing in so many parts of the world. Such global successes warm the sense of patriotism of Soviet people. Moreover they learn little about the costs of such policies. Thanks to the state monopoly of the mass communications media and political information, few people have a clear conception of the economic drain resulting from the Soviet conduct of foreign policy (i.e., the cost of military and nonmilitary aid programs) and the magnitude of the resources devoured by the constant modernization of the Soviet military machine. Moreover, it seems that the Soviet regime largely succeeded in convincing its people that all Soviet moves abroad are basically defensive. Nor is the Soviet public informed of mass attitudes toward the Soviet Union in parts of the world where *official* support is given to Soviet policies (East Europe in particular). And on the occasions when unwilling allies need to be coerced (viz., Poland, Hungary, Czechoslovakia), Soviet patriotism and insecurity can be invoked.

We shall doubtless never know the exact nature of the beliefs Soviet leaders have in their system, in Marxism-Leninism, in their historical mission. Yet it can hardly be denied that having expropriated a Messianic-millennial ideology they must find it easier to justify and maintain an assertive posture in international affairs. It is quite possible that Soviet leaders are beginning to take their ideology more seriously, especially those parts which prophesy the doom and decline of the capitalist world. There is a good deal in the behavior of Americans (and Western Europeans too, for that matter) that begins to make certain predictions of Marxism appear plausible.

Two final points need to be made in concluding these gloomy reflections. My impressions of the moods and attitudes prevailing in American society are heavily colored by the mass media and the academic setting. Neither should be taken as the source of representative or reliable information, or insight about the American condition today, although both are symptomatic of many social processes of the present. However, even distorted representations of American reality, such as the mass media often convey, have a certain self-fulfilling quality.

The reasons sketched in this chapter provide a basis for pessimism about the part played by the United States in East-West relations. Nothing would please me more than to be proved wrong in regard to all major propositions and predictions I have made here.

Postscript 1982

Developments during the past six years since this chapter was written, unhappily bear out its gloomy analysis and predictions. Soviet global assertiveness has continued and American responses have remained feeble, though slightly more vigorous than under the previous administration. In addition to its advances in Africa (noted in the chapter), the Soviet Union expanded its influence in Indochina, showed no hesitation to send its troops to pacify Afghanistan, encouraged (and cooperated with) its Polish representatives to impose a military dictatorship, successfully supported guerrilla movements in Central America (gaining allies in Nicaragua and Grenada), and, most recently, hastened to seize the opportunity to extend its influence in South America as well by offering assistance to Argentina when she was at war with Britain.

On their part, the United States and NATO countries have of late talked more about the need to forestall such developments and in particular to match the buildup of Soviet military power, but they have done little. Several NATO countries have cheerfully continued their trade relations with the USSR, even providing inexpensive credits and in the process allowing themselves to become increasingly dependent economically on the Soviet Union (as in the case of the gas pipelines to Western Europe). In turn, the United States under President Reagan lifted the grain embargo imposed by President Carter after the Soviet invasion of Afghanistan and reimbursed banks for overdue interest payments on loans to the Polish military dictatorship.

To be sure, even the feeble gestures aimed at reversing the growing political and military imbalance on the part of the United States and NATO (such as increasing military appropriations) provoked much indignation and cries of reviving the cold war on the part of the Soviet Union, its allies, and sympathizers, as well as groups and individuals in the West who were neither. Opposition to draft registration in the United States was among the symptoms of the unwillingness on the part of many segments of the society, and especially the college educated, to take any steps requiring even minimal commitment to national defense.

In the United States as in Western Europe, large antinuclear protest movements arose—in what measure inspired, encouraged, or supported by the Soviet Union remains debatable[8]—to combat American and Western rearmament in the context of a freeze on the production and deployment of nuclear weapons. As was noted earlier, these movements have suffered from an unbalanced concern with American (Western) as opposed to Soviet military might and policy, and they have been capable of bringing pressure only on American and Western policy makers but not the Soviet Union.[9] It is an interesting question why, after thirty-five years of living "in the shadow of nuclear destruction," as of 1981–82 there has been a sudden upsurge of apprehension among so many Western Europeans and Americans about the prospect of nuclear war. Whatever the Soviet contributions to the spread or organization of such concerns and movements, their indigenous roots cannot be disputed. Perhaps it has been due to a combination of resentment against the Reagan administration (and its reallocation of resources from welfare to the military), the fear that the Western attempts to resist further Soviet expansion would lead to conflict (hence the corresponding acquiescence in Soviet penetration of the Third World), plus a leavening of Soviet efforts and organizational skills.

Some of the American attitudes touched upon in the article could also be characterized as forms of what I called elsewhere "therapeutic appeasement." The latter differs from ordinary appeasement by ingeniously and circuitously justifying the need for appeasement not by the strength but the weakness of the power to be appeased. This type of appeasement is far more acceptable psychologically (and therefore politically) than one which legitimates the same by reference to the superior strength of the adversary since by doing so one admits to weakness, or fear, or both. By contrast, appeasement justified by reference to the insecurity of the other side makes the appeaser appear to be more adult, mature, and rational.[10] Why fight over Angola or Afghanistan? Let them have it if they really want it, if they really think that it will make them happy. Let them gratify their irrational impulses (bred by insecurity) and they will soon come to their senses. The approach outlined here reflects a transfer of the therapeutic perspectives applied in interpersonal relations to the sphere of international relations.

Six years after this chapter was written I can only foresee continued Western retreat and Soviet advance in diverse parts of the world unhindered by Soviet domestic problems, but made easier by the domestic economic-social problems in the Western world.

Notes

1. At the time of writing this, it was reported that North Korean soldiers bludgeoned to death two American officers in the demilitarized zone. The American official response consisted of angry words deploring the incident. The U.S. representative in the United Nations decided not to call a Security Council meeting "this time" and was content to make a report to the Council about the atrocity. Given the U.S. response to the hijacking of the *Pueblo,* it is hardly surprising that the North Koreans consider such violent provocations a risk-free activity.
2. "Reluctance" in the case of Angola should be replaced by "refusal."
3. For example, it has become virtually impossible on most American college campuses to make any favorable comment or assessment of American society without confronting scorn, skepticism, or outright hostility. It may be noted here that although the activism and political protest of the 1960s are a thing of the past, student values and attitudes changed much less than behavior.
4. A. Hacker, *The End of the American Era* (New York: Atheneum, 1970), p. 143.
5. (1982): Americans can certainly understand and become indignant about *violations* of human rights—what they find difficult to conceive of are *societies without any human rights* in which, consequently, no such violations occur! This is a distinction that goes to the heart of the recent dispute about the difference between totalitarian and authoritarian societies. While the dispute flared up in the wake of an article by Jeane Kirkpatrick ("Dictatorships and Double Standards," *Commentary,* Nov. 1979) and its applicability to U.S. foreign policy, the issue of the differences between totalitarian and nontotalitarian dictatorships has long been recognized and much discussed by political scientists.

   The vehemence provoked by these distinctions is related to its policy implications under the Reagan administration that regards totalitarian regimes (which are coincidentally also Marxist-Leninist at this point in time) more of a menace to the United States than authoritarian ones (which generally tend to be more "right-wing"). At the same time, it has also been argued, and quite plausibly so, that a right-wing dictatorship (such as, say, the current one in Argentina) can be morally more repugnant than a Marxist-totalitarian one, as the former engages in more overt violence than the latter. It may be suggested that what differentiates totalitarian systems from other dictatorships is (among other things) their innovative and efficient techniques of social control which the coercively more primitive authoritarian regimes do not possess. Such efficiency often translates into higher levels of intimidation among the population which in turn reduces the need for overt violence.

6. An entire organization is dedicated to this proposition: The Citizens Exchange Corps, Inc. of New York, which promotes such informal get-togethers between "ordinary" Soviet and American citizens in order to reduce international tension through personal contact and understanding.

7. Quoted in P. Hollander, *Soviet and American Society: A Comparison* (New York: Oxford Univ. Press, 1973), p. 24.

8. See, for example, Bukovsky, "The Peace Movement and the Soviet Union," p. 281, and Rael Jean Isaac and Erich Isaac, "The Counterfeit Peacemakers: Atomic Freeze," *American Spectator,* June 1982.

9. The Soviet resolve to keep the nuclear freeze movement totally one-sided, that is, anti-Western, has been reflected in their refusal to tolerate *any* peace demonstration within the Soviet Union (unless, of course, organized by the authorities themselves) which makes reference to Soviet armaments as well. (See, for example, "7 West Europeans Detained in Soviet—Tourists in Red Square Sought to Unfurl a Sign Opposing World Arms Spending," *New York Times,* 20 April 1982; "Soviet Hauls a Shipborne Western Protest Group Out to Sea," *New York Times,* 4 June 1982; "Soviet Police Bar Disarmament Meeting," *New York Times,* 14 June 1982.)

10. For related points, see also the following chapter: "Revisionism."

19.
Revisionism

The following essay is a review of *The Giants: Russia and America,* by Richard J. Barnet (New York, 1978). There are three things wrong with this book, which is both a product and an example of the revisionist school of the cold war. The first is the author's image of the Soviet Union; the second, his perception of the United States; and the third, his idea of Soviet-American relations.

To begin with, Mr. Barnet's image of the Soviet Union: this may be summed up as that of an insecure, bumbling giant. The giant had a difficult childhood, and its traumas continue to bedevil him in adulthood; this is why he must continue to throw his weight around, to brag, and to pretend to be the strongest of all giants. But one would be wrong to take the aggressive rhetoric or the ideology behind the rhetoric too seriously, for in reality this giant is mature and responsible and anxious to preserve the status quo.

How does Mr. Barnet deal with facts that are difficult to square with this image? There are always, it turns out, special explanations. Thus the Soviets only became involved in Angola because the circumstances were "irresistible" and it was "a special situation not likely to be repeated." (Ethiopia, one supposes, is yet another such special situation.) The spread of Soviet control over Eastern Europe was a purely defensive measure. The Soviet Union showed commendable restraint in not giving all-out support to the Portuguese Communist party. There was nothing the Soviet Union could have done to discourage the Arabs from attacking Israel in 1973. The invasion of Czechoslovakia "symbolized Russia's moral weakness, not its strength." In other words, even where Soviet aggression may be acknowledged to exist, Mr. Barnet believes that it is to be treated gently and with understanding, approached in the spirit of the psychotherapist who is reluctant to judge actions of his patient which may have been induced by the underlying traumas of childhood.

As for the United States, it gets no such benefit of the doubt. America in Mr. Barnet's view is stronger than the Soviet Union, more cohesive and stable, more warlike and hostile. Where Soviet aggression must be seen in context and treated with compassion, and hostile Soviet rhetoric, in particular, must never be taken seriously, "American ideological fervor" is a real threat to world peace and must be taken very seriously indeed.

The main differences Mr. Barnet sees between the Soviet Union and the United States are those which can be used to justify a more critical stance toward the United States; for the rest, he sees similarities—a growing convergence between the two nations. This convergence, he argues, has been brought about through the technological modernization of Soviet society, which has made it more and more "American," and also by a growing similarity between the elites running the two countries, including a similarity between their misperceptions of one another's society. It is these misperceptions which Mr. Barnet finds responsible for much of the hostility between the United States and the Soviet Union, and it is these which he would like to see reduced in the interests of mutual reconciliation. He stops short of adopting the philosophy of the Citizens Exchange Corps—that if enough Russians and Americans discovered one another's human essence over good food, drinks, and talk, the problems between the two countries would be practically eliminated. but he too seems to believe that personal contacts between elites are of utmost importance and that greater weight should therefore be given to after-dinner and cocktail-party conversation than to what is printed in *Pravda*—a proposition which some other "experts" in Soviet-American relations also seem to regard as self-evident.

While one can question many of the specific points and the major arguments advanced here, the greatest liability of this volume is the author's addiction to highly dubious and sometimes grotesque parallels between the two societies and their foreign policies. The book opens with the following statement: "Each player depends upon the other not to upset the table . . . each imputes to the other a master plan that tends to be a mirror image of its own." And it continues in this vein throughout:

> In the years of coexistence . . . what each society has produced, how each has spent its money, how much secrecy each has craved, and how each has treated the rest of the world have been substantially determined by what a roomful of men in the White House and Kremlin thought their counterparts were doing or were about to do. . . .

> The one thing American politicians and Soviet politicians have usually agreed upon since the beginning of the cold war is that they are engaged in an ideological struggle. . . .

> . . . the official eschatology in both Washington and Moscow still embraces the fantasy of mass conversion [of the other side].

And on and on. John Foster Dulles's view of communism was the "mirror image" of the Communist view of capitalism. If there were no free elections in Eastern Europe, neither were there any in the American South. The massive, orchestrated, all-embracing vilification of the United States by the Soviet Union is equated with the author's recollection of "American comic-strip caricatures of the Soviet Union in this [cold war] period." Academic institutions "in both countries" are at the service of the government and intelligence-gathering operations, and "scholars at the [Moscow] Institute for the Study of the United States are in much the same position as scholars at the Harvard Russian Research Center or at the Columbia Institute of Russian Studies." "The military establishments on both sides subscribe to the same basic principles" and "constitute a potent political force with which the political leadership must negotiate." In short, Soviet-American relations during the cold war came down to "a history of mutually reinforcing misconceptions." "The madness of one bureaucracy sustains the other."

In its refusal to concede that there are fundamental differences between the American and the Soviet systems and their foreign policies, this book is typical of a certain American mind-set. But what explains the reluctance to confront such differences? Why the fascination with convergence theory and the relentless search for symmetry and "mirror images"?

I can think of several explanations. A major one is that if we can believe that the Russians are not so different from us, are in fact becoming more like us every day, then they also become less threatening. One can "understand" that Russians want cars, washing machines, suburban homes, and trips abroad, and one can therefore "understand" the mentality of a leadership which says it wants to provide them with such amenities but has to balance its domestic priorities against its foreign-policy objectives. The notion of convergence even succeeds in making such qualities as greed, corruption, and bumbling positively endearing, and somehow preferable to ideological purity, dedication, or adherence to principle.

There is also the persistent lure of a technological-economic determinism. Insofar as the Soviet Union has become a modern industrial society, it cannot be all that different from our own—so the argument goes. Economic rationality presses for similar solutions to similar problems; the pursuit of efficiency is incompatible with ideological dogmatism. This idea is especially reassuring because of its apparently hard-nosed, quasi-scientific underpinnings: it is not wishful thinking, but merely an acknowledgment of how modern industrial societies *must* operate. So too with Mr. Barnet's particular emphasis on the similarities of the two elites, which rests on the currently fashionable idea that in our times entrenched bureaucracies shape the course of international relations (bureaucratic determinism).

The belief in American-Soviet similarities also derives from a genuine difficulty which pragmatic people have in accepting that others take ideas and ideologies seriously. Surely, if American politicians running for office or trying to stay in office don't mean what they say, can Soviet functionaries be different? The notion that their-elites-are-as-bad-as-our-elites is probably rooted in a generalized mistrust of those who hold power. As such it is certainly a healthy impulse. Yet it unfortunately obscures more than it illuminates.

The same applies to the "mirror-image" perspective which Mr. Barnet embraces wholeheartedly, and which facilitates his explanations of the two countries' behavior. The "mirror-image" perspective allows one to take a more "objective" view of Soviet-American relations: both systems may be seen to be at fault, for each has its own vices which mirror those of the other. We have McCarthyism and racism; they have Stalinism and the purges. We are obsessed with money and profit; they are obsessed with ideological conformity. Yet as with the notion of a growing similarity between the two societies, the policies or actions that are alleged to mirror one another turn out on closer inspection to have little in common.

Mr. Barnet does have some reservations about the benefits of convergence; in fact he acknowledges that it may lead to greater Soviet assertiveness in international affairs. But he reaches this conclusion by arguing that the Soviet military bureaucracy has become a mirror image of the American and is *therefore* more aggressive. This is entirely characteristic of the benign attitude he takes toward almost everything the Soviet Union says and does; of his pervading suspiciousness toward American policy makers; and of his spurious attribution of symmetry to two highly dissimilar regimes. There must be better ways to pursue the possibilities of peace and international stability than through misreading the nature of both Soviet and American society.

20.
Reflections on Anti-Americanism in Our Times

In the course of the last quarter century or so, the United States has become a nearly universal scapegoat symbol. It has been denounced in countless speeches and editorials, on posters, in radio broadcasts, and over television, as well as in private conversations, for the ills of the world, for the problems of particular societies, and even for the unhappiness of individuals. No country has had more hostile demonstrations in front of its embassies around the world, or more of its libraries and cultural missions abroad ransacked, or more of its policies routinely denounced in the United Nations and other international organizations. More American flags have been burned, in and outside the United States, than the flags of any other country. More American diplomats and politicians traveling abroad have been subjected to abuse and violence. Jacques Barzun observed: "As a nation whose citizens seek popularity more than any other kind of success it is galling (and inexplicable) that we, the United States, are so extensively unpopular."[1]

Anti-Americanism is one of the most significant, widespread, and intellectually neglected cultural, political, and social-psychological phenomena of the last few decades.[2] Few parts of the world are free from it; it is found in countries officially friendly toward and allied with the United States as well as those officially hostile or neutral; in countries with social-political systems similar to the American as well as in those diametrically opposed; among both developed and underdeveloped nations and on all continents.

Anti-Americanism is many things to many people. Its manifestations range from official policy to highly personal hatreds, from theoretical examination and indictment to "gut reactions," from mass hysteria to reasoned analysis. It is a global phenomenon, originating in diverse conditions, meeting different needs, and serving different political, economic, ideological, cultural, and psychological purposes. Anti-Americanism, I would suggest, has three major dimensions: the critique of the American political-economic system, of American culture, and of the American character.

In order to understand anti-Americanism, one must try to classify its numerous types or varieties. To begin, three major sets of distinctions may be made: *First,* there is the anti-Americanism of non-Americans, as distinct from the anti-Americanism of Americans. *Second,* anti-Americanism may be official or unofficial, that is, anti-Americanism as a government policy and fostered by official propaganda (as in the Soviet Union or Cuba), and anti-Americanism as a spontaneous impulse independent of governmental encouragement and propaganda. A *third* major distinction may be made between political and cultural anti-Americanism, which at times appear separately.

Further distinctions could be made between the anti-Americanism of intellectuals (American or other) and the anti-Americanism prevalent among other social strata; between the anti-Americanism of Western Europeans and of Latin Americans—two fairly distinct regional varieties—or, more generally, between those in industrially developed and underdeveloped countries. Looking to its ideological roots, one might also distinguish between anti-Americanism rooted in some version of Marxism-Leninism (which places the United States in the role of the arch-imperialist country and fountainhead of capitalism) and that which originates in some conservative or traditional belief that looks upon the United States and what it stands for as the most perniciously effective agent of modernization and change. In the latter critique, Americanization brings in its wake cultural homogenization, spiritual impoverishment, and the sundering of traditional social bonds.

Let me suggest five major attributes of the United States that attract worldwide animosity and make America the most likely candidate for becoming a near universal scapegoat.

1. *Too much is known about the United States.* No society can escape criticism when there is as much information disseminated about it as there is about America. By any standard of international or historical comparison, more is known about the United States around the world than about any other country in our time or in the past. That much of this information is shallow or stereotyped contributes to the "image problem." Thus a precondition of anti-Americanism is publicity: certain things have to be widely known in order to be denounced and criticized. Even misperception and distortion require some information. Unknown lands or social systems cannot be denounced or become targets of hostility. A combination of distance and misinformation or stereotyped information provides an ideal breeding ground for hostility toward a country or culture. For much of the world, the United States is distant in reality but familiar in some of its characteristics because of the mass media and the

penetration of some of the more questionable cultural products of American society into the cultural marketplaces of many countries.

2. *Affluence.* The wealth of American society, in an exaggerated or realistic version, and the affluence of so many individual Americans is well known around the globe. It invites many negative responses, including simple envy, sour-grapes critiques of "soulless American materialism," and cries of social injustice (in this perspective the United States becomes a symbol of global inequality, of the maldistribution of resources and material advantages). It is among the paradoxes of worldwide anti-Americanism, and obviously related to the appeal of American material comforts (so often denounced), that millions of people around the world still try to emigrate to the United States.

3. *Pervasive global cultural presence.* American movies, magazines, and TV programs reach not only into Canada, Mexico, and Western Europe, but also into much of the Third World (unless it is Communist controlled and therefore determined to stem the tide of subversive entertainment). Such cultural presence not only contributes to the global awareness of the United States and of American mass culture and its material products, it also offends the upholders of indigenous tradition and culture and the bearers of elite cultural values everywhere. Nor is the self-portrait projected by the American mass media particularly flattering. While the worldwide popularity of these American cultural offerings is undeniable, this very popularity generates further condemnation of the perniciousnes of American mass culture by local intellectuals, opinion leaders, and guardians of indigenous traditions.

The global American cultural presence is supplemented by the physical presence and high visibility of Americans in many parts of the world. Probably no other country in history has sent forth as many travelers (mostly tourists) as the United States. Notwithstanding the economic benefits of such tourism, the large-scale physical presence of Americans in places like Western Europe, the Caribbean, and Latin America has not increased the fund of goodwill toward things American. The fault does not lie with the travelers. In few parts of the world, if any, do the "natives" like recurring invasions of well-heeled strangers. The major images of the traveling American are not calculated to win minds and hearts abroad: the American tourist of the conducted tours shepherded from bus to cathedral; the wealthier individuals buying up antiques or real estate and driving up local prices; or the hippie invader bedding down in a sleeping bag near the old fountains in the center of town. These stereotypes of the traveling American tend to combine with those disseminated by American popular culture and mass media, often intensifying the distaste for American culture and styles of life.

4. *The anti-Americanism of Americans.* Much of the global anti-Americanism feeds on and reflects the anti-Americanism of Americans. People do not think well of those who do not think well of themselves. A large proportion of American intellectuals and opinion leaders do not think well of their country, its social and political system or cultural values. Few foreigners fail to be impressed by such a propensity to guilt, self-criticism, and lack of collective self-confidence.

5. *The combination of great power with the weakened will to use it.* Until recently, the United States was the unrivaled military superpower of the world. American science, technology, and industry created an awesome military machine, and yet all this power, all the nuclear submarines, missiles, and bombers failed to achieve America's political objectives. Soviet influence was not contained nor the Iron Curtain rolled back nor Cuba prevented from becoming a Soviet satellite (and an aspiring exporter of revolution in Latin America and Africa). Other Third World countries were not deterred from siding with the USSR (or China) in and outside the United Nations, nor was the global drift toward left-wing authoritarian and anti-American regimes halted. The list of unaccomplished American foreign policy goals could be extended. The most notable failure of military might was, of course, Indochina, with Vietnam, Cambodia, and Laos becoming Communist-dominated, despite the extended and profligate use of American military power. The image of the ineffectual bully emerged in the wake of the Vietnam fiasco. America appears as the big, bumbling country that can be taunted, teased, and abused with relative impunity.

Let us examine first the anti-Americanism of Americans. In many ways, the anti-Americanism of Americans is the prototype and fountainhead of all other forms of anti-Americanism. From American anti-Americanism, others can borrow themes, arguments, or illustrative material for any particular criticism or attack on the American political-economic system, culture, or personality. The anti-Americanism of Americans, like anti-Americanism in general, is not a systematic ideology or clearly elaborated social criticism. it is more of an impulse, an emotion, a set of beliefs. The anti-Americanism of Americans—articulated by estranged intellectuals—rests on the agonized belief that contemporary American society is possibly the most evil society ever known in history—a belief highly congenial with unfamiliarity with the major facts of history that comes so naturally to Americans of all persuasions.

The conviction about the exceptionally unjust and peculiarly oppressive nature of the United States has been held and elaborated by people like Daniel Berrigan, Noam Chomsky, Howard Bruce Franklin, Paul Goodman, Lillian Hellman, Gabriel Kolko, William Kunstler, Norman Mailer,

Herbert Marcuse, C. Wright Mills, Victor Navasky, Charles Reich, Theodore Roszak, Philip Slater, Susan Sontag, Robert P. Wolff, and many others in the last two decades. The perceptions of the most vocal and well-known American critics of American society have much in common. A few examples make the point.

For Mailer, as for many other critics, the uniquely deadening qualities of American life were the most hateful, a viewpoint that resembles Marcuse's despair over the efficiency of the System in forestalling beneficial social change. (The latter proposition was expounded at some length in Marcuse's *One Dimensional Man.*) Mailer contrasted the crucial defects of American society with revolutionary Cuba:

> We live in a country very different from Cuba. We have had a tyranny here but it did not have the features of Batista; it was a tyranny one breathed but could not define; it was felt as no more than a slow deadening of the best of our possibilities, a tension we could not name which was the sum of our frustrations. We all knew that the best of us used up our memories in long nights of drinking, exhausted our vision in secret journeys of the mind; our more stable men and women of some little good will watched the years go by—their idealism sank into apathy. By law we had a free ballot; was there ever a choice? We were a league of silent defeated men. . . . In silence we gave you [Castro] our support. You were aiding us, you were giving us psychic ammunition, you were aiding us in that desperate silent struggle we have been fighting with sick dead hearts against the cold insidious cancer of the power that governs us, you were giving us new blood to fight our mass communications, our police, our secret police, our corporations, our empty politicians, our clergymen, our editors, our cold frightened bewildered bullies who govern a machine made out of people they no longer understand.[3]

A somewhat similar vision informs the dark observations of anthropologist Jules Henry about American culture: "When fear penetrates all aspects of culture and becomes a dominant driving force, the culture freezes in fixed attitudes of attack and defense, all cultural life suffers, and the Self nearly dies in the cold."[4]

Most American critics of American life and culture had no difficulty linking inauthenticity, depersonalization, and anxiety (to name only a few ills of American society) with technology. In fact, the frequent association of the United States with inhuman, wasteful, or outright destructive technology has been a potent source of anti-Americanism among Americans more than non-Americans. This has been the case particularly in the contexts of the Vietnam War, the assault on the physical environment, and profligate domestic consumption patterns.

Marcuse considered technology so deeply implicated even in domestic repression that he felt that automobiles too served subtle repressive functions by allowing workers submerged in debilitating drudgery to sublimate their aggression by getting behind the wheel: "If this aggressiveness were not sublimated in the speed and power of the automobile it might be directed against the dominant powers."[5]

What seemed to enrage the most embittered American critics of the United States—and gave their critiques the quality we are trying to convey here—was what they perceived to be the peculiarly insidious combination of repression, injustice, and corruption, on the one hand, with a certain flexibility, benevolence, and tolerance on the other. Several widely used concepts introduced by the critics—such as "welfare-warfare state" (Chomsky), or "repressive tolerance" (Marcuse), "corporate liberalism," and "liberal fascism"—reflect this combination of something desirable with something abhorrent. Hence the critics' alarm over the possibility that this system remains capable of legitimating itself and their apprehension that its vices are not sufficiently apparent to the masses wallowing in false consciousness, or to the technocrats who are bought off by shares of power and prestige. (It was precisely such concerns on the part of numerous critics that led to the exhilarating anticipation in the 1960s of political polarization and to the hope that the System would be provoked into becoming more *intolerantly repressive!*)

It is the firm belief in the uniquely evil (or distasteful) character of American society and culture that distinguishes the American critic of American society from the native critics of other Western societies, of which more will be said. The anti-Americanism of Americans may be considered a particularly diffuse, intense, and embittered form of alienation, often suffused with a sense of personal injury, shame, and despair. It differs significantly from the attitudes of the social critics of other nations, with the possible exception of the guilt feelings of many post–World War II Germans. Nobody calls an alienated Frenchman anti-French (or Italians anti-Italian or Britons anti-British). Estrangement and social criticism in these and other societies do not carry the same flavor as they do in the United States. For one thing, the alienated Frenchman rarely leaves France, either on vacation, in self-exile, or as an emigrant. Nor will he despise French food, or movies, or the design of French cars, or the manners of his fellow countrymen. In short, his estrangement is more limited, more specific, and less of a cultural and personal affair. One cannot detect in the alienated Frenchman (or Italian or Briton) the uncertainties, the unease, the guilt-ridden qualities discernible in so many alienated Americans.[6] The anti-American Americans often insist that there is something uniquely and basically wrong, not only with the

American social-political system, but also with the American people, with their tastes, values, habits, consumption patterns, and ways of life.

To the extent that the anti-Americanism of Americans is primarily an attribute of American intellectuals, these attitudes may reflect the long-standing problems of American intellectuals in a business society, the traditions of their relative social isolation, and their elitist condescension toward those more brutally immersed in the "cash nexus" of daily life. There may also be a cultural lag that explains the lingering resentment of intellectuals about their limited recognition in society at large—a state of affairs that no longer exists. Certainly, there are some uniquely American social and historical conditions that predispose the American intellectual to the attitudes sketched here.

Consider the confessions of a singularly estranged and critical group of Americans, admirers of Castro's Cuba, the members of the Venceremos Brigade who volunteered to cut sugarcane in Cuba:

> White people [i.e., most members of the Venceremos brigade] . . . came to Cuba with only the most fragile sense of themselves as people. . . . They were often paralyzed with shame and despair over the values which a competitive, individualistic and racist middle class culture had instilled in them.

Or

> Amerika [*sic*] does a lot of ugly things to people. It puts walls between them. . . . Amerika tries to make pieces of everything. . . . Not long ago I was in pieces. All the experiences of my life had conspired to fragment my understanding. . . . I suffered from the prime Amerikan problem: middle class consciousness, the inability to feel.

Or

> I can fight the system because I truly hate it. I hate how it has warped the people of our country. How it tries to warp me and everyone it can. It lives off the weakness that all people have and perpetuates those weaknesses. Amerika will rip you up—tear your guts apart from the inside.[7]

What is one to make of such hatred especially on the part of people—young, white, middle- and upper-middle-class college students or dropouts—who, in no objective, verifiable sense have been deprived, disadvantaged, or victimized by their society? While there have been upper-class rebels at other times and places in history, in contemporary America there has been a striking and highly standardized expansion of the rebellious, alienated stance unrelated to objective conditions or to the deprivations of the critic. It may be more than conjecture to suggest that there is a great deal of personal unhappiness and anguish behind such strident and sweeping rejections of America.

How is one to account for the savage hostility of such a gentle servant of God as the Reverend Daniel Berrigan (no inexperienced youth), who calls Americans "savages of the West," "joyless" inhabitants of a "prison society"? Berrigan was also convinced of the "genocidal intent and execution . . . beyond any reasonable doubt" of the bombings in Vietnam and considered "the American ghetto and the Hanoi 'operation' . . . a single enterprise . . . total war in both cases." To be sure, some of this bitterness was the product of the Vietnam War and of the methods used by the American forces. Yet his other claims and linkages—of genocide and domestic racial discrimination and the Vietnam War, of "disease and malnutrition [being] a systematic method of destruction of minority peoples in our ghettos,"[8] bespeak an implacable hatred of American society. It reflects the determined search for human malevolence without which the passionate rejection of any social-political system is incomplete. In the minds of such native anti-Americans, everything that is bad has to be systematic, deliberate, and interconnected. Vietnam, race relations, poverty, environmental problems, bad TV programs, fins on cars, plastic on kitchen tables—all add up to a subtly repressive (or "repressively tolerant") conspiracy of nameless, faceless, joyless, death-dealing men at the top, members of the Establishment, of the monopoly-capitalist, liberal-fascist-corporate system.

Tom Wolfe's parody of the social criticism of American intellectuals captures many of the main themes and emotional tones of the phenomenon:

"A small group of nameless, faceless men" . . . now dominates American life. In America a man's home is not his castle but merely "a gigantic listening device with a mortgage"—a reference to eavesdropping by the FBI and CIA. America's foreign policy has been and continues to be based upon war, assassination, bribery, genocide, and the sabotage of democratic governments. "The new McCarthyism" . . . is already upon us. Following a brief charade of free speech the "gagging of the press" has resumed. Racism in America has not diminished; it is merely more subtle now. The gulf between rich and poor widens daily, creating "permanent ghetto-colonial populations." The decline in economic growth is causing a crisis of capitalism, which will lead shortly to authoritarian rule and to a new America in which everyone waits, in horror, for the knock on the door in the dead of the night, the descent of the knout on the nape of the neck.[9]

The centerpiece of American anti-Americanism in our times is not the detailed, specific institutional criticism (such as one might have encountered among the alienated in the 1930s), but the more general claim that the social system, besides being unjust, exploitative, oppressive, and fascistic deforms and cripples the individual personality. It prevents people from experiencing authentic feelings, joy, spontaneity, good human fellowship. To be sure, this basic charge is associated with the by-now familiar reproaches against American society: that it is overcommercialized, materialistic, inauthentic, leveling/homogenizing (but, for other critics, also elitist), wasteful, overly individualistic, overbureaucratized; that it misuses technology, drives wedges between people, polices the whole world, mistreats the poor, ransacks the Third World, and, of course, is racist to the core. In short, in the old New Left parlance, the United States is "the belly of the monster" (of world capitalism, imperialism, neocolonialism, and racism).

Anti-Americanism in the Third World is another major species of the phenomenon. In many instances—for example, in India and some African countries—it is more a matter of official, or semiofficial policy, or an attitude of elite groups, than a mass phenomenon. Latin America may be a special case in the Third World, since it has been most exposed to American economic, political, and cultural influences, and consequently anti-American resentment may go beyond the ranks of intellectuals and other elites. In general, the United States stands accused in the Third World of economic domination or of neglect and indifference, or of support for the neocolonialism of European powers. Furthermore, the view has gained ground in Third World countries that the Western world, and the United States in particular, is morally bound to provide reparation or restitution for the ills of colonialism and past exploitation, that an international redistribution of wealth is called for, and the wealth of the United States (and other Western countries) is illegitimate. Hence American aid is both demanded and resented. As the richest of the "have" nations, there is little hope for the United States to overcome this type of hostility, which is intensified by well-known examples of American wastefulness and depletion of environmental resources. Hostility toward the United States also feeds on a somewhat outdated conception of race relations in the United States and an even more archaic image of the alignment of the countries of the world. In this perspective, the protagonists are frozen into old roles: The United States and Western European nations remain the rich, cold-hearted villains, while the oil-rich Arab countries retain their places in the impoverished Third World as far as their ideological-political alignments and continued modest contributions to the United Nations budget are concerned.

Poor countries, more than rich ones, need scapegoats to account for their unhappy situation. If the former colonial powers become less and less plausible targets of blame with the passage of time—though a good try is still being made from time to time—the United States, because it is the richest, most powerful white nation (often allied with the former colonial powers), irresistibly becomes the prime candidate for scape-goating.

Anti-Americanism in Western Europe is more cultural than political. Although it rests on the pervasive American cultural and physical presence, most Western Europeans have no serious objections to American troops or political ties. Here too anti-Americanism is preeminent among in-tellectuals and other elite groups, both Marxist and conservative, who fear the erosion of local cultural values and standards (or business interests). Marxist intellectuals are anti-American all over the world for obvious reasons: The United States is the keystone of what is left of the worldwide system of capitalism. The anti-Americanism of some European intellectuals, such as the late Bertrand Russell or Jean-Paul Sartre, has been just as intense and obsessional as that of their American counterparts. Insofar as there is anti-Americanism in Eastern Europe, it is due to a sense of letdown: The United States did not live up to the political hopes and expectations of East European nations, either on a global scale or in relation to their particular political fates.

It should not be thought that anti-Americanism is a totally irrational phenomenon, a form of scapegoating or prejudice without any foundation. However, most of the American vices, whether in foreign policy, in the national character, or in cultural orientation, are neither unique nor so serious as to provide the kind of condemnation and revulsion we have witnessed.

Consider the following inventory of unattractive American traits as seen by foreigners, according to an American social critic of impeccable credentials, Dwight MacDonald:

> Americans appear to other nations to be at once gross and sentimental, immature and tough, uncultivated and hypocritical, shrewd about small things and stupid about big things. In these antinomies fatally appears our lack of style.[10]

While the charge of "lack of style" has haunted generations of American intellectuals (and social classes above the lower ones), it is obviously not a charge to warrant murderous indignation. But there is more to this criticism than meets the eye. The lack of style is not merely a matter of taste or a problem of diminished aesthetic sensibilities. The lack of style, a surface phenomenon, points to deeper connections: to the lack of values, or the confusion of values. I suspect that what many foreigners despise and dislike about American society, or about individual Americans, is the confused groping for a style or for values and standards. The American spectacle of a moral and aesthetic free-for-all, of the astonishing ups and downs of moral (and philosophical-ideological) fashions, the rapid switches from Leninism to vegetarianism, from thoughtless wastefulness to obsessive conservation, from preoccupation with issues of foreign policy to fixation on the domestic, from singing the praise of monogamy to acclaiming open marriage—the American "openness to change" is what often disturbs, shocks, or antagonizes the outside observer most. It is not self-evident why this should be the case, since openness to change is associated with flexibility, innovation, initiative, an open mind, and many other good things. Yet there is a thin line between "openness to change," on the one hand, and suggestibility, inner uncertainty, inability to discriminate, and moral confusion, on the other.

I believe it is this moral-ethical (and aesthetic) confusion of Americans that, in the final analysis, may provoke the greatest hostility or, at least, ambivalence, everywhere. This is so, I believe, because in a sense these attitudes may be the shape of things to come. If one can speak of "Americanization" in various parts of the world, it means, among other things, the export of confusion, of high and easily frustrated expectations, ethical relativism, nonmaterial insecurity, forms of spiritual malaise. All these factors are associated with secularization and the decline of traditional values and social organization. In this field, as in many others, the United States has the unquestioned lead.

The "First New Nation" image (the title of S. M. Lipset's book published in 1963) continues to haunt Americans and non-Americans alike. This "first new nation" was founded—and continued to live on and off—what Daniel Boorstin called "extravagant expectations." In few countries of the world is there a comparable popular awareness of social ideals or of ceremonial values as in the United States. Eighteenth-century values and ideals survive with amazing vitality in the minds of many Americans, who keep judging their society (and perhaps their personal selves as well) in the light of such values. In few parts of the world, and rarely in history, has there been such a keen awareness of and concern with the gaps between ideal and actual, theory and practice, collective aspirations and their realization. This may account for the peculiarly bitter and self-hating quality of the anti-Americanism of Americans, and especially of American intellectuals. However, not even the most bitter critics of the United States consider American culture and society a total, unmitigated failure.[11] Even the Marxist critics must and do admit that American capitalism created the most productive economic machine that has ever existed. Perhaps it is this curious mixture of success and failure, of partially realized high ideals, that affronts and enrages—and unites—the anti-Americans of the world. You cannot completely write off the United States, or give up on it, but neither can you endorse it wholeheartedly. For many Americans the admonition to "love it or leave it" poses an impossible choice.

Postscript 1982

Since this piece was written, several new and significant eruptions of anti-Americanism took place in different parts of the world lending support to the points made prevoiusly.

The frenzy of anti-Americanism that was displayed in Iran (and included the taking of hostages) belonged to the species which arises out of the offended sensibilities of the custodians of traditional values and ways of life. Iranian anti-Americanism, religious in its inspiration, was perhaps the clearest example of the fusion of anti-Americanism with the protest against modernization, and especially the modernization of social values (modern technology, especially if military in its applications, was quite acceptable to the upholders of tradition in Iran). Hostility to the United States also had some specific political components on the part of those who opposed the regime of the Shah which, in turn, had rested on American support.

Two other recent outbursts of anti-Americanism deserve mention. In Western Europe, the new wave of anti-Americanism has been linked to the antinuclear (or disarmament) movement which, as noted before, largely fixes the blame on the United States for the arms race and international tension and expresses greater concern with American missiles yet to be deployed than with Soviet ones already in place. In Germany and Italy, small terrorist groups exhibit a particularly intense and fanatical anti-Americanism culminating in acts of violence against Americans or American property.

Most recently, the British-Argentinian war over the Falklands has produced somewhat unexpectedly an upsurge of hostility toward the United States (more than toward Britain), not only in Argentina but all over Latin America, suggesting the huge reservoirs of such sentiments ready to be mobilized by particular events. In this case, it was the American support of Britain that triggered these sentiments and a perception of the United States as perfidious and hostile toward Latin America. In this, as in many other instances, hostility toward the United

States rests on (often outdated) conceptions of overbearing American power, openly or surreptitiously exercised. Thus anti-Americanism, especially in the Third World, often incorporates in its imagery heroic victim-underdog countries pitted against the cunning, ruthless, and powerful United States.

Notes

1. "The Man in the American Mask," *Foreign Affairs* (April 1965).
2. Anti-Americanism, as far as I know, has no historians; I cannot refer to any authoritative works on the subject. It is in itself interesting why so little has been written about anti-Americanism, and why so few intellectuals and social scientists have been puzzled by it, and sought to account for it. Evidently, Americans as well as non-Americans have come to take it for granted by now. This is all the more thought-provoking, since before the middle of this century and through much of the eighteenth and nineteenth centuries the global image of the United States (to the extent that such a thing existed) was rather positive.
3. *The Presidential Papers* (London: Deutsch, 1963).
4. Suggestively entitled *Culture Against Man* (New York: Random House, 1965).
5. "Marcuse Defines His New Left Line," *New York Times Magazine,* 27 Oct. 1968.
6. Or equivalents of such sentiments: "We, the American people—We: affluent, corrupt, dehumanized, brutalized, chauvinistic, racist, white America—we share the guilt for U.S. policy and for the atrocities" (Advertisement in the *New York Times* News of the Week, 30 Nov. 1969). Along these lines, it may not be farfetched to suggest that if the white race is the cancer of mankind, as Susan Sontag proposed, she would presumably regard the United States as the cancer of the white race.
7. Members of the Venceremos Brigade were mostly college or graduate school students or dropouts from academia and may best be considered aspiring or marginal intellectuals. I would guess that a large portion of them have since completed their studies and pursue today some profession or middle-class occupation. See also Sandra Levinson and Carol Brightman, eds., *Venceremos Brigade* (New York: Simon and Schuster, 1971).
8. *Night Flight to Hanoi* (New York: Macmillan, 1968).
9. *Mauve Gloves & Madmen, Clutter & Wine* (New York: Farrar, Straus and Giroux, 1976).
10. *Discriminations* (New York: Crossman, 1974).
11. For some of its critics America redeems itself, in part, by allowing a small elite of aesthetes and intellectuals the gratifications of the mind. Susan Sontag has written: "I live in an unethical society that coarsens the sensibilities and thwarts the capacities for goodness of most people but makes available for minority consumption an astonishing array of intellectual and aesthetic pleasures" (*Trip to Hanoi,* New York: Farrar, Straus and Giroux, 1968).

21.
Comparative Sociology in the United States and Why There Is So Little of It

At the 1980 annual meetings of the American Sociological Association, the only session explicitly and open endedly devoted to comparative sociology[1] entitled "Comparative Social Systems" attracted a peak audience of twenty-seven (during much of the session there were only about fifteen to twenty in attendance). Of the five individuals on the platform three spoke with accents betraying their non-American origins (the chairman and two of the presenters).

It is tempting to view the information disclosed here as symptomatic of the state of comparative sociology in the United States, which not only remains the preoccupation of a minority within the profession, but also appears to attract a minority of the foreign born. What I am suggesting is that the apparent indifference toward comparative sociology signifies not so much a lack of interest in matters comparative but rather in matters outside the United States and especially in the ways they compare with the state of affairs here. Thus it is noteworthy that even when American sociologists show interest in phenomena outside their country—which is not often the case—it tends to lack the comparative perspective and instead takes the form of area or case study. To draw once more on my experience as session organizer for "Comparative Social Systems," I can report that approximately half of all papers submitted for consideration were in fact single case studies and made not the slightest pretense of being comparative. Evidently, some of our colleagues regard themselves as comparativists simply by virtue of not studying American society. They would argue, I presume, that comparison is always implicit when you investigate the unfamiliar or less familiar case.

Since probably few would seriously challenge the proposition that comparative sociology is not widely cultivated in the United States and that this is regrettable, I will devote most of this paper to an inquiry into the likely explanations of this state of affairs. If one were to rank order the various types of sociological research and teaching on the basis

313

of comparative and noncomparative concerns, I suspect that we would come up with something approximating the following classification: (1) Probably close to 85 percent of the research done (and courses taught) deal with substantive issues in the American context alone (some of this may be comparative chronologically, but probably much of it focuses on the American present. (2) Perhaps 10 to 15 percent of the work may involve non-American case studies sometimes equated with comparative sociology. (3) The remaining 5 percent or so may be divided between comparison of several non-American cases and those which contrast some American phenomena with the non-American. The relentless, if in many ways understandable, yet epistemologically unsound and theoretically constraining, preoccupation with American society persists among the majority of American sociologists. A few relatively recent exceptions, no matter how notable in their isolated grandeur, will not undercut this generalization.[2]

The evidence of the neglected state of comparative studies need not be confined to attendance figures at professional meetings devoted to their cultivation. The indications are everywhere that comparative sociology, and primarily its cross-cultural or cross-national variety, has remained on the margins of American sociology. The limited development of historical sociology may at least in part be explained by the same circumstances.[3] It may be argued that historical sociology has two strikes against it as far as most American sociologists are concerned. When involved with no non-American subjects, it suffers from the same liabilities as comparative sociology (of which more will be said in this chapter), while its focus on the past further reduces its appeals. On the other hand, the practice of historical sociology may lend itself more readily to the social-critical, unmasking temper and thereby can make a more successful connection with what has become a large part of mainstream sociological activity today. American sociologists are less averse to looking at the past when by doing so they can "demystify" the present; that is, connect the critique of present-day institutions and practices to their antecedents and put current social criticism on more solid foundations by showing the historical roots of unappealing contemporary phenomena.

A perusal of leading journals, course listings at universities and colleges, the programs of national or regional sociological meetings, as well as the books reviewed and advertised reveals and confirms that cross-cultural comparisons—especially of a more substantive kind—are infrequently made by American sociologists. While it may be true that some of the leading figures in American sociology did, in the last decade or so, produce significant comparative studies (those cited previously), such pioneering works[4] do not seem to have much of an impact on the profession as a whole, on much of the research being carried out and the courses taught. There are virtually no texts on comparative sociology (what comes closest to a text is a volume which presents "a codification of cross cultural analysis."[5] There seems to have been a greater interest in the methodological problems of comparative studies than in comparative investigations themselves.[6] Introductory (or more specialized) textbooks rarely invoke the experience of other societies, except perhaps in connection with race and ethnic relations. Interestingly enough, even some of our major theoreticians such as Talcott Parsons, Robert K. Merton, and C. Wright Mills rarely drew on the experiences of societies other than the American. (According to a somewhat unkind joke heard around Harvard in the 1960s, Talcott Parsons's perspectives on social control were influenced by his observations of the disciplined and largely self-regulated flow of traffic between suburban Belmont, where he lived, and Harvard.)

Some of the circumstances that plausibly account for the all too modest cultivation of the comparative field—and what it amounts to, the limited interest in the world outside—have remained fairly constant. Doubtless de Tocqueville already observed that there was a singular American preoccupation with American society and culture connected with the pride in its achievements and the assurance that this was a society profoundly different in its intentions and accomplishments from all others, past and present. Stanislav Andreski, a British sociologist, has suggested that American collective self-centeredness and difficulty in understanding other cultures is also connected with the "cultural consequences of immigration and assimilation, as the latter entailed insistence on the superlative qualities of things American and a desire to shed disreputable foreign ways."[7] There was also, initially, geographic isolation and material self-sufficiency making it easier to ignore the rest of the world. While both of these conditions are things of the past, some of the habits they created have not disappeared and recent historical events have done much to revitalize them. I am referring to the post-Vietnam isolationism and the associated sentiment that the dangers and complications, political and military, of the outside world were best left alone as involvement with them proved costly and counter-productive. Admittedly, it is a big leap from the opposition to military intervention in Southeast Asia (or other distant parts of the world) to the reluctance of sociologists to conduct cross-cultural research. Yet when a society reverts to its historic preoccupation with itself, it creates an ethos hardly conducive to raising questions about the world outside, to comparing the familiar with the unfamiliar. And when many intellectuals, including sociologists, feel strongly that their society is in certain ways uniquely deformed—as many have felt since the 1960s—they will not have much interest and energy left to invest in other societies. It has come to be an article of faith among liberal intellectuals, and most American sociologists fall under this heading,[8] that instead of what was seen as destructive and pointless foreign entanglements, attention and resources must be devoted to the problems at home. This position was at once persuasively pragmatic and appealingly idealistic as it stressed that charity must begin at home and that both the political authorities and intellectuals have a prime obligation to understand better and solve the problems of their own society.

To this one may add that American education, never noted for its dedication to the task of acquainting the young with the world outside, has been very much a part of these recent trends. Fervently embracing the fashionable notions of "relevance," secondary schools as well as institutions of higher education dropped language requirements, fled even from the pathetic remnants of geography which were sometimes subsumed under "social studies" (that peculiar hodgepodge of diluted or sugarcoated fragments of sociology, current events, and history), and deepened their commitment to *not* teaching the history of other countries, and most certainly not in any chronological or conceptual order. This is to say that American education, higher and lower, has done little to provide a basis for the development of interest in other cultures—neither before nor since the 1960s. A presidential report on the teaching of foreign languages and international studies provides recent substantiation of these observations.[9]

Thus for most Americans, sociologists included, the United States remains the measure of all things. Both education and the mass media have contributed to this. In all probability, such a collective self-centeredness, reflected in American sociology, is also associated with American individualism and its intensified varieties in more recent times.[10] Fascination with the collective self and preoccupation with one's ego go well together.

There are other, more specific and consequential contributions to the condition being sketched here; they are to be found in the predominant impulses which draw people to sociology in the United States. The first one is the desire to create or cultivate a science of society. There are those who wish to become scientific sociologists and, therefore, their prime concern is the attainment or refinement of methodological precision, measurement, quantification, testing. For those in this group, comparative studies of a cross-national character present unnecessary hazards and complications. It is easier to deal with one case (or setting) than with several. Furthermore, the type of data they find scientifically respectable is more readily available in the United States; so are data-processing institutions and organizations, and, most importantly, the funds necessary for large-scale, easily quantifiable research which has policy implications. Understandably, the various government agencies and even most private foundations are more interested in supporting research related to the United States than other countries—an added incentive to stay with American society as the basic research topic. Moreover, the more scientifically oriented sociology is also more expensive (because of the need for large samples, computer analysis of data, trained interviewers, etc.); hence the issue of funding is critical. Thus funding itself promotes a bias to favor issues and research topics pertaining to American society. Even when more respectable data are collected and made accessible in other societies, comparison with their American counterparts presents problems. Data collecting procedures are not fully standardized cross-culturally; moreover, for American sociologists unfamiliar with other societies such information is inherently more difficult to interpret.

Among the scientifically minded, there is yet another reason for shying away from comparative sociology. It is the specter of ethnocentrism which raises its head when cross-cultural comparisons are made. Such comparisons create strong temptations to make value judgments which the scientifically minded want to avoid. Many such sociologists may also feel that despite the achievements of American social scientists in collecting and analyzing information about American society, much more remains to be learned, so why bother with other cultures when almost any theoretical-intellectual concern can be pursued more safely and with better financial support in a methodologically more respectable manner in the American context?

The other major impulse that prompts Americans to become sociologists—the desire to pursue the dictates of a developed social conscience—also militates against the comparative approach. Those who belong to this category are probably even more numerous than the previous contingent. I am referring to all who become sociologists because of some altruistic-idealistic concern with the nature of American society and especially its shortcomings. Many of them study the institutions and problems of the United States in order to find solutions to specific problems, to devise proposals for remedial action. Others engage in similar activities without the ameliorative design and are content to play the part of the social critic who exposes the defects of the system, hoping that this will hasten its collapse. Neither of these orientations is conducive to interest in other societies.

For better or worse, most American sociologists are deeply interested in and involved with their own country. Many have what may be called a love-hate relationship with their society. To use another cliché, they can neither love it nor leave it—nor leave it alone. A large portion of the work of such sociologists is devoted to the documentation of the many divergences between the American dream and reality, to the depiction of the countless disparities between the ideals and actualities, ceremonial values and daily institutional practices. They give every indication of being shocked by such discoveries as if they had believed that such phenomena were a rarity in history and the discrepancies between social ideals and practices a peculiar liability of contemporary American society. These critics of society pursue their task in a curious intellectual-theoretical vacuum which does not readily accommodate comparative perspectives. Most of them seem genuinely uninterested in other societies and feel that their duty is to study, expose, unmask, improve, or transform—as the case may be—their own. They find the experience of other lands irrelevant, operating still in a spirit of American exceptionalism, an attitude which may be considered a cultural lag.[11]

The recent rise and popularity of Marxism among younger sociologists has not done much to alter this situation despite the comparative affinities of Marxism, except perhaps making the study of industrially underdeveloped, or "Third World" countries more popular, especially insofar as they could be portrayed as victims of the United States and other Western countries, and thus joined to other streams of social criticism. By and large, these more recent Marxist strains in American sociology served more to strengthen the domestic social-critical tendencies rather than enrich comparative perspectives. Thus, for example, the "world system" studies have functioned, in many instances, as vehicles to illuminate the *global* malignancy of American institutions and influences. It may also be noted here that many of the recent "world system" studies suffer from the curious neglect of the rather extensive noncapitalist parts of the "system" and that, in turn, in the discussions of the capitalist world the United States and the American-dominated multinational corporations loom large.

It is not only the intensely critical view of American society that diverts attention from cross-cultural endeavors but also the more out-of-date admiration of the "advanced" character of American institutions. Thus a reluctance to compare the United States to other countries may also be founded upon the premise that the former, being at the apex of some developmental scheme, will not long remain significantly different since other societies will sooner or later come to assume many characteristics of the United States (a viewpoint usually associated with emphasis on the inexorable consequences of industrialization, urbanization, and secularization)—and if so, why then should one bother with comparing transient differences? Thus the convergence theory, for example, used primarily to account for the imputed similarities between the United States and the Soviet Union, has failed to stimulate many specific studies designed to gauge the actual growth of similarities between the two countries. (There used to be a way of looking at the Soviet Union, "as in effect just another fast developing area with a big trade potential . . . as though the Revolution and the doctrines of Marxism-Leninism were puerile incidents, temporary deviations from the ultimate forward movement of the world alongside businesslike American lines.")[12]

Thus the preoccupation with American society, which for most sociologists precludes the development of comparative interests, has many sources. These include the traditional, idealistic American exceptionalism (i.e., that in this society lofty ideals could and should be realized, etc.); the practical, problem-solving, ameliorative bent; the concern with scientific precision and methodology; and since the 1960s the intensification and institutionalization of social criticism. It is in some ways curious that this institutionalization of social criticism in American sociology has remained so single-mindedly focused on the ills and defects of American society and has failed to give rise to a broader and theoretically more rewarding "critical sociology" which would have examined comparatively the flaws and contradictions of various social systems and not only those of the contemporary American one. Not only has the domestic social criticism (or critical study) failed to stimulate the development of a broader comparative, critical curiosity about social-political arrangements in other lands, but occasionally the opposite occurred: fierce social critics of the United States were transformed into guileless enthusiasts, taking leave of their critical faculties as they contemplated other societies and their declaration of good intentions.[13] More often, however, the singular preoccupation with the United States has precluded even this type of interest in other societies. Most typically we find a determined avoidance of studies which would compare aspects of American society with those of others. It is no mystery why this has been the case. The critic of American society, sociologist or not, basically has two options. Either he must be capable of contrasting American society with greatly or significantly superior alternatives (an exercise that has become increasingly difficult for various historical reasons) and thereby strengthen his critique of American social-political arrangements, or the issue of alternatives, that is, of comparative evaluation, has to be abandoned altogether. Apart from a few and often transitory exceptions, most critics opted for the second course of action. They abstained from comparison.

Comparing American society with others cannot but undermine or shatter the certainty—a novel form of ethnocentrism—that maintains that in its irrationality, corruption, injustice, or sheer viciousness American social structure is unsurpassed. It is a belief that can be upheld only as long as little is known about other societies. Such a perspective, to which more than a few of American sociologists are bound by strong emotional ties, has become entrenched over the past decade and a half and could not survive serious comparative scrutiny. If the latter were to be carried out, the social critic would be deprived of any lingering, unarticulated hope or belief about the superiority or preferability of other social-political systems. As a rule, impassioned social criticism cannot flourish unless it is based at least implicitly on the belief that social arrangements and institutions superior to those rejected in the familiar society are feasible and are to be found elsewhere. Should the critic harbor suspicions that in fact these cannot be found, he may prefer not to look too closely at the alternatives.

While it is both tiresome and customary to predict the persistence of the status quo, it has some justification if one ventures to speculate about the prospects of comparative sociology in the United States. The sociological imagination falters as one searches for conditions which would in the conceivable future significantly alter the situation sketched in this chapter. Thus if American society continues to experience the types of domestic problems and difficulties that in the past and in recent times have stimulated the bulk of sociological research and upon which both the problem-solving and social-critical impulses have fed, then it is hard to imagine how new interests in societies outside the United States would develop. Correspondingly, as long as there remains a paucity of inspiring models or superior alternatives abroad, offering lessons worthy of study and eventual emulation, it is again difficult to see what will provide the impetus for turning to other cultures and for reducing the preoccupation with American society.

Nevertheless, the remote possibility cannot be ruled out that eventually both the problem-solving and social-critical impulses will abate as American sociologists experience a sense of surfeit with their own society and, at the same time, confront the limited practical contribution their discipline has made to solving its problems. Likewise, the realization may spread, even without the benefit of comparative research, that American society is not uniquely flawed and qualified to be the singular object of social criticism (and moral outrage). Thus intellectual energy may be freed for the comparative study of societies, including that of America. Under such circumstances, a new wave of interest in other nations and cultures may arise, not inspired by the search for practical remedy or uninformed admiration, but by a more profound interest in the old puzzles and questions of social existence and the human condition. Such a curiosity may not only signify the revitalization of comparative research; it may also lead to the birth of better theories of society than we presently have.

Notes

1. There was one other session at these meetings making a comparative claim entitled "Schooling: Comparative Studies." However, judged by the titles, three of the four papers presented in this session were case studies (on Israel, Brazil, and an unnamed African society, respectively). Some sessions not explicitly comparative occasionally included comparative papers (e.g., in a session entitled "Values, Cultures and Belief Systems" one paper compared the tolerance of free speech in the United States and West Germany). There were, however, very few such instances of comparative topics under other substantive headings. According to my estimate, no more than a dozen papers presented at the 1980 Annual Meetings of the American Sociological Association could be called comparative in the cross-national or cross-cultural sense. The total number of papers presented was approximately 800. There was also a panel discussion of comparative relevance entitled "The World-Economy and Competing States: One System or Co-Determination?"

2. See, for example, Reinhard Bendix, *Kings or People* (Berkeley: University of California Press, 1978); Irving L. Horowitz, *Three Words of Development*, 2d ed. (New York: Oxford University Press, 1972), and *Genocide: State Power and Mass Murder* (New Brunswick, N.J.: Transaction Books, 1976); Alex Inkeles, *Becoming Modern* (Cambridge: Harvard University Press, 1974); Barrington Moore, Jr., *Social Origins of Democracy and Dictatorship* (Boston: Beacon Press, 1966), and *Injustice* (White Plains, N.Y.: Pantheon, 1978); Theda Skocpol, *States and Social Revolution* (New York: Cambridge University Press, 1979); Charles Tilly, Louise Tilly, and Robert Tilly, *The Rebellious Century* (Cambridge: Harvard University Press, 1975); Immanuel Wallerstein, *The Modern World System* (New York: Academic Press, 1974); and Paul Hollander, *Soviet and American Society: A Comparison* (New York: Oxford University Press, 1973).

3. Victoria E. Bonnell, "The Uses of Theory, Concepts and Comparison in Historical Sociology," *Comparative Studies in Society and History* 2(1980):156–73.

4. It is also interesting to note that the works referred to compare societies other than the American. Apparently, the most infrequently undertaken are comparisons between American society (or some aspect thereof) and others.

5. Robert M. Marsh, *Comparative Sociology* (New York: Harcourt, Brace, and World, 1967).

6. See, for example, Ivan Vallier, ed., *Comparative Methods in Sociology* (Berkeley: University of California Press, 1971).

7. Stanislav Andreski, *Prospects of a Revolution in the USA* (New York: Harper and Row, 1973), p. 31.

8. See, for example, Ladd and Lipset, in B. Bruce-Briggs, ed., *New Class?* (New Brunswick, N.J.: Transaction Books, 1979); also ch. 16 of this volume.
9. President's Commission on Foreign Language and International Studies, *Background Paper and Studies* (Washington, D.C.: U.S. Government Printing Office, 1979).
10. See, for example, Christopher Lasch, *The Culture of Narcissism* (New York: W. W. Norton, 1978); Andrew Hacker, *The End of the American Era* (New York: Atheneum, 1970); Tom Wolfe, *Mauve Gloves & Madmen, Clutter & Vine* (New York: Farrar, Straus Giroux, 1977).
11. See, for example, Daniel Bell, "The End of American Exceptionalism," *Public Interest* 41(1975):193–224.
12. Claude Cockburn, *Crossing the Line* (London: MacGibbon and Kee, 1958).
13. Examples of such attitudes may be found in C. Wright Mills, *Listen Yankee* (New York: McGraw-Hill, 1960); also in Paul Hollander, *Political Pilgrims* (New York: Oxford University Press, 1981).

22.
Society and Intellectuals:
The Persistence of Estrangement
and Wishful Thinking*

The time has come or perhaps is already overdue for a reexamination of our thinking about intellectuals and their relationship to society in the Western world, and particularly in the United States.[1] For far too long both social scientific and popular thinking have been dominated by conceptions and stereotypes of intellectuals that have become increasingly questionable and divorced from reality. Not only have the attributes and behavior of intellectuals changed in this century, their social role has changed too, and more significantly than is generally recognized. We will be in a better position to reevaluate the relationship of intellectuals to society and their social functions once we are clear about what intellectuals are and what they are not.

It is useful at the outset to specify what groups of people and particular individuals I have in mind, and their chronological and historical context. While the remarks that follow are broadly based on observations of prominent Western intellectuals since the late 1920s, I am especially mindful of the attitudes which were most apparent in the 1930s and 1960s and have become prominent again in the 1980s. When talking about Western and especially American intellectuals I refer only to that vocal, important, and influential group whose attitudes and beliefs are known to us by virtue of their public expression. Since no one has ever taken a census of the values and attitudes of all or most Western intellectuals, generalizations are bound to be limited to those who took the trouble or had the opportunity to express their beliefs in their writings or in the mass media.[2]

Perhaps the major source of the entrenched and persisting misconceptions about the nature of intellectuals may be found in an excessive attribution of rationality. Intellectuals have for some time been seen, thanks particularly to the work of Karl Mannheim, as a group capable of more rational perception of the social world than most other people. Such a view rested in turn on Mannheim's belief that, due to their "free-floating" social situation (not firmly or unalterably implicated in the web of class membership), intellectuals were able to rise above particular social interests (which distort and mold sociopolitical perspectives). Their perceived disinterestedness was the basis of their alleged greater rationality, objectivity, powers of discrimination, and capacity for penetrating social criticism. Somewhat akin to the Marxist notion of the proletariat (which had only its chains to lose), intellectuals, having no stake in the established class structure,[3] had little to lose by examining it without flinching, by going beneath the facade, by not taking for granted whatever was given. For far too long such assumptions have held sway and enjoyed virtual immunity from rigorous critical scrutiny and by such default became part of the conventional wisdom about the nature of intellectuals.

The idea of the intellectual as outsider acquired currency and has become entrenched. It was a glorified status but also peculiarly limited in its implications as to *what* makes one an outsider besides not working for the government or big corporations. Employment at big universities, foundations, publishing houses, or the mass media were mostly compatible with the images of the integrity and inspiration conferred by the outsider status. Persisting romanticized conceptions of such "detached" or "marginal" intellectuals (sheltering especially in academia) have overlooked the rise and development of the new and powerful subcultures which have demanded and rewarded conformity to their own values and norms no less than other institutional settings and subcultures. The early vision of intellectuals—rootless, free-floating, detached from major social institutions and influences, free of the stranglehold of vested interests—has become increasingly dated, due partly to the social and economic changes which multiplied the number of people who could lay claim on the appellation "intellectual" and which produced the various employment opportunities noted above. Mannheim probably would have recognized the momentous importance of these developments on the outlook, capacity for original thinking, iconoclasm, and nonconformist impulses of intellectuals. One of the results of such subculture formations has been the growing standardization of the social perception of intellectuals and the increasingly stereotyped and predictable character of their social criticism and world view.

While intellectuals have become better integrated, structurally speaking, their estrangement[4] persisted and acquired a certain respectability. Even the most vehement denunciations of the social order ceased to be viewed as acts of defiance, nor was any risk attached to them—political, economic, or social. On the contrary, such critiques have become a badge of belonging to the subcultures here discussed. Alienation and rejection of society could no longer be meaningfully associated with nonconformity, dissent, or innovative criticism; estrangement itself has become a new subcultural norm, a new form of conformity. This state of affairs contrasted with earlier times, described by William Barrett: "For the intellectual the avant-garde position may lose its special enchantment when it becomes commonly accepted: after all, it may be held now in a vulgar way and not for his lofty reasons. There is then the temptation to develop some more *outre* position just to be different."[5] This is no longer the case. At least since the mid-1960s many intellectuals no longer want to be different from their audiences or followers. They ceased to be the avant-garde; they look for ever-expanding audiences and thrive on the applause of the like-minded. When hundreds of thousands (or millions) of people act out jointly their "nonconformity" it does become a new form of conformity—as happened to many forms of social criticism, deviant values, "alternative" lifestyles, and attitudes associated with the counter-culture of the period. Intellectuals earlier thought of as highly individualistic, have in more recent times increasingly displayed a craving for community. Not only has this been apparent in the 1960s and early 1970s when many sought to embrace, at least temporarily, youth movements and massive social protest—and the forms of communitarianism those under thirty had developed—their political ideals and projections in the twentieth century as a whole have almost invariably reflected the desire for a sense of community. My analysis of the political aspirations and hopes of intellectuals in recent times,[6] shows that political systems and ideologies have been largely rated according to their potential or perceived accomplishments in creating community. Every single political system Western intellectuals admired and idealized between the 1920s and 1980s was seen as offering the realization of communal aspirations. Increasingly, contemporary liberal and radical intellectuals have rejected individualism as arid, alienating, dehumanizing, and isolating, and have also sought meaning and purpose in nonpolitical group settings: academic, therapeutic, or quasi-religious. While intellectuals have become integrated into society through affiliation with major social and economic institutions, a felt marginality survived regardless of their income, employment, or opportunities for self- and public expression and influence.[7]

Another set of misconceptions regarding the nature of intellectuals may be traced to the long process of secularization and its impact on those experiencing it. By virtue of their association with the Enlightenment, intellectuals have been rightly seen, for almost two centuries, as the cutting edge of secularization, pioneers of the demystification of the world, capable of confronting human existence without the comforting myths of religions. It was widely assumed that intellectuals, more than most people, have a lesser need for some transcendent belief system. But as is vividly shown in their political ideals and aspirations (more on this below), intellectuals turned out to be as much or more afflicted by the pangs and pains of secularization than other mortals. Perhaps it was their "rationality" or search for meaning that paradoxically predisposed them to looking for underlying meaning and purpose in human existence and the social world. Unexpectedly, intellectuals emerged in the front ranks of those to whom a world from which the gods had retreated (as Weber put it) has become hard to bear. This intense need for sustaining values, a sense of purpose and meaning, constitutes one of the most often overlooked attributes of intellectuals. Awareness of this need is of crucial importance for revising our thinking about them as it has had great bearing on their major defining characteristic: the capacity for critical thinking and questioning.

The discomfort experienced by intellectuals in an increasingly secular world was not the only factor exerting pressure on them to become involved with the articulation of values which could provide a new sense of purpose. The declining functional importance of religious institutions left a gap in the articulation of social values which had to be filled by some group. Although religious functionaries have continued to fight a valiant rear-guard action to preserve their role and authority in articulating moral ideals and concerns, intellectuals have increasingly taken over these activities. Another overlooked function of intellectuals is the public ventilation of moral concerns, the formulation of ceremonial values (for example in commencement speeches), and the analysis of gaps between social ideals and everyday practices. Today intellectuals have largely replaced the clergy as the major agents of public moralizing in their roles as teachers, writers, contributors to the mass media, and foundation officials. Since this has been a gradual development and since it has coexisted with the persistence of more traditional sources of moral authority, its significance has not been fully recognized.

The intellectuals' need to believe has crystallized in our time around some variety of socialism or Marxism. Such ideological attachments led to the suspension or discarding of what used to be regarded as the major defining characteristic of intellectuals: their critical thinking, their capacity for social-political criticism and demystification. Ever since the October Revolution of 1917, a large and influential segment of Western intellectuals has been engaged in trying to find an identifiable physical and social setting where the ideals and values of socialism and Marxism could be located, embodied in observable social, political, and economic institutions, visible in the behavior of ordinary people as well as in the inspired dedication of their leaders. As Walter Goodman put it, "the faithful do seem to need a place to which their faith can attach itself."[8] Despite a long series of historical revelations and disappointments in political systems defining themselves as socialist, every new contender for such a designation has been enthusiastically received and given every benefit of doubt. Arnold Beichman wrote:

> For Marxism the jury is always out. Marxism in practice—whether in Moscow, Peking, Havana or the rest—is always defined out of existence as distorted by various historical factors. Democracy, however, never has its incidental sins dismissed in this way. As a result Marxism itself never has any crises . . . Marxism as part of reality is never involved with reality.[9]

Leon Wieseltier commented on a more specific manifestation of the same attitude:

> Noam Chomsky was . . . serene about the developments in Poland. "What lessons are to be drawn from the imposition of martial law in Poland? the answer in my view is: virtually none." In a sense this is true; Chomsky never learns. At least not from misery that comes from Moscow. The developments in Indochina, however, or Central America, are always full of lessons. There was something that Chomsky did say about Poland, though, that deserves study. He denied that the matter had any bearing upon either "socialism" or "communism."[10]

The need to believe and the associated quest for moral certainty may sometimes also lead to its paradoxical counterpart: moral relativism. Many intellectuals who reject their own society because of its social injustices and drift into the admiration of other political systems which promise the eradication of such defects end up justifying and rationalizing the flaws of the alternative system on pragmatic grounds as problems of growth, transient aberrations, measures of self-defense, or trivial blemishes rendered insignificant by the overall context and to be vindicated by the future. In short, questionable means to overwhelmingly laudable ends. Such judgments have often led to double standards. While double standards are not a singular failing of intellectuals, their political utterances and judgments in recent times testify to the startling degree to which they are prone to their use. The passionate partisanship of double standards also conflicts with the conventional wisdom about intellectuals which attributes to them higher levels of rationality, objectivity, and detachment, and thus a lesser likelihood of being carried away by political passions and bias. It is always in the service of political commitments and to salvage political beliefs that double standards arise; they represent ways of redefining reality, of forcing sociopolitical phenomena into compartments of right and wrong established by a priori commitment rather than evidence. Correspondingly moral indignation or outrage is stilled or inflamed depending not on *what* was done but *who* had done it.

How did such developments in the outlook and predisposition of a sizable number of Western intellectuals—including some of the most distinguished and creative ones—come about? How did intellectuals become so adept at the suspension of their critical faculties, let their guard down and part from their finely tuned analytic instincts, abandoning their sensitivity to sham, posturing, and contradiction? How did their political passions and commitments emerge, like a veritable stone wall to be placed between themselves and the sociopolitical facts of life they wished to ignore or view through the distorting lens of wishful thinking? Why and how did so many intellectuals in our times manage to make the most astounding and, in retrospect, embarrassing, misjudgments about political systems like the Soviet one under Stalin, China under Mao, Cuba under Castro, and other assorted Third World dictatorships? These were regimes which imprisoned, tortured, executed, or "merely" exiled millions of people of all social classes and treated their own intellectuals no better. They were at best silenced and deprived of the chance to function as intellectuals—at any rate as intellectuals are supposed to function. For substantial periods of time none of these events were noted, or if noted given weight as relevant to judging the true essence and intentions of the political systems involved. Yet such misjudgments, misperceptions, rationalizations, and apologetics did little damage to the credibility of intellectuals in general—as a value-formulating elite or spokesmen for moral rectitude—or that of particular individuals upholding and propagating such misconceptions. For example Corliss Lamont, a foremost apologist of the Soviet Union under Stalin (and still sympathetic to the Soviet regime), recently had a chair in civil rights named after him at Columbia University (to be sure, he provided the money for it); Noam Chomsky's reputation has largely survived his strenuous attempts to minimize the massacres of the Pol Pot regime in Cambodia; John K. Fairbank, who extolled the virtues of Mao's China during the Cultural Revolution, has remained an unchallenged authority in academic circles; few criticized Susan Sontag for her early fevered praise of Castro's Cuba (though many did after she dramatically revised her views of communist dictatorships in general); the parishoners of William Sloan Coffin, Jr. have not confronted him about his sanguine appraisals of North Vietnamese communism; we have yet to hear any criticism or self-criticism regarding John Galbraith's assessment of the splendid economic performance of China under Mao; and if Jonathan Kozol engaged in any soul-searching over his views about the humanity of the Cuban regime (in light of its treatment of wheelchair-ridden poets and other writers, among other things) it has escaped my attention. Such examples could be multiplied.

There has been little if any pressure, either originating in the larger intellectual community or within the individuals concerned, prompting self-examination or reappraisal on the part of those who insistently and exuberantly confused repression with progress and political rhetoric with social reality. There have been few reassessments comparable to the serious self-scrutiny of the God-that-failed variety of an earlier generation of intellectuals who unequivocally tore themselves away from the veneration of the Soviet Union and the movements it inspired and often controlled in the West.

I suggest two related reasons why such developments have not taken place in more recent times, that is, since the 1960s. First, because the ethos of anti-anticommunism has become so entrenched that, although it is certainly no longer expected of intellectuals to approve of or admire particular communist regimes (especially the Soviet Union), explicit rejection or criticism of such regimes is still viewed with distaste[11] (more on this below). Second, today the subculture of estrangement—powerful enough to shelter and provide moral support for even the most embittered social critics—takes a tolerant view of the misjudgment of communist societies, incurred, as it were, in the cause and context of rejection of one's own society. In these circles what matters is criticism of American society—that confers the bona fide—whereas criticism of communist societies (or public revision of overly favorable views earlier held of them) is viewed as a diversion from the real task of probing the defects of the United States. Moreover, in these subcultures it may justifiably be feared that in light of a close critical analysis of communist systems the American may end up looking better.

Double standards have tenaciously prevailed in the evaluation of American society on the one hand and those, on the other, claiming socialist credentials and objectives. Highly critical in one setting, outright credulous or tolerant in the other—these have been the surprising attitudes of large numbers of American intellectuals through much of this century. Despite the all too obvious lessons of history, these attitudes have remained ingrained and remarkably persistent. For instance, even at a time when more sober reflection about the Vietnamese communist regime has arisen among segments of the antiwar movement and public opinion at large, Staughton Lynd could still aver that "I believe that Vietnamese Communism, like Communism in the Soviet Union, China and Cuba, has improved life for the majority . . . while repressing minorities."[12] Lynd has of course merely reiterated an article of faith of many intellectuals of similar persuasion: that at the expense of civil liberties (which anyway only a minority needs) the majority lives better in such societies. No amount of evidence—including the massive outflow of citizens under extremely hazardous conditions who could rightfully be thought of as belonging to the "majority," that is, ordinary men and women and not the upper classes or refined intellectuals—altered such preconceptions on the part of Lynd and company.[13]

This brings us to another perceived attribute of intellectuals that needs rethinking and revision: the assumption that they are deeply and un-equivocally committed to personal, political, and intellectual freedom and especially free expression. Even the briefest immersion in the vast literature produced by intellectuals about societies which have thoroughly and meticulously extinguished such freedoms makes it clear that many Western intellectuals' commitment to intellectual freedom is selective at best. Consider the case of Nobel Prize-winning Gabriel García Márquez. On the one hand he knows that Cuban writers are imprisoned for no good reason and he even intercedes on behalf of at least one of them (Armando Valladares). At the same time he holds the conviction that "progress . . . lies . . . in Latin America with Fidel Castro."[14] Besides what one may suspect to be questionable and limited information at his disposal about the progress Castro achieved, this attitude suggests that Márquez considers the repression of intellectuals an insignificant factor in the equation, a price worth paying for the other assumed benefits, for "progress." Apparently the repression of intellectuals will not make him alter his cordial relations with Castro's Cuba (although he prefers to live in Mexico, thus resembling a long line of Western admirers of communist countries who almost invariably opted for life in the Western societies they despised). And while Márquez and other Western intellectuals expect and take for granted intellectual freedom in Western societies, this does not enter to any appreciable extent into the balance of assets and liabilities of their own societies; it does not reduce alienation. Perhaps they share Marcuse's view that such freedom merely conceals repression, that tolerance is ultimately repressive. And although such freedom represents an obvious and essential condition for their own occupational, social, material, moral, and political survival, they have succeeded on innumerable occasions to overlook or justify its absence in putatively socialist, progressive, or revolutionary societies. These attitudes suggest that when such intellectuals are persuaded that those in power are men of good will, intellectual freedom loses importance. Under such conditions intellectuals might as well become mouthpieces of the benevolent leaders and autonomy becomes a superfluous luxury.

The benefit-of-doubt posture among intellectuals has also reemerged recently in the context of Soviet-American relations and disarmament.

While American policies and leaders are viewed with profound scepticism or deep suspicion, the Soviet Union, while no longer idealized as in the 1930s, is often viewed more sympathetically on account of its—always justified—insecurities and apprehensions, benefiting from a "therapeutic perspective." It is upheld by such diverse intellectuals as Richard Barnet, Stanley Hoffmann, Jerry Hough, George Kennan, Marshall Shulman, and especially Theodore von Laue.[15] While such scholars regularly call on the United States to "understand" Soviet policies (and at the same time to accommodate to them), no such kindness is extended to the United States. The attitudes of such intellectuals toward the Soviet Union may be described as that of "a social worker dealing with a patient who may do odd things now and then but means well"—as Walter Goodman put it discussing the corresponding editorial policies of the magazine *The Nation*.[16] It has also become characteristic of such intellectuals to play down the differences in values which separate the superpowers and which have created recurring conflict. Thus not only Noam Chomsky, but more surprisingly George Kennan and Ronald Steel too managed to keep under control their moral indignation over the Soviet-supported repression in Poland, considering it a legitimate expression of superpower interest in their backyard (though not the American attempts, however hesitant, to stem the multiplication of pro-Soviet regimes in Central America). Of such attitudes it was observed that:

> The detachment of Kennan and Steel is disturbing, because it suggests that at least among some intellectuals, American liberalism is losing its identity. It has become the address for a wide array of alibis—détente, neoisolationism, anti-anti-Communism, realpolitik, and a politically paralyzing case for nuclear disarmament. These are all reasons to walk away from Poland.[17]

In a similar spirit, Arthur Schlesinger, Jr. pleaded for better relations with the Soviet Union by arguing that "disagreement over *civic values* does not justify tensions that threaten nuclear war."[18] [Emphasis added.]

It may finally also be asked whether intellectuals are more capable of taking disinterested moral stands than anyone else—an important question in light of their increasing involvement with the elaboration, analysis, or propagation of moral values and ethical principles. Insofar as their political attitudes and preferences serve as a guide, the answer is clearly negative. A fairly thorough examination of the political attachments of Western and primarily American intellectuals (such as I had undertaken in *Political Pilgrims* and which I continue to pursue) suggests that their moral judgments, indignation, and compassion tend to be determined far more significantly by the parties involved in the actions or policies under scrutiny than the acts themselves and their consequences. Whether intellectuals find particular forms of behavior morally deplorable or excusable, acceptable or unacceptable, depends far more on the identity of the parties involved than the behavior itself. This is another area where double standards are easy to detect. As long, for example, as such intellectuals are satisfied that one particular group (nation, political movement, or system) represents The Victim and another The Victimizer, their judgments will flow along predictable channels. The problem is that perceptions and definitions of who are the victim and victimizer, underdog or topdog are often dated, stereotyped, idiosyncratic, and determined by ideological bias. For a handful of loyalists even the Soviet Union can qualify as the perennial underdog; its actions and policies, no matter how aggressive, seen as essentially defensive. Such perceptions will not be shaken by any amount of nuclear armaments, huge standing armies, the power of the KGB, and the often demonstrated willingness and ability of the regime to ruthlessly suppress entire nations, groups, or particular individuals.

The centrality of rationality and critical spirit in the makeup of intellectuals may be questioned on other grounds as well. It is hard not to be impressed by the uses made of the concepts "socialism" and "fascism" respectively, each having become a fetish precluding the need for further thinking once these labels have been applied. The polemical attribution of fascism as the most widely accepted symbol of evil has become especially prominent since the 1960s in the United States, as it gradually became a generalized term of derogation. Similarly, once the label "socialist" has been successfully affixed to a country or movement, the necessity for a more thorough and critical examination of the phenomenon so labeled tends to be removed. In such and other instances intellectuals often displayed severely diminished powers of discrimination. This was also the case when, in the 1960s and early 1970s, the United States was regularly compared to Nazi Germany; when violent criminals were misidentified as freedom fighters or great creative artists (as in the famous case of Norman Mailer and Henry Abbott);[19] when Gore Vidal compared the military occupation of Poland to the "occupation" of the United States by corporations;[20] when Arthur Miller, reflecting on the power of *The New York Times,* said that "not in Poland, not in Czechoslovakia, the Soviet Union or Rumania is the control so narrow over what goes on the stage as in this country." [21] Nor were powers of discrimination prominent when George Wald, Nobel Prize-winning professor emeritus of Harvard, declared that "we Americans . . . are the most brainwashed people in the world";[22] or when Raymond Hunthausen, archbishop of Seattle, was quoted: "I say with a deep consciousness of these words that Trident [the American nuclear submarine] is the Auschwitz of Puget Sound."[23] It may also be recalled that in the 1960s not a few academic intellectuals entertained the view that college students were "Niggers" (due to their oppressed state), and a prominent professor of English literature, Louis Kampf (who headed the Modern Language Association) opined that the Lincoln Center, being an elitist institution, deserved to be urinated upon and smeared with excrement, while Herbert Marcuse related the possession of automobiles in the United States to repressive government.

Why does estrangement persist among so many intellectuals either as an engulfing state or at least as a low-grade, diluted consciousness, self-evident attitude, or conditioned reflex? After all, what used to be seen as a major cause and condition of alienation, structural marginality, has virtually disappeared. Most of those claiming intellectual status have found a home in universities, colleges, publishing houses, foundations, branches of the government, the media. Occupationally and materially secure intellectuals have emerged as one of the most influential social strata, many of them recipients of both symbolic and tangible honors and recognition, most of them at least reasonably prosperous. While one may associate the most recent upsurge of social criticism and estrangement with the Reagan presidency and all it entails—particularly the rise in unemployment and the substantial decline in the condition of the poor (as was the case in the 1930s)—it must be remembered that estrangement was no less intense at more prosperous times (1960s), when unemployment was low, welfare programs expanding, and affluence was assailed as "empty" and spiritually debilitating or repressive in subtle ways.

Large segments of Western intellectuals have been estranged in good economic times and bad, and their social criticism was not dependent on the state of the economy, although in times of crisis it intensified, reaching higher levels of eloquence and indignation. Economic conditions are not the only factors intensifying estrangement as the 1960s in the United States indicate: racial issues and what is seen as an unjust war could be others. The eruption of social criticism connected with the status of ethnic minorities surfaced at a time when their condition was rapidly improving, while in previous decades intellectuals had viewed Blacks and other deprived minorities with far greater equanimity although their condition showed little improvement. Treating the Vietnam war as a cause for social criticism and the rejection of American society also begs the question, since to a considerable degree attitudes toward the war were predicated on attitudes toward American society. The more vehement the criticism of U.S. involvement and the greater the sympathy toward the Vietcong and North Vietnamese was, the more animosity there was among critics toward American social arrangements and institutions.

At least for some, and especially the most vocal critics of the war, "Vietnam offered the key to a systematic criticism of America," as Susan Sontag wrote in *Trip to Hanoi*. As Jerry Rubin put it (in *Do It*): "If there had been no Vietnam war we would have invented one." Perhaps the propensity to estrangement among American (and Western) intellectuals may be thought of as something relatively constant, an underlying reservoir of attitude, which may expand or contract in its expressions or display depending on external social and historical circumstances.

In looking for the causes of the persistence of estrangement beyond and beneath the observable defects of social institutions, we must note that present alienation among Western intellectuals has become a powerful tradition that created a well-defined subculture of its own, especially in academic settings. Alienation and the rejection of society has come to be passed on, as other cultural values, from one generation to the next, explicitly and implicitly. The worthlessness of the society one lives in has become for many a given premise, an article of faith no longer in need of proof, analysis, or argument, though proofs or illustrations are often adduced to strengthen or confirm predispositions.[24]

Paradoxically, high expectations toward one's own (Western) society continue to prevail, especially in the United States. This is all the more peculiar since that same society is rejected and written off, while anger and indignation over its failure to deliver remains unabated. These attitudes are most pronounced in the United States, where high sociocultural expectations are deeply and historically ingrained. It is only in light of such exceedingly high expectations that the depth, aggrieved quality, and persistence of estrangement can be understood. While the great material wealth of the United States is often evoked as the ostensible explanation for the bitterness with which societal deficiencies are viewed—an unrealized potential—these high expectations are not limited to material well-being. Far more is expected and desired: a sense of community, fraternity, meaning, purpose, self-realization and fulfillment, authenticity (whatever that means for the critics)—the semiarticulated hope of transcending the human condition. Here again the fruits of secularization are apparent as pressures for meaning intensify in a world which has become increasingly meaningless and threatening.[25] Socialism, communism, and the revolution have all been concepts and imaginings suffused with religious meaning. As Irving Howe noted in his autobiography of the more recent merging of such sensibilities: "Many of those drawn to the New Left politics were really trying to satisfy formless religious hungers."

The persistence of alienation is also connected with the refusal, on the part of the younger generation of intellectuals, to learn *any* lessons from history. The disincentives for such learning originate in the need for hope. Intense rejection of one's own society is not feasible, neither psychologically nor philosophically, unless one can juxtapose an alternative vision to the existing state of despair and defective social institutions. If injustice, scarcity, oppression, exploitation, selfishness, greed, power lust—are seen as endemic and universal, indignation about their presence in one's own society would be tempered. But Western intellectuals in our times have had a series of inspiring (if short-lived) alternatives and ideals against which to measure the flaws of their own society. An increasing number of such sociopolitical systems have arisen and provided firmer foundation for the rejection of their own society.

The appeals of Soviet society waned after more was learned about the purges, the Moscow Trials, the collectivization campaigns; or after the Nazi-Soviet Pact, Soviet treatment of Eastern Europe, Khrushchev's revelations at the 20th Party Congress, the treatment of Jews in more recent times, or new methods of handling dissent in psychiatric hospitals.[26] The attributes which elicited enthusiasm toward the Soviet Union were readily transferred to Castro's Cuba, Mao's China, and North Vietnam. When Chinese official revelations (milder but analogous to those of Khrushchev) following Mao's death cast doubt on the admirable qualities of China (earlier celebrated by traveling intellectuals), there was still Cuba to cast in the role of the authentic socialist state under its original charismatic revolutionary leader. When Cuba's image was somewhat tarnished by the persecution of homosexuals and intellectuals and when it sent waves of refugees to American shores, enthusiasm somewhat subsided too. Simultaneously Vietnam, the new unified one, gave rise to the boat people and only the most determined among the supporters of the Vietnamese Communists could convince themselves that the United States was to be blamed for these refugees (or for the massacres of the Pol Pot regime in Cambodia).

Yet none of these disappointments have terminated the quest for more authentic incarnations of socialism. Certainly the lessons of the 1930s, of pro-Soviet fellow-traveling have not been learned by many members of the more recent generation of intellectuals. (As Irving Howe put it, "sometimes the New Left resembled a society for resurrecting The God That Failed.") Quite a few of their elders too have forgotten or willfully suppressed these lessons in the new, invigorating atmosphere of the 1960s when, once more, it became more important to be passionately hostile to American society than to be right about the evils of the Soviet Union and similar systems. It was sufficient for Lillian Hellman to sum up her misjudgments of the Soviet Union by noting that "we were mistaken about the degree of democracy in the Soviet Union"—as William Barrett observed in *The Truants*—and in a similar vein Corliss Lamont wrote (in his recent autobiography) about the Soviet Union in the post-Stalin period that it "still falls short of being a true democracy"— an admission similar to suggesting that Nazi Germany fell short of according complete respect to all ethnic groups.

It is equally symptomatic that present admirers of the Soviet Union like Angela Davis can attract sympathetic "overflow crowds" on liberal campuses (such as the University of Massachusetts at Amherst),[27] while former social critics who had radically revised their views of American society (and correspondingly of socialist countries they earlier admired) like Eldridge Cleaver earned "boos and hisses" at Yale University for saying that the "U.S. [is] the freest and most democratic country in the world."[28]

For Andrew Kopkind the lessons of Vietnam included nostalgic recollections of his guided tour of North Vietnam during the war which allowed him to marvel at the "exhilirating spirit of common struggle and collective good will" he encountered there. In the same breath, he responded to Susan Sontag's criticism of communist regimes (Vietnam included) as follows:

> She [Sontag] seems to have forgotten that politics is history, not philosophy; that revolutions are responses to reality, not to theory; that the nature of all things is contradiction, not equilibrium. North Vietnam was, and is, a Communist state—proceeding (dialectically, dare I say the word?) in its development according to the forces and furies of the real world. Then, that society may have expressed more truth and justice . . . than now, but perhaps less than it will in the future. And what about the truth and justice in Lyndon Johnson's democracy? Yes and no. The point is that it makes little sense to me to stop time and freeze place if there still is a vision of a human face.[29]

A case study in obfuscation and muddled evasion. Yes and no. Whatever the North Vietnamese did—why not talk about Lyndon Johnson? (It reminds one of the old Soviet joke in which a polite inquiry about a delayed subway train or meal in a restaurant provokes the retort: "And how about the KKK and the lynchings in the South?") What Kopkind seems to say, in his convoluted way, is that ends justify means and that the North Vietnamese had no choice but to do things one may not like (he delicately refuses to call a spade a spade). To his credit he made no reference to breaking eggs when one makes an omelette.

The continued outpouring of refugees from countries claiming to be socialist—whether in Indochina, the Caribbean, or Eastern Europe— rarely inspired serious reflection or a rigorous rethinking of the nature of these systems. The refugee phenomenon was sometimes dismissed by associating them with the *ancien régime* (the minority that did not benefit from the salutary social changes), viewing them as merely economic refugees, blaming their exodus on forces external to the systems concerned (e.g. the United States in Indochina), or by viewing these refugees as people of a low level of political maturity who suffered from false consciousness, failing to grasp the beneficial nature of the new regimes.

Such attitudes fed on the continued need to locate *somewhere* greener pastures than those in Western societies. If it was no longer possible to idealize the Soviet Union, China, Cuba, or Communist Vietnam, some intellectuals found a substitute in the more intangible Third World, distinguished by its generally non-White inhabitants, victimized status (by the West or the forces of capitalism), and vague accusatory rhetoric and revolutionary promise. Those looking for something more specific picked, from time to time, countries like Tanzania, Ethiopia, Angola, Mozambique, or even Albania, while Iran under the Ayatollah earned the admiration, at least for a while, of Richard Falk and Ramsey Clark. Closer to home in Central America, Nicaragua and the guerrillas in El Salvador have emerged as prime targets of idealization and admiration, perhaps because as Peter Shaw suggested, "there has to be at least one approved insurgent movement on the Left at any time."[30] Such insurgents are especially appealing as they represent revolutionary promise short of fulfillment and untarnished by the reality of established power. Ramsey Clark, among others, effortlessly switched his enthusiasm from Iran and (earlier) North Vietnam to Nicaragua where he found an exceptionally "high commitment to human rights."[31] A reporter of *The New York Times* informed his readers that "Nicaragua's revolution breaks the mold." Besides American intellectuals and opinion makers thrilled by this latest incarnation of revolutionary purity and promise, it was reported that "Managua today is being occupied by a fresh-faced army of back-packing youth in shorts and hiking boots. They are left-wing students on holiday from Europe, here to see the revolution firsthand."[32] This was the same regime characterized by one of its former supporters, Humberto Belli (also a sometime editorial page editor of *La Prensa,* the main source of opposition to Somoza and subsequently to the Sandinistas), as follows:

> When the revolution triumphed they were seen as heroes, loved and admired by a grateful people. But soon afterward, the behavior of the

Sandinista leaders undercut their own support. They started to ride in Mercedes Benzes. . . . They would parade through the city with motorcades and live in the best houses of the members from the old regime. They literally took over the best neighborhoods . . . Las Colinas, one of the richest neighborhoods of Managua was taken over by the Sandinista leadership. The Somocistas used to live there. . . . They [the Sandinistas] have put chains around the neighborhood and have guards to check your ID. They have private swimming pools, tennis courts and bars. . . . The romantic aura around the Sandinistas has evaporated [not for their American and Western European admirers though]. . . . They are constantly asking people to make sacrifices but not sharing them. There are special sections in the military hospital where Sandinista members can go for special treatment, while the average Nicaraguan will wait in line for hours.[33]

It has a familiar ring for all those who lived under Marxist one-party regimes or know for other reasons about the forms the distribution of elite privilege takes in "socialist" countries. Even Libya under Qadaffi found its admirers among estranged Westerners as indicated by the visit of two West German leaders of the Green party, a major organ and reservoir of estrangement in Western Germany. Apparently they were just as impressed by him as were other generations of political pilgrims by Stalin, Mao, and Castro: "We entered [his] tent reverentially and paid rapt attention to his words. In contrast to the petty-bourgeois fussiness of our Bundeskanzler [Helmut Schmidt] Qadaffi radiates a ceremonial dignity."[34] Even the Soviet-imposed Afghanistani regime found defenders among Western academics as reflected in the recent *Revolutionary Afghanistan* by Beverly Male (published in London), defending the "revolutionary violence" of the regime as other intellectuals have done at other times in other places. And on some American campuses too Soviet policies in Afghanistan found their defenders as on the occasion when "in the fall of 1980, the CIA interviewed [at the University of Michigan] . . . for positions within the Agency. The recruiters were met by about fifty demonstrators. One carried a sign which read: 'Extend the gains of the October Revolution to Afghanistan.' "[35] While such apologetics may be dismissed as foolish or eccentric, they rarely elicit the kind of moral revulsion they deserve and which is provoked by attempts to defend questionable American policies.

The continued indulgence of erstwhile or persistent defenders of Marxist police states contrasts sharply with the hostility with which Susan Sontag's soul-searching was received by many—an attitude which testifies to the vitality of estrangement that grips many intellectuals. To have said, as Sontag did, that "*every one* of these countries [where a Leninist party has taken power and rules] is a tyranny that oppresses workers and corrupts intellectual life"[36] flew in the face of the political pieties which still prevail in what used to be called the adversary culture. Sontag's critics were angered without trying to challenge seriously, if at all, her assertion by pointing to communist systems where her generalization would fail to apply. Anti-anticommunism explains these attitudes and especially the apprehension of many intellectuals about being identified as anticommunists, without necessarily being procommunists. Sontag said on the same occasion: "Much of what is said about politics by people on the so-called democratic left [where a very large portion of intellectuals belong] has been governed by the wish not to give comfort to 'reactionary' forces. . . . We were unwilling to identify ourselves as anti-Communists because that was the slogan of the right."[37]

The attitude is almost daily confirmed. Thus it was revealed in a recent interview with García Márquez that "while he has a . . . distrust for Communist apparatchiks . . . he voices this view only privately so as 'not to play into the hands of the Right.' "[38] (Half a century ago Soviet sympathizers used to confess to the same motives when explaining why they did not publicly express their knowledge of Soviet policies they themselves felt repelled by.) Hence anti-anticommunism has two main components. One is the fear that an indictment of all communist regimes would extinguish the flickering hope that there may yet emerge an authentic incarnation of socialism. Secondly there is the haunting fear that admitting to anticommunism without some mental reservation establishes a tainted kinship between the intellectual and the unsavory political forces and characters on "The Right."

The connection between such attitudes and reluctance to rectify grave and sometimes ludicrous political misjudgments is close, as Dennis Wrong pointed out in his criticism of Victor Navasky's book (*Naming Names*)—a characteristic product of the anti-anticommunism school. He wrote:

> If complicity with Stalinism had been an isolated occurrence, a bizarre intrusion of the darkness of Russian despotism into the restless lives of overprotected Western intellectuals, the idea of *pas d'ennemis à gauche* might regain some plausibility. But the radicalism of the 1960s disabused us of this prospect by repeating the earlier, more painful experience in diluted form in relation to other communist tyrannies. *Many left-wing intellectuals now seem incurably prone to a "back to the old drawing board" attitude when political myths they fervently embraced only yesterday are exposed as evil illusions, an attitude which prevents them from learning anything or even from undergoing the pain of real disillusionment.*[39] [Emphasis added.]

Misinformation about existing societies (believed to be superior to one's own) makes a contribution to estrangement by creating largely illusory counterpoints to defects of the familiar social system. The prior estrangement predisposes the intellectual to find virtue in distant places, and when finding it allows him to condemn his society all the more harshly and justify his alienation more fully. Idealization of unfamiliar societies does not depend on solid information about them. Besides favorable predisposition and receptivity, the major precondition of their idealization is massive ignorance which visits rarely dispel, especially given the conducted tour aspects of these "fact-finding" tours.[40]

There remains another circumstance less frequently discussed which enters into the attitudes and values associated with intense social criticism and rejection of Western society. Being or becoming a social critic has come to play an important part in the sense of identity and self-esteem of many Western intellectuals. There is substantial ego gratification to be derived from such a stance, in addition to the endorsement and applause of one's fellow social critics and the considerable subcultural supports and rewards flowing in this direction, including opportunities for publishing and invitations to be on the lecture circuit. The role of the social critic is also attractive because of its self-evident moral underpinnings. He can display a level of awareness of the ills of society, not given to others; he belongs to an elite of the enlightened, formerly a beleaguered avant-garde of dissenters, more recently an establishment of its own. Being a social critic in the United States has become in some ways the best of all possible worlds, one which can combine idealism with security, idealism with material and status rewards, passion with safety, and political commitment with group support. There is also something deeply satisfying about drawing the world's attention to evil and injustice; by doing so the critic has automatically placed himself into the ranks of the virtuous, whose heart is in the right place. His is a social role inextricably involved with ethical principles and good intentions. While the benefits for the self are incidental byproducts of the stands taken, they create a warm, enduring glow of self-satisfaction— a process which in turn reinforces and prolongs the alienated stance.

In the light of twentieth century experience—especially the duality of domestic social criticism and the hopeful suspension of disbelief of the political pilgrimage—it is no longer possible to entertain the idealized conception of the relationship between estrangement and the social roles of intellectuals. There is more evidence than one would wish for to indicate that alienation by itself does not create, let alone guarantee, either critical clarity, political wisdom, or personal integrity. Contrary to what we used to believe, the most prized qualities of intellectuals, particularly the application of critical reason and rational discernment, are not always furthered by alienation. Estrangement produces its own illusions, even a false consciousness of its own.

Notes

*Preparation of this chapter benefited from a grant provided by the John M. Olin Foundation.

1. A discussion of the characteristics of intellectuals and their social roles in non-Western societies is a totally different and more constricted topic, since intellectuals can only play a significant role in societies that permit and institutionalize free expression and public debate, i.e. Western societies.
2. In addition to the names mentioned in this chapter, my comments have been stimulated by the writings and public utterances of intellectuals such as Bettina Aptheker, Herbert Aptheker, Paul Baran, Henri Barbusse, Simone de Beauvoir, J.D. Bernal, Bertolt Brecht, Daniel Berrigan, David Caute, Claud Cockburn, Alexander Cockburn, Malcolm Cowley, Jerome Davis, David Dellinger, John Dewey, John Dos Passos, Theodore Dreiser, W.E.B. DuBois, John K. Fairbank, Richard Falk, Lion Feuchtwanger, Louis Fischer, Howard Bruce Franklin, Joseph Freeman, John K. Galbraith, Felix Greene, Tom Hayden, Granville Hicks, E.J. Hobsbawm, Leo Huberman, Julian Huxley, Arthur Koestler, Jonathan Kozol, Corliss Lamont, Saul Landau, Harold Laski, Owen Lattimore, Eugene Lyons, Mary McCarthy, Maria Antonietta Macciocchi, Norman Mailer, C. Wright Mills, Jan Myrdal, Scott Nearing, Pablo Neruda, Romain Rolland, Jean-Paul Sartre, Orville Schell, George B. Shaw, Upton Sinclair, Philip Slater, Edgar Snow, Lincoln Steffens, Anna Louise Strong, Paul Sweezy, Ross Terrill, Harry F. Ward, Beatrice Webb, Sidney Webb, H.G. Wells, Edmund Wilson, Ella Winter, and Howard Zinn—among many others.
3. This is a highly questionable proposition. Intellectuals do have a very high stake in any social order that allows them to function as intellectuals. Such a viewpoint is neither widely recognized nor given sympathetic reception by many intellectuals. The reason is that the social systems which have most characteristically provided intellectuals with amenities for free expression and safeguarded intellectual freedom have historically been bourgeois or capitalist societies toward which many intellectuals feel a strong aversion on other grounds, which overwhelms whatever grudging appreciation intellectual freedoms may evoke.
4. Estrangement and alienation are used interchangeably throughout this chapter.
5. *The Truants* (Garden City: Anchor Press, 1982), p. 93.
6. Paul Hollander, *Political Pilgrims* (New York: Oxford Univ. Press, 1981).
7. This was exemplified by sentiments among media intellectuals: "There was a distinct feeling that, despite the high pay and the access to powerful media that TV writers and producers enjoy, they are still part of a despised underclass" (Ben Stein, *The View from Sunset Boulevard* [New York: Basic Books, 1979], p. 28).
8. "Hard to Digest," *Harper's* (June 1982).
9. "The Spell of Marxism," *Policy Review* (Summer 1982).
10. "Ideas in Season," *Partisan Review* (no. 3, 1982).

11. A former minister of justice for the Vietcong Provisional Revolutionary Government and currently a political refugee, Truong Nhu Tang, observed in another context: "Public opinion in the free world is not yet ready to support resistance to the Vietnamese communists or their Russian patrons. There is still a confused feeling that those who are against communism must be reactionary while those who are progressive will necessarily support the socialist regimes of this world" ("The Myth of a Liberation," *New York Review of Books,* 21 October 1982).

12. *The New York Times,* Letters to the Editor, 2 July 1979.

13. It is safe to assume that Lynd does not know or does not wish to make much of such information, that—as another political refugee and former Vietcong activist put it—"The flow of political prisoners within Vietnam and the flow of refugees out of Vietnam included large numbers of former Viet Cong freedom-fighters, socialist revolutionaries, nationalist intellectuals, and religious activists who have learned in their flesh the consequences of embracing the Communists as allies. American progressives, it is fervently hoped, will never have the opportunity to learn the same lessons in the same way" (Doan Van Toai and David Chanoff, "Learning from Viet Nam," *Encounter* [Sept.–Oct. 1982]).

14. *The New York Times Book Review,* 5 Dec. 1982.

15. Von Laue, a historian of modern Russia, is distinguished by extending such therapeutic understanding to Stalin himself.

16. "Hard to Digest," *Harper's* (June 1982).

17. Leon Wieseltier, "Liberals against Liberty," *The New Republic,* 10 Feb. 1982.

18. *Wall Street Journal,* 17 Aug. 1982.

19. Of this instance a commentator noted: "There is a tendency to believe violence on the Left is somehow justifiable. Had Jack Abbott substituted for the phrase Marxist-Leninist, Hitlerian-Mussolinian, I do not think Mailer would have written the introduction to this book" (Michiko Kakutani, *New York Times Book Review,* 20 Sept. 1981).

20. See *Partisan Review* (no. 3, 1982).

21. "A Report from the American Writers Conference," *Wall Street Journal,* 16 Oct. 1981.

22. *The New York Times,* 22 Oct. 1982.

23. *The New York Times,* 19 Apr. 1982.

24. This state of affairs was not uniquely American. Of West Germany it was reported that "never before in our history have we seen the spectacle of politicians and pastors, pedagogues and best-selling writers, teachers and hit-songsters, all vying with each other to impress our children with the ugliness of the prospects facing them, with the horror . . . of all of life's problems that will soon overwhelm them disastrously" (Helmut Schoeck, *Encounter* [Dec. 1982]).

25. Here one may point to a curiously contradictory development. Whereas intellectuals have increasingly moved toward transcendental or teleological concerns, whatever the terminology in which they have been couched, the clergy by contrast has increasingly moved away from transcendental or metaphysical preoccupations, especially in the United States, seeking instead to rejuvenate their churches or denominations by immersion in secular, social, and political affairs and causes.

26. Two recent developments provoked relatively little attention, analysis, or indignation in the United States: (a) the Soviet practice of chemical warfare in Afghanistan and Indochina and (b) the emerging case for Soviet complicity in the assassination attempt on the pope. Apparently the ruthlessness involved has been too unpleasant for Western scholarly analysts, politicians, and the media to contemplate.
27. *Massachusetts Daily Collegian,* 14 Apr. 1980.
28. *The New York Times,* 25 Feb. 1982.
29. *The Nation,* 27 Feb. 1982.
30. *Encounter* (June-July 1982).
31. *Newsweek,* 1 Mar. 1982.
32. *The New York Times,* 30 Dec. 1981. For a prototypical wishful assessment of conditions in Nicaragua, combined with an apology for its undemocratic practices see also Carlos Fuentes: "Give Nicaragua a Chance," *The New York Times,* 18 Jan. 1983.
33. *Freedom at Issue* (Nov.-Dec. 1982).
34. *Encounter* (Sept.-Oct. 1982).
35. *Commentary* (Nov. 1982).
36. *The Nation,* 27 Feb. 1982.
37. Ibid.
38. *New York Times Book Review,* 5 Dec. 1982.
39. "Obsessed with the Fifties," *Partisan Review* (no. 31, 1982).
40. For further discussion of this issue, see my article "Political Hospitality," *Society* (Nov. 1981).

Name Index

Abbott, Henry Jack, 332, 342n
Adorno, Theodor, 5
Amalrik, Andrei, 99
Andreski, Stanislav, 76n, 315
Andropov, Yuri, 77n
Aptheker, Bettina, 341n
Aptheker, Herbert, 341n
Arendt, Hannah, 187–88
Armstrong, John A., 109
Aron, Raymond, 220
Artemiev, V. P., 83, 101n
Atkinson, D., 229
Azrael, Jeremy R., 229

Bakunin, Mikhail A., 242
Bao, Ruo Wang, 126n, 208, 214
Baran, Paul, 221, 341n
Barbusse, Henri, 341n
Barmine, Alexander, 85
Barnet, Richard J., 295–98, 331
Barrett, William, 325, 336
Barron, P., 210
Barzun, Jacques, 299
Baudet, Henri, 256
Bauer, Raymond, 53n, 204, 217, 232n
Beauvoir, Simone de, 262, 263, 267,
  269, 341n
Beichman, Arnold, 327
Bell, Daniel, 322n
Belli, Humberto, 337
Bendix, Reinhard, 76n, 321n
Berger, Bennett, 13n
Berger, Peter, 13n, 142, 207, 214, 229,
  251n
Berlin, Isaiah, 54n, 248, 250n
Berman, Harold J., 102n, 215
Bernal, J. D., 341n
Bernard, Jessie, 160n
Berrigan, Daniel, 262, 264, 269, 302,
  306, 341n
Bettelheim, C., 222

Bialoguski, M., 101n
Billington, James H., 125n
Bird, Caroline, 160n
Birnbaum, Norman, 281n
Black, Cyril, 101n
Bloch, S., 214
Bonnell, Victoria E., 321n
Boorstin, Daniel J., 309
Bowles, Samuel, 209
Boyd Orr, John, 269
Brecht, Bertold, 341n
Breslauer, G. W., 210
Brezhnev, Leonid, 141, 165, 195, 287
Brightman, Carol, 280n, 311n
Bronfenbrenner, U., 209
Broyelle, Claudie and Jacques, 227,
  229
Bruce-Briggs, B., 322n
Brzezinski, Zbigniev, 77n, 101n, 114n,
  212, 218
Bukovsky, Vladimir, 99, 227, 281n
Burgess, Guy, 90
Burton, N., 222
Butterfield, Fox, 31
Byrnes, R. F., 204

Calzon, F., 210, 212
Carter, Jimmy, 291
Castro, Fidel, 5, 194, 206, 207, 212,
  213, 217, 218–19, 223, 224, 232n,
  258, 263, 264, 266, 275, 303, 305,
  328, 335, 338
Caute, David, 218, 264, 341n
Ceauscescu, Nicolai, 217
Chalidze, V., 99, 227
Chanoff, David, 342n
Chomsky, Noam, 302, 304, 327, 328,
  331
Chou En-lai, 263
Clark, Ramsey, 276, 337
Cleaver, Eldridge, 336

345

Clytus, John, 222, 225
Cockburn, Alexander, 341n
Cockburn, Claude, 322n, 341n
Cocks, Paul, 129, 212
Coffin, William Sloan, Jr., 328
Cohen, J. M., 204
Cohn, W., 218
Committee of Concerned Asian Scholars, 223, 280n
Connor, Walter, 141, 220, 226, 227
Conquest, Robert, 214, 281n
Cowley, Malcolm, 341n
Cranston, Maurice, 218

Dallin, Alexander, 210, 229
Daniels, Robert V., 116
Davis, Angela, 336
Davis, Jerome, 341n
Deak, I., 142n
Dellinger, David, 341n
Deriabin, Peter, 90
Dewey, John, 341n
Dimitrov, George, 217
Djilas, Milovan, 113, 216
Doan Van Toai, 214, 342n
Dominguez, Jorge, 204, 212, 222, 225, 228
Dos Passos, John, 341n
Draper, Theodore, 207
Dreiser, Theodore, 341n
DuBois, W.E.B., 341n
Dulles, John Foster, 296
Dumont, René, 218, 219, 222
Dunham, Vera, 51, 208
Dunn, Ethel, 150
Durkheim, Emile, 118, 245

Eberstadt, Nick, 227, 229
Eddy, Sherwood, 279
Edwards, Jorge, 214
Engels, Friedrich, 105, 189, 201, 207, 208, 210

Fagen, R., 208, 213, 223, 232n
Fainsod, Merle, 68, 114n
Fairbank, John K., 223, 328, 341n
Falk, Richard, 337, 341n
Feiffer, George, 77n, 205, 214, 215, 228

Feuchtwanger, Lion, 259, 261, 263, 266, 341n
Field, Mark, 227
Firestone, Shulamit, 159n
Fischer, M. E., 217
Fisher, Louis, 101n, 341n
Flacks, R., 203
Frank, Jerome D., 126n
Frank, Waldo, 257, 261, 265
Franklin, Howard Bruce, 302, 341n
Freeman, Joseph, 341n
Frolic, Bernard, 31, 142n, 213, 223, 231n
Fuentes, Carlos, 343n
Fukuyama, Francis, 196n

Gagnon, J. H., 245
Galbraith, John K., 328, 341n
Gamberg, H., 251n
Gasiorowska, Xenia, 51
Geiger, Kent, 229
Gerschenkron, Alexander, 51, 159n
Gitelman, Zev, 229
Goldman, Marshall J., 230
Goodman, Paul, 302
Goodman, Walter, 326, 331
Gorer, Geoffrey, 115
Gorky, Maxim, 172n
Gottwald, Klement, 217
Goytisolo, J., 213
Graham, Billy, Rev., 278–80
Greene, Felix, 341n
Greer, Germaine, 158n
Grigorienko, P. G., 99
Gromyko, Andrei, 180
Guevara, Che, 224, 264, 266

Hacker, Andrew, 156–57, 285
Halperin, M., 204, 207
Haraszti, Miklos, 12n, 113, 141, 230
Hart, Armando, 209
Hayden, Tom, 261, 265, 269, 341n
Hazan, B. A., 208
Hebert, Jacques, 272
Hellman, Lillian, 302, 335
Henry, Jules, 303
Herf, Jeffrey, 13n
Hermassi, E., 203
Hicks, Granville, 341n
Hirschman, Albert, 9

Hiss, Alger, 287
Ho Chi Minh, 206, 217, 264, 266, 270
Hobbes, Thomas, 211
Hobsbawm, E. J., 341n
Hoffmann, Stanley, 331
Hoge, Warren, 281n
Hollander, Gayle, 208
Hollander, Paul, 13n, 77n, 142n, 205, 206, 212, 213, 214, 220, 222, 223, 224, 229, 231, 232n, 322n
Horowitz, Irving Louis, 210, 213, 214, 222, 228, 230, 231, 321n
Hough, Jerry, 74, 77n, 141, 331
Howe, Irving, 334, 335
Howe, Louise Kapp, 160n, 161n
Hoxha, Enver, 201, 205, 206, 217
Huang, Joe C., 164, 166, 167, 168, 169, 172
Huberman, Leo, 341n
Hunthausen, Raymond, 332
Huntington, Samuel P., 220
Huxley, Aldous, 64
Huxley, Julian, 260–61, 263, 341n

Inkeles, Alex, 13n, 76n, 126n, 142n, 204, 205, 232n
Isaac, Rael Jean and Erich, 294n

James, C. Vaughan, 165, 166, 170, 172
Jancar, Barbara W., 229
Johnson, Chalmers, 129, 132
Johnson, Hewlett, 279
Jones, Jim (Rev.), 183–84

Kakutani, Michiko, 342n
Kampf, Louis, 333
Karnow, Stanley, 229
Karol, K. S., 222
Kasenkina, Oksana, 86
Kassof, Allen, 76n
Kaznachaev, A., 86
Kennan, George F., 331
Kenworthy, Eldon, 281n
Kharchev, A., 150, 151
Khomeini, Ayatollah, 277
Khrushchev, N. S., 21, 56, 87, 109, 122, 123, 227, 335
Killian, Lewis, 246

Kim Il Sung, 201, 206, 217, 218
Kirkpatrick, Jeane, 77n, 293n
Kluckhohn, Clyde, 204
Koestler, Arthur, 341n
Kohak, Erazim, 183
Kolakowski, Leszek, 206, 251n
Kolko, Gabriel, 302
Kollontai, Alexandra, 145, 147
Konrad, George, 113, 141, 220, 227, 230
Kopkind, Andrew, 336
Korbonski, Stefan, 129, 132
Korchagin, Pavel, 168
Kosinsky, Jerzy, 118, 120, 121
Kozol, Jonathan, 328, 341n
Kunstler, William, 302

Labin, Susan, 214
Ladd, Everett, 322n
Lamont, Corliss, 328, 336, 341n
Lamont, Corliss and Margaret, 259, 261, 269
Landau, Saul, 276, 341n
LaPalombara, Joseph, 114n
Lapidus, Gail W., 229
Laqueur, Walter, 196n
Lasch, Christopher, 322n
Laski, Harold, 341n
Lattimore, Owen, 272, 341n
Laue, von, Theodore, 54n, 74–75, 331
Leites, Nathan, 39, 116, 205
Lenchevsky, Oleg, 87
Lendvai, P., 208, 209
Lenin, Vladimir Ilich, 4–5, 53n, 105–107, 116, 134, 189, 191n, 201, 205, 207, 208, 210, 226, 242, 254, 287
LeoGrande, W. M., 212
Leonhard, Wolfgang, 118, 119, 120
Levinson, Sandra, 280n, 311n
Levy, M., Jr., 52n
Lewis, Oscar, 204
Leys, Simon, 29, 31, 113, 208, 222
Lifton, Robert Jay, 125n
Lion, Jill A., 102n
Lipset, Seymour Martin, 250n, 309
London, Ivan D., 232n
Lowenthal, Richard, 206, 207
Ludz, P., 142n
Lukács, Georg, 5
Luttwak, Edward, 11

Lynd, Staughton, 261, 265, 269, 329
Lyons, Eugene, 341n

Macciocchi, Maria A., 341n
MacDonald, Dwight, 308
Mailer, Norman, 257–58, 302, 303, 332, 341n
Male, Beverly, 338
Malenkov, G. M., 52n, 108
Mandel, William M., 160n
Mannheim, Karl, 323–24
Mao Tse Tung, 17, 24, 125, 173n, 201, 205, 206, 213, 214, 217, 218, 223, 224, 227, 229, 263, 266, 328, 335, 338
Mao, Mrs., 158
Macuse, Herbert, 5, 180–81, 211, 303, 304, 330, 333
Marcuse, Jacques, 214
Markov, Georgi, 100
Márquez, Gabriel García, 330, 339
Marsh, Robert M., 321n
Marx, Karl, 43, 105, 134, 189, 201, 207, 208, 210, 223, 243, 287
Matos, Huber, 212
Matthews, Mervyn, 114n, 220, 221
Mathewson, R. W., 52n
McCarthy, Mary, 341n
McDowell, E., 204
McRae, Duncan, Jr., 248
Merton, Robert K., 248, 315
Mesa-Lago, Carmelo, 128, 204, 209, 219, 225, 227, 228, 229
Meyer, Alfred G., 51n, 54n, 67–74, 110, 113, 114n, 116, 135
Mickiewicz, E., 208
Milgram, Stanley, 187–88
Miller, Arthur, 332
Mills, C. Wright, 73, 245, 303, 315, 322n, 341n
Moody, Mary Jane, 102n
Moore, Barrington, Jr., 68, 146, 321n
Moore, Wilbert E., 76n
Myrdal, Jan, 341n

Naimark, Norman, 143n
Navasky, Victor, 302, 339
Nearing, Scott, 341n
Nekrasov, Viktor, 87
Nekrich, Alexander, 230

Nelson, L., 209, 222, 225, 228
Neruda, Pablo, 341n
Nettler, Gwynn, 242
Nimigeanu, Dumitri, 101n
Nimkoff, Meyer F., 146
Nixon, Richard, 287

O'Dell, F. A., 208
Ostrovsky, N., 168

Padilla, Herbert, 5
Parish, W. L., Jr., 204
Parsons, Talcott, 315
Perevedentsev, V., 149, 150
Petrov, Vladimir and Evdokia, 86, 90
Philipson, Lorrin, 103n
Pipes, Richard, 288
Pirogov, Peter, 102n
Podhoretz, Norman, 191n
Pol Pot, 216, 328, 335
Powell, David E., 77n, 226, 228

Qudaffi, Muhamar, 338

Rakosi, Mathias, 201, 217
Reagan, Ronald, 11–12, 291, 293n
Reddeway, Peter, 214
Reich, Charles, 303
Reinhold, R., 204
Revel, Jean Francois, 13n
Riding, Alan, 13n
Rigby, T. H., 216
Ripoll, C., 213, 281n
Robespierre, Maximilian, 242
Rolland, Romaine, 341n
Roszak, Theodore, 302
Rougemont, Denis de, 255
Rubin, Jerry, 334
Russell, Bertrand, 308

Sakharov, Andrei, 221, 226, 227, 228
Salkey, Andrew, 281n
Sartre, Jean Paul, 262, 264, 308, 341n
Schell, Orville, 341n
Schlesinger, Arthur, Jr., 331
Schoeck, Helmut, 342n
Shaw, George Bernard, 255, 259, 262, 268, 279, 341n
Shaw, Peter, 337
Shawcross, William, 229

Shelley, Louise, 227
Shils, Edward, 53n, 251n
Sholokhov, M., 36
Shulman, Colette, 102n
Shulman, Marshall, 331
Silverman, B., 224
Simon, W., 245
Simmons, E. J., 52n
Sinanian, S., 142n
Sinclair, Upton, 341n
Sinyavski, A., 53n, 99, 163, 208, 223
Skocpol, Theda, 321n
Slater, Philip, 303, 341n
Slonim, M., 52n
Slusser, Robert M., 101n, 210
Snow, Edgar, 341n
Solomon, Peter H., 231
Solzhenitsyn, Alexsandr, 99, 187–91
Sontag, Susan, 8, 258, 265, 271, 303,
    311n, 328, 334, 336, 338–39
Stalin, I. V., 27, 33–34, 39, 47, 50,
    51, 55, 63, 74–75, 81, 85, 108,
    109, 123, 147, 148, 164, 165, 166,
    172n, 188, 189, 201, 206, 214, 217,
    254, 263, 266, 273, 289, 328, 338
Steel, Ronald, 331
Steffens, Lincoln, 341n
Stein, Ben, 341n
Stojanovich, Svetozar, 113, 210, 216,
    217, 219, 226
Strong, Anna Louise, 341n
Strumilin, S. G., 146
Struve, G., 52n
Szamuely, Tibor, 114n
Sweezy, Paul, 341n
Szelenyi, Ivan, 113, 141, 220, 227

Tarsis, Valeri, 114n
Terrill, Ross, 341n
Tertz, A., 52n
Thomas, J., 210
Tilly, Charles, Louise and Robert,
    321n

Tito, Josiph Broz, 217
Tocqueville, Alexis de, 288, 315
Tomasic, Dinko A., 116
Treadgold, Donald W., 114n
Triska, Jan F., 129, 132
Trotsky, Leon, 113, 147, 216, 217,
    242
Trudeau, Pierre Elliot, 272
Truong, Nhu Tang, 342n
Turkel, G., 203

Ulam, Adam, 68, 116, 205, 206
Urban, George, 217

Valladares, Armando, 276, 330
Vallier, Ivan, 321n
Vidal, Gore, 332
Vogel, Ezra, 70, 204

Wald, George, 332
Wald, Karen, 209
Wallace, Henry, 272
Wallerstein, Immanuel, 321n
Ward, Harry F., 341n
Webb, Beatrice and Sidney, 341n
Weber, Max, 3, 106, 111, 267, 326
Wells, H. G., 341n
Whyte, Martin King, 126n, 142n, 204,
    208, 209, 222, 232n
Wieseltier, Leon, 327
Will, George F., 281n
Wilson, Edmund, 341n
Winter, Ella, 262, 341n
Wolfe, Bertram, 218
Wolfe, Tom, 306
Wolff, Robert P., 303
Wolin, Simon, 101n, 210
Wooton, Barbara, 265
Worsley, Peter, 214, 224
Wrong, Dennis, 339

Zeitlin, M., 209
Zinn, Howard, 341n

Subject Index

Abortion, 120, 147, 149, 150
Adversary culture, 339
Advertising, 178–79, 250, 260
Affluence, 9, 10, 177, 245, 249, 256, 301, 333
Afghanistan, 141, 143n, 182, 193–96, 202, 291, 292, 338, 343n
Africa, 11, 141, 182, 202, 276, 291, 302
Agriculture, 109, 176, 218
Albania, 100, 129, 137, 141, 142n, 143n, 202, 205, 217
Alcoholism. See Drunkenness
Alienation, 11, 156, 224, 226, 230, 232n, 249, 257, 258, 259, 265, 277, 278, 285, 304, 323–43
American Sociology, 3–4, 202–204, 241–51, 313–22
Angola, 141, 143n, 182, 194, 202, 276, 284, 287, 290, 292, 293n, 295, 337
Anomie, 156, 245, 247, 248
Anti-Americanism, 299–311
Anti-Anti-Communism, 329, 331, 339
Anti-Semitism, 94, 182
Area studies, 130, 203, 313
Arts (the), 109, 147, 163, 164–65, 208, 223, 262
Atomization, 213
Auschwitz of Puget Sound, 333
Authoritarian. See Authoritarianism
Authoritarian personality, 48
Authoritarianism, 27, 75, 76, 148
Automobiles. See Cars

Baptists, 279–80
Belief System, 138, 188
Berlin Wall, 96–97, 230
Birth rates, 148–50, 158
Boat People. See Refugees
Border controls, 2, 79–103, 215; coastal, 209

Bulgaria, 100, 141, 202, 217
Bureaucracy, 2, 5, 67–73, 105–14, 121, 129, 147, 187, 213, 214, 216, 298
Bureaucratization. See Bureaucracy
Business, 11, 195, 255, 287
Businessman. See Business

Cambodia, 141, 143n, 202, 216, 302, 335
Camps, corrective labor, prison, etc., 2, 187–91, 208, 225, 272, 279
Campus, 157, 245, 293n, 336
Capitalism, 6, 71, 206, 209, 211, 220, 226, 242, 267, 287, 296, 300, 306, 307, 308, 310, 337
Capitalists. See Capitalism
Capitalist society, countries, 55, 94, 138, 147, 189, 226, 262, 274
Cars, 4, 58, 62, 65, 157, 175–76, 178, 179, 221, 222, 269, 297, 304, 306, 333, 338
Cash nexus, 257, 305
Censorship, 164, 171
Chemical warfare, 196n, 343n
Child care, 147, 154, 158, 221
Child-rearing, 27, 146, 155
China, 5–6, 17–29, 75, 100, 113, 125, 129, 140, 143n, 148, 158, 163–73, 202, 204, 205, 209, 210, 213, 215, 216, 225, 253–76, 302, 328, 329, 335, 337
Citizens Exchange Corps, Inc., 294n, 296
Clergy, 273, 326, 342n
Coercion, 3, 7, 34, 51, 56, 69, 70, 75, 109, 188–89, 190, 197–200, 206, 210–16, 225
Coercive institutions and apparatus. See KGB
Cold War, 68, 69, 135, 193–96, 199, 286, 292, 296, 297

Collective (the), 22, 37–39, 44, 47, 118, 120, 124, 125, 167, 172n, 183–84, 209, 223, 275
Collective Farms, 61, 176, 229; farmers, 290
Collectivism. *See* Collective (the)
Collectivization of land, 171, 229, 335
Columbia Institute of Russian Studies, 297
Comintern, 119
Committee for the Defense of the Revolution, 213
Communism, 56, 62, 67–77, 169, 172, 195, 227, 296, 334, 342n
Communist: character, 21–22; morality, 19, 49, 172n, 223; society, 43, 223, 232n, 286
Community, 8, 184, 185, 256, 258–59, 260, 264, 265, 267, 274, 325, 334
Consumer attitudes. *See* Consumption
Consumer goods. *See* Consumption
Consumption, 64, 65, 149, 157, 176–77, 181, 222, 257, 285, 305
Contraceptives, 26, 149
Convergence, 67, 70, 76n, 110, 296–97, 298, 319
Corruption, 185, 229, 297
Counter-Culture, 9, 13, 157, 325
Crime, 67, 137, 225, 226, 227, 228, 262, 332
Critical Sociology, 205, 319
Criticism and Self-Criticism, 38, 41, 44, 115–26, 328
Cuba, 5, 75, 76, 100, 129, 143n, 194, 202, 204, 208, 209, 210, 212–13, 214, 215, 225, 253–78, 290, 300, 302, 303, 305, 328, 329, 335, 337
Cult of personality, 25, 123, 206, 217–19
Cultural Revolution (the), 29, 170, 205, 209, 216, 221, 223, 229, 275
Czechoslovakia, 100, 141, 143n, 199, 202, 217, 290, 295, 332

Democracy, 259, 283, 327, 336
De-Stalinization, 166
Détente, 194, 283–84, 296, 331
Determinism (cultural, economic, historical, social), 73, 75, 133, 188, 241–51, 297, 298

Deviance, 22, 25, 118, 216, 226, 325
Deviant behavior. *See* Deviance
Discrimination (ethnic, racial, sexual), 155, 220, 225, 229, 258, 259, 306
Disenchantment, 140
Dissent, 158, 160n, 181, 190, 199, 213, 214–15, 216, 340
Dissenters, dissidents. *See* Dissent
Divorce, 121, 147, 154
Divorce rates, 148, 150, 151, 158, 159n, 178
Double standards, 75, 327–29, 332
Draft registration, 292
Drug addiction, 225
Drunkenness, 63, 67, 225, 226, 228

East Germany, 96–97, 99–100, 141, 143n, 194, 202
Eastern Europe, 6, 50, 75, 80, 128–42, 164, 181, 183, 199, 200, 202, 206, 221, 223, 225, 231, 251, 290, 295, 297, 308, 335, 337
Education, 19, 28, 63, 109, 133, 152, 154, 203, 205, 208–209, 215, 220, 223, 228, 241, 244, 262, 274, 288, 316
Egalitarianism. *See* Equality
El Salvador, 141, 196n, 276–77, 337
Elite, 35, 89, 111, 117, 125, 133, 136, 137, 140, 147, 163, 205, 207, 209, 220–22, 285, 296, 297, 298, 307, 340
Elite groups. *See* Elite
Elitism, 108, 219, 307, 333
Emigration, 89, 97, 98–99, 230, 315
Enlightenment, 264, 325
Equality, 5, 138, 155, 219, 222, 261, 263
Escapism, 46, 64, 65, 137, 228, 231
Estrangement, 10–11, 249, 256–57, 274, 275, 277, 304, 323–43
Ethiopia, 141, 143n, 182, 194, 202, 295, 337
Ethnic groups, 6, 137, 150, 190, 333, 336
Ethnocentrism, 71, 164, 317, 320
Evolutionary optimism, 131, 134, 141
Exile, 190, 191n, 328
Expectations, 11, 139, 149, 151, 152, 156, 180, 184, 191, 228, 241–51, 274, 286, 308, 309, 334

False consciousness, 211, 304, 337, 341
Family, 18, 25, 27–28, 87, 145–61, 232n
Family instability, 137, 225, 229
Fascism, 68, 332
Fellow travelers, 256, 264, 335
Feminism, 10, 145–61
Foreign Policy, 130, 193, 243, 283–94, 295–98, 308, 309
Functionalism, 3–4, 145, 210–11

Gay liberation, 155
Grain embargo, 291
Green Party, 338
Grenada, 141, 194, 202, 278, 291
Guerrilla movements. See Guerrillas
Guerrillas, 194, 196n, 276–77, 337
Gulag. See Camps
Guyana, 183–84

Harvard Russian Research Center, 297
Homosexual(s), 155, 335
Hooliganism, 55
Hospitality. See Techniques of Hospitality
Housing, 58, 62, 65, 138, 154, 177–78, 180, 221, 222, 227, 229–30, 338
Hungarian Revolution (1956), 200
Hungary, 2, 5–7, 12n, 35–36, 75, 100, 141, 143n, 175–85, 199, 202, 217, 227, 290. See also Hungarian Revolution

Identity, 156, 178, 185, 264, 265, 267, 340
Immigration. See Emigration
Incentives, 220–25
Individualism, 18, 19–20, 48, 65, 118, 120, 149, 156–57, 180, 184, 242, 285, 316, 325
Indochina, 6, 76, 141, 194, 230, 277, 291, 302, 337, 343n
Industrialization, 33, 49, 50, 81, 131, 133, 134, 207, 254, 318
Industrial society, 110, 133, 180, 211, 257, 297

Inequality, 182–83, 210, 219, 220–25, 257, 267, 301
Informers, 83, 213–14
Intellectuals, 7–8, 10–12, 21, 73, 95, 116, 139–40, 185, 189, 195, 206, 214, 245, 249, 253–81, 284–85, 300–303, 305, 306–309, 311, 315–16, 323–43
Internal Passport, 215, 227
Intimidation, 136, 294n
Iran, 310
Isolationism, 195, 284, 315, 331
Israel, 93–94, 99, 295
Izvestia, 59, 60, 91

Jewish. See Jews
Jews, 2, 94, 99, 182, 184, 188, 335
Juvenile delinquency, 64, 65, 67, 137, 149, 225, 227, 228

KGB (state security organs), 2, 5, 77n, 82, 83, 87, 100, 136, 139, 190, 200, 208, 213–14, 221, 224, 332
Komsomol (young communist league), 37, 55, 62, 82, 83, 117, 224, 272

Laos, 202, 302
La Prensa, 337
Latin America, 302, 307, 310
Left (the), 157, 257, 302, 337, 339. See also New Left
Legitimacy, 96, 134–37, 201, 205–209, 211, 216–17, 219, 220
Legitimation. See Legitimacy
Leisure, 25, 28, 55–65, 157–58, 181, 218
Liberalization, 131, 200
Libya, 338
Literature, 33–54, 163–73, 208, 209, 223
Living standards, 220, 264

Magadan, 272
Manual labor, 21, 209
Marxism, 2, 4–5, 7, 9, 17, 39, 113, 189, 201–231, 249, 251, 256, 291, 310, 318, 327
Marxism-Leninism, 10, 21, 43–44, 75, 83, 119, 138, 172n, 188, 201–31, 290, 300, 309, 319

Marxists. *See* Marxism
Mass media, 17, 24, 61, 65, 97–98,
    109, 121, 123, 134, 147, 193, 208,
    211, 214, 223, 254, 259, 268, 274,
    288, 290–91, 300–301, 316, 323–24,
    326
Mass society, 187
"Me Decade," 184
Media. *See* Mass media
Mental illness, 87, 184, 225
Middle class, 12, 157, 245, 247, 287,
    305
Migration. *See* Emigration
Mirror images (Soviet–American),
    295–98
Modernity. *See* Modernization
Modernization, 6, 51, 59, 71, 106,
    111, 131, 132, 133, 142, 151–53,
    158, 187, 206–207, 220, 228, 290,
    296, 310
Mongolia, 129, 202
Moral certainty, 327; indignation, 244,
    260, 320, 327, 331; relativism, 327;
    responsibility, 188; standards, 22,
    28, 120, 180
Morality, 22, 28, 120, 180, 223,
    242–43
Mozambique, 141, 143n, 194, 202,
    276, 337
Multinational corporations, 318

Nationalism, 80, 198
Nationalities, 137
NATO, 194, 291, 292
Nazi Germany, 71, 332, 336
Nazism, 9, 13, 68, 187–89
Negative hero, 34–35, 44–48, 169. *See
    also* Positive Hero
New Left, 9, 257, 307, 334, 335
New Man, 50, 57, 71, 185, 209,
    220–25, 266
New Socialist Man. *See* New Man
New Soviet Man. *See* New Man
Nicaragua, 6, 141, 202, 276, 277, 278,
    281n, 291, 337
Nonconformity, 216, 324–25
North Korea, 75, 100, 129, 143n, 202,
    217, 218, 225
North Vietnam, 129, 143n, 253–75,
    277, 335, 336, 337

Nuclear disarmament. *See* Nuclear
    freeze
Nuclear freeze, 10, 277, 278, 292,
    294n, 310, 330, 331

October Revolution, 80, 208, 326, 338
Old people, 137
One-party states, 7, 113, 197–200,
    201, 207, 212, 219, 338
One-party systems. *See* One-party
    states
Order of Maternal Glory, 150

Palace Communes, 146
Participation, 5, 139, 140
Party (the), 4, 5, 19, 23, 25–26,
    37–39, 41–43, 48, 57, 82, 83, 107,
    109, 112, 113, 115, 117, 123, 125,
    130, 147, 164, 173n, 208, 213,
    216–20, 222, 272, 273
Party-aristocracy, 178
Peaceful coexistence. *See* Détente
Peasants, 6, 59, 115, 156, 171, 176,
    219, 229, 265
Pilgrims (ideological, political),
    253–82, 340
PLO (Palestine Liberation Organiza-
    tion), 277
Pluralism, 51, 71, 73, 128, 131, 277,
    283, 286
Pluralistic. *See* Pluralism
Poland, 5, 7, 75, 100, 141, 143n,
    197–200, 202, 232n, 290, 331, 332
Pollution, 229
Poor (the). *See* Poverty
Positive hero, 34–44, 167–69. *See also*
    Negative Hero
Post-Stalin period, 63, 87, 190, 215,
    336
Poverty, 221, 226, 243, 244, 257, 258,
    259, 306, 307
Pravda, 55, 60, 83, 112, 148, 296
Prisons, 254, 262–63
Privacy, 17–29, 56, 58, 62, 65, 158,
    175–85
Private. *See* Privacy
Private entrepreneurs, enterprise, 176,
    229
Privilege, 113, 138, 176, 216, 220–22
Progress, 116, 133, 191

Projection, 288–89
Proletariat, 20, 217, 324
Propaganda, 19, 21, 25, 33, 88, 91, 93, 94, 163, 169–70, 171, 194, 223, 278, 279, 281n, 284, 300
Prostitution, 147, 254
Protestant ethic, 288
Pseudo-charisma, 217
Pseudo-participation, 139, 290
Public health, 226–27, 228, 254, 264
Public property, 136, 227
Public Security Office (bureau), 213, 273
Purges, 47, 53n, 55, 69, 109, 232n, 298, 335
Puritanism, 26, 40, 46, 153, 167, 169, 185
Purpose, 2, 8, 55, 256, 259, 261, 326, 334

Rationing, 221–22
Refugees, 230–31, 335, 337, 342n
Religion, 6, 254, 325, 334; secular, 274
Religiosity. *See* Religion
Renaissance Men, 264
Repressive tolerance, 304, 306, 330
Revisionism. *See* Revisionists
Revisionists, 18, 74, 165, 172n, 205, 295–98
Romania, 137, 141, 202, 332
Rural areas, 58, 113, 177, 229, 230

Sandinistas, 337–38
Scarcity, 113, 140, 206, 221, 248, 265, 335
Secrecy, 97, 98, 212
Secretiveness. *See* Secrecy
Secularization, 67, 152, 248, 267, 274, 309, 318, 325–26
Self-fulfillment, 146, 157, 241, 257, 264, 274, 285, 334
Self-realization. *See* Self-fulfillment
Sense of purpose. *See* Purpose
Sex, 26–27, 40, 147–48, 153, 159n, 169, 180; education of, 153
Sex roles, 149, 150
Sexual. *See* Sex
Social criticism, 10, 11, 241, 245, 246, 249, 256, 260, 261, 304, 314, 318,

319, 320, 324–25, 333, 340
Social injustice, 260
Social justice, 5, 221, 267, 274, 286
Social mobility, 67, 140
Social problems, 137–38, 141, 225–31, 248, 256, 286
Socialism, 5, 6, 8, 12, 20, 23, 56, 127–43, 172n, 185, 189, 206, 209, 224, 226, 249, 254, 272, 273, 275, 286, 290, 326, 327, 332, 334, 335, 339
Socialist Commonwealth, 141, 194
Socialist realism, 33–51, 163–73, 208, 223
Solidarity (movement), 141, 197–98, 232n
South Vietnam, 182
South Yemen, 141, 143n, 182, 194, 202
Soviet Constitution, 219
Soviet Union, 1, 2, 5–6, 10, 50, 51, 68, 73, 74, 75, 79–103, 105–13, 123, 125, 129–40, 145–61, 163–73, 176, 183, 187–91, 193–95, 198–200, 202, 206, 207, 210, 214, 215, 216, 251, 253–82, 283–94, 295–98, 300, 302, 319, 328, 329, 331, 332, 335, 336, 337. *See also* Party (the)
Spontaneity, 42–44, 106–107, 108, 167, 307
Stakhanovites, 82
Standard of living, 176–77, 181, 183
State (the), 5, 6, 113, 185, 210–16, 222
State Security Organs. *See* KGB
Stratification, 138, 175, 220–25
Structural-Functionalism. *See* Functionalism
Subcultures, 324–25, 329, 334, 340
Suicide, 225
"Survivals," 22, 226
Symbionese Liberation Army, 183
Synanon, 183

Tanzania, 337
Techniques of Hospitality, 268–73, 279
Technocrats, 9, 134, 304
Technology, 9, 80, 153, 187, 258, 302, 303, 304, 307, 310

Television, 55, 58, 61, 63, 64, 176, 276, 299, 301, 306
Therapeutic appeasement, 292–93, 295–98, 331
Third World, 8–9, 202, 203, 229, 276, 286, 292, 301, 302, 307, 311, 318, 328, 337
Thought reform, 117
Totalitarianism, 2, 7, 17, 26, 28–29, 33–36, 50, 67–76, 79, 98, 106, 110, 111, 148, 165, 293n

United Nations, 194, 284, 293, 299, 307
United States, 1, 8, 12, 73, 74, 75, 86, 93, 94, 100, 135, 145, 146, 151, 154–58, 176, 178, 180, 182, 183, 190, 193–96, 203, 241–51, 256, 274, 277, 278, 283–94, 295–98, 299–311, 323–43
Urban areas, 59, 113, 230
Urbanization, 67, 131, 318
USSR. *See* Soviet Union
Utopia, 183–84, 207, 254, 274
Utopia-seekers. *See* Utopia

Vandalism, 225
Venceremos Brigade, 242, 263, 266, 305
Vietcong, 276, 277, 333
Vietnam, 10–11, 100, 143n, 195, 202, 217, 225, 229, 275–76, 278, 285,

302, 303, 306, 315, 335, 336, 337
Vietnamese Gulag, 214
Violence, 2, 3, 136, 190, 210, 211, 213, 258, 293, 294n, 299, 310, 338
Volga Germans, 99

"Weather" underground, 183
West (the), 92, 100, 124, 181, 182, 189, 256, 259, 276, 283, 292, 306, 329, 337
West Germany, 92, 93, 99, 338, 342n
Western democracy, 141, 257, 293
Western Europe, 181, 249, 256, 278, 286, 291, 301, 308
Western society. *See* Western democracy
Western world. *See* Western democracy
Westernization, 64
Wholeness, 8, 247, 265, 267
Wishful thinking, 288–89, 297, 323–43
Women, 23, 60, 65, 145–61, 228, 229, 261, 262
Workers, 4–5, 56, 59, 82, 219, 224, 227, 229, 261, 273
Working classes. *See* Workers
World War II, 2, 80, 81, 86, 91, 94, 123, 151; post-, 304

Young Communist League. *See* Komsomol
Yugoslavia, 129, 130, 137, 139, 142n, 217, 230